Backpack Ambassadors

Backpack Ambassadors

How Youth Travel Integrated Europe

RICHARD IVAN JOBS

The University of Chicago Press   *Chicago and London*

The University of Chicago Press, Chicago 60637
The University of Chicago Press, Ltd., London
© 2017 by The University of Chicago
All rights reserved. No part of this book may be used or reproduced
in any manner whatsoever without written permission, except in
the case of brief quotations in critical articles and reviews. For more
information, contact the University of Chicago Press, 1427 E. 60th St.,
Chicago, IL 60637.
Published 2017
Printed in the United States of America

26 25 24 23 22 21 20 19 18 17   1 2 3 4 5

ISBN-13: 978-0-226-43897-9 (cloth)
ISBN-13: 978-0-226-46203-5 (paper)
ISBN-13: 978-0-226-43902-0 (e-book)
DOI: 10.7208/chicago/9780226439020.001.0001

Library of Congress Cataloging-in-Publication Data

Names: Jobs, Richard Ivan, author.
Title: Backpack ambassadors: how youth travel integrated Europe /
    Richard Ivan Jobs.
Description: Chicago; London: The University of Chicago Press, 2017. |
    Includes bibliographical references and index.
Identifiers: LCCN 2016044002 | ISBN 9780226438979 (cloth: alk. paper) |
    ISBN 9780226462035 (pbk.: alk. paper) | ISBN 9780226439020 (e-book)
Subjects: LCSH: Youth—Travel—Europe—History. | International travel—
    Europe—History—20th century. | Europe—History—1945-
Classification: LCC G156.5.Y6 J63 2017 | DDC 914.04/550835—dc23
    LC record available at https://lccn.loc.gov/2016044002

♾ This paper meets the requirements of ANSI/NISO Z39.48–1992
(Permanence of Paper).

FOR KIM, GRETA, AND EZRA

Contents

1   Map of Cold War Europe. © Martin Lubikowski, ML Design 2016.

Backpack Ambassadors

Youth travel was both my inspiration and aspiration for this book. In 1997, I was a twenty-seven-year-old Rutgers University graduate student living in Paris, researching my dissertation. Two friends of mine with whom I had backpacked in India a couple of years earlier, Mark and Ari, visited me there. During their visit, the three of us took a trip to Amsterdam. This was actually my third time there. I had first visited Amsterdam as a Eurailing backpacker in the summer of 1990. While there with Mark and Ari, it occurred to me how much I liked the city, and how much I would like to spend some prolonged time there, as I was doing in Paris. That got me thinking about how I would like to spend time in lots of different places around Europe. I asked myself whether I could develop a research project that would enable that. While researching my book *Riding the New Wave: Youth and the Rejuvenation of France after the Second World War* (Stanford University Press, 2007), I discovered a variety of materials indicating that there was a significant social and cultural component to European integration, in addition to the straightforwardly economic and political elements, and that youth and young people were central to this project of international reconciliation from below.

For example, a series of studies from the mid-1990s pointed out that individual mobility was greatest among those between the ages of fifteen and twenty-four. In Europe, this age group accounted for a quarter of all cross-border traffic. An extraordinary fifty million young Europeans had traveled abroad, and another twenty million desired to do so. A fifth of all tourist journeys worldwide

1

2   Backpackers walking toward Central Station, Amsterdam, May 1973. Photograph by Rob
Mieremet. National Archives of the Netherlands/Anefo, license by CC-BY.

were by young people aged fifteen to twenty-five. Their travel was characterized by a desire to be in the company of their peers, and hence
they selected destinations where they could meet such people. They also
liked to spend less in order to travel longer; they liked to move around,
viewing this as part of their personal development, particularly if they
considered themselves middle class. In Europe, they accounted for about
one hundred million border crossings annually, and this transit was
overwhelmingly intra-European. The studies emphasized international
youth travel as an integrating factor in a united Europe. However, although institutions such as the European Union (EU) and the Council
of Europe were promoting youth mobility at the time—indeed, they had
sponsored the studies—their programs were all fairly new, developed in
the 1980s and implemented in the 1990s.[1] Thus, although the formal in-

stitutions of European integration recognized and idealized the impact of transnational youth mobility on postwar Europe, they had contributed little institutional support to encourage or develop it.

The mass travel of young backpackers that began in Western Europe was a profoundly new phenomenon unique to the postwar period. This book is a history of youth travel in Europe, and how this cross-border mobility fostered a European social and cultural integration between the end of the Second World War and the end of the Cold War. The young, through their travels, transgressed politically constituted territories in ever-widening patterns. In doing so, they developed a transnational travel culture vital to the broad ideological trajectory of postwar Europe. Meanwhile, the practice of independent youth travel itself spread across borders, incorporating more and more young people from more and more places, reaching well beyond Europe and young Europeans. By studying the practice of travel by the young and the emergence of youth as a transnational social body in the postwar period, *Backpack Ambassadors* emphasizes a profoundly social and cultural integration, in addition to an economic and political one. By investigating the cultural practice of youth travel as a case study, it argues for a less EU-centric approach to the writing of European integration history. This book is not a history of the European Union or its antecedents. The development of youth travel worked at times with the institutional, technocratic efforts at formal integration, at times against them, and at other times outside them altogether. European integration is usually treated as a top-down affair, but this book is a cultural history that looks at the story from the bottom up, revealing how state policy and social activity interacted.

The postwar travel of the young between the various nations of Europe was intended to promote international cooperation and understanding. This would help the people of Western Europe avoid future violence and national aggression by developing an amicable familiarity with peoples and places. This project is integral to understanding the historical development of European integration by showing how Western European states and societies, through public-private partnerships, sought to surmount cultural divides and promote civic discourse through the international travel of the young. In the postwar period, the young of Western Europe were encouraged to interact and think of themselves as a transnational community based on age. Interestingly, the young individuals interconnecting Europe through circuitous travel were not exclusively European. Their geographic origins were increasingly diverse, ranging from North and South America to the Antipodes, Asia, and Africa. The policies of the United States government, and the activities of young Americans, figure prominently throughout this story: U.S. foreign policy promoted integration, and young Americans helped shape European travel culture, with more than a million traveling to and through Europe each year by the 1970s.[2] Still, although their numbers were quite large, backpacking in Europe was not as much an American phenomenon as it was a European one.

Akira Iriye has led the way in considering the international relations of cultural organizations.[3] Several historians have focused on the role of young people who participated within and through such formal organizations, including the European Movement, rendering visible their political work in foreign relations, especially within the ideological struggles of the Cold War.[4] While these studies demonstrate the integral role of the young acting through larger adult-led paradigms, *Backpack Ambassadors* builds on work that looks at informal practices outside such structured and organized leisure or political movements by considering the transnational mobility of young people and its role in developing the postwar social body of youth.[5] The study of international relations has understandably operated in a paradigm that frames the national state as the key actor. Looking at the broad impact of transnational youth travel enables us to emphasize the horizontal dimensions of integration emerging from social activity, rather than just the vertical dimensions descending from the political activity of diplomats negotiating international treaties. While these backpackers were not ambassadorial in the sense of acting in the direct service of the state, their interactive mobility suggests a different kind of international relations.

Indeed, young people often considered themselves, with justification, to be especially transnational when compared to their older counterparts. Their aspirations and activities in the twentieth century led them to seek possibility through mobility, whether for work or leisure, politics or culture, education or immigration, identity or community. They often saw their mobility as a distinct privilege of their age.[6] Youth as a life stage, cultural concept, and social group is characterized by movement: as an individual life stage, it marks the transition from childhood to adulthood; as a cultural concept, it is symbolic of vibrant activity, dynamic rejuvenation, and unruly commotion; and as a social body, it is defined by an articulated and flexible unity of cultural practices that extend across time and space, even if the exact parameters of what counts as youth and who counts as young vary by period and place. The accelerated contacts between the young themselves have given shape to the social body of youth, and by extension to society as a whole. Indeed, what we think of as youth is a transnational invention of industrial modernity, while the proliferation of postwar youth cultures arose from the transnational dynamics of the baby boom, the high material standards of living, and the expansion of education, secularization, and mass media.[7] Accordingly, the role that the young play as youth within society has changed.

The concept of "rites of passage" comes from cultural anthropology and describes the formalized rituals used to mark an individual's or group's change in social status. When applied to the young, it commonly denotes the movement from youth to adulthood. "Rites" refers to the ritualized ceremonial aspects of sanctioned behavior held in common by the community, while "passage" denotes the episodic advancement along a path, course, route, or threshold. Importantly, the passage takes place between multiple groups, with the young acting as intermediaries, and the rites they perform serve to bind the various social groups together as a community. Most often, the ceremony marks the integration of the young into the adult community on terms set and controlled by the latter. However, if we focus on the agency of the young on their own terms and consider the practices that emerge from their own sociability, we no longer see being young merely as being preparatory for being adult, but instead recognize how the young themselves create youth.[8]

In the case studied here, the informal rites developed out of the passage. Youth hostels and rail passes, for example, provided a systemic infrastructure for youth travel, the continuity of which crossed national borders and overlay Europe in ever-denser matrices, beginning in the north and west before expanding into the south and east. In Western Europe between 1946 and 1960, the number of youth hostels doubled, the number of hostel members tripled, the number of hostel beds quadrupled, and the number of overnight stays in hostels more than quintupled. In the 1970s, Eurail and Interrail youth passes provided affordable mobility to millions of young people from around the world, enabling them to crisscross Western Europe in their rail-riding peregrinations. This networked infrastructure preceded formal integration and helped shape a repertoire of social behaviors, the accumulation of which aggregated into patterns of cultural practice. The cultural practice of independent youth travel, in turn, evolved over time, proliferated across space, and incorporated more practitioners, thus becoming, at the same time, more condensed and more diffuse. Through the agency of the young, backpacking became ritualized as a new form of passage, with associated habits and behaviors that were laden with symbolic meaning. As a travel practice, it has spread across the globe, and while heterogeneous, it retains the strong association with youth.

Youth backpacker travel was distinguishable from other forms of young cross-border mobility. It was a voluntary movement, not compelled by circumstance or external force, and was of a touristic character, if in a new form. Thus, while migratory guest workers or conscripted soldiers or political refugees may have been young and on the move in Europe, their mobility was distinct from that of backpackers, even if at times the different groups' practices might intersect, overlap, or conflict. State and society privileged who could travel, when, where, and how. Access to mobility acted as a stratifying factor of inclusion and exclusion. Over time, the distinctions of class, gender, and nationality diminished, but those of race and ethnicity persisted, as we will see. Even among backpackers, the more their travel resembled vagrancy or migration, the more negatively it was perceived by the general public and the more forcefully it was regulated by the state. The integrative elements of their mobility were accompanied by processes of delimitation and othering that also constituted a form of Europeanization.

Travel and tourism are being reconsidered by scholars for the transnational role they have played in international relations, as large numbers of people moved across borders in pursuit of leisure. This was nowhere more evident than in postwar Western Europe, where mass leisure and personal mobility were embraced as democratizing forces that empowered a broadening middle class, spurred economic development, and encouraged transnational encounters.[9] There has been quite a bit of historical research on tourism as consumption and leisure, but surprisingly less emphasis on the historical study of travel as transnational mobility.[10] The simultaneous rise of mass tourism and international youth culture were intertwined phenomena of postwar consumer capitalism as it expanded the market of leisure across Western Europe. Time and cost barriers to travel were dramatically lowered, while the political barriers to cross-border traffic also diminished. Leisure mobility changed from aspiration to expectation, in part as a result of interwar legislation such as the 1936 French law guaranteeing paid vacations and the British Holiday with Pay Act of 1938. Considerable scholarly attention has been placed on the production of identity, including national identity, and its entanglement with travel and tourism.[11] There is a growing focus on the phenomenon of youth travel as well, though not yet much by historians.[12]

The social field in which these young travelers interacted spanned borders, giving rise to a cultural practice that had an integrating effect on Europe. By following their movements, tracing their circuits, and identifying their behaviors across national borders, we learn that the nation is not effaced by such transnational endeavors, but instead operates in a broader context of dynamic social processes. One prominent scholar has written, "If social history rewrote history from the bottom up, transnational history proceeds from the outside in."[13] As national boundaries were crossed more and more often, their symbolic power was eroded through routine, yet not dissolved, as the nation continued to condition and shape the mobility of the young. In following backpackers' trajectories, we can see how their experiences transcended existing boundaries while creating new ones and doing the same for travel practices. The networks of youth travel acted as a circuitry interconnecting more and more of Europe as the transnational flows and practices perforated nation-state territorial containers.

Transnational circulations are being studied for what they can tell us about the social and cultural impact of modern mobility.[14] Sociologist John Urry thinks that contemporary society can best be understood as consisting of interlocking systems of mobility, virtual and physical, informational and demographic, local and transnational.[15] Fellow sociologist Zygmunt Bauman has written at length about the twenty-first century's "liquid modernity" of unstructured, fluid states of flows and circulations, an era of software rather than hardware, and of uncertain, shifting paradigms in which humanity is compelled to keep moving.[16] Travel and tourism are major dimensions of this mobile liquidity, as globally they constitute the world's largest industry. As a case study of the history of youth travel, *Backpack Ambassadors* considers the infrastructures that condition movement, the hidden and conspicuous passage of people and things, the contact zones of cultural exchange, the tensions of individual agency and structural constraint, and the interrelation of the mobile with the immobile, but it does so in ways that provide a significant historical dimension that explains how this mobile world came about.[17]

Travel and mobility are creative activities of the human condition that have been shared across time and place, especially, if not uniquely, in the West. Gilgamesh and Odysseus were tested by their wanderings, gaining self-realization through the endurance of ordeal.[18] Herodotus has the distinction of being both one of the world's first historians and one of its first travel writers, for his histories are as much travelogue as chronicle. In many ways, the ancient Romans invented vacations and tourism. Naples became the first holiday resort, with second homes for the Roman elite, who also traveled to Egypt to tour the pyramids and to Greece to see temple ruins, even leaving graffiti, which is still visible, scrawled on the walls to mark their visits. An ancient map guidebook, the *Tabula Peutingeriana*, recommended routes, marked tourist sites, and indicated facilities such as hostels and inns along the Roman roadways.[19]

The medieval knight established his freedom within the feudal hierarchy through travel, codifying the connection between spatial mobility and social mobility. The Renaissance praised the value of travel as an educational recommendation.

The "Grand Tour," a long and leisurely trek through Europe that was customarily undertaken by aristocratic young men in the seventeenth and eighteenth centuries, combined the chivalric tradition of the young knight with that of the Renaissance scholar, a systematized cultural practice that indelibly associated extended European travel with youth and personal development.[20] The medieval guild tradition of the journeyman's *Wanderjahr* developed into working-class apprenticeships on the road, away from home. In 1765, Diderot, in his famous *Encyclopédie*, talked about travel as something that enriches the mind and reduces prejudice. The Romantic poets of the early nineteenth century, such as Wordsworth, Keats, and Byron, turned travel and tramping into an aesthetic experience, as did the Beat poets and novelists of the mid-twentieth century.[21] The Grand Tour, meanwhile, became more middle class and evolved from a lengthy sojourn to a summer excursion of a month or two.[22]

Modern vacationing emerged in the industrial economy of Europe in the mid-nineteenth century, with a rapid internationalization of practices and standards that developed into mid-twentieth-century mass tourism. Beach resorts like Ostend, spas like Vichy, tour companies like Thomas Cook, and guidebooks such as *Baedeker* became well established in the second half of the 1800s, supporting a growing international market of well-to-do tourists. To be a part of European modernity was to be on the move, by rail, ship, or carriage, and later by bicycle, automobile, or airplane. The making of the modern tourist was also the making of the modern citizen. The nationalist potential of tourism was evident as a tool for nation building, while the democratization of leisure became an aspiration of welfare states.[23] The economic boom of the postwar decades led to a broadening of the middle class, an affluence expressed in the development of 1960s mass tourism.

The postwar mobility of the young stemmed from an interconnected social experience that developed into a new travel culture, centered in Europe and defined by a fluid yet coherent set of values and practices. Over time, this circuitous transnational mobility helped to interconnect European economies, states, and peoples. It was integral to the establishment of the principle, unique to Europe, of free movement across open borders. Today, mobility is enshrined in article 45 of the EU Charter of Fundamental Rights, guaranteeing the freedom of movement to all EU citizens, while travel has in recent decades been used as a policy tool for building European identity, just as it had been used to build national identity a century earlier.

Early accounts of European integration focused on elite figures involved in diplomatic negotiations within a history of ideology and political movements. Later the focus of study shifted away from "great men" toward the role of the state and national interests, but still viewed through a diplomatic lens. More recent work has taken a comparative approach but still prioritizes the nation, while the study of non-state actors has been largely limited to business associations and trade unions that worked closely with technocratic elites. What has been lacking are multilateral, multi-archival transnational histories that emphasize non-state actors as agents of integration beyond the sum of national European policies.[24] *Backpack Ambassadors* is such an investigation.

Historians such as Kiran Klaus Patel have called for new ways of looking at the process of European integration outside, and as distinct from, the political and economic framework that led to the creation of the European Union.[25] Working backward from its establishment overemphasizes the singular role the EU and that of its various predecessors in the integration of Europe. Instead, we should consider the plurality of integrations, the multiple interconnections, and the variety of ways in which Europe became more integrally interactive, whether economically, politically, technologically, socially, or culturally. By embedding the history of the European Union within broader international structures and transnational networks, we decenter it in ways that acknowledge the historical activity of non-governmental actors, young travelers among them.

This can take a variety forms. One strategy is to think about Europeanization as distinct from, or at least a complement to, formal integration. Europeanization is a flexible lens through which to consider the intensification of intra-European connections, exchanges, and entanglements that does not, by necessity, imply a teleological progression toward political union, nor even a singular ideological pursuit.[26] For example, there has been considerable work focused on questions of infrastructure, particularly regarding transport, energy, and telecommunication systems.[27] Likewise, in postwar Western Europe, there was a proliferation and convergence of welfare states, parliamentary democracies, and regimes of consumer capitalism. Meanwhile, cultural studies of integration have been limited to the internal dynamics of cultural practice within the EU bureaucracy, or to official cultural policies through which the EU has tried to inculcate a European identity.[28] Few scholars have considered the cultural practices that emerge from transnational social interaction among the people of Europe as a community—and the contribution that this process has made to integration. As this book demonstrates, the emergence of mass youth travel is an ideal case for illuminating these dimensions.

Backpack Ambassadors traces this cultural integration process from 1945 to 1992. It opens at the moment that Western Europe confronted the violent legacy of two world wars, and it concludes at the end of the Cold War and as European integration was redefined by the Maastricht Treaty. It details the institutional and governmental programs that various countries used in the years following the Second World War to promote fraternity among their populations via the travel and interaction of the young. It also considers the emergence of independent youth travel and how this separate process often complicated the official pattern of integration, while still contributing to it in unofficial ways. Thus it investigates the overlap of inter-state and non-state transnational activities and actors.

There is a long history of intra- and extra-European circulation through labor exchange, merchant trade networks, agricultural migrations, military campaigns, religious pilgrimages, imperial bureaucracy, study abroad, and tourism, but the mass travel of young backpackers was a new development, unique to the postwar period. The dynamic interaction of their circulation can therefore teach us a lot about the specific context of Europe in the decades after the Second World War and how youth mobility shaped major political developments of the era: from postwar reconstruction to Cold War rivalries; from the reconciliation of France and West Germany to the protests and countercultures of the 1960s; from the legacies of imperialism to European unification. I hope that by looking through the window of youth travel, readers will be able to survey the changing landscape of Europe in the decades after the Second World War and, in doing so, understand the relevance of this period for contemporary concerns about borders and migration.

ONE

Youth Mobility and the Making of Europe

Odette Lesley, a young Londoner, marveled at all the people she had met from around the world during the Second World War. She found that these encounters gave her a profound desire to travel when the conflict was over, and this was something she felt she shared with others her age. "We realized that there was a very big new world out there, that we knew nothing about at all. All I knew, for instance, was my little bit of north London, where I'd been brought up; the local streets, my neighbours, and the local dance hall. But I was hearing these marvellous stories, and they opened up horizons to such an extent that I thought I might even see those places one day. I might go there. And I felt a strong sense of independence as a girl that I'd never felt before. It was so exciting, I felt anything was possible."[1] Lesley's enthusiastic expression of liberation and autonomy tied to mobility and international travel was typical for the period and for her age, as young Europeans began to travel on an unprecedented scale in the years following the war.

Meanwhile, Anne O'Hare McCormick, the respected foreign correspondent for the *New York Times*, wrote in her column "Abroad" about the need for clarity in the European postwar settlement. She thought that some form of European unity was in order, which was rightly being demanded by the young in particular. What they wanted was "a large world like yours," she quoted a young Frenchman as saying, "where you can move freely across State lines and feel at home anywhere." McCormick claimed that the young envisioned a continent "not without nations . . . but without customs or passports." However, this was in jeopardy, she insisted. As the Allies divided Germany and the continent into rigid zones of influence, there was a danger of young Europeans becoming part of the problem rather than the solution. "These citizens of tomorrow are no longer the material for unity, within their own country, with neighboring countries, or in the United Nations."[2] To her mind, the internationalism of European youth, expressed through their desire for unfettered mobility, was essential to Europe's peaceful future, to the problem of Germany, and to recovery in general. If Odette Lesley expressed a youthful desire for independence and mobility to explore the world and meet new people, Anne McCormick advocated a rationale for state policies to harness this mobility to serve the purpose of stabilizing postwar Europe.

In the years following the Second World War, Western Europeans, through private and public initiatives, invested significant resources to send the young across national borders and to welcome young travelers from abroad. They did this in a variety of ways: through the establishment, expansion, and transformation of their national youth hostel networks, shifting the focus away from domestic and toward international travel; through the proliferation of international work camps where the young could labor for the reconstruction of Europe in fraternal camaraderie; and through the organization of the European Youth Campaign, aimed at uniting the continent through the abolition of border controls. In short, the young of Europe were encouraged to visit, encounter, and engage other nations and nationalities. All of these endeavors were intended to help Western Europe recover from the violent hostility of the recent past by facilitating youth mobility across national borders. Nationalist and internationalist endeavors were deeply intertwined as the young were treated as assets in the national humanitarian and reconstruction projects.[3]

This cultural internationalism had its roots in the interwar period, was focused on reconciliation between belligerent nations, and was premised on the interpersonal interaction of the young.[4] International hosteling, American study abroad, Franco-German youth exchanges, and pan-European federalism all originated in the 1920s and 1930s. While the vitality of internationalism in the interwar period is often overlooked, given the vehement nationalism with which it competed, it relied on transnational structures and activities of non-state actors just as its postwar successor would.[5] As part of the 1940s postwar reconstruction in Western Europe, international gatherings of young people labored to restore and build hostels, railways, parks, and schools. As a component of this endeavor, the international travel of European youth was promoted generally, but Germany and young Germans were targeted specifically, in an attempt to integrate them into a broader European community by bringing western youth to occupied Germany, and by encouraging travel outside the occupied zones by young Germans. Indeed, in the decades after the Second World War, many young Germans, who had a somewhat troubled relationship with nationality, used travel as a means to Europeanize themselves.

Meanwhile, the young themselves began to travel in greater and greater numbers, using and shaping the development of a vast infrastructure to support their mobility. The frequency of their travels and the routes of their itineraries brought them in contact with one another through a transnational expansion of social space that was regionally limited to the western half of the continent. As organized exchange groups or as independent hitchhikers, these young travelers began to recognize themselves as a cohort with shared interests via their circuits of travel in Western Europe. Because of the informality of these social relations, they were indirect as well as largely imagined, yet they were powerful nonetheless. Thus, in the postwar period, there was a complex top-down and bottom-up process of policies and demand regarding youth mobility, which led to the emergence by the 1960s of a vast new travel culture; this, in turn, helped give shape to Western Europe as a democratic and "Europeanized" social space.

The Cultural Internationalism of Hosteling

The first youth hostel was the brainchild of Richard Schirrmann, a teacher in Altena, Westphalia, who liked to take his students on days-long rambles through the surrounding hills and forests. He envisioned the availability of overnight accommodations throughout the German countryside to facilitate hiking and exploration by the young. In 1909 he set up the first youth hostel in a school, but with support from the local *Landrat*, he was able to move it to the old fortified castle of Altena in 1912. Schirrmann's idea emerged in the context of an existing widespread hiking culture among young Germans, known as the *Wandervögel* or *Zugvögel*, or "migrating birds," whose shelters were often called "nests."[6] By 1913 Schirrmann had already established eighty-three youth hostels in the hills of the northern Rhineland.[7] While the onset of the First World War disrupted this expansion, soon thereafter momentum was restored, with much of the hostel equipment bought cheaply as army surplus. There were twelve hundred German youth hostels by 1921, and twenty-one hundred a decade later, with the number of overnights in 1931 reaching a staggering 4.2 million.[8] In the Weimar era, the German youth hostel movement became a respected national institution, independent but enjoying the support of national and local government, providing a common meeting place for young people from a variety of backgrounds. The scope of the youth hostel membership in terms of class, gender, and region was remarkable as the association successfully managed to navigate the difficult political climate of the 1920s.[9]

Schirrmann's original vision was limited to his own country; he had no aspirations for an international movement. Nevertheless, in the 1920s the concept began to be duplicated elsewhere, usually by young people who had visited Germany and then brought the idea back home.[10] The first youth hostel outside Germany was founded in Zurich in 1924, with the concept spreading the next year to Basel, and then elsewhere in Switzerland. Next was Poland, where the government was particularly keen on the possibilities of hostels for nation building. Then, in quick succession, youth hostel organizations were founded across Western and Northern Europe. By 1931 they were in Denmark, Norway, the Netherlands, Belgium, Scotland, England, Wales, Ireland, and France. Each of these was a local endeavor, using the German association as a model, but taking on attributes specific to its own national context.[11]

Indeed, in many ways the national was paramount. A Hamburg businessman funded a program to build hostels on Germany's perimeter in order to emphasize a German cultural identity on the nation's margins.[12] The Swiss hostels were not eager to welcome foreign visitors, and discouraged them with higher fees while reserving beds for the exclusive use of Swiss youth. In Basel, the hostel's first annual report stated frankly that it intended "to ensure that youth hostels should not be overrun by foreigners."[13] In Poland, youth hostels were a government rather than private initiative. The Polish government wanted not only to help the young appreciate the beauty and variety of their new country, but also to "awaken in them a feeling of national pride, and encourage a positive attitude towards the State."[14] This functional use of youth travel to serve national integration was common throughout the various networks where the young were encouraged to discover and appreciate their homelands and fellow countrymen through hosteling. While bicycling around Sweden in the mid-1930s, for example, Gösta Lundquist marveled at the new patterns of contact between young workers, farmers, and students via the new Swedish hostel network; he commented in his journal that "out of this, something must grow," reflecting his sense that this was a positive development for the Swedish community because hosteling was fundamentally in tune with the egalitarian vision of social democracy.[15] Yet here, too, the Swedish Tourist Association, which had established the hostel system with nearly three hundred hostels and more than seven thousand beds by 1939, was overtly nationalist, refusing to join the International Youth Hostel Federation (IYHF) until 1946 to avoid the required reciprocity, and strictly limiting accessibility to foreign youth in favor of native Swedes of whatever age.[16]

The most overt nationalist politicization, unsurprisingly, was in Nazi Germany. In early 1933 the Nazis took power, and that spring they took over the German Youth Hostel Association, just as they eventually eliminated all independent youth movements by absorbing them into the compulsory Hitler Youth.[17] The number of German youth hostels shrank by 25 percent under the Third Reich, even though they were used as places of political and militarist indoctrination for groups of "Aryan" youth. While the Nazis viewed group travel and tourism as an effective tool of nationalism, independent travel was firmly discouraged; effectively, it was considered to be vagabondage.[18] A young Frenchman who witnessed these dramatic changes noted that in 1932, German youth hostels had already become politicized spaces for competing ideologies: "the uncommitted were few," he wrote, and "everyone had taken sides." A year later, in 1933, he found the hostels completely taken over by Nazism, with portraits of Adolf Hitler and rousing renditions of the Nazi anthem "Horst Wessel" sung by the common-room fire.[19]

Yet throughout the 1930s, even as the Germans forfeited leadership in the hosteling movement and the tension between European nation-states escalated, efforts were made to establish a structure for an international organization. The first international conference of youth hostel associations took place in Amsterdam in 1932. The International Youth Hostel Federation was founded soon thereafter to coordinate and organize the practical problems of international travel by the young within the different national hostel networks. For example, the IYHF focused on designing and adopting a standardized pictogram sign language, arranging bilateral agreements of membership reciprocity, getting the individual networks to agree on and conform to standard policies, and helping new youth hostel associations get established.[20] Although the internationalist impulse dates from this period, it was after 1945 that hosteling became a forceful proponent of cultural internationalism as a distinct contrast to its more national or domestic posture of the interwar period. That is, there was a fundamental ideological shift as a result of the Second World War.[21]

At its most basic level, cultural internationalism says that a more peaceful world order can be achieved through interpersonal interactions at the sociocultural level across national boundaries. Internationalism itself dates to the late nineteenth century. In fact, internationalism and nationalism have been parallel developments, but the historical peak of internationalism arguably came after the Second World War, when nationalism was blamed as the root cause of two devastating world wars. Whereas much of the internationalism of these postwar years was legal or economic, it was also focused on the capability of ordinary individuals to promote better understanding through collaborative endeavor. Europe was the center of this sort of internationalism.[22]

This kind of cultural internationalism had its origins in the wake of the First World War, when "Europe" became a component of national redefinition. The aftermath of the Great War led to a multitude of attempts to rebuild European relations in political, economic, social, and cultural terms. Although they diverged with national interests and competing visions, such movements deliberately developed an ideological Europeanism.[23] Throughout the 1920s, French and German Europeanists, for example, sought to change hostile attitudes through the intercultural contact of elites engaged in transnational collaboration and networking; but in the 1940s, such efforts became more democratic and shifted to reach a much broader audience with a heightened emphasis on the young.

Under the leadership of Jack Catchpool, the IYHF would see its task in the postwar period as not simply to promote hosteling, but in doing so to rebuild Europe and serve the international community more broadly by promoting friendship and cooperation in the face of deadly chauvinist nationalism. In his 1946 presidential address to the IYHF conference, the first to take place in eight years, Catchpool proclaimed that "with the help of our organization . . . bonds of friendship and understanding may do more to prevent future wars than the work of statesmen and diplomats. We must work single-mindedly to re-establish the facilities which existed before the War and to extend them enormously. . . . We must encourage young people to regard a holiday abroad as their right and privilege," because "we have an apparatus in our hands which may do much to heal the wounds of our broken world."[24]

Indeed, internationalism became the animating force undergirding the expansion of hosteling in the postwar period. A new, profoundly idealistic and egalitarian optimism governed the hostel movement and was represented publicly by the indefatigable Catchpool: "We strive to bring together the peoples of the world, so that around the common-room fire, or sharing a common meal, or wandering along the trail, they may learn to appreciate each other's viewpoint and outlook, and realize that we are a world brotherhood."[25] In 1946, each hostel began hosting an annual "International Weekend" to give full attention to the international character of youth hosteling.[26] As the Danish minister of education explained, "there is no age better to start with in the international field than the young and there is no better way of starting friendships between young people than the free intercourse across all frontiers and the arrangements for housing the young wanderers under a common roof."[27] In response to the growing demand by the young for international travel, IYHF secretary Leo Meilink, a Dutchman, stated that in the new postwar order "we will all have to live in an international way."[28]

In 1948, Catchpool implied that the internationalist impulse of hosteling was its most compelling and significant feature; indeed, it was its greatest contribution to humanity.[29] Because of the successful efforts he witnessed in the years immediately following the war, Catchpool grew increasingly emboldened in his vision of hosteling to serve internationalism. He described hostelers as "youthful ambassadors" and speculated that in the years to come, the IYHF would be a worthy recipient of the Nobel Peace Prize.[30] "To-day," he concluded, "all nations are interdependent, and to attain lasting liberty and equality, we must practise fraternity too, on an international scale."[31] The new IYHF constitution stated plainly that its purpose was "to foster understanding and goodwill between nations, particularly by facilitating international travel."[32] By the end of the 1950s, the cultural internationalism of hosteling was viewed as a resounding success in bringing the young of Western Europe closer together, and in turn, bringing the countries of Western Europe closer together as well.[33]

Hosteling fit well within the larger Allied assumption that the reconstruction of democracy in Europe would require the advancement of liberal individualism.[34] Postwar liberal parliamentary democracy itself would become a defining feature of Western Europe, while its establishment was a site of Europeanization.[35] Catchpool had stressed the need for an aggressive expansion of hostel networks to spread not only the good work of internationalism, but also democratic practices. The hostel was, he said, "the nursery for our democracy." It taught responsibility and good citizenship by training young people to be self-reliant and to think and work for themselves. It brought together in companionship the young of varied social backgrounds, some rich, some poor, some urban, some rural, some boys, some girls. It taught a moral order through the interaction of young men and young women working with a common purpose. It taught democratic methods through the debate and committee work of governing and managing hostels and hostel networks.[36] Because the young served on local and national committees, volunteered for work parties, and cooperated in the administration and development of local hostels, hosteling was considered effective training in democracy. As Catchpool said, "The increasing part taken by young people in the control and organisation of hostels, in every country, is, I believe, the finest training they can have in the duties and responsibilities of citizenship in a democracy."[37] Accordingly, the 1950 IYHF constitution articulated a democratic egalitarianism, stating that "hostels shall be resting places where young people of every nationality and circumstance can meet in friendly atmosphere" with "no barriers or distinction of race, colour, religion, or class."[38] This may seem innocuous today, but it represents a significant ideological shift from the years before the war.

A unanimous motion passed at the 1946 conference of the IYHF stated that the movement ought particularly "to help the moral resuscitation of youth."[39] In 1947, Leo Meilink stressed that hosteling was primarily an educational movement, and not simply tourism.[40] An article from an American pedagogical journal entitled "Youth Hosteling: Social Travel toward Democracy" found hosteling to be "a rugged, simple, friendly, democratic way of living." By allowing the young to know and love their homeland through personal observation, and by promoting "common physical, mental and spiritual excellence" among them, the author concluded that hosteling was "a great potential force for character education and for education for democracy."[41] Another study published the same year made the connection between democratic practices and internationalism explicit by stating that hosteling "tends to encourage and develop cosmopolitan attitudes" and "international sympathy" through "contacts fostered by the youth hostel [that] are characteristically democratic." That is, "one of the significant results of the commingling of young people in the democratic milieu of the youth hostel has been the development of international friendship. In short, hostel membership together with mutual interests and activities minimized national prejudices."[42]

In a different article, the same sociologist concluded that hosteling was a superb example of the social distance theory of social problems, which says that generally, the better the understanding and fellow-feeling between individuals and groups, the fewer the social problems. His study concluded that bringing together young people from a variety of economic and international backgrounds through the common practice of hosteling contributed to "the elimination of physical distance," which then "leads to a diminution of social distance." The "leveling function" was most important because "the hostel is thus a working democracy." Even though language created barriers, he claimed that in the unique context of hosteling, the desire to overcome foreign languages itself facilitated sociability.[43] The proponents of hosteling argued that it could be used as an effective tool to foster democracy in postwar Europe by training the young in democratic practices informed by an internationalist worldview; hosteling, as such, was viewed as integral to the cultural reconstruction of Western Europe.[44]

The Work of Cultural Reconstruction

The first postwar conference of the IYHF established four immediate objectives: reconstruction in Western Europe with an emphasis on international work parties; facilitation of international youth travel in the difficult circumstances of postwar Europe; training and international exchanges of youth hostel wardens; and the reestablishment of a democratic youth hostel system in Germany.[45] The physical reconstruction of youth hostel networks proceeded at a remarkable speed, with the formerly occupied countries of Western Europe reaching their 1939 usage level by 1947. The average size of European youth hostels increased from twenty-seven to forty-seven beds between 1946 and 1950.

The war had taken a terrible toll on the continental hostel networks. In the summer of 1939, there had been forty-six hundred youth hostels recording more than 11 million overnight stays, with 40 percent of the total number of hostels in Germany alone. Demand for accommodations that summer far exceeded supply.[46] During the war, most hostels were raided for equipment, others were taken over to be used as soldiers' barracks, and many were destroyed outright. By 1946, the numbers had dropped to eighteen hundred youth hostels with 2.3 million overnights, with most of these outside continental Europe.[47] Where combat had taken place, the numbers were grim. There were nine youth hostels remaining in the Netherlands, France had fewer than fifty, and the number in Germany had been reduced from over two thousand to a few hundred.[48]

Voluntary international work camps served the purpose of building, repairing, and improving hostels, while simultaneously promoting international camaraderie among the young volunteers. As the *Birmingham Post* enthused, these young people "are to be envied for the chance of foreign travel and of working alongside youth of other countries; for the stimulating exchange of experiences, hopes and ideas in those wide-ranging common-room talks after the day's work is done; and for the satisfaction which comes of having put something of oneself into a house for others."[49] Already in the summer of 1946, there were four hundred English hostelers working on seven projects stretching from Norway to Italy. There were dozens of projects to build or repair hostels each year. In the summer of 1949, a group of thirty young people from eleven countries ventured to the island of Ameland off the Dutch coast to turn the ruins of a German radar station into a youth hostel. In a twenty-minute documentary, "A Song for Ameland," they were promoted as part of a "youthful army" of international volunteers mobilized across Europe to rebuild the continent, working toward a future of peace and camaraderie.[50]

Youth Service Camps sprang up all over Europe in the wake of the war. Financed by voluntary contributions and organized by a wide variety of associations, the camps recruited young men and women with an average age of twenty to spend anywhere from a few weeks to a few months laboring in the reconstruction of cultural and educational resources such as hostels, parks, and schools, and sometimes infrastructure such as railways and roads. The mobilized labor was secondary to the primary goal of "strengthening the democratic goodwill and human solidarity" of the young. Thus, while the task might be the completion of a structure, the focus was on cultivating good citizenship within an international community.[51] An internal report by the French military government enthused about the effectiveness of youth work camps sponsored by Service Civil International in their zone of occupied Germany.[52] In the summer of 1948, the head of the French occupation, General Pierre Koenig, compellingly lobbied the French government to allow young Germans into France to work in camps there. While Koenig recognized the delicacy of the situation and the reservations of the French government, he insisted on the demonstrated moral value of the international work camps, and of the desire for young Germans to meet and reconcile with other youth while learning about democracy in foreign cultures.[53]

Through the leadership of UNESCO, the Temporary International Council for Educational Reconstruction (TICER) was set up in the winter of 1947–48 as a centralizing and coordinating agency for twenty-five international organizations operating voluntary work camps in more

3   International Youth Work Camp at Burg Liebenzell, near Stuttgart, West Germany, 1953.
Bundesarchiv, Bild 194-0666-33/photo: Hans Lachmann.

than sixty countries. TICER was dedicated to facilitating educational and cultural reconstruction in war-devastated areas. The bulk of its work supported the international youth camps spread throughout Europe after the Second World War by helping them to pool resources and expertise, promoting their activities, and acting as an intermediary for them.[54] The camps, most of which took place during summer vacation, varied in size, from a dozen to several hundred to several thousand workers. In 1948 there were 135 camps in twenty European countries with over thirty thousand young volunteers from more than fifty nations.[55] Notably, the geographic distribution of these projects had not yet been disrupted by the hardening divisions of the Cold War, and they could be found across the continent. Yet in 1949, the number of camps sponsored in Eastern Europe dropped precipitously as the international service organizations were no longer welcome to operate there, and the visa and travel restrictions became markedly more difficult.[56] As a result, many such organizations were reconceived in the context of the Cold War as fighting the spread of communism.[57]

In the pre–Cold War moment, there were significant projects that garnered world attention and brought together large numbers of European youth in what would soon become the eastern bloc. Among them were the reconstruction of the village of Lidice in Czechoslovakia and the construction of the Youth Railways in Yugoslavia. In 1942 the Nazis had razed Lidice, shooting all the men and sending the women and children to concentration camps. After the war, volunteers came from around the world to help the survivors rebuild. The work camp there was the finish line of a 1947 international relay race, with the young competitors arriving from the four corners of the continent, having begun at other sites of Nazi brutality, such as Oradour in France and Hammerfest in Norway.[58]

While the efforts at Lidice emphasized recovery from the brutality of the nationalist past, the work in Yugoslavia was focused on a modern and internationalist future. In 1946 and 1947, leftist youth came from all over Europe to help build the "Youth Railways" of Brčko-Banovći and Šamac-Sarajevo. The 100-kilometer-long Brčko-Banovći line was built in the summer of 1946 by several thousand young people, including a few hundred foreign volunteers. Their days were spent in hard labor, while their evenings were occupied with cultural and athletic activities. The Yugoslavs used the success of this initial endeavor to mount a massive recruiting campaign for the summer of 1947 to bring in young people from abroad to work on the Šamac-Sarajevo Railway. The promotional materials tapped into the internationalist zeitgeist by declaring "the Youth Railway" as "a major contribution to the strengthening of fraternal solidarity and mutual co-operation between the youth of different countries."[59] That summer, more than two hundred thousand young men and women worked as laborers for various lengths of time, building five tunnels and seventeen bridges, leveling slopes, and putting up embankments, while laying nearly 250 kilometers of track.[60] The vast majority of the participants were from Yugoslavia, itself a multinational state that was using youth labor on construction projects and youth leisure in summer holiday camps as a means of reconciliation to heal the terrible national, ethnic, and political divisions of the war.[61] There were also several dozen "international youth brigades," organized according to nationality and totaling several thousand workers. The head of the British youth brigade was an enthusiastic twenty-three-year-old, E. P. Thompson, who went on to become a renowned historian whose first book was a collection of essays about the experience. He described a kind of internationalist and egalitarian idyll: while the young were building the railway, he said, "the Railway was building a new generation" and teaching them "democratic initiative and self-government and the true values of community living." At the end of their work, each foreign brigade was sent for a week or so on a tour of Yugoslavia, at which point many would break off to continue traveling independently in order to explore Southern Europe, most often Italy.[62]

As part of its postwar efforts to promote youth travel in Europe as a means of recovery, the IYHF targeted Italy as a destination for international travelers, as well as to help young Italians become travelers themselves. The country had no youth hostels, however. Although it had been a priority destination for other young Europeans dating back centuries to the aristocratic Grand Tour, there was no tradition among Italian youth of going on prolonged rambles by foot or bicycle, nor of group travel to other countries, nor even much in the way of student exchanges. Young people were not attracted to each other as a social group in Italy in the same way as elsewhere in Europe; the social group of "youth" developed later there, solidifying in the 1960s.[63]

Efforts to establish youth hostels in Italy proved difficult. In fact, because there was seemingly no demand for hostels by young Italians themselves, it was initially proposed that other national associations build their own hostels in a new "Youth City" to be developed in Rome.[64] This idea was rejected, however, as being antithetical to the hosteling movement, particularly because it would segregate hostelers according to nationality. Instead, the first Italian youth hostel opened in 1946 in a former fascist youth center in the Italian Alps, followed by three others in 1948. By 1950 there were twenty-four hostels, but membership in the Italian Youth Hostel Association was anemic at less than two thousand.[65]

Elsewhere on the Southern European periphery, Francisco Franco's regime began actively promoting Spain as a travel destination for other Europeans. One of the first of many state-led initiatives was the establishment in 1955 of a youth hostel organization. Initially the Spanish government set up impromptu youth hostels during the summer months in schools and at residential colleges, with separate accommodations for boys and girls aged fourteen to twenty-one. The regime quickly decided that it was most interested in attracting foreign youth, and it sought to join the IYHF to gain the advantages of reciprocity. For its part, the IYHF insisted that the Spanish youth hostels be independent from the government, that the upper age limit be abolished for foreigners, and that permanent hostels open to both sexes be established. The Spanish agreed to the reforms, most reluctantly to mixed accommodations, and gained IYHF membership in 1957.[66] In 1959, hostels in Spain had fifteen thousand overnights by Spanish members and fifteen thousand foreign overnights, with five thousand Spanish members hosteling abroad.[67] Within ten years, the cross-border hosteling traffic had grown significantly, with ninety thousand foreign overnights in Spanish hostels, while Spanish youth spent twenty-eight thousand nights abroad but only forty-five hundred in Spain.[68]

European tourism to Spain began in earnest in the late 1950s and expanded in an extraordinary way over the next decade and a half. Between 1959 and 1973, the annual number of foreign visitors to Spain grew from three million to thirty-four million.[69] Spain was a primary beneficiary of the shift from upper-class leisure travel to mass tourism that characterized the economic prosperity of the era. The welfare states of Western and Northern Europe guaranteed two to three weeks of paid holiday, while the growth of private and public transport—planes, trains, and automobiles—brought sunny Spanish beaches within reach.

The late Franco regime intentionally encouraged foreign tourism as a way to combat Spain's isolation from Western Europe. Spain had not been a belligerent in the war or a recipient of Marshall Aid; nor was it a member of NATO or involved in the official efforts at economic integration. It wasn't a welfare state democracy, either. Thus, in multiple ways, it stood apart and distinct from Western Europe, and its marginality was largely based on such difference. Tourism, then, became a useful auxiliary to the complexities of formal diplomacy through informal exchange, commercial and otherwise. The Franco regime was interested in the economic development and foreign currency that tourism would bring to Spain, but quite significantly, it also imagined tourism as a way to Europeanize the country.[70]

Governments varied in their explicit support of hosteling, but were on the whole keen to develop their networks in the postwar era. The IYHF was successful in lobbying Western European governments to reduce barriers to youth travel between countries by modifying passport, visa, and currency requirements, providing travel facilities and transportation at reduced cost to the young, and investing in the reconstruction and expansion of hostel networks. The Italian government officially recognized the new Italian Youth Hostel Association, and provided it with startup grants and funding.[71] The British government paid 50 percent of the cost of new hostels; the Norwegian government provided interest-free loans; the Dutch government gave grants; and the new West German government made the construction of youth hostels a centerpiece of its 1950 Youth Plan (*Bundesjungendplan*), easily outpacing the government funding of any other hostel association.[72]

Unsurprisingly, conditions immediately after the war had been most dire in Germany. The widespread destruction, the conditions of supply, and the division of the country into zones of Allied occupation made typical youth travel there a near impossibility. Initially, those youth hostels that remained intact were being used for more urgent needs, as hospitals, schools, or refugee housing. At first, the Allied powers occupying Germany viewed the hostel system as part of the Nazi infrastructure, and were reluctant to revitalize it. The American military authorities had planned to confiscate all remaining Bavarian youth hostels as part of their denazification program in the American zone, but a public outcry convinced them to reconsider.[73]

Beginning in the fall of 1945, the leaders of the American, British, and French hosteling associations urged their respective military governments occupying zones of Germany to restore the existing hostel buildings to their original purpose. They argued that hosteling could be a powerful tool in the Allied program of reeducation aimed at denazifying and democratizing Germany.[74] At the February 1946 IYHF executive meeting, it was agreed that hostels in Germany were "of the utmost importance for the future of Europe. It concern[s] the re-education of the German youth. . . . When hostels [are] used in the right way, they might be important instruments in the re-education of youth to democratic feelings and to mutual understanding and friendship."[75] A special committee was set up to advise the western occupying powers about the vital

4   An Anglo-German work party rebuilding the Weissenbrunn youth hostel in West Germany, 1948. Courtesy of Hostelling International.

part that hostels could play in the reeducation of German youth, particularly through international contact with other young people.[76] The Allied Control Council was convinced and assisted the IYHF endeavors with funding and logistical support.[77]

In February 1946, Leo Meilink, the secretary of the IYHF, addressed young Germans over Radio Luxembourg. "The youth of Germany," he said, "must not be excluded from our international community. In this closely inter-related world, everyone can find a place and cooperate in the life of the community. We are delighted that the founders of the

German youth hostel movement have taken up their work again, and are determined to rebuild the movement in its original and genuine form. We urge you all to cooperate, and we promise that we will give you all possible assistance."[78] Jack Catchpool was essential in establishing international work parties in the British zone of occupation, where British and German youth together reconstructed damaged youth hostels. He led the first party of volunteers to Hamburg in the summer of 1947. In this regard, he drew upon his past experience as an Englishman helping to build hostels in Ireland in the thirties, where "[we] tried to say with the work of our hands, how sorry we were for all the many and grievous misunderstandings of the past."[79] In the following two years, teams of young volunteers from several countries worked at dozens of sites in the British, American, and French zones, while German hostelers and hostel wardens visited Britain, the United States, and France.[80] International work party volunteers paid their own expenses and brought their own tools, food, sleeping bags, and other equipment.[81] The military governments provided indispensable equipment for the refurbished hostels, donating field beds, tents, blankets, and kitchen utensils.[82] In 1946, as a matter of official policy, the French military government made a thorough and systematic accounting of German hostels in its zone, detailing the condition, proximity to the nearest railway, and recommendations for improvement and possible expansion of each.[83] For the French, the restoration of hostels and exchange of youth would become an integral part of their strategy to reconcile and partner with West Germany.[84] By the end of 1948, 339 youth hostels were operating in the western zones of occupation, with 1.5 million overnights. In 1949, with the approval of the occupying powers, the German Youth Hostel Association was reestablished, and in 1950 it was readmitted to membership in the IYHF.[85]

There was, of course, tension and lingering animus toward Germany and German hostelers. For example, the official language of the IYHF had been German in the 1930s, but it was changed to English in 1946, with some members adamantly refusing to hear German spoken at all. Even the elderly father of hosteling, Richard Schirrmann, who was no Nazi, was treated with trepidation. Later there was some difficulty in the restored Dutch hostels regarding the preponderance of young Germans traveling there in the early 1950s. Some found the Germans not to be deferential enough, to lack tact and sensitivity given the recent and harsh occupation.[86] Similarly, the young Dutch who chose to travel to Germany in these years referred to it as "missionary work" (*missiewerk*), their reluctant duty to convert young Germans into Europeans.[87] In light of the war's legacy, the German hostel group reported to the IYHF on the welcome surprise that young people from Western Europe and the United States had come to visit them, and to work side by side with young Germans. The Germans themselves were still "waiting for the opportunity to travel abroad and make contacts with the youth of other countries, but at present passport and money regulations make this almost impossible."[88] This would remain the case until the currency reform of 1948 and the loosening of border controls in 1950.

Looking back, leaders of the youth hostel movement found that "the social changes brought about by the war had, in general, a favorable effect on the youth hostel movement in Europe."[89] It is not hard to see why. At the first postwar meeting of the Executive Committee, the IYHF made it clear that it wanted to stimulate international travel as soon as possible, because it saw this as a mechanism for reviving the use of hostel systems and, more importantly, as a means to establish common goodwill in the wake of the war. To get around currency restrictions, the IYHF set up an exchange coupon system, whereby hostelers could buy a voucher in their own country to be exchanged for an overnight stay in another.[90] Next, they lobbied governments to ease passport and visa controls for the young. As a result, during the reconstruction period, a time of continuing hardship and austerity, there was a sharp increase in the use of hostels by foreign visitors in Western Europe generally. For example, the total numbers of foreign overnights for Belgium, Denmark, France, the Netherlands, Norway, and Switzerland increased 600 percent between 1946 and 1949, from 65,000 to 390,000. A quarter of this international usage was attributable to British hostelers, who remained the most active until young Germans were able to travel in large numbers in the 1950s.

Young people in the United States were eager to travel in Europe as well. Their dilemma was not currency, but transportation. In coordination with the American Youth Hostel Association, Catchpool had tried for years to implement a plan for "Youth Ships" that would transport young travelers cheaply back and forth across the Atlantic Ocean. In 1947, the U.S. government released two troopships to do just that, but they were still unable to meet demand. In May 1948, the American Youth Hostel Association created a nonprofit organization to provide charter flights across the Atlantic at half the standard airfare. In 1949, three thousand American hostelers traveled to Europe by plane, and five hundred by ship.[91] The Organization for European Economic Cooperation (OEEC), set up as part of the Marshall Plan, was very impressed with the

European hostel network, deeming it ideal in the "necessary moral and material requirements" for youth travel, but they were concerned that the explosion in European demand for hostels would leave no room for young Americans. They considered this "a matter of extreme urgency," as they wanted to accommodate as many American youth as possible and encourage them to travel through Europe, in order not only to build a sense of transatlantic community but, more importantly, to bring in as many American dollars as possible.[92] In fact, the OEEC and the European Recovery Plan (ERP) both prioritized international and transatlantic tourism as a mechanism for restoring economic fluidity and capturing American dollars.[93] By 1960, young Americans would be second only to young Germans in the international usage of hostels. By 1965, a survey showed that 11 percent of all U.S. college students had traveled to Europe before graduation.[94]

Over the 1950s, there was a 66 percent increase in the number of beds provided by the seventeen youth hostel associations of Western Europe. It was a new era of purpose-built hostels supported lavishly by public funds. It was also the beginning of the shift to urban hosteling. Originally, hostels were located in the far reaches of the countryside; the first city hostel was established in Munich in 1927, recording forty-five thousand overnights in its first year.[95] By the 1950s, municipalities recognized the need for and value of youth hostels, particularly with the growth of international rail travel by the young. Hamburg and Copenhagen both built 350-bed hostels, in 1953 and 1955 respectively; a 200-bed hostel opened in London in 1959. In London, Paris, Copenhagen, and Oslo, groups of young volunteers sprang up in the late forties and early fifties to welcome and host foreign guests arriving during the summer at their city hostels. They would show their young visitors around and invite them to social events or to their homes. Although these groups had disappeared by the end of the decade, they demonstrate the international goodwill initiative that marked youth hosteling in the postwar years, as well as the variety of strategies adopted by Western European cities that invested municipal resources to attract foreign youth.[96]

In the early 1950s, the French UNESCO Commission proposed that the organization's member states establish a series of "International Youth Cities" in the major metropolises of Western Europe. These were intended to be campuses that could accommodate large numbers of young people traveling abroad (the proposal for Paris was for two thousand beds), provide cultural programming about the host country, and encourage international contacts and friendships among the young. The proposal pointed out that the existing hostel system, while an admirable endeavor, was unable to meet demand during peak season, and did not offer a sufficiently systematized curriculum of cultural internationalism. Although the idea generated interest in other countries—Denmark and the Netherlands, for example—not even the French Commission was able to secure the funding, although it did manage to have Le Corbusier draw up some initial plans.[97]

As each year brought a new record for foreign overnights in hostels, those who did not or could not travel abroad could still have an international experience. By the end of the 1950s, a clear trend was emerging: hostels themselves were becoming predominantly international spaces.[98] "In some cases there will even be more foreigners in a youth hostel than national members. Young people of limited means, who want to meet foreign people, need therefore not go abroad, but will find the international atmosphere at their own youth hostels."[99] Such a shift could be quite rapid: in France, foreigners made up only 25 percent of hostel overnights in 1952, yet by 1954 they made up 59 percent.[100] Recognizing this shift toward international travel by the young, a Dutch student organization saw that there was a need to help the growing influx of young visitors from abroad. In 1958 it published a guidebook specifically targeting these young travelers to help them make sense of the Netherlands, with the first entry astutely offering insight into Dutch beer and gin (*jenever*).[101]

Meanwhile, thousands of hostelers from elsewhere in Europe were descending on Italy, without young Italians themselves doing much traveling. The first Italian youth hostel dated from 1946, and by 1950 the 24 Italian hostels recorded 27,000 overnights by foreigners, with only 3,000 by Italians themselves. By 1960, foreign usage of the 75 Italian hostels was an astonishing 350,000, second only to West Germany, but the disparity with Italian usage remained, with only 50,000 domestic overnights.[102] This meant that the Italian youth hostel system was international from the outset; unlike systems elsewhere in Europe, it was designed for and frequented by foreigners. Aldo Pessina, the head of the newly constituted Italian Youth Hostel Association, found that he needed to teach young Italians how to be travelers.[103] Slowly but steadily, the practice would develop among young Italians, in tandem with the growing tourism of Italians generally.[104] Rome even hosted a conference on how the young could help the larger public develop a more European consciousness; the participants' conclusions emphasized travel among the young of the European Economic Community above any other measure.[105] Likewise, the Young Italian Federalists used the hostel system as a "school" for travel to promote Europeanism.[106]

5   French backpackers arrive at the Vatican in Rome, September 1950. ANSA/Corbis.

In 1946 there were 1,800 youth hostels worldwide; in 1960 there were 3,700. In 1946 there were 50,000 beds and 400,000 members; in 1960 there were 220,000 beds and 1.3 million members. In 1946 there were 2.3 million overnights, with 75,000 of those by foreigners; in 1960 there were 14.7 million total overnights, with 3 million of those by foreigners.[107] International usage of hostels grew by 237 percent in the 1950s. Notably, 40 percent of this international usage of Western European hostels in 1960 was recorded by young citizens of five countries: West Germany, the United States, Canada, Australia, and New Zealand. In 1950 their proportion had been less than 10 percent. This vast influx from North America and the Antipodes was coupled with the pent-up demand for travel among young Germans.[108] Thus, what we think of as "the West" was articulated within a community of young transnational travelers moving about within the spatial confines of Western European hostel networks.

The Problem of Germany

West German officials consciously used travel as a tool to reconcile Germans with their European neighbors in the aftermath of the war by promoting tourism to West Germany. Likewise, West German tourist associations saw travel abroad as a way to integrate Germans into the larger European community. The rising number of German tourists was not always so welcome. Complaints about Germans "occupying" beaches abounded, particularly given the German habit of demarking territory in the sand, often with the use of a flag; and the French were much less enthusiastic about bilateral youth exchange programs than were the West Germans.[109] West Germans, meanwhile, actively sought to attract western tourists to dispel what they saw as unfair prejudice against them due to Nazism and the war.[110] In the first six months of 1952, for example, West Germany had one million foreign visitors, almost all of whom were Westerners.[111] By 1953, West German hostels already had the largest number of incoming and outgoing international travelers.[112] In 1957, the Munich youth hostel hosted young people from sixty-one different countries.[113] At the same time, not only did young West Germans record the most overnight stays in youth hostels abroad, but they nearly doubled the next highest number (the UK).[114] The first year in which the number of West Germans who traveled abroad was higher than the number of foreigners who visited the Federal Republic was 1958. Among all Germans, those under twenty-one traveled the most.[115] Personal encounters through the transnational practices of travel in the postwar decades helped to foster the Westernization and internationalization of young Germans.[116] It was intended to do so.

In the decades following the war, mobility typified German society. Initially this was largely an experience of displacement, as migration and improvisation became a skill set for survival. Residents moved around within western Germany to a profound degree and for all sorts of reasons, and this uprooted mobility had lingering aftereffects, including securitized border controls.[117] As their prosperity rose, West Germans quickly became the world's most avid travelers.[118] This included a rising acceptability among Germans of independent youth travel abroad. This unstructured and informal travel practice focused on encountering other people more than it did on touring museums or visiting sites. In turn, these transnational experiences had a profound effect on the worldview of many of these young people.[119] For West German youth in particular, travel could be a means to become European.

In midcentury Germany, there was a familiar trope about the young as "border crossers" (*Grenzgänger*); they were seen to be liminal, fluid, mobile, and transgressive, willfully crossing boundaries of all sorts.[120] The poetry of Wolfgang Borchert is suffused with images of the mobility of the young at the end of the war. In "Railways, by Day and by Night," he compares his generation to trains, coming and going, rumbling on, never stopping, with no fixed home nor destination. "They are like us. . . . They are always wanting to go somewhere. Nowhere do they stay."[121] His most famous prose poem, "Generation without Farewell" (1945), concludes: "We are a generation without homecoming, for we have nothing we could come home to, and we have no one to take care of our hearts—so we have become a generation without farewell and without homecoming. But we are a generation of arrival. Perhaps we are a generation full of arrival on a new star, in a new life. Full of arrival under a new sun, in new hearts. Perhaps we are a generation full of arrival at a new love, at a new laughter, at a new God. We are a generation without farewell, but we know that all arrival belongs to us."[122]

Mobility had an inherent positive value in postwar Germany. However, though the desire was strong, few people could actually travel abroad during the Allied occupation.[123] A young group who called themselves "Großfahrt 1946" tramped around Germany, from Berlin to Mecklenburg to Stralsund, to gain some understanding of what had happened to the country and its people. In the process of wandering through a destroyed Germany, they were trying to understand themselves, too. These kinds of self-reflective tramping trips around Germany in the years of occupation and reconstruction were common, in part because it was so hard to get out of the country. In the summer of 1949, a group of young people set out for Rome but were stopped at the border because they had no papers. They wanted to go abroad to see what was going on there, but to do so independently rather than as part of some organized exchange. One young man out of a group of five who managed to get across the border in the summer of 1947 explained it this way: "Every one of us endeavors, wherever he stands, to win space, to widen horizons, to meet people, and to argue with them. . . . Our great longing is to leap over the borders to get in touch with the outside world."[124]

When Bob Luitweiler, a twenty-eight-year-old American, was tramping around Europe in 1948, he visited an international work camp outside of Stockholm, where Gertrude Hertling, a young German volunteer, said to him in excellent English, "You cannot imagine how isolated the German youth are. First, as a result of the Nazi regime, then during the War, our youth have been cut off. Now the occupation forces allow us to take no more than five dollars out of the country. You can't go far with that. How can our German youth, locked into occupied Germany, learn the meaning of democratic ways?" Inspired, Luitweiler soon thereafter founded Peacebuilders (later known as Servas), the first hospitality network of hosts intended to give young Europeans, and particularly young Germans, the opportunity to visit neighboring countries at very little cost by providing accommodations. He spent the late 1940s and early 1950s hitchhiking around Northern and Western Europe, successfully recruiting hosts by tapping into the emerging enthusiasm for the practice of youth travel there.[125]

In 1950 the borders of West Germany were opened, and large numbers of young people began to go on tramping expeditions abroad. Importantly, however, their possibilities for travel were circumscribed, as the eastern border of West Germany was increasingly regulated and controlled. Thus the Cold War division of Germany and Europe did much to determine their direction of travel, which was restricted to the western half of the continent and even a little bit beyond, such as North Africa. In 1952, a group of a dozen youth, aged thirteen to twenty-two, traveled across France to Algeria. "We went because we were fascinated by France and wanted to build bridges with the young French and Muslims," one of them wrote.[126] This desire for international contact with other young people was typical at the end of the war. In an editorial entitled "What We Want to Do," a young man claimed that what youth in Germany wanted more than anything was to meet and understand the young of other countries because they felt so isolated and cut off.[127]

Twenty-one-year-old Dieter Danckwortt of Bonn wrote an article in the *Hannoversche Neueste Nachrichten* in 1946 blaming the terrible situation in Germany on the older generation. Hundreds of letters came in response, some supportive, most condemning. Danckwortt responded that it was up to the young to reform Germany, and that they could do so only by joining with young people from other countries: "Because of our feelings of camaraderie with this young Europe," he wrote, "we must make connections with the young from other countries as soon as possible to force our freedom from officials." This youthful camaraderie would "demand and foster community." He also wrote of "the thirst for international cooperation" among the young of Germany. The authorities and older generation should get out of the way and stop hindering contact.[128] At the 1948 opening of a new youth hostel at Kamp built by international volunteers, a young French Europeanist, Jean-Anet d'Astier, proclaimed a solidarity of generational purpose: "if there remains a Franco-German problem," he said, "it is because our parents and grandparents lacked the resolve" to fix it. The young needed "to think European"; moreover, there could be "no Europe without Germany."[129]

Doris Ackermann was fifteen years old in 1949 when she went to Denmark with twenty-four other young boys and girls from Düsseldorf. "We were ready to make international friends," she said, by spreading goodwill in the wake of the war. The Danish grandmother of her host family told her, "I never wanted to speak or see German again, but you are such a sweet girl." Ackermann was overwhelmed by the possibilities of reconciliation that international contact offered to her as a young German. She became active in internationalist meetings and conferences for young Europeans. "We became richer. We Düsseldorfers learned a lot that year, including about democracy."[130]

Young Germans began traveling abroad independently in large numbers during the 1950s. Hitchhiking was common; indeed the "autostop" had been a common practice for getting around within Germany during the years of occupation, so for large numbers of the young to take it up as a means to travel outside Germany was no great surprise. In many ways it came to characterize the new culture of German youth travel in the 1950s. While their parents might head south for a relaxing vacation, the young tended to travel north and west as part of a self-conscious *bildungsreisen*, or coming-of-age journey, which kept them on the move.[131]

For some, this travel became a means of atonement, a way to distance themselves from the Nazism of their parents but at the same time to learn about it and reach out to their generational comrades across the border.[132] Bernward Vesper, the son of a Nazi poet, recounted just such an impulse and his encounters in his autobiography, *The Trip* (*Die Reise*): "I met on the streets, in the youth hostels, in the cars Danes, Norwegians, Swedes, English, Americans, and French. And while I set out with the angst of being humiliated, which I felt as a German whose land was occupied, humbled, and hated by the enemy, I found myself instead in an international brotherhood." Vesper made a point of visiting sites of Nazi aggression across Europe as a kind of penance: "And what was revealed precisely before the monument for the Danish resistance fighters murdered by the Germans, and later in Coventry and Oradour, was that all of us viewed the war as a matter of the older generation."[133] Vesper had discovered a generational and international camaraderie through his travels that helped him both to understand and to displace the war's legacy.

A similar impulse was depicted in Bernhard Schlink's bestselling novel *The Reader*, about young Germans coming to terms with the Nazi past in the early 1960s. The young protagonist, transfixed by a trial of perpetrators, seeks to understand the Holocaust. "I decided to go away," he says, because in order to confront this past, he must leave West Germany. He would have preferred to go to Auschwitz, but the Cold War made that difficult: "it would have taken weeks to get a visa." So instead he hitchhiked to France to visit the Struthof concentration camp in Alsace. Although he had been gone only a few days, upon his return "I walked through the city as though I had been away for a long time; the streets and buildings and people looked strange to me."[134] He wanted to both understand the crime and condemn it; to bring himself closer to it, but at the same time also to declare his distance from it.

This was part and parcel of the larger dilemma of German nationality, which young public intellectual Hans Magnus Enzensberger confronted directly by asking in 1964, "Am I German?" He said that to him, the nation-state was anachronistic in an international age, at least in Western Europe, and that "my nationality, then, represents something expected of me by others." In fact, he said, for Germans, the extinction of nationality was a goal, an objective, and as such, a socially galvanizing force.[135] For many young West Germans in the 1950s and 1960s, nationality was a dilemma, but one that they could circumvent through internationality.[136] This had been encouraged as a matter of official policy. For example, an internal report by the French occupation authorities in the 1940s concluded that German youth generally lacked faith in democracy and found communism appealing. However, they were also drawn to Europeanism. The report suggested that international reconstruction camps, hosteling, and youth exchanges could be a means by which to encourage this Europeanism, and through that to develop democratic tendencies among German youth.[137] Even West German chancellor Konrad Adenauer felt similarly: "the people must be given a new ideology," he said to his cabinet. "And it can only be a European one."[138] The idea of Europe, he and others hoped, could supplant the void left by the collapse of German nationalism while challenging the appeal of communism. In fact, Adenauer and others were building on a strong undercurrent of German Europeanism that predated the rise of Nazism and communism.[139] One way to accomplish this was to encourage and support the young's demand for freedom of movement across national borders. Such policy had the added benefit of distinguishing West Germany from its rival, East Germany.

Republikflucht and Cold War Mobility

As early as 1952, the new East German regime identified *Republikflucht* (flight from the republic) as a serious problem for the state, with the young constituting a high proportion of those leaving the country. Concerned by the rising numbers of young East Germans fleeing to the West in the 1950s, authorities in the German Democratic Republic (GDR) built a formidable barbed wire border fence, strictly limited familial visits, disallowed student exchanges, and began to discourage any contact whatsoever. The most effective measure was the 1957 Pass Law, which severely restricted cross-border traffic.[140] Still the young kept leaving, primarily through Berlin. Thousands even had jobs or went to school in the western half of the city, commuting back and forth daily without great difficulty. The Freie Deutsche Jugend (Free German Youth [FDJ]), established in 1946 as a comprehensive youth organization not only to socialize the young but to train them and harness their energy for the socialist future, began to post activist members at train stations and on subway platforms to discourage young border crossers from their habit of frequenting West Berlin for work, school, or leisure; the regime feared that many of them would end up settling there permanently. Between 1957 and 1960, 36 percent of those who fled west were between the ages of fifteen and twenty-five, double their proportion of the population.[141] In total, between 1952 and the building of the wall in 1961, more than 2.5 million East Germans fled to the West, and half of them were under the age of twenty-five.[142]

The authorities in West Berlin encouraged young East Germans to spend time there. They offered reduced ticket prices at cinemas, hosted free concerts, and kept shops full of youth culture merchandise. In the mid-1950s, American financial support helped institute a program to draw East German youth to the "island of freedom" for cultural and leisure pursuits. East German adolescents could get reimbursed for travel expenses as well as receive a per diem provided by their young West Berlin escorts, who were also given a per diem. Within a year, about eight thousand young East Germans had visited Berlin through the program. This coincided with a larger effort to fund visits by East German youth to West Germany through relatives, schools, and churches. Many stayed in West German hostels, while a few even had home stays with American families living abroad. In 1955, about twenty-one thousand East German youth received travel aid of some kind through these programs funded by the United States. It thus becomes clearer why East German officials grew alarmed and imposed tight restrictions on youth travel in 1957.[143] Leading up to the building of the Berlin Wall, the state patrolled trains and buses, set up roadblocks, and created a system of informants to try to contain the population. In the year before the wall was built, fifty thousand East Germans were detained on suspicion of *Republikflucht*. Meanwhile, thirty thousand East Germans had left via the unguarded exit to West Berlin in the month of April alone.[144]

On the morning of 13 August 1961, Berliners awoke to find their city divided by a closed border of barbed wire and armed guards. By 17 August, the first concrete elements were already in place, and an efficient operation proceeded to erect a reinforced concrete wall punctuated by guard towers encircling West Berlin. Cut off from work and school, social and family life, former border crossers would face unemployment and discrimination; they would be suspect, harassed, and denied jobs, and some would even be arrested. It isn't surprising that most of those who tried to cross the formidable new boundary were young: Conrad Schumann, a nineteen-year-old soldier, abandoned his post and jumped across the wire; Ursula Heineman, a seventeen-year-old waitress, squeezed through an unnoticed gap; Gunter Litfin, a twenty-four-year-old tailor, was fatally shot while trying to swim across the Spree River; Peter Fechter, an eighteen-year-old bricklayer, was shot while trying to jump the wall and bled to death in no-man's-land, out of reach but in view of those on the other side. West Berlin police had to break up a crowd of 150 young people who were attempting to cut down the barbed wire border fence from their side. Students at the Free University of West Berlin began forging documents for friends on the other side of the wall; fake passports produced by the "Girmann Group" enabled several thousand to escape. Twenty-two-year-old Harry Seidel was the first to dig a tunnel from West to East in June 1962, through which fifty-four fled. Two Italians studying in West Berlin, Domenico Sesta and Luigi Spina, got funding from the American television network NBC to build a long, wide tunnel. A cadre of forty-one students, several from abroad like Sesta and Spina, dug the tunnel to the East while being filmed for television. Twenty-nine escaped before the passageway filled with water.[145] Between 1961 and 1989, the multilayered border proved highly effective in retaining the East German population. Those who managed to get across tended to be impetuous youth, with the most famous border incidents of the era involving the young.[146]

The degree and kind of popular mobility in each bloc helped to define the Cold War in Europe, setting the West off from the East, while controlling movement across the Iron Curtain itself gave definitive form to the comparative mobility networks on each side of it. Eastern Europe had a history of restricted mobility compared to its western counterpart well before the onset of the Cold War.[147] Over time, the mobility of people on both sides became increasingly transnational and frequent, as did travel across and between the two zones. Indeed, the freedom to travel, or lack thereof, was a determining factor in ending the European Cold War, just as it had been in initiating it. In popular memory, the Berlin Blockade of 1948–49, which restricted movement, is often seen as the beginning of the Cold War, just as the 1989 opening of the Berlin Wall, which restored mobility, marks its conclusion.

Of course, the division of Germany was one of the definitive acts of the Cold War. The potential for Soviet influence over a unified German state was one of the reasons the Allied West accepted a divided Germany, as well as why integrating West Germany into the western bloc became fundamental to French security plans specifically.[148] Likewise, the double containment of a renascent Germany and expanding Soviet influence led the United States and others to support the early efforts at uniting Europe.[149] European integration mitigated the marginalization of Belgium, Italy, and the Netherlands in the developing Cold War security apparatus.[150] Thus, while the Cold War did not prescribe the ways and means by which the integration of Europe proceeded, it did provide an important impetus and stability, as well as contribute to the shape and form that formal integration would take, differentiating and defining Western and Eastern Europe.

At the height of the Cold War in the mid-1950s, the influential political scientist Karl Deutsch and his associates argued that the free transnational mobility of persons would be an essential component in guaranteeing the success of the North Atlantic security community. He claimed that the mobility of the average person was far more important to the security of the West than the mobility of goods or money. For Western Europe to become a pluralistic society united in mutual security in the face of potential Soviet aggression, states needed to encourage free movement across their national borders by reducing border controls and increasing the frequency of personal contact. Recognizing that states might be concerned about unwanted labor migration or even permanent settlement, Deutsch suggested that youth travel for study or tourism would be a low-risk way to initiate such policies incrementally.[151] Young people were at the center of a global struggle for influence, through both formal organizations and informal cultural practice. Public and private policies of this era promoted an informal integration through the transnational mobility of youth as a component of Western European Cold War politics.[152]

The European Promise of Youth Mobility

For young advocates of European integration, the free mobility of youth across the borders of Western Europe held the promise of uniting Europe as a bulwark against communism. The Western European Union looked to the effectiveness of youth travel as a form of international relations that was "breaking down the frontiers between young people" and thus creating a common European cohort.[153] The international travel of the young on a massive scale could help render the borders of Western European nation-states inconsequential, they felt. In this way, transnational cultural contact through travel became a means of activism for young enthusiasts of European integration.[154]

Youth mobility was a key component of the 1950s European Youth Campaign, an umbrella organization that coordinated and funded multiple independent youth groups favorable to integration, run for and by young people who desired a united Europe.[155] The European Youth Campaign, in turn, was a key component of the European Movement, a high-profile international political group that promoted and lobbied for political integration. The European Youth Campaign's newspaper, published in four languages with shared but not identical editorial content, promoted international travel by the young. It described programs, camps, and offices, provided contact information, featured travelogues on various countries, profiled the experiences of individual travelers to encourage interest, and advocated for the freedom of movement through its editorial content, such as a front-page story in 1952 celebrating the removal of passport controls between Scandinavian countries. Another article imagined a "Europe without frontiers" ten years in the future, or in the words of a young Frenchwoman who was asked what a united Europe would mean to her, "the ability to travel more easily . . . no more customs barriers, no more visas or passports, no more currency limitations."[156]

This promotion of mobility was part of a larger effort to unite Europe by uniting the young through personal interaction. The European Youth Campaign and the Young European Federalists sponsored pen pal schemes, international friendship programs, rallies, conferences, international caravans, the twinning of towns in different countries to foster stronger ties, and essay contests that asked contestants to write a welcome letter to an imagined young European visitor from another country.[157] A 1954 flyer from West Germany made an appeal in this way: "Youth calls to you from across borders: You are from Europe. You are still in Europe. We welcome your visit to us. You are one of us! Bon voyage to you as you move on. There, too, you will find people like us, like you: European!"[158] Their goal was to raise a European consciousness among the youth of Europe, particularly through interpersonal interaction, while advocating for policies in the interests of youth generally. The European Youth Campaign's international membership peaked in the mid-1950s at tens of thousands, while the group maintained a substantial annual budget of several hundred thousand dollars, the bulk of which came, unbeknownst to them, from the CIA, which hoped that the youthful appeal of Europeanism might counter that of communism.[159]

In the early 1950s, the European Youth Campaign, including particularly the Young European Federalists, conducted a publicity campaign demanding the abolition of borders and freedom of travel for the young in the name of building a united youth and a united Europe. In December 1952, three hundred students from ten countries burned a border post on the Franco-Italian border while demanding a Europe with unfettered mobility.[160] Dozens of similar protests took place on the shared borders of Western Europe in the early 1950s. The first was at Wissembourg on the Franco-German border in August 1950, where hundreds of youth from nine countries converged on the border post from both sides carrying banners that declared "Europe Is Here" and "We Demand European Citizenship," and then proceeded to dismantle the frontier barriers and build a bonfire with the remnants while customs officials looked on. In their official statement they demanded "a European passport giving freedom of travel throughout Europe" while noting that "Europeans have marched to the frontier, not to fight each other, but unified in their desire to abolish frontiers."[161] In January 1952, hundreds of Dutch and German youth gathered at Wyler, a village on the border between the Netherlands and Germany, to celebrate the passage of the Schuman Plan. They set the border gate on fire while brandishing placards stating "Away with Borders!" and "Long Live Europe!" In May 1953 in Liège, hundreds of Belgian, Dutch, and German youth went so far as to burn an effigy of a border customs official as a symbolic auto-da-fé before proceeding the next morning to demonstrate at the triangulated point of their shared borders. At the European Youth Assembly at The Hague in October 1953,

6   "Youth Wants Europe." One of several border protests by the European Youth Campaign, this one at Menton on the French-Italian border in December 1952. Keystone Pressedienst, Hamburg.

the young brought their own border markers with them to toss onto a bonfire, while thousands chanted "Eu-ro-pa!," "En Avant!," "Vorwärts!," "Vooruit!," and "Avanti!"[162]

Border controls emphasized to young Europeanists that a united Europe was yet to be created, and thus the shared borders became a strategic point of political protest, a territorial space ideally suited for collective or individual political action. Some considered the illegal transgression of borders to be an effective means to undermine and perhaps dismantle frontiers altogether by demonstrating their absurdity. *Jugend Europas*, the German newspaper of the European Youth Campaign, celebrated young travelers who were arrested for illegal border crossings as "courageous demonstrators for a United Europe." This sort of travel behavior was interpreted as direct political action: "Border, passport, visa? There are no such obstacles to a true European!"[163] The promotion of youth mobility, illegal or not, was a central tactic of the young Europeanists who sought to unify the western half of the continent.

Perhaps the most fruitful endeavor in this regard was the European Youth Campaign's effort to coordinate international rail travel for the young, laying the groundwork for the future Eurail and Interrail passes. At the European Youth Assembly at The Hague in October 1953, the delegates passed a unanimous resolution advocating a common European passport for the young, with consistent and reduced rail fares for their international travel. They claimed this to be elemental to the free circulation of ideas and peoples, which was itself, they said, fundamental to a democratic Europe.[164] As a result, there were prolonged negotiations with national railways to standardize reduced fares for international rail travel by European youth. At a 1955 conference in Rome, representatives from more than forty youth organizations, ranging from hostels and scouting to the Catholic Church and the YMCA, met with representatives from the tourist and rail groups of Western Europe. The various attendees repeatedly emphasized the moral imperative of international youth travel to reconcile and stabilize Western Europe. Such journeys needed to be "rapidly multiplied" because inexpensive, accommodating, and efficient rail travel was the key to developing an effective "social tourism." Social tourism was a phenomenon of the postwar welfare states of Western Europe, which were seeking to widen and democratize access to leisure in ways that were purposeful and often politically engaged.[165] The term was used throughout their discussions to denote a form of travel that was more about interacting with other people than it was about vacationing or sightseeing, and it was something they viewed as being uniquely characteristic of youth travel. They saw it as their duty to promote and enable this social tourism that would create an ennobled democratic citizenry. The representatives pored over comparative data from more than a dozen countries trying to see how they might be able to harmonize policies. They debated at what age limit fares should be decreased for individuals or groups. They discussed whether the price for all travel by the young ought to be lowered, or only that specifically designed to build Europe; they decided on the former, in that even informal independent travel had a "moral" role to play in developing a peaceful and stable Europe. To their way of thinking, the international mobility of the young was an inherent good.[166]

Not surprisingly, getting the national railways to accommodate requests to reduce fares for all international youth travel—and to do so in a common, harmonized fashion—was difficult. Yet incremental progress was made, including new rail passes and more readily available information about such fares, as well as the introduction of standardized student and youth identity cards to qualify for those reductions.[167] Meanwhile, the committee lobbied the Council of Europe for reforms as well, and in December 1961, the organization's member states, sixteen countries in all, agreed to allow young persons to travel on collective passports as a way to promote youth travel between their countries.[168]

The Merits of Independent Youth Travel

Others were not so sanguine about the benefits of independent youth travel. Winfried Böll, a West German Social Democrat, wrote an article for *Jugend Europas* in which he criticized in no uncertain terms the supposed moral benefits of youth mobility. He was particularly concerned with the emergent trend among young travelers of tramping about without sufficient financial means. He recognized that these "free riders" considered themselves to be "poor Germans" but "good Europeans." Yet this practice smacked too much of vagabondage, and rather than building character and independence, it denoted an overreliance on the benevolence of others. Böll was scandalized by the idea of young men and women traveling and camping together. How, he wondered, could this be a moral good for the young or for Europe? This form of travel was dangerous for both, he wrote. Böll warned about scantily clad young women hitchhiking in Italy who unwittingly got themselves into trouble.[169] Of course there were real dangers. The 1955 murder in France of a twenty-six-year-old Briton, Janet Marshall, lent credence to such worries about independent travel, especially for young women. Marshall had been on a bicycle tour and had stayed at the Amiens Youth Hostel the night before she was molested and murdered along a roadside by Robert Avril, a forty-three-year-old vagrant who had already served time for rape and theft.[170] The sensational crime gave support to those like Böll who argued that youth travel needed to be structured, pedagogical, and chaperoned for the benefit and security of both the young and Europe.

The West German Catholic Church agreed. Christian churches exercised considerable authority in 1950s West Germany as the adjudicators of good and evil; they placed sexuality at the center of their moral concerns.[171] Travel to Italy and especially to France had a long association with erotic fantasy and sexual fulfillment among Germans, helping to trigger unease about young people going abroad on their own.[172] Independent travel was by definition unchaperoned and unsupervised. Church officials worried about the emerging trends in youth travel and referred to hitchhiking in the 1950s as "degenerate"; to hitchhike was to indulge in selfish individualism, and to do so in another country, they thought, was the height of egoism. In this, they had the support of Pope Pius XII, who wrote a note to the West German Church in 1959, entitled "Christian Conceptions of Travel," in which he characterized young people who traveled for amusement as troublingly self-indulgent.[173] Indeed, West German Catholic organizations had been pushing back against international youth exchanges since the mid-1940s, when a host of such programs had been set up with France. In the early 1950s, the leaders of the West German Catholic Church worried about the growing fashion of youth tourism abroad, believing that young Germans should take the time to explore and appreciate their own country and fellow countrymen rather than tramp through Italy or Spain. While the Church was concerned about the dissolution of the German national body, it remained interested in organizing cross-border youth contacts when they directly served its interests by being specifically faith-based or anticommunist.[174] The Catholic Church throughout Western Europe was ambivalent about the hostel movement in the 1950s, with several separate Catholic hostel organizations in place due to worries about the seeming moral turpitude of independent youth travel.[175] Others were much less moralizing, but still questioned whether travel in general led to a European consciousness, or if only specific forms of organized pedagogic travel did so, something that would come under much greater scrutiny in the 1960s.[176]

After Sweden joined the IYHF in 1946, hostels in the country were required to give foreign youth priority in lodging. The steady influx in the number of foreign youth traveling there in the 1950s led to debates regarding the "foreigner problem" of unruly youth. The leaders of the Swedish Tourist Association were particularly disturbed by hitchhiking foreigners, whom they blamed for introducing the practice of such undignified begging to Swedish youth, and generally corrupting the wholesome goodness of Swedish hosteling.[177] Even the IYHF debated whether to welcome hitchhikers because it was concerned that hitchhiking might not be compatible with the true hosteling spirit. It smacked a bit too much of vagrancy and didn't promote self-reliance. In

7   A backpacking hitchhiker in France, 1951. The "autostop" quickly became a preferred
mode of independent youth travel. Licensed by Gamma-Rapho. © Keystone-France.

the end, although hitchhikers were not barred from hostels, the practice
was discouraged. It did, however, have the salutary effect of spurring the
IYHF to work for cheaper public transport—namely, rail.[178]

The sense of self-liberation and independence that backpacking, rail
travel, and hitchhiking seemed to offer to the young was, for many of
them, the whole point. As Bernward Vesper remarked, "This feeling of
being really alone . . . freed me." Hans-Christian Kirsch's 1961 novel
Mit Haut und Haar described young hitchhikers as having come from
"bombed cities, between borders and in escape," but now as "awake, free,
and unbound."[179] One can appreciate the bold exhilaration of seventeen-
year-old Julie Thomas from the southern coast of England, who spent
the summer of 1950 hitchhiking around France and staying in youth

hostels while her parents thought she was working as a fruit picker in the foothills of the Alps. The following summer, she hitchhiked across France to Spain and back again. At one point, she joined more than thirty other young hitchhikers riding south in the back of an empty melon truck. She was part of a society of young travelers whose numbers seemed to grow each summer. She found the sense of adventure and community among the young travelers who would assemble and disperse astonishing in retrospect, and she continued to hitchhike in Western Europe throughout the 1950s. As she said, "in those days not long after the war, we didn't worry about a thing."[180]

This wasn't true only for Europeans. In the 1950s, Canadian hostels held information sessions on hitchhiking in Europe as a way to further one's civic education and personal independence through travel. Valeen Pon spoke at hostels about how she had discovered art and history through her 1949 hitchhiking trip with two girlfriends across the length and breadth of Europe. In 1954, Lydia Paush, Diane Marchment, and Imogene Walker gave advice on what to pack, where to go, and what to do based on their hitchhiking trip. After their trip, Georgia Papas and Loraine Irvine encouraged other young people to hitchhike as well, letting them know that Canadians were well liked in Europe.[181]

In 1961, inspired by a stranded German backpacker he had met in Singapore, twenty-two-year-old Teo Eng Seng hitchhiked and took trains across the post-imperial network of Malaysia, India, Iran, and Turkey to reach Europe. In Bulgaria he felt unwelcome, as if he were under surveillance and being followed. This changed markedly in Yugoslavia, which he found very hospitable, and where it was easy to get rides. He attended a Boy Scout Jamboree in Austria and enjoyed Vienna very much. His most difficult experience was in Germany, where on multiple occasions police chased him from the roadside or shooed him away from an opportune hitchhiking spot such as a gas station. Eventually he was picked up by a woman in a red sports car, who hosted him for a night before sending him on his way to the Netherlands, France, and finally London, where he settled for a time to go to art school. As an aspiring artist and illustrator, he was excited to visit museums and see great works of art, but it was the journey itself that had most thrilled him.[182]

French and American officials were surprised to find that the surge in American postwar tourism was characterized more by the young than by the newly prosperous middle-aged they had so eagerly sought.[183] In the early 1950s, the American Express office in Paris had to enlarge its public bathroom to accommodate the growing number of young Americans tramping through Europe who were using it as a washroom. In 1960, a U.S. Foreign Service officer complained that young Americans out of cash and in need of a loan to get home were now showing up daily.[184] Many of them were students who had come to France for the rapidly expanding collegiate study abroad programs.

American study abroad programs had their roots in the interwar period, when Smith College, Marymount College, and the University of Delaware began Junior Year Abroad programs to France for language study. Similar programming eventually began to expand to other Western European countries, but in the 1950s France was still the top destination.[185] In the postwar period, study abroad programs began to proliferate beyond elite East Coast colleges, in part due to encouragement and subsidy from the U.S. government and in part due to student demand, with more than forty programs and ten thousand American students in Europe in 1960. The Council on Student Travel (CST) was founded in 1947 to coordinate American study abroad programs, particularly by aggregating transatlantic transport. Over the 1950s, however, the CST shifted away from accommodating study abroad to become an agency promoting youth tourism generally; the latter was outpacing the former as study abroad increasingly became a conduit for American independent youth travel within Europe.[186]

Foreign students from Africa, however, experienced things differently. First, whereas American study abroad students tended to be white, single, middle-class women in their early twenties, hoping to learn a language and have some fun, foreign students from Africa were black men several years older, often married, elite if also penurious, who were seeking professional degrees and experience. Whereas sub-Saharan African students numbered only a few thousand in France in the 1950s, they dominated the overseas student population in the UK. In the context of decolonization and the Cold War, African students were prized as a means of maintaining connections and wielding influence in a postcolonial world as the UK competed with the United States and the Soviet Union for foreign students. Though they came from the British Commonwealth, they were subject to much closer state supervision than other foreign students (which was true for African students in France as well).[187] They moved through imperial networks to the metropole, but once there, they often found their mobility circumscribed. In the late 1950s, British authorities identified a dozen Kenyan students who were planning to travel to mainland Europe as potential communist sympathizers. London officials interfered with the students' plan for European travel, concerned that they either would become radicalized as communist agents or were at risk of becoming destitute and indigent. As a result, the UK put new restrictions in place constraining African students there from further travel abroad.[188] In France, Algerians were guaranteed freedom of movement into and within the metropole as a result of the 1947 law declaring Algerians to have all the rights and duties inherent to French citizenship. In practice, however, Algerian mobility was monitored and curtailed through a variety of policies prompted by the dual concerns of migration and the war of independence.[189]

Significantly, the participants in American study abroad programs were, and still are, overwhelmingly young women. In the 1920s and '30s, independent travel and socializing by young American women studying abroad was firmly discouraged by their programs and host families. Instead, they were expected to participate in group touring under the supervision of appropriate chaperones. By the 1950s, however, young women were adhering to such strict social mores less and less, and began increasingly to experience the freedom and adventure offered by independent travel. Elizabeth Simmons and her roommate, both from Smith College, spent a weekend with two young men touring Belgium by motorcycle; later, during Easter break, Elizabeth went to Spain with two other women from her program along with two French men.[190] The youth mobility practiced by Elizabeth and other young women demonstrates a shift in gendered spatial practices. Historically gender has been defined, at least in part, spatially—the classic ideological binary of public and private mapped a masculine and feminine idealization of space and the appropriate forms of movement through that space. Relative flow and relative fixity, with masculinity as mobile and femininity as static, varied by class, race, ethnicity, and nationality, but operated as a system structuring mobile practices.[191] The postwar agency of young women moving independently through the networks of youth mobility—hostels, hitchhiking, and the like—disrupted these norms. Young women, like men, found the independence of youth travel liberating. By 1960, exchange and study abroad programs that promoted group travel were finding more and more that the young traveler "does not want to be 'organized.' He wants to have his independence and his private sphere safeguarded."[192]

A Dutch study showed that freedom, comfort, and a good hot meal were most appreciated by young travelers, while a clear substantial majority disliked the leadership of adults. The independence and freedom that hosteling offered was its most desirable quality to them.[193] The Danish, for example, worked hard to establish a "friendly atmosphere" in their hostels so as to "avoid any kind of authority" that might alienate visiting hostelers.[194] A German study confirmed that making new friends with other young people while remaining on the move rather than staying put were the two top travel preferences of the vast majority of young travelers.[195] By 1962, three-quarters of all German youth travel abroad was being done independently.[196] The postwar years in Western Europe gave birth to a profound new phenomenon of independent youth travel that developed fully on a massive scale in the 1960s and 1970s, with the most desirable aspect being not a particular destination but rather the chance to encounter other young people.

Some of this is best illustrated by literature. The renowned Dutch author Cees Nooteboom wrote his first book at age twenty. Largely based on his own itinerant travels, *Philip and the Others*, published in 1955, traced the wanderings of Philip Vanderley as he hitchhiked around Western and Northern Europe, sometimes staying in youth hostels, sometimes not. The "others" in the title explicitly refers to those he encountered and communed with while traveling—including young people from America, Australia, Belgium, Denmark, England, France, Ireland, Sweden, and West Germany—and was, Nooteboom later explained, explicitly meant to convey the diversity and community of Europe.[197] Indeed, Philip travels with others for a while, then goes off on his own, then hooks up with some other "others" for a stretch. He spends a few days in Paris with Vivien, an Irish lass who has pitched her tent outside the youth hostel, providing the two of them with intimate privacy. The characters in the book all seem to be searching, to be on a personal quest without knowing exactly what they are looking for, while congregating as impermanent communities. This is exemplified by Philip, who tries to track down a Chinese girl by hitchhiking around Europe scrutinizing hostel registries; in the end, he catches up to her in Denmark and travels with her through Scandinavia.[198]

Similarly, English author David Lodge's autobiographical novel *Out of the Shelter* is based on his 1951 travels to West Germany when he was sixteen. Lodge didn't write the book until the late 1960s, and he did so then only because, he explained, of "a feeling that my experience had a representative significance that transcended its importance for me personally."[199] That is, Lodge looked back upon the personally transformative quality of his travels as revealing a larger cultural shift for young people and for Europe generally that in retrospect he felt was quite evident. The novel is a kind of postwar *bildungsroman*, in which coming out of the shelter is meant to convey both the end of wartime conditions and mentalities and the end of adolescence. Timothy, the protagonist, comes of age by being on his own, and comes to terms with the "hereditary enemy," Germany, through his transnational travel, though in truth he spends most of his time with young Americans, including Gloria Rose, with whom he has his first sexual adventures.

Meanwhile Colin MacInnes's famous novel *Absolute Beginners* (1959) is shot through with the mobility and internationalism of the emerging youth culture. In a 1958 interview, MacInnes said that he considered the postwar young to be "internationally-minded," though not necessarily in a self-conscious way, "but intuitively so."[200] The eighteen-year-old protagonist of the novel dashes about London on his scooter, articulating his identification with an age group rather than a social class, one that he declares to be international and recognizable from their common culture. He laments that he has not yet traveled, has not been hitchhiking across the continent like so many others, although he also mocks "the hitch thing" derisively as having become so commonplace as to be a cliché. Still, the novel ends as he sits in an airline terminal with a ticket for Oslo, reflecting on the interconnectedness of the world and the young, and his intention to explore both.[201]

Even Agatha Christie recognized the new phenomenon and made youth hostels and youth mobility central plot points in two of her novels from the mid-1950s, *Hickory Dickory Dock* (1955) and *Dead Man's Folly* (1956). In the first, a youth hostel is the main setting for murder, while in the second the comings and goings of international youth to and from a nearby hostel provide cover for one of the murderers to slip away in disguise as a young Italian tourist carrying a rucksack down the road.

A rather different kind of road trip is depicted by Ingmar Bergman in his classic 1957 film *Wild Strawberries*. Isak Borg drives from Stockholm to Lund to receive an honorary degree. The seventy-eight-year-old Borg is a successful and well-off doctor who has grown cold and withdrawn in his old age, having retreated into a kind of self-imposed isolation. Along the way, he picks up three young hitchhiking travelers—two young men, Anders and Viktor, and the irrepressibly cute Sara—who are headed to Italy together. Although Sara is traveling with two men, she declares herself a virgin, to make things clear. They all are dressed like day hikers, one has a guitar, and their boundless vim and youthful enthusiasm serve as a contrast to the dour, sad, lonely man in the midst of a kind of existential crisis. Their intended trip is a contrast to his as well: he journeys through his past, they to their future; he is at the end of his journey, they are at the beginning of theirs. Once in Lund they get a ride to Hamburg, and their journey continues. For Bergman, at least, hitchhiking and foreign travel was closely associated with a new, youthful era of Swedish and European postwar modernity.

Youth Mobility and the Making of Europe

An American political scientist, Ronald Inglehart, conducted a series of studies in the mid- to late 1960s that shed light on the matters of youth, mobility, and European internationalism. He found that internationalism did not diminish commitment to the nation-state. He expected to find a positive correlation between a general internationalism and support for European political and economic integration, and did, but he also learned a great deal more. Overall, Germans were the most favorable to internationalism, followed closely by the Dutch, then the French, with the British further behind the others.[202] He also found a significant gap between adults and youth in their degree of Europeanness, with more than 90 percent of the young people in the three European Economic Community (EEC) countries under study favoring European unification—"about as near to a unanimous verdict as one is likely to come in survey research." When the data was broken down by age cohort, Inglehart discovered that the younger one went, the greater was the Europeanism. Importantly, he concluded that it was not their youth per se that had made them more European, but the specific context within which they had been young—namely, the postwar climate of internationalism and cooperative endeavor, the expansion of secondary and higher education, and the increase in trade and exchange of persons. The specific circumstances of their socialization, Inglehart said, accounted for their markedly different attitude in comparison to the older cohorts.[203]

With further study, Inglehart found that foreign travel was an even greater predictor of support for European integration than was age cohort. Nor was it simply that those who were more likely to travel were already pro-European; rather, foreign travel itself generated internationalist sentiment. As one might expect, affluence and education were factors—the higher the social class or educational degree, the more likely one was to be pro-European—yet this was not so strong an indicator as foreign travel or age. This suggested to him that the massive expansion of intra-European tourism (the growth of which was annually doubling the growth of the booming 1960s economy), particularly by the young, would have significant long-term implications. He concluded that the younger and more traveled one was, the more likely one was to be pro-Europe. Foreign travel had increased dramatically among nearly all segments of the European population with the advent of mass tourism in the 1960s, but it was particularly profound among the younger cohorts.

Despite the shorter number of years that they had lived, those between the ages of twenty and twenty-four had already done more foreign travel than those older than fifty-five. Inglehart's study showed that an astonishing 74 percent of German respondents aged twenty-one to twenty-four had visited two or more foreign countries; for young Belgians the number was 69 percent, for the Dutch 65 percent, for the French 48 percent, and for the Italians 29 percent.[204] Although the proportion for Italy might seem discrepant from the others, the fact that over a quarter of the young Italian respondents had visited two or more countries by the mid-1960s is itself remarkable and indicative of a dramatic cultural shift underway, since there had been virtually no independent tourist travel by young Italians whatsoever until the 1950s.

The response to the 1966 flood in Florence demonstrates these changes. On 4 and 5 November of that year, the Arno River flooded Florence, leaving behind a ton of mud for every person in the city and devastating the artistic and historical patrimony there. The churches, museums, and libraries, all filled with invaluable Renaissance treasures, were completely inundated with mud, in some places as deep as twenty-two feet. Young people immediately began showing up to help, becoming known to Florentines as *gli angeli del fango*, "the Mud Angels." Over the winter of 1966–67, more young volunteers spontaneously arrived to help clean up Florence. Most were Italian, but a significant number came from much farther away. They cleaned mud out of the Basilica di Santa Croce, carried priceless paintings out of the Uffizi galleries, and brought food and fresh water to the elderly who were still in their upper-floor apartments. These youthful workers were not organized, nor had they been recruited. They simply showed up. Young Europeans dropped what they were doing and boarded trains or hitchhiked or drove south. Many had already been on the road, and simply shifted their itinerary to gravitate toward Tuscany. Mayor Piero Bargellini, already overwhelmed with the disastrous state of his city, had to scramble to accommodate them. He arranged to house them in idle sleeping cars and coaches in the Florence rail yard, set up a central office at the Uffizi to dispatch them daily to the places where they were needed, and managed to organize a canteen to feed them in the kitchen at the Galleria dell'Accademia.[205] One Florentine commented that even before soldiers arrived as part of the official government response, "the city was already in the hands of the young."[206]

There was tremendous turnover in the winter months, as some Mud Angels would stay a few days, others a few weeks. They listened to music while working, smoked cigarettes on break, and had only a little energy

8 The multinational Mud Angels at rest on the mud-covered floor of the Biblioteca Nazionale, Florence, November 1966. Photograph by Swietlan Nicholas Kraczyna. Used with permission.

left for carousing at night. Because of the polyglot nature of the young workers, the archivists and preservationists had to devise a color-coded card system to track and process each item. It is unclear how many Mud Angels there were in total, or even exactly where they had come from. There were likely at most only a few thousand, yet given their mythic status in Italy, one would think the number was ten times that.[207]

In London, when Mark Bradley and a friend saw the harrowing images of Florence on the BBC, they took two hours to load up a car and then spent two days on the road, arriving to work for two weeks as part of a human chain passing texts and documents up out of the cellar stacks of the Biblioteca Nazionale. "We didn't understand much," Bradley later recalled, "but there was great excitement." Pietro di Muccio de Quattro was a twenty-year-old law student in Rome who spent seven days working in Florence, dumbfounded by all the young people there from so far away: "My right hand held a Japanese hand, the left an American one. It was the fourteenth or fifteenth of November. How the hell did they get here from all over the world so soon?" Mireille Bazin from Reims came down with thirty other art students during their holiday break. William Michaut commented that "despite the language barrier, we lived in intense communion."[208] Ignacio Serrano Garcia from Valladolid said that he and the other Mud Angels came to Florence out of a sense of duty to the European patrimony there, while Riccardo Lanza from Milan explained the harmony among the young Mud Angels by saying, "it was something already present in our generation . . . with more or less means, [we] had travelled in Italy and abroad and had often relied on the solidarity between us."[209] The Mud Angels of 1966 were an expression of the internationalist instincts, transnational travel, and generational solidarity that had developed out of the postwar mobility of youth.

Youth Mobility and Transnational Europeanization

Non-governmental actors, in addition to nations and states, have played a profound role in the evolution of postwar international relations, and the young have been central to such endeavors.[210] A preoccupation with state-centered activities limits our understanding of European integration, as does a teleological vision that sees the history of integration as leading inexorably to the political or economic European Union.[211] Europeanization and integration have taken many forms.[212] Transnational networks of shared interests and practices, among them independent youth travel, have played a profound role in the cultural integration of Europe. Hosteling underwent a form of harmonization and integration as it reoriented itself in the postwar period toward an emphasis on building transnational networks of youth travel, inspired by an ideological cultural internationalism meant to reconcile the peoples of Western Europe. That is, the institution of hosteling was meaningfully Europeanized in this era. Meanwhile, by providing cheap accommodations and thousands of facilities, international hosteling played an important part in the democratization of travel and the emergence of mass European tourism in the years of postwar prosperity.

Of course, Europe as a whole underwent a process of political, economic, and cultural Europeanization in the twentieth century, which accelerated after the Second World War.[213] The member countries of the Common Market recognized that the mass tourism of intra-European travel in the early 1960s was "one of the principal forces forging the New Europe," and that, given the projected growth, potentially "no corner of Europe" would be "immune to this form of Europeanization." Thus the EEC itself expected travel and tourism to expand "Europe" beyond the original six members of the Common Market through the transnational contact of its young people.[214] In the mid-1960s, the Organization for

Economic Cooperation and Development (OECD, formerly the OEEC) had ongoing discussions about the explosion in independent youth travel. The participants were thrilled with the exponential growth and value of youth tourism for developing a "European consciousness," but they also recognized it as a phenomenon distinct from mass tourism in general. The habits, attitudes, destinations, and means of travel were distinctive for the young who moved more frequently in less-planned itineraries. The OECD wondered how it might help develop infrastructure to accommodate the predicted territorial expansion of youth travel outward, potentially helping to advance the institutional integration of Europe to new member states in the travelers' wake, perhaps even eastward.[215]

In the summer of 1962, Diethard Beck and his friend Rolf departed Mainz, West Germany, in a rusty old car and set out for the Balkans in search of adventure. They looked for other young European travelers to hang out with, but began to encounter them in significant numbers only once they reached the beaches of Greece.[216] While there were certainly other young people traveling about the East, the culture of youth travel as such was confined to the areas considered to be Western. Diethard and Rolf were the exceptions that proved the rule. Such circuits of travel have had a long history. As Thomas Nugent's 1756 guidebook to the Grand Tour indicates, the spatial pattern of the traditional aristocratic trip was limited even then to what would eventually become the six original members of the European Economic Community—Belgium, the Netherlands, Luxembourg, France, Germany, and Italy.[217] Likewise, these same eighteenth-century circulations were what originally gave rise to the very concepts of a Western and Eastern Europe.[218] Consistently, the emergence of the modern tourist industry in the nineteenth century conceived "Europe" as the area west of a north-south axis stretching from today's border between Sweden and Finland down to that between Italy and Slovenia.[219] Diethard and Rolf had chosen to travel through Yugoslavia, which was a desirable option for independent youth travel in part because the rest of Eastern Europe had largely been closed off, but also because it occupied a kind of privileged position as a legitimate (non-Soviet) communist country open to exploration.[220] In contrast, when Bob Luitweiler ventured through Eastern Europe in the 1950s trying to recruit hosts for Servas, he found himself isolated and harassed, and unable to generate any interest; in Bulgaria he was arrested five times in ten days.[221] Yugoslavia was a place where "Western" Europeans could go to explore "Eastern" Europe without great difficulty, while the sparse number of young travelers there was yet another indication of its difference from the West, although this would soon change.

Pierre-Yves Saunier has written that the transnational approach to history is particularly useful for thinking about the entangled connections and linkages that help generate human circulations and flows across national borders. The social relations that emerge from such encounters often lead to new social, economic, political, or cultural formations.[222] In the postwar period, the cultural practice and social relations of youth mobility, constrained by the geopolitical limits of the Cold War, geographic proximity, and institutional infrastructure conducive to their travel, helped constitute the social space of Western Europe. The French theorist Henri Lefebvre has talked about how space is not an inert, natural, or preexisting given, but rather an ongoing production of social relations. That is, in our conceptual understanding, space is not simply an agglomeration of peoples and things spread across a territory; it is produced by the cultural meaning that emerges through social practice. This is particularly so when symbolic meanings develop through the spatial relationships of human activity.[223]

The postwar transnational practice of youth travel helped to "Europeanize" Western Europe and Western Europeans through the interpenetration of a circumscribed geographic space that was increasingly seen to stand for Europe as a whole. This is true even though many of these travelers were not themselves members of the Common Market or even from Europe; the growing numbers of young North American, South American, and Australian travelers, for example, were helping to generate a European social space through the patterns and frequency of their itineraries. These were highly determined circuits of travel through hostel networks, reconstruction camps, and border controls, which all served largely to limit and circumscribe where one could and would travel, whom one would meet, and what one might do. The act of traveling in and of itself was a productive activity generating new understandings and meanings for youth.[224] Yet while the patterns of youth mobility were structured by social class, gender, race, and nationality, at the same time they were not fixed or predestined; it was a flexible and inconsistent mobility that emphasized freedom, independence, improvisation, and individual agency.

Of course, the social configuration of geographic space does not necessarily correspond to the territoriality of nations.[225] The growing youth circulation across national borders expanded the social space of "European" activity even though it did not encompass the entirety of the continent.[226] This process of Europeanization was not uniform or even necessarily intentional.[227] It, too, was flexible and inconsistent. As a cultural practice, it had the quality of a "transnational socialization" leading young travelers to be increasingly favorable toward integration, as Ronald Inglehart's research had shown.[228] This Europeanization relied on transnational structures, movements, and practices, such as hostel networks, federalism, and hitchhiking, while transnational mobility itself was often influenced by varied understandings of internationalism that were together helping to generate a new, integrated social space.[229] As Mitch Perko from Essex described his teenage years of travel in the 1950s, "It was an awakening and an education—a wide-eyed look at the world, albeit geographically limited [but with] a very European feel."[230]

TWO

Journeys of Reconciliation

A 1966 conference held in Starnberg, West Germany, focused on the burgeoning phenomenon of international
travel and tourism by the European young. Coming from a
dozen Western European countries, the participants had expertise from various academic disciplines, policy institutes,
commercial entities, and private organizations. The conference was hosted by the Institute for Tourism, founded by
Heinz Hahn in 1961 as a social-scientific interdisciplinary
research institute dedicated to critiquing and promoting international travel and tourism.[1] The meeting was premised
on the notion that international youth travel was a public
matter, the concern of government, society, and commerce
alike. A Frenchman from the Council of Europe suggested
that it ought to awaken feelings of European solidarity, feelings of belonging to a European generation. A Bavarian youth
leader emphasized that international youth travel could and
should serve the educational function of tolerance for others, which, he thought, explained why it had become an important and meaningful part of West German foreign policy,
particularly toward France.[2] Helmut Kentler, a psychologist
from Berlin, stressed that the roots of this phenomenon were
in the years of Allied occupation immediately following the
Second World War. He pointed to a profound connection
between culture, travel, reconciliation, and Europe:

We grew up under a fascist regime that isolated us from all outside
influences. I remember well the first time I listened to a jazz record,
and how it just stopped me in my tracks, how I stood helpless in front

of a Picasso painting, how I was beside myself the first time I read translated works of modern literature from France, Britain, and America. A difficult learning process began. We hurried to try and get to these places where all things new came from. But for us, the borders were still closed. Then something surprising happened: representatives of foreign youth associations came to us, and with them politicians, writers, and artists. They met with us and we developed friendships. That was the beginning of the excitement for Europe that grabbed the young. We wanted to tear down the border posts; we did just that and met the youth of Europe. Organizations of understanding grew like mushrooms, mostly founded by students, authorities responsible for youth, or youth syndicates. They all wanted to serve the cause of international youth, and they set out to arrange exchange partners and take on the administration of organizations. No one could have anticipated that years later an industry of youth tourism would develop from these organizations of understanding.[3]

As Kentler suggested, these postwar journeys of reconciliation and efforts at interpersonal contact among European youth had become intimately bound up with the project for European integration in general. In the years immediately following the Second World War, Germany was the focus for international exchanges, because the population there was considered to be isolated from the rest of Europe. Private organizations, with government support, led these efforts and hoped to use the cultural practice of travel to promote internationalism among the young of Europe, beginning with Germany. This preceded and corresponded to the endeavor establishing institutions designed to achieve the economic and political integration of Western Europe. As in that undertaking, France and West Germany served as the engine driving the cultural practice of youth mobility as an effective means of international relations. In the decades following the war, these bilateral and intergovernmental efforts at reconciliation through personal interaction among the young suggest ways in which the integration of France and West Germany developed on a popular level and in a sociocultural fashion that anticipated and accompanied the more institutional process of political and economic negotiation.[4]

For all the focus on economic and political union, the integration of Europe was initially a response to the disintegration of Europe in two horrific wars. The primary impulse behind reconciliation and integration was to recover from the most recent war while preventing another, and the subsequent economic and political matters were efforts in that regard, too.[5] Of course, reconstruction, the rise of the superpowers, the Cold War, imperial decline, and economic viability in a global marketplace were all primary factors of integration as well. It is important not to forget, however, that the reconciliation of peoples, rapprochement, and the avoidance of war were an initial impetus to integration and arguably its most significant accomplishment, particularly in light of the violence of the fifty years prior to this period. A more general, more diffuse, but no less profound integration was happening outside the official diplomatic treaties and institutions, often with some form of official government support, but often through private initiative. On the one hand, these sorts of endeavors included transnational networks of infrastructure through the development of transportation and energy grids, for example.[6] On the other hand, the social relationships and cultural practices of daily life were being utilized to reconcile the peoples of France and West Germany via the mobility of the young in the decades following the Second World War. Importantly, these journeys of reconciliation tended to be organized, structured, and planned, in contrast, and often in response, to independent youth travel.

The economic and political integration of Europe in the second half of the twentieth century through the European Coal and Steel Community, the European Economic Community, the European Union, and related institutions, policies, and agreements was largely an elite-driven, technocratic, and undemocratic affair. The governments of France and West Germany led these diplomatic endeavors. Through the French military government's policies in its zone of occupation in Germany, the partnership of France and West Germany to host a European Youth Rally in 1951, and the establishment of the Franco-German Youth Office in 1963, we can see the ways in which these governments sought to harness the proliferation of international youth travel to serve their national interests of reconciliation and integration through a social and cultural dynamic that rewarded grassroots initiative with intergovernmental support.

An Occupation of Reconciliation?

While the French plan for the zones of occupied Germany was initially aggressive in its objective to dismember the state, dismantle the military, and grab the economic resources of the Ruhr, it was clear that Britain and the United States would not accept such draconian measures, particularly as tensions with the Soviet Union began to develop. Instead, Allied policy quickly shifted to stabilizing a democratic Germany with the hope of creating a bulwark against Soviet influence. The western occupying powers diverged on the methods, but all agreed on the necessity of German reeducation, with a particular focus on young Germans. The privileged position of the young in the Allied efforts to stabilize and rejuvenate German society was evident in the July 1946 amnesty provided by General Lucius Clay of the American zone to German youth born after 1 January 1919. Similar policies were instituted in the other zones of occupation, and all were premised on the notion that the young could not be held responsible for the actions of the Nazi state, and that the best hope to denazify and democratize Germany lay with them.[7]

The French occupation authorities chose a cultural emphasis for their German reeducation programs, with one focus on interpersonal interaction through the exchange and travel of French and German youth.[8] Their goal was to get young Germans to appreciate and understand the other peoples and cultures of Europe, and also to get Westerners to accept young Germans as peers. In the years of the Allied occupation, a host of programs were established to send Germans to the United States, the United Kingdom, and France, but it was more common for the young from other countries to go to war-torn and occupied Germany. The French were the first to initiate such policy, in 1946, and had by far the most extensive programs, eventually involving tens of thousands of young people.

Whereas the American and British policies of denazification used legal channels to focus primarily on the German leadership, the French adopted a more cultural strategy intended to target the German people as a whole. Thus the French military government, under the leadership of General Pierre Koenig, emphasized prosecution less and reeducation more. They designed this reeducation to combat what the French military saw as the isolation of Germany, with the aim of bringing the Germans back into the mainstream of European culture, albeit a European culture that the French military defined in a way that was rather Francocentric. During the Allied occupation, the French reopened schools and universities in their zone of southwestern Germany before the other Allies. They published millions of new textbooks, outpacing the British by two to one and the Americans by seven to one. They undertook a vast expansion of French language instruction for young and old, which was compulsory for the former. They brought in hundreds of French language instructors, who taught not only in schools but also in four newly founded French institutes at Freiburg, Tübingen, Mainz, and Trier.[9] They established and equipped cultural centers and libraries. They founded an entirely new university at Mainz. French theatrical and choral groups toured the occupied zone, as did major art exhibitions. The International Bureau of Liaison and Documentation (BILD), set up in 1945, promoted Franco-

German mutual understanding through public education via its bilingual magazine *Documents/Dokumente*.[10] Emmanuel Mounier helped form the Committee for Exchanges with the New Germany in 1948, which organized public debates, lectures, and conferences between French and German intellectuals and dignitaries.[11] In 1951, the Franco-German Historians Agreement set out to reform school textbooks through a cooperative endeavor generating a shared historical narrative.[12]

These policies were pursued despite the great bitterness among the French toward the brutality of the German wartime occupation of France, with the deprivations and rationing of those years still ongoing. In this respect, General Koenig's policy of friendship and accommodation with the Germans of the French zone was a bold initiative.[13] Koenig even proposed placing German orphans and the offspring of French occupation soldiers with French families permanently. French social workers traveled throughout Germany identifying potential candidates for adoption, but when German church leaders denounced the emigration scheme as kidnapping, French authorities abandoned the project.[14] Such proposals likely fed into the early 1950s fear in West Germany that young German men were being abducted into the French Foreign Legion, an unfounded moral panic that emphasized a sense of helplessness and victimization at the hands of the Allies who had been targeting German youth.[15]

French authorities concluded that the best programs in this overall cultural strategy were those that facilitated a "very free exchange of opinion between French, German, and foreign students who effectively and favorably confront each other's point of view."[16] Gatherings at which such frank confrontation was avoided were seen as the least successful.[17] The lack of problematic incidents resulting from such open dialogue surprised the occupation leadership; a respectful if cautious rapport predominated at these encounters.[18] The leadership designed the youth camps and exchanges to address past conflict and future peace. A young German socialist who participated in a camp at Württemberg noted that not only did the young French and Germans get along, but the camaraderie evoked a "sentiment of solidarity" among the participants. A young German Catholic woman emphasized the "considerable political importance" of the camp as a means of reconciliation. In the words of a young Frenchman, "the young Germans welcomed us with a lot of trust. I think that they hoped, in return, to secure ours, which for my part they have."[19] The informal interaction of large numbers of French and German youth distinguished French occupation policy from that of the other Allies.

A restricted report by the Allied Control Council from the summer of 1947 detailed the contacts and relationships between German and Allied youth with respect to each zone of occupation. Allied policy prioritized international contact with German youth as a means of postwar reconciliation and institutional reconstruction. The differences between the American, British, and French policies emerge in the kinds of contacts that were emphasized and the scale on which they were carried out.

The Americans focused on youth organizational leadership and on establishing or reestablishing a host of institutional programs—secular, religious, political, and recreational—for the young. They hoped to foster pluralism among youth movements to counter the monolithic influence of the Hitler Youth. Youth clubs predominated, where American soldiers played sports with young Germans, watched movies, or listened to music. The American zone authorities helped German youth leaders attend international conferences and brought Allied youth leaders to the American zone to help the Germans establish or reestablish their own organizations, such as the YMCA, scouting, sports groups, and hostels. For example, the Americans sponsored conferences in Munich and Frankfurt in the summer of 1947, where youth leaders from more than a dozen countries in Europe and North America addressed several thousand young Germans and advised them on how to set up and manage youth organizations. The American programs limited interpersonal contact between young Americans and young Germans to visits by German youth leaders to the United States, and to a fairly extensive pen pal correspondence scheme.[20] The well-known American Visiting Experts and Cultural Exchange Program did not focus on the young. In 1947, its first year, it sponsored 81 exchanges, and, in 1948, 354.[21] By 1955, a total of about twelve thousand West Germans had visited the United States through this program.[22] While interpersonal interaction was a key component of American policy, it centered on the political, economic, and cultural elite of a democratic West Germany, rather than the young more generally.

In addition to a focus on youth leadership and organizations, the British used their zone to target education through conferences, lectures, summer vacation courses, and university partnerships, as well as a variety of small-scale student exchanges, at both the university and the secondary level.[23] In early 1947, British occupation authorities handed responsibility for education in their zone back to the Germans. They instead began to focus their educational efforts on "bringing Germans into contact with modern developments in other European countries" as a "practical contribution towards the cultural integration of Germany into Europe" through parapublic pedagogy. The British brought German youth leaders to the UK for training courses with British youth leaders, while they set up youth leadership training centers in their zone, particularly at Vlotho. In 1948–49, they sponsored visits by about a thousand young Britons to Germany, while approximately fifteen hundred young Germans went to Britain.[24]

In their report, the French emphasized that direct contact between ordinary German youth and the youth of Allied and other foreign countries was, for them, a fundamental strategy of denazification and democratization in general, but also, more importantly, a strategy of reconciliation particular to the Franco-German relationship.[25] This was one reason that their zone, unlike the others, intentionally pursued a policy of fraternization between their occupying forces and local Germans; in fact, they often lived together.[26] Thus, the French military government emphasized contact between the French and German leaders of youth organizations, like the Americans, and educational partnerships and exchanges of students, like the British, as well as substantial interpersonal interaction among young French and Germans themselves. As early as 1946, more than a thousand French youth visited with young Germans in the French zone of occupation. By 1948, fifty thousand French children had attended summer camps in the Black Forest region of West Germany.[27] Meanwhile, a traveling exhibit entitled "A Message from French Youth" spent eleven months touring a dozen cities in the French zone of occupation, reaching an audience of more than 150,000 young Germans.[28] A delegation of young leaders representing the major French youth organizations visited all four zones of occupation in March 1947 to assess the state of German youth and identify constructive steps for rehabilitation.[29]

Such programs attempted to develop a mutual sympathy for these two cultures, so riven by conflict, by utilizing the young; these activities later merged into programs for the reeducation of older age groups, too. Compared to the British and Americans, French occupation authorities had the distinct advantage of territorial proximity, which enabled them to pursue their policy aggressively over the years of zonal occupation. Additionally, they built upon a host of programs in the interwar years that were similarly designed to bring together the French and German peoples through their young.[30] Most importantly, the French occupation demonstrated an ideological commitment to using interpersonal contact as a tool of foreign policy designed to achieve, first, reconciliation, and, second, cooperation in the emerging European context, with both designed to serve French concerns for national security.

The French military government concluded that the main way to achieve a lasting Franco-German cultural accommodation was through the internationalism of the young. Raymond Schmittlein, the director of public education in the French zone, summarized these policies in 1949 as a "liberation" designed to "break the chains on German youth." Schmittlein insisted that only by freeing German youth from chauvinist nationalism and replacing it with humanist internationalism could French security be achieved and a tolerant, democratic Europe emerge.[31] His office decided that the best way to liberate German youth was to expose them to new ideas through direct contact with the young of other European countries within the contexts of universities, youth movements, and youth leadership.[32] In response to demand, in 1945 the French Military Government of the Occupation created the Department of International Meetings, headed by Jean Moreau, to coordinate, facilitate, and encourage international contact, particularly among young French and Germans.[33] They hoped that, through contact with French and European youth organizations, they might be able to reconstitute the pre-Nazi pluralism of German youth groups.

A variety of French youth organizations, predominantly confessional and ideological, were also reaching out to like-minded German youth in the French occupation zone and sought the help of the military government there to do so. In 1945, several private groups began petitioning the occupation authorities for permission to operate in the French zone. A total of thirteen hundred young French people spent part of the summer of 1946 in meetings and camps with young Germans in the Rhineland and the Black Forest. Catholic, Protestant, socialist, scouting, and hosteling groups were the most active and had taken the initiative to establish contact themselves. General Koenig's staff welcomed them particularly because of their internationalist character, seeing it as "one of the most certain and effective means" to counter the nationalist or fascist tendencies of German youth. In fact, the Department of Public Education in the Occupied Zone wanted not only to facilitate an expansion of these kinds of contacts, but "to give all such initiatives a more and more pronounced international character because it does not seem desirable to limit contacts to a Franco-German dialogue."[34] Therefore, it sought to "provide possibilities for contact with the exterior world."[35] Though the primary participants were French and German, from the outset the programs were also open to other nationalities, particularly Belgian, Dutch, and English, with some disappointment in the inability to get Soviet youth to participate. Ensuring the participation of other nationalities complicated matters, but "in a time when frontiers have lost much of their significance and are in any case permeable to ideas, it is necessary to facilitate, orient, and control this circulation so as to benefit German youth as much as possible."[36] The objective was to place Franco-German reconciliation within a broader international context, and one that served the purpose of French strategic aims—namely, long-term security. The legacy of the war itself posed the primary obstacle.

While they intended for the camps to generate discussion about the difficult conditions in the occupied zones and to address the lingering acrimony from the war, French authorities also meant to promote fraternity and solidarity among the young through recreation. Twenty-two-year-old Robert Vannet went skiing for two weeks in the Tyrol, and found the unexpected camaraderie he experienced there overwhelming: "the new generation has arrived!" he exulted.[37] The Ministry of National Education helped recruit and select French participants from politically and religiously "neutral" youth groups. From the outset, the occupation government intended these first camps as pilot programs, with a plan for rapidly improving and expanding interpersonal contacts among the young as a matter of official policy, as "the first step toward the establishment of fraternal relations" that would ensure peace.[38] They developed policy and procedure as they went, getting more efficient and more effective year by year. The initial programs in 1946 experienced problems related to military permits and passport controls, a shortage of appropriate facilities for the large numbers of participants, the scarcity of goods and foodstuffs, a lack of discipline among the young, and an insufficient number of bilingual group leaders and interpreters.[39]

Already by the winter of 1947–48, the programs had expanded significantly. The international youth camp in the Tyrol alone hosted more than fifteen thousand young people from all over Europe, with French and Austrians in the majority. The youth hostels in the French zone of Germany hosted thousands of European youth coming to Germany for organizational leadership meetings, vacation camps, and language and other short-term instruction. These young travelers had priority in terms of transport and supplies in what remained rather austere conditions in the occupied zones; they were accommodated in all sorts of ways, such as being allowed to travel on collective visas and passports.[40] The Koblenz newspaper *Rhein-Zeitung* reported on a 1948 meeting at the Stahleck Castle, amazed that hundreds of youth from a variety of Western European countries came to the French zone in order to befriend young Germans.[41] Not long after, an article in *Nouvelles de France* celebrated the efforts of the French occupation to establish a rapport among European youth: "The success of these contacts, the ties of friendship and reciprocal understanding that they sustain between the young of different nations, and the frankness with which they address current problems merit being emphasized and encouraged for the future."[42] In May 1949, a European Youth Camp took place in the French zone at St. Goar, located on the Rhine at the foot of the Loreley Rock. Juventus, a group that would evolve a year later into the Young European Federalists, sponsored the one hundred mostly French and German campers.[43]

By 1948, German youth began to take part in activities in France, including participating in a winter camp at Chambon-sur-Lignon, a national hostel meeting at Dunkirk, and an annual pilgrimage of French students to Chartres Cathedral.[44] The *Rheinischer Merkur* marveled at the success of such international contacts, and particularly the reception of young Germans in France.[45] The first German visits to France were individual rather than group affairs, however. More than a hundred young Germans visited and stayed with the families of French friends they had made at previous camps and meetings. French youth organizations soon followed, with invitations to group gatherings in France.[46] Nevertheless, there remained significant ambivalence among the French, as several organizations had trouble placing young Germans with French host families. Indeed, even though French groups initiated and organized such programs, throughout the 1940s and 1950s West Germany proved to be the more eager partner.[47] Nevertheless, Wolf-Dieter Wardeiner, a twenty-eight-year-old West German, anticipated studying in Paris with trepidation. Yet he found the interaction between French and German students there to be "extraordinarily precious," and marveled at the fun to be had as part of an international gathering of young people at a Parisian club, where he "danced with a French, Dutch, Swedish, German, and Italian girl," one after the other. The "deeply meaningful friendships" that came from "so many directions" surprised him, particularly those with the French. He returned home planning to do his part to "contribute a little to a humane understanding between these long divided peoples."[48]

In 1946, approximately fifteen hundred young people were involved in the French programs; by 1950, more than ten thousand were taking part every year.[49] The French government found an eager partner with the 1949 establishment of the Federal Republic of Germany, which quickly set up offices to facilitate youth travel, offering a per diem to any young person visiting West Germany as well as to any young German going abroad, and creating a special office to oversee exchanges between West Germany and France.[50] Government leaders in both countries hoped that the continuation of these interactions and meetings could play a political role in the reconciliation of their countries. In a letter to the French foreign minister, Robert Schuman, in 1951, André François-Poncet, a former ambassador to Germany and now the high commissioner of the French occupation, having succeeded General Koenig in 1949, said that he believed these transnational encounters had done more good than any of the other policies pursued during the occupation.[51] Indeed, the French authorities regarded the traditional means of transmitting culture through expositions and conferences as outmoded and ineffective; interpersonal interaction best transmitted cultural appreciation, they felt, as demonstrated by the variety of independent programs run by private organizations that had been doing just that.[52]

This systematic use of international youth encounter that had become a primary policy objective for the French occupying authorities was something they considered to be genuinely innovative.[53] When the new federal government of West Germany sought Allied support for its 1950 Youth Plan (*Bundesjungendplan*), the Americans and British were enthusiastically supportive, while the French demurred, saying that they wished to concentrate on international visits and exchanges rather than on projects internal to West Germany.[54] In March 1949, the French consul in Freiberg wrote to the French ambassador to West Germany about his concerns regarding the efficacy of youth travel and exchange in the efforts to achieve Franco-German reconciliation and thus French national security. "We risk committing a grave error in judgment," he wrote, because so many of his colleagues were "convinced that the Franco-German problem can easily be resolved through an intense cultural action among German youth." He pointed out that there had been similar efforts in the 1920s and 1930s, when all sorts of Franco-German associations constituted themselves in the interests of rapprochement, and which did not turn out to be very effective in securing peace, to say the least. However, there remained a "unique historical opportunity" because the French policy of postwar contact with European youth had exposed young Germans to the possibility of a European federation. He suggested that France should combine the cultural project with the political one. In the interests of French security, he recommended using interpersonal interaction with other young people to give German youth a Europeanist ideology through French guidance in order to counter the influence of the "nationalist communism" emerging in the East. He and others proposed that bilateral contact between French and German youth could be used to achieve France's national security goals via the Cold War context of multilateral Europeanism.[55]

Europe on the Rhine: The 1951 Youth Rally at Loreley

The French foresaw international youth meetings and exchanges as a means to combat isolation, demonstrate commonality, further understanding, initiate dialogue, and promote reconciliation as well as stabilize German democracy.[56] The French occupation authorities hoped to expand these youth meetings to accommodate an even broader international base.[57] In fact, the 1946 "Message from French Youth" train exhibition through occupied Germany was followed by a 1948 tour that included Austria, Belgium, Germany, Italy, and Switzerland.[58] In the early 1950s, when the efforts at European political and economic integration were significantly underway and beginning to occupy the public mind, the issue of "Europe" and "European youth" overlay these earlier endeavors. François-Poncet recognized this explicitly, and thought that the ongoing talk of European unity offered an opportunity to further Franco-German reconciliation.[59] Thus, the efforts to reconcile France and Germany became part of the endeavor to integrate Europe; likewise, the new institutions of an integrated Europe played an increasing role in the rapprochement of these formerly belligerent peoples by design.[60]

Foreign Minister Schuman's 1950 proposal to coordinate coal and steel production, known as the Schuman Declaration, articulated the primary goal as reconciliation between France and West Germany, with the simultaneous intention of moving toward a federal Europe through a common foundation of economic development. A year later, France, West Germany, Belgium, Italy, Luxembourg, and the Netherlands, which would collectively become known as the Europe of the Six, signed the Treaty of Paris, creating the European Coal and Steel Community (ECSC). A host of other proposals and negotiations—some successful, some not—developed over the course of the 1950s, culminating in the 1957 Treaty of Rome, which among other things established the common market principles of the European Economic Community (EEC). One consequence of the Schuman Declaration and the quick establishment of the ECSC was that it took the European project out of the halls of technocratic negotiation and thrust it into the public consciousness.

The public debate about Europe shaped the ongoing discussion about youth mobility and its role in integration. It was believed that personal interaction between French and German youth would lead not only to reconciliation between peoples but to a more broadly integrated Europe, which in turn would help prevent a future war between France and West

Germany. The French Europeanist Raoul Dautry pointed out in late 1950 that the future of Europe must not simply be about building institutions; it was also essential to establish rapport among peoples. The former would fail without the latter. The best way to ensure such success was through the young, he insisted.[61] A Franco-German article from 1951 argued the need for a European youth identity to secure a peaceful future. This European consciousness, the authors asserted, could best be achieved by promoting meetings and exchange opportunities for the young.[62] A discourse had emerged that emphasized youth mobility as a necessary component of a peaceful Europe, a conclusion that built upon those of Karl Deutsch and his team of political scientists, who had said that the free mobility of persons was a much more important factor in establishing international security than the exchange of goods or money.[63]

In the context of 1950s Franco-German Europeanism, a narrative developed that travel, particularly by the young, could lead to a brighter European future free from belligerency and war. An article in a French newspaper noted that a European youth rally would fit into the broader emergent phenomenon of youth mobility. Sometimes these young people traveled in twos or threes, it said, but often they were alone. With their hands in their pockets, their packs on their backs, and their wrinkled shirts, "we recognize them easily." The young men and women traveling around Europe, be it in Rome, in Innsbruck, or in the woods of Finland, "want to leave home and go ever farther, pushing back the frontiers that have kept them tethered for too long." Perhaps, the paper suggested, this was the best way to come to understand and love a foreign country and a foreign people. In short, it recognized that these meetings and the travel of the young were part of an interconnected and intracontinental process.[64] The German historian Wilhelm Treue argued in 1954 that throughout the modern era, travel had been the fundamental component in developing a European consciousness. Travel, he thought, had knit Western Europe together in such a way as to make European unity a possibility.[65] Not long thereafter, a UNESCO paper agreed, stating, "the common European culture of today is largely due to the exchange of students."[66] Meanwhile, a Bonn newspaper marveled about all the different places around Europe where thousands of young people from that city were spending their summers, often in camps of various kinds, where they were meeting and befriending young people from other countries.[67] French diplomatic experts recognized that "a contempt for frontiers" had developed: "people were on the move, by necessity or by taste; and little by little, a new kind of international relations was born." They saw that the desire to move around after the stifling years of war, the curiosity and impatience of youth, the facilities of modern transport, and the growing interdependence of European countries all favored the blossoming of an active movement for international exchange. For them, it was particularly important that this new kind of international relations was cultural, postwar, and young.[68]

In the summer of 1951, French occupation authorities joined Konrad Adenauer's new West German government in cosponsoring the European Youth Meeting, which was held at the Loreley Rock overlooking the Rhine.[69] From late July to early September, young people traveled there from all over Western Europe for one of five ten-day-long camp experiences organized around the possibilities of European integration. The Loreley camp took place in the context of the final negotiations for the European Coal and Steel Community and the early discussions of a European Defense Community; prominent leaders, intellectuals, and politicians came to give speeches and workshops promoting the European ideal. The Franco-German organizers intended for the rally to use the transnational interaction of the young as a means of postwar reconciliation and European integration under the leadership of France and West Germany.[70]

The camp was an inter-Allied effort. Not only did all the western occupation commissions offer their official sanction and support, but they also contributed to the financial cost and provided other support services such as military transportation—for example, the Americans flew young Berliners over the closed border to Loreley—as well as the majority of the equipment needed for the camp. The Americans provided tents, the French donated cooking gear, and the Germans offered foodstuffs, much to the later chagrin of the French, and even the English, who grumbled about Germany as "the land of eternal sausages."[71]

Although the Bundesjugendring, West Germany's umbrella youth organization, was the official sponsor, the idea for the meeting, and much of the planning, originated with the French occupation authorities, specifically the department in charge of promoting international meetings and exchanges, whose members had been thinking about such a gathering since 1948.[72] This staff, led by Jean Moreau since 1945, was preparing to leave Germany as the occupation officially ended, and they viewed the meeting at Loreley as the culmination of their efforts to reconcile the young of Germany and France, as well as an opportunity to work hand in hand with their German counterparts within a new framework of European integration.[73]

9   The European Youth Rally at Loreley, September 1951. Historical Archives of the European Union, CS 94. © Claus Schöndube heirs.

The location of the meeting atop the Loreley Rock, with its commanding views of the Rhine valley and an undulating landscape of steep vine-covered hillsides cascading down to the river's edge, had obvious symbolic overtones, with the river as a historical thoroughfare of international encounter and nationalist conflict now transcended. François-Poncet's poetic speech to the campers in mid-August emphasized that this great river was the very place where a European culture first took hold at the end of the Roman Empire, as part of the earliest attempts to forge a European identity. Neither German nor French, but a combination of all that was Frankish and Carolingian, the Rhineland was Franco-German through and through. "As in the past, so in the future, the Rhine will be one of the arteries of the coming Europe," he said. It was "Europe's river, a river of peace and of unity."[74] Heinrich Heine, an early proponent of Europeanism, wrote the famous Romantic poem "Die Lorelei," known to generations of German schoolchildren, about the old folk legend of the Lorelei maiden. Most importantly, and more practically, the location offered proximity to rail lines with direct access to the major cities of Western Europe, and a dense network of nearby youth hostels that could help move the young into, out of, and around the region.[75]

The camp was divided into five sessions, with participants staying for ten days each. The organizers placed great emphasis on providing a high-quality cultural program and invited young people between the ages of sixteen and twenty-five, who often came as part of a youth organization or applied in groups.[76] Individual groups pursued their own particular agenda in the mornings. A lecture forum usually took place every other day at midday, with the speakers including such prominent European political personalities as former Belgian prime minister Paul-Henri Spaak, a staunch Europeanist, and Robert Aron, a French political intellectual. Topical study groups focusing on social, economic, political, and cultural themes such as "The Young Citizen and the State" and "Ways of European Cooperation" filled the afternoons. Workshops helped the participants develop skill and talent in artistic endeavors such as photography, dance, and puppetry. Professional cultural programming from across Western Europe predominated in the evenings, with the goal of showcasing the rich cultural heritage of the various nationalities present. On one evening campers watched a performance of *Le Cid* by Jean Vilar's theater troupe; on another they listened to a Bavarian choir; and on still another they watched a screening of Vittorio de Sica's *Bicycle Thieves*. Camp organizers expected the young not only to develop an appreciation for the artistic heritage of other countries, but also to recognize the common European quality of western civilization that united them all.[77]

Three large demonstrations punctuated the camp: the opening ceremony ("Youth Calling Europe"), the main rally in mid-August ("Youth Building Europe"), and the closing ceremony ("Youth Experiences Europe"). For each of these, thousands of young people, in addition to the resident campers, arrived in Loreley by train and bus. The rhetoric of speeches and rallies affirmed a discourse of youth as the future who would build a new and better Europe.[78] As the *New York Times* described, however, the whole affair lacked the rigid orchestration of political theater one might have expected: "Except for the introductions of speakers in the big open-air theatre on the plateau above the famous cliff, there were no translations and no effort to keep the young people's noses to the conference grindstone. In a free and easy manner on a perfect summer morning, the groups strolled past the upper tiers or sunned themselves on the grassy slopes, listening to speeches when they understood the language or appreciated the ideas."[79] The young editorial staff of the Loreley newspaper, *Camp*, wrote that the young came to "get to know and understand each other," and that they wanted to "learn to love each other and thus build the new Europe."[80] Recalling the devastation of the war and the Holocaust and seeing nationalism as the root cause, the editors concluded frankly, "Our aim is to live in peace with each other instead of being killed in a future war."[81]

The project went from conception to execution in a little over six months—a remarkable achievement, but one that nevertheless produced a number of difficulties and disagreements.[82] In the end, the French did as much as the Germans in organizing and preparing the camp, maybe more, and not without considerable friction. In fact, Moreau concluded that a disastrous failure had been avoided only because the French intervened capably to counter German shortcomings, whether in recruiting young people from across Europe or actually running the daily programming.[83] A Belgian headline boasted, "French Inspiration and German Organization, or the Recipe for Success."[84] Yet in reality it was more characteristic of Roy Willis's description of Franco-German relations as "organized disagreement."[85]

In spite of it all, the French, the Germans, and everyone else considered the camp to have been a success. About seven thousand young people stayed for a full session, another seven thousand stayed for a few days, and scores of others visited on day trips from and to the surrounding region. In total, at least thirty-five thousand young people from twenty countries had been there: 60 percent from Germany, 20 percent from France, 10 percent from Great Britain, 4 percent from the Netherlands, and less than 2 percent from Belgium and Italy. The young were recruited, organized, and housed according to nationality. The gender split was two-thirds boys, one-third girls.[86] Participants reported the most enthusiasm about the cultural activities, particularly those that involved international teamwork, such as joint theater productions. Moreau concluded that the daily cooperation in fertile cultural work despite the challenge of language showed that there "already existed a European sensibility," one that he felt had been evident in the burgeoning cultural exchanges since the end of the war.[87] He also reported that because of the goodwill of the campers, their openness and desire to know one another, they had avoided conflict despite the legacy of the war. The young, he claimed, were prepared to "internationalize" themselves. He contrasted their experience with that of the adult organizers, among whom overcoming language barriers and national temperaments posed greater problems, he thought.[88]

The organizers tried very hard to use the meeting at Loreley as a platform to promote Europeanism not only to the young, but to the broader public. Identical stories appeared in dozens of newspapers in multiple languages as journalists repeated verbatim the releases provided by the Loreley press office. The intended audience was, of course, Western Europe, with a special effort to convince Germans in particular that they, too, belonged to Europe. That summer, more than fifteen hundred articles about Loreley appeared in the German press alone, the vast majority overwhelmingly positive.[89]

While the official press releases emphasized folklore and the colorful camp life, the conservative newspaper *Rheinischer Merkur* set off a scandal with an article entitled "Lorelei with Red Hair," which claimed that the camp had been infiltrated by French communists.[90] As one example, it pointed to an article by a young Frenchman in the camp newspaper expressing opposition to the rearmament of Germany. There was an uproar in the German press for a couple of weeks, with accusations flying back and forth as the camp got caught up in the domestic politics of Cold War West Germany. Yet the episode allowed those at Loreley to emphasize that these young people had the freedom to criticize and express political opinions, and that European youth had a right to self-determination, as well as a will to shape the continent and society in their interests.[91] The outcome, they implied, contrasted the camp with another gathering that competed for the loyalty of Europe's young that summer, this one in East Germany.

For two weeks in August 1951, the leftist World Federation of Democratic Youth held its biennial rally, the World Youth Festival, in East Berlin. Twenty-six thousand young people from 104 countries attended the event, which was sponsored by the East German state and the Soviet Union, and two million young East Germans had some kind of connection with it, though apparently there was little interpersonal interaction between the bulk of German youth and foreigners, who were housed separately and provided with distinct programs.[92] "For Peace and Friendship" was the official theme of the festival, and much of the rhetorical content was antimilitarist, yet in a paramilitary sort of way, and meant as an implicit condemnation of the ongoing discussion to rearm West Germany through either NATO or the European Defense Community (EDC). The activities centered around sports competitions during the day and cultural performances in the evenings, both of which were undertaken according to nationality. The rally focused on Communist Party officials and dignitaries, with the young doing a lot of marching and parading in uniforms.

Through their sponsorship of the World Youth Festival that year, the Soviets intended to demonstrate the legitimacy and sovereignty of the new German Democratic Republic by welcoming youth from around the world, communist or not. They also wanted to show an openness that defied Winston Churchill's recent description of Eastern Europe as having been closed off behind an Iron Curtain. In the middle of the summer, the strict border protocols into the Soviet zone of occupied East Germany were suspended in order to process the tens of thousands of young people who were already headed to the festival from the West. Western officials responded in multiple ways, first and foremost by hastily organizing the rival European Youth Meeting at Loreley, but also by closing their side of the border, denying passport and visa applications, limiting access, and harassing western youth trying to get to Berlin. While the East Germans and Soviets lessened their border controls, the West Germans and Allies intensified theirs.[93] In July, an additional eleven thousand armed West German police were deployed along the Lower Saxony border with East Germany, while to the south the American military supported the expanded patrols of the Bavarian border police. The West German government ordered that East Germany be sealed off. Working in twelve-hour shifts, the West German police and American military sought to prevent what were deemed to be illegal border crossings by the young into, across, and from West Germany to East Germany. Along this inter-German border, thousands of West German and Western European youth were intercepted on buses and trains, in cars, and even on foot and on bicycles, as individuals and as groups. Once detained, most were sent home; others were taken to a temporary transit camp set up at Wabern, or to a holding facility in Fulda for those deemed to be agents of the East German FDJ youth movement, of which there were many, who were sent to recruit, coordinate, and accompany attendees.[94]

American reports from the Bavarian border with East Germany indicated that the young West Germans came from all over the republic and represented a cross-section of social class; they ranged in age from children to young adults, with about a third of the total female, and while most didn't seem particularly political, there were, according to official reports, "fanatics" among them.[95] The West German press followed the story, particularly focusing on the many East German *agents provocateurs* trying to stir up West German youth, but they also noted the large numbers of detained youth, some of whom were surprised by all the fuss, including Gerhard Berger and Hans Schmidt from Essen, who had brought along their girlfriends, Hilde and Jenny, on a vacation getaway of sorts to Berlin, with the promise that their expenses would be paid by the East German FDJ.[96] Tens of thousands of others made it across the border, but not without conflict. About a thousand young people armed with clubs and brass knuckles attacked the border in the Maroldsweisach forests, one of many violent confrontations that led to gunfire.[97] In total, three young West Germans were reportedly killed trying to evade the West German border police, though deaths along the border in this era were not uncommon.[98]

In the UK, the issue of the closed border became a public scandal with potential international implications when 280 young British delegates were arrested and detained in Saalfelden, Austria, by U.S. soldiers from the American zone of occupation there.[99] One student from the London School of Economics was even roughed up and required eight stitches to his forehead. The young Britons had been dogged the whole way, by officials in London who had delayed their paperwork, by port authorities in France who had questioned their credentials, and finally by the U.S. military policemen who arrested them in Austria. They eventually made it to the festival, late and feted as heroes, by doubling back through Italy and up through the Soviet zone. A few years earlier, in 1947, British occupation authorities in Austria had refused to allow 105 young Danish volunteers to proceed to Yugoslavia, where they intended to work on the Youth Railways, while the United States refused to allow any of its young nationals to enter Yugoslavia as well.[100] These incidents raised the question, to the delight of the eastern bloc, of who, exactly, had militarized the border and was determined to limit access. Whose Iron Curtain was it? Indeed, the entire 1951 episode was in large measure designed for propaganda purposes, to highlight the ways in which the West was as responsible for the hardening of the border as the East. The Berlin Blockade and Airlift had left the impression that the Soviet bloc was determined to maintain a secure and restricted border, when in fact the earliest strict enforcement of border controls and placement of physical barriers had been implemented by the West, and by the American military specifically.[101] During the festival itself, at the urging of their hosts, foreign attendees mostly shunned West Berlin, venturing there rarely. Yet this was not true for the massive numbers of East German youth who had come to Berlin for the festival. They, in fact, were keen to explore the western half of the city. Some of them, it was reported, did not return to East Berlin, indicating the onset of *Republikflucht*.[102]

While it is clear that in large measure the organizers had planned the meeting at Loreley as a counter-event to the Berlin World Youth Festival, they avoided presenting it as such. They seemed to want the comparison to be indirect and implicit rather than straightforward and explicit.[103] Unsurprisingly, the coverage in both the *Times* and the *New York Times*, though limited, emphasized the Cold War contrast between the two events. The *New York Times* referred to youth headed to Berlin as "young Reds." A letter to the editor of the *Times* complained about the lack of coverage of Loreley in comparison to the rally in Berlin, where the communists were "waging a cold war to capture the hearts and minds of young people."[104] The *Christian Science Monitor* described Loreley as a meeting of youth from "the free countries of Europe," there for "an enthusiastic manifestation of European friendship and democratic understanding."[105] A writer for *Le Monde* concluded that if the goal of Loreley was to be a western counterpart to the massive youth festival in Berlin, then it had fallen short in terms of overt politicization. After all, where were all the parades? He concluded, however, that the intangible search for a "European spirit" by the thousands of campers at Loreley demonstrated that the meeting there had offered a more truly democratic experience.[106]

A British official who attended the ten-day opening session at the Loreley gathering reported on the "distinct anti-communist tinge running through the proceedings," and while he remained a Euro-skeptic, he saw its value in terms of the Cold War: "I am myself very impressed by the strength of the European idea to kindle the German young. It is the only idea or ideal strong enough to stand up to the East."[107] Because the emerging Cold War had heightened their sense of urgency, in 1949 British occupation authorities had sought a broad "policy to capture German youth for the west," but were unsuccessful in securing financing from London. Alternatively, in 1950, the British began discussing the possibility of finding someone to sponsor and organize an international youth festival as a means of "binding German youth to western ideals" to counteract communist efforts in the East.[108] Thus, the French idea for Loreley had fit very neatly into British plans. Young Germans, they thought, were nostalgic for the order, ideological certainty, sense of purpose, and collectivism of Nazism. Because of this, the rise of Marxism might prove to be powerfully seductive. One alternative was to "Europeanize" German youth.[109] In this regard, the internationalism of Europe served as a conceptual counterweight to the internationalism of communism to capture German and western youth.[110] This lent a sense of expediency to getting Loreley put together quickly in order to compete with the Berlin rally. All in all, Loreley fit well within the "double containment" policy of countering Soviet influence in Europe while containing a resurgent Germany by integrating it into the West.[111]

One distinction between the Loreley and East Berlin gatherings was that the former was premised much more as a means of reconciliation for the past than was the latter. To accomplish this, the rally at Loreley sought not to portray a monolithic ideological bloc, but to permit a confrontation between points of view, and enable the young of various countries to encounter and engage each other, particularly regarding the legacy of the war. An eighteen-year-old Englishwoman wrote a letter of thanks to the organizers of the Loreley meeting, saying that the opportunity to know and befriend young Germans and appreciate the friendly German character had counted as a profound "discovery" for her. Older people at home in England wouldn't understand, she wrote, but "it will be up to us to convince them."[112] A young Frenchman, whose mother had died in a German bombardment and whose father had spent the war in a concentration camp, confided, "After three days here, I have nearly forgotten all that [the Germans] made me suffer." Another young Frenchman emphasized that there should be no rancor when remembering the war: "To build Europe, we must join hands with the young of the new Germany."[113] *Die Neue Zeitung* emphasized the campers' seriousness of purpose in their casual exchanges: when, for example, a young Englishman asked whether the rest of Europe should be concerned about the union of the new German state, a young German responded that he did not want to give up those new democratic bonds, and that it should not impede the building of Europe; indeed, the two endeavors should be complementary.[114] A young Briton wrote that "not the saving of Europe but the discovery of the European" had motivated the young to come to Loreley.[115] The special correspondent for *La Nation belge* described the camp as "an Internationale of friendship" where there was no hierarchy, but instead an egalitarian camaraderie prevailed.[116] Moreau concluded that, above all, Loreley had had a considerable influence on German youth, who welcomed thousands of young foreigners to their country and experienced a continental and generational camaraderie.[117]

Though there was some talk of further meetings like Loreley, none came to pass.[118] A financial mess and lingering acrimony among the organizers were among the reasons. Rather than sponsor massive international meetings, the French and Germans would focus on bilateral cooperation and exchange, while the European Movement would concentrate on the European Youth Campaign. As early as 1948, French authorities worried that interpersonal contact between the young of France and Germany might falter in the post-occupation period. While private groups continued to initiate and expand the number of programs and contacts, they needed help to sustain their endeavors, particularly given the complications of making transnational arrangements. The occupation authorities foresaw that a future government department should not only help coordinate and facilitate such private efforts at exchange, but financially subsidize them as well, even if the programs themselves remained in private hands. They saw growing German enthusiasm, too, as more and more German groups began to take the initiative and issue invitations to partner with French groups. Such a government program would enable an ongoing Franco-German reconciliation, to be pursued vigorously through the "impact of quotidian politics" of the young on the old.[119] In 1953, Jean Moreau accepted an appointment to run the new Office of International Meetings within the Cultural Affairs Division of the French Ministry of Foreign Affairs to develop programs and facilitate exchanges with other European countries, including a permanent commission dedicated to Franco-German youth relations that would work with its West German counterpart through intergovernmental cooperation.

In 1954, France and West Germany signed a cultural accord to promote and expand interaction between their peoples, such as youth exchanges and the new phenomenon of "twin-towning." No longer limited to what had been the French zone of occupation, such popular contacts between the two peoples began to multiply rapidly through grassroots efforts.[120] Twin-towning had begun during the occupation with the help of French authorities, and it grew steadily as a grassroots means to foster contact between French and German communities, again with an emphasis on the young. The *New York Times*, astounded at the phenomenon, ran a feature article in 1960 focused on Dijon and Mainz, noting that the Franco-German efforts at twinning appeared to be the most rich, involving, and fruitful of the worldwide movement. It claimed that the investment in the endeavor by ordinary people, rather than simply politicians or business interests, made the Franco-German twinning uniquely effective.[121] In early 1958, the French minister of foreign affairs reported to the minister of national education that he viewed the recent exchanges between young French and Germans to have been successful in improving relations between the two peoples, and thus an expansion of such programs was highly desirable from a foreign policy point of view.[122] Whereas the rally at Loreley had been a multilateral European endeavor under Franco-German leadership, renewed efforts at youth exchange advanced along a bilateral, intergovernmental trajectory. These postwar efforts at reconciliation through youth mobility culminated in a friendship treaty and the founding of the Franco-German Youth Office.[123]

The Franco-German Youth Office

In the early 1960s, while the European Commission of the EEC focused on a multilateral approach to harmonize the six economies of the Common Market, Charles de Gaulle and Konrad Adenauer pursued a bilateral strategy of cooperative integration through the 1963 Elysée Treaty, otherwise known as the Franco-German Friendship Treaty.[124] Adenauer, who sought to anchor West Germany firmly within the orbit of Western Europe, a policy known as his *Westpolitik*, initiated the idea for the treaty, but de Gaulle controlled the agenda, as he sought to secure for France a central position of strength on the continent as a counter to the influence of the United States and United Kingdom. Indeed, the Franco-German Friendship Treaty was promulgated in the same month, January 1963, that de Gaulle first vetoed British membership in the EEC.[125] Both de Gaulle and Adenauer hoped that the agreement would foster intergovernmental cooperation between France and West Germany as the basis for a dominant position in European affairs that would serve their distinct national interests.

To promote this treaty as a means to reconcile their peoples, Adenauer undertook a tour of France in the summer of 1962, and de Gaulle then visited Germany that fall, with extensive press campaigns for each as public relations. On 9 September at Ludwigsburg, de Gaulle addressed the young of West Germany in German, and told them that it would be up to them and their French counterparts to make the Franco-German friendship viable. While it was the task of governments to organize economic and political cooperation, he said to German youth, "you must do your part, and the French young theirs, to ensure that all circles among you and us are brought closer together, get to know each other better, and are bound more intimately." This was essential for a peaceful future, he concluded, because only the mutual friendship of the French and German peoples could provide the cultural foundation upon which a European political union could be built.[126] Although each of them remained somewhat ambivalent about the other and their nations' partnership, de Gaulle and Adenauer claimed that the key to reconciling peoples of all generations, classes, or regions was for the young to serve as the vanguard, penetrating French and German society effectively and thoroughly.

While the 1963 Elysée Treaty proposed several elements for cooperation between the two nations, including a military one, the focus of the treaty, and the only substantive accomplishment to come from it, was the Franco-German Youth Office (L'Office franco-allemand pour la jeunesse/ Deutsch-Französisches Jugendwerk), which was created for the purpose of facilitating personal contacts between the young of France and Germany.[127] By the early 1960s, the political class in both countries had come to accept that the cultural integration of France and West Germany could best be achieved through the mass mobility of the young. Ideally such visits would be organized, coordinated, and structured as group travel designed to serve national interests—and also moral ones, as unease about the supposed dangers of independent youth travel had grown. A French Catholic parenting publication, expressing concern about the morally dubious appeal of independent travel to Great Britain, where the young might surrender to the sexual and commercial delights of Swinging London, advised its readers to consider carefully the need to control adolescents abroad, through either placement with Catholic host families or organized group travel.[128]

The Franco-German Youth Office (FGYO) was (and is) a bilateral, integrated entity, independent of either state but given a generous budget by both. It initially had a French and German staff with a French director, followed five years later by a German director, and offices in both Paris and Bonn, with the headquarters fluctuating between the two capitals. The first effort coordinated by the FGYO took place in the summer of 1963, with a couple dozen young French and Germans meeting on the battlefields of Verdun—an obviously symbolic beginning.[129] In the early 1960s, the years immediately preceding the founding of the agency, there had been approximately 25,000 youth contacts per year between France and West Germany, substantially more than either had with any other country. After the introduction of the agency in 1964, France and West Germany averaged more than 300,000 youth contacts per year. By 1968, the FGYO had helped 1.8 million young Germans and French come together through over 35,000 programs; by 1978, the number reached 4 million; by 2003, over 8 million had participated in more than 250,000 programs. Relatedly, with the help of the FGYO, the number of officially twinned French and West German towns doubled between 1963 and 1968, to reach a total of 350.[130]

The French and West German governments designed the FGYO as an umbrella organization to facilitate, underwrite, and expand the variety of existing cultural exchange programs, the bulk of which were private. It had an annual budget of 100 million francs, jointly contributed by both governments, with 90 percent of its outlay going directly to subsidizing exchanges.[131] It worked with groups from a broad range of philosophical, confessional, educational, and political dispositions. It helped support leadership exchanges for youth organizations, work camps, vocational internships, town-twinning, vacation camps, individual and family exchanges, sporting events, educational exchanges, linguistic programming, artistic programs, agricultural programs, apprenticeships, and more. The FGYO not only expanded the volume of exchange, but it democratized

10   The first FGYO youth camp, summer 1964, Berlin. Used with permission of DFJW/OFAJ.
      © DFJW/OFAJ.

the base of participants and oversaw the quality of the programming, which was designed to promote "the incumbent role of youth" as a vanguard to definitively reconcile the two peoples.[132]

From the outset, the FGYO had intended to increase the numbers of working-class and rural youth who participated in exchanges. Though it had some success in expanding the opportunities, young people couldn't always afford to get away for a couple of weeks, if they were willing to go at all.[133] Inevitably, those who participated in FGYO activities had the means and time to travel. Also, they had the inclination. The young who went on these trips chose to do so; a significant process of self-selection largely limited participants to those who were most amenable, or at least not overtly hostile, to such encounters. Many of the programs were bilingual, for although the percentage of young Germans who spoke French was growing, their numbers weren't growing as fast as the numbers of those who spoke English: in the mid-sixties, about 15 percent of Germans under age twenty-five spoke some French, whereas 35 percent spoke some English. Still, more young Germans spoke French than the other way around.[134] In its 1968 evaluation, the FGYO recognized that it needed to improve language study more effectively through long-term programming, perhaps combined with apprenticeships and internships; this educational and professional direction typified the office in the 1970s.[135]

One successful endeavor that was funded and encouraged by the FGYO but neither designed nor run by it was the sister programs "Connaissance de la France" and "Wir entdecken Deutschland." The French government launched "Knowing France" initially in 1960 to familiarize the young of France with the distinct regions of their own country through domestic travel programs. It was quickly adapted in 1964 to serve the goals, and thus garner the subsidies, of the new Franco-German Youth Office. At the same time, "We Discover Germany" began in West Germany. These bilingual programs lasted roughly two weeks and sponsored approximately fifty young persons aged eighteen to twenty-five, divided evenly between French and German. Together, the young of France and West Germany would jointly explore a region, learning about its heritage, folk customs, and economy by meeting with prominent persons as well as interacting with local youth. The goal was to get the young participants to think about how these regions would participate in the building of Europe.[136] In 1966, for example, "We Discover Germany" ran forty-nine programs all over the country, including four in West Berlin. Some were rural, some urban, but each was designed to introduce the particularities of a given locale to young French and Germans from elsewhere.[137] Thus "Knowing France" and "We Discover Germany" were designed not only to bring the young of the two countries together in a joint endeavor, but also to educate them about the particularities of a given place, its people, landscape, and economy, in the context of their country and, more largely, Europe. In 1968, the two programs combined for a total of 162 sessions with five thousand participants, a tiny portion of the roughly three hundred thousand youth contacts that year.[138]

The influential teen magazine *Salut les copains*, which commanded a 40 percent share of the total French youth publication market, ran a special issue dedicated to profiling West German youth and youth culture. *SLC* had already been pursuing an editorial policy of placing French pop culture within a Europeanist context, one that put particular emphasis on West Germany.[139] In 1964–65, when the young musician Johnny Hallyday was conscripted and stationed in Offenberg, West Germany, the media reveled in his symbolic potential for reconciled youth: Hallyday stood for both a French patriot doing his duty and a pop celebrity in the burgeoning international youth market.[140] In 1965 *SLC* sent three young reporters to West Germany, who recounted their experiences there in a kind of travelogue exposé: Hervé, who had never been there and recorded his personal encounters along the northern coast; Benjamin, who was taken around Hanover by Ria so that he could get an insider's point of view; and Jean-Marc, who reported on the style, fashion, and attitudes of "Our German Cousins." The feature concluded with a transcribed interview with six young West Germans—Arne, Harald, Horst, Karen, Karl, and Sibylle—who had been living in France for a few months and talked about France, French youth, Franco-German relations, German reunification, and European integration, as well as boys and girls and pop stars. The entire special feature emphasized a mutual admiration society.[141]

Annual surveys showed a steady increase in the favorable opinions that the young of France and West Germany held toward one another and their respective countries. A poll from fall 1968 indicated that 76 percent of French youth and 89 percent of West German youth regarded exchange between their countries as an important part of their present and shared future.[142] In 1973, 83 percent of West German youth and 86 percent of French youth expressed a desire to visit and get to know their counterparts across the Rhine.[143] Studies had also shown that young French and young West Germans were much more favorably disposed to each other than were their elders, and that this was due in part to the social bonds and cultural proximity that had emerged through personal experience.[144] Monika, a twenty-seven-year-old German who had a professional internship in France, wrote: "now I better understand the French and their worries, I understand their mentality, and I can state that I helped put an end to the prejudices against Germans lodged in many French hearts. I worked with the French, and while they found me typically German, I showed them that the German soul has nothing to do with discipline and boastful songs of war." Patrick, a twenty-one-year-old French welder who served an apprenticeship in Germany, said that his experience "proved that Europe is not just a fantasy, but something real and concrete."[145] In the view of agency officials and politicians, the statistical and anecdotal evidence suggested a causal link between interpersonal contact and Franco-German reconciliation, particularly when viewed within the matrix of European integration.

Accordingly, some young people began to view these interactions as more than simply about reconciliation for past conflict; they saw in them the foundation for a future Europe. When Isabelle Mouré was twenty-one, she spent a year studying German abroad. The following summer, in 1973, she hosted some of her new German friends at her family's house in Savoy. Her grandmother sternly chided her, invoking the dead: "You know, your grandfather would not be pleased to see all these Germans in his house." Rather than feeling remorse, Isabelle felt invigorated, for she understood her grandmother's displeasure: Isabelle took her bearings not from the past, as did her grandmother, but from her hopes for the future. She found that the statement represented for her and "for all us Europeans, an immense and thrilling challenge to take up."[146] Gaby Lafitte, a polyglot Alsatian who traveled through France, West Germany, Belgium, the Netherlands, Switzerland, England, and Italy to study languages, lavished praise on the FGYO, stating that the objective of her exchanges was not simply "language training, but rather partnership training for the future of Europe."[147] Not merely comfortable with Germans, these two considered their travel experiences to be the basis of their Europeanism.

Studies published in the late sixties had shown that the general publics in France and Germany were favorably disposed to European integration, but that this was especially true for the young French and Germans.[148] The young tended to be more internationalist than their elders across the countries of Western Europe. Political scientists concluded, however, that this was not due to the fact of their being young, but rather to the context within which they were young, to the specific social and cultural experiences of this particular age cohort. Among the most important factors, they determined, was the effect of postwar exchanges and foreign travel. Moreover, the generational disparity in attitudes toward integration was most pronounced, they found, in France and West Germany, the two countries that had most aggressively pursued a cultural policy of reconciliation through the mobility of the young.[149]

It needs to be emphasized that these endeavors were organized and state-sanctioned. They were arranged and implemented by organizations, which then sponsored the groups and structured the travel. For example, occupation authorities had carefully vetted the private groups that were initially allowed into the French zone to organize programming there. The young who were brought to Loreley had largely been recruited through youth organizations, drawn for the most part from their leadership. The FGYO vastly expanded the numbers and kinds of young people involved, but still operated through organized group travel that had the imprimatur of the state. This may help explain the surprising fact that in the 1960s slightly more young women than young men participated in FGYO programs.[150] On the one hand, their social class gave them the means and opportunity, while on the other hand, the structured, organized, and chaperoned group trip gave young women the moral cover to do so. This constituted a marked contrast to the unstructured, independent travel that we associate with young itinerant backpackers.

By the tenth anniversary of the FGYO, many considered Franco-German reconciliation to be an accomplished fact. One newspaper asked, "Why a Franco-German Youth Office in 1975?" The reason had been clear in 1963, it said, but reconciliation was now complete. "After rapprochement," the paper advocated for an all-out "policy of integration," again emphasizing youth mobility between France and West Germany to establish sympathetic understanding as a prerequisite for broader European integration.[151] In the 1970s, the success of the FGYO began to serve as a model for a multilateral, European-wide program.[152] Even the *Frankfurter Allgemeine* looked to the organization as "a model for Europe" premised on mobility.[153] Meanwhile, *Le Monde* predicted "fewer dollars, more deutschemarks" as it declared French tourism to be entering a "European age."[154]

Indeed, the FGYO had been created in 1963 "for the young of both countries to serve Franco-German cooperation, and through it, to serve Europe as well."[155] Gerhard Schröder, the West German minister of foreign affairs who negotiated the treaty, later admitted, "we hoped that this cooperation would evolve toward a political union." Part of the intention behind the treaty was to establish regular intergovernmental consultations, an autonomous institutional apparatus of bilateral cooperation to help set the precedent for future Franco-German collaboration and intergovernmental autonomy in other areas; the FGYO was meant to serve as a model for integrated endeavor.[156]

In West Germany more so than in France, politicians had emphasized from the outset that this cultural cooperation would embolden a political Europe. The 1963 treaty and the youth office were working in pursuit of a united Europe, they said, and there could be no political Europe without a social reconciliation with France.[157] Some West German politicians pressed the government to forgo the bilateral Franco-German Youth Office altogether, and instead create a multilateral European Youth Office. The opposition Social Democrats put forward this proposal in 1963, opining that if the goal was actually to build Europe for the long term, the project should start immediately. Adenauer and his government insisted that France and West Germany had a special role to play in making integration possible, and that Europe could unite only with Franco-German reconciliation. The expansion to a European-wide program, they argued, would be a risky distraction.[158] French politicians followed the debate in West Germany closely, particularly after the Bundestag voted in February 1964 in favor of a European-wide office.[159] Both governments held their bilateral ground, however, and insisted that the FGYO was the best means to ensure their national interests as a precondition to Europe's future.[160]

Efforts to develop a European Youth Office continued in West Germany, despite the FGYO's insistence that bilateral programs would be more effective than multilateral efforts owing to the principle of reciprocity, and that any European office should merely help coordinate a network of bilateral arrangements.[161] West Germany, in fact, actively used bilateral youth exchange as a component of foreign policy aimed at reconciliation with former enemies, most evidently with France, but also in its concurrent program with Israel and later, in the 1970s and 1980s, with East Germany and Poland.[162] As one German official put it in 1966, "Travel, and above all travel, leads to genuine personal contact and exchanges of ideas. It is an excellent means for young people to build a balanced view of Europe, where the young as members of national groups can encounter each other and work together." Thus governments must recognize and develop "the role that the extensive exchange of youth will play in the shaping of a Europe tomorrow."[163] France's enthusiasm for the FGYO centered on the fact that it was *not* a European institution. De Gaulle, at this point, had developed a rather obdurate position vis-à-vis the Common Market. In the end, the FGYO successfully resisted efforts to turn it into a European-wide program.[164] Those efforts led instead to the establishment of the European Youth Centre, founded in Strasbourg in 1972 by the Council of Europe. Recognizing the achievement of reconciliation, the FGYO shifted its emphasis in the 1970s to improving the educational and professional quality of the exchange experience.[165] Specifically, the office became more focused on individuals' careers via study abroad or agricultural, artisanal, and professional apprenticeships.[166]

Across the Channel, similar ferment developed once the value of these social and cultural relations to the groundwork of European political and economic integration became apparent. Slowly, the British recognized that their lack of cultural relations had contributed to their inability to gain access to the Common Market. In 1967, a young Member of Parliament, Frank Judd, doggedly pursued his government to find out why it was not making international exchange programs a priority. During Parliament Question, he asked, given the government's commitment to entry into the Common Market, was it not "sad that in the past 15 years we have fallen so badly behind the rest of Western Europe in this respect?"[167] Indeed, in the mid-1950s, the British government had decided to scale back its already limited programs with Europe and focus its meager efforts instead on the Commonwealth. The Commonwealth Youth Trust sought to promote relationships among the young of the British metropole and its former colonies. The hope was that forging sentimental ties between young people would foster economic interconnectedness in a decolonizing world, and in so doing help combat the spread of communism as well. In 1961, a proposal for a vast Commonwealth Youth City to be built in London resulted instead in a commitment of money to expand the British hostel system.[168] The Commonwealth was performing poorly as an economic unit relative to trade with the continent. By 1965, the six states of the EEC had become the largest single market for British exports, while trade within the EEC was growing twice as fast as trade with nonmembers.[169]

The UK did, in 1965, expand its cultural programming, particularly youth exchange, with West Germany, but France, and Charles de Gaulle in particular, was blocking British efforts to join the Common Market at the time.[170] The Duncan Report at the end of the decade explicitly recommended that the government, through the British Council, pay much more attention to Western Europe, specifically France, and that it emphasize personal contacts among the young in doing so.[171] In 1970, the UK helped sponsor a paltry eighteen thousand exchanges between Britain and *all* member countries of the European Community.[172] This was a stark contrast to the more than three hundred thousand youth exchanges being organized annually between France and West Germany alone. The British concluded that expanding cultural relations must become an essential part of the British strategy in political negotiations for entry into the Common Market. They admired particularly the success of Franco-German efforts at reconciliation through interpersonal contact among the young.

France became the main target of the UK's new efforts at cultural work, and youth exchange became the primary method. The FGYO was repeatedly used as an example of the kind of endeavor Britain needed with France, and Western Europe generally, to facilitate British entry into the EEC.[173] After de Gaulle's resignation and the ascension of Georges Pompidou to the French presidency in 1969, the British saw their opportunity. A series of visits by President Pompidou, Prime Minister Edward Heath, and high-level ministers led to a joint declaration committing their governments to facilitating more interpersonal contact between the French and British, with the bulk of funds allocated for youth exchange.[174] British officials conducted a confidential study of the FGYO to explore how they might duplicate its success. They concluded that they simply could not afford to match the scale of it, and instead chose to expand significantly the British Council's presence in France, with an emphasis on youth exchange to match programs the UK already had with West Germany.[175]

The U.S. State Department felt similarly. In the mid-1960s, the U.S. Interagency Youth Committee (IAYC), established by President John Kennedy in 1962 to counter communist influence on the young, commissioned three confidential reports on the "young elites" of France, Great Britain, and West Germany in order to evaluate their attitudes toward the United States and make recommendations to improve them.[176] All three reports, by different authors, credited the remarkable success of the Franco-German Youth Office in improving relations between France and West Germany and offered it as a model for what the United States might do as part of a cultural policy of foreign relations. While they each reported that they had observed no significant upsurge in hostile attitudes toward America, they were troubled by the growing intra-European mobility of youth, and worried about the effect this might have on U.S. interests there. They suggested that the U.S. government consider negotiating similar bilateral exchanges to avoid cultural estrangement, as the young in these countries seemed focused less and less on America and more and more on Europe. Each author offered the opinion that the increasing transnational mobility of youth was generating a positive predisposition toward Europe, perhaps at the expense of the United States. The report on young Britons noted that such exchange programs were limited for the UK, but predicted that as Britain ramped up its efforts to join the EEC, it would be in the UK's national interest to develop robust bilateral exchanges, particularly with France.[177]

The strategically cultural process of European integration described here happened largely outside the institutional apparatus of political and economic integration. The FGYO and similar programs were bilateral agreements between individual nation-states, not programs of the European Commission or other European entities. In the mid-fifties, the European Coal and Steel Community organized vacation camps in Italy for the children of workers from member states. The 1951 ECSC treaty had established a social service imperative meant to focus on quality of life for workers. As president of the ECSC Commission, Jean Monnet thought these camps were a great idea not only for the young themselves, but for what he foresaw as the social consequences of European integration. While the ECSC held camps in 1955, it postponed later ones indefinitely, and the program fell by the wayside.[178] Similarly, the European Commission began sponsoring exchanges for young workers in 1963, but the program suffered from a lack of attention and dissipated gradually until it was absorbed by other, grander schemes in the 1980s.[179]

While the discourse of regeneration and rejuvenation and of youth as the future of Europe was deployed persistently by federalist Europeans, such as those at Loreley, it remained a largely rhetorical posture drawing upon the language of nationalist mobilization. European institutions demonstrated no real commitment to the young in terms of policy or programming.[180] In fact, although the young had been a target group for the promotion of Europeanism, the European Community (EC) did not begin to address the young in significant ways until the late 1970s, with such entities as the Europe Youth Forum, established to advocate for the young in an advisory role to the European Commission, and in the 1980s with work programs and extensive exchange and travel policies.[181] A 1983 European Commission study pointed to the remarkable success of the Franco-German Youth Office and other bilateral arrangements, and claimed that for the future development of the European Community into the European Union, "a political community depends on mutual understanding among its people," and that massive multilateral youth exchanges among member states would be the best mechanism for establishing a popular foundation for political union.[182] Over the 1980s, the European Commission developed the Youth Exchange Scheme (YES) for Europe, a program officially launched in 1990 to stimulate and improve the quality of youth exchanges among member states in the EC. Its initial goal was to enable eighty thousand young people between the ages of sixteen and twenty-five to stay for a week or more in another member state. The European Commission cited the success of West Germany, France, and the United Kingdom in their efforts at bilateral youth exchange as a means of international relations.[183] Indeed, the Franco-German Youth Office provided the design pattern for YES for Europe, which used as a template the FGYO's decentralized, supportive role subsidizing the bilateral and multilateral exchanges developed by national agencies and private associations.[184] Thus the EC eventually began to promote large-scale exchanges among the young in the late 1980s, particularly with the YES for Europe program (later renamed Youth for Europe), as well as the concurrent, and more famous, European Community Action Scheme for the Mobility of University Students program (Erasmus), established in the 1990s for university student exchanges among member states. The European Commission recognized the viability and success of these sorts of programs in facilitating integration, and that it had been outside EC policy, at the national level and through bilateral cooperation, that these kinds of achievements had been made.[185]

Cultural Integration

To celebrate the fiftieth anniversary of Charles de Gaulle's famous 1962 speech to West German youth, French president François Hollande and German chancellor Angela Merkel met in September 2012 at Ludwigsburg, where Merkel finished her speech with a line in French: "Long live Franco-German youth, long live European youth!" Her statement made clear the implied binational foundation of European integration: that the youth of France and Germany were the core of European youth. In 1971, Georges Pompidou claimed that Franco-German bilateral relations had provided the foundation for European integration as a whole, and that the most important thing that had enabled Franco-German reconciliation, in his view, was the youth exchanges.[186] A 1980 political cartoon by Swiss cartoonist Hans Geisen depicts French president Valéry Giscard d'Estaing and German chancellor Helmut Schmidt standing before a tableau showing de Gaulle and Adenauer pushing little Marianne and Michael to play together, while in the foreground Marianne and Michael, now grown, need no further encouragement. Such attitudes reflect the sense that promoting interaction among the young served the national interests of France and West Germany. This corresponds with Alan Milward's assertion that far from undermining the European nation-state, integration stabilized it and served the interests of it. However, unlike Milward, but like Pompidou, we can conclude that a profoundly cultural process based on young people's interpersonal interaction accompanied and supported the political or economic policies by design.[187]

The policies of the postwar Allied occupation targeting the young made significant contributions to later Franco-German European cooperation.[188] Through the programs that proliferated throughout the French occupation zone, the Loreley youth rally, and the FGYO, we see a strategic impetus to develop cultural relationships in order to make political ones possible. European integration has had a fundamentally social and cultural component that has operated largely outside the familiar political and economic institutions of integration, and has relied heavily on the practice of European youth mobility to achieve familiarity, if not camaraderie.[189]

Many viewed the rally at Loreley as a failure because it did not establish an active and ongoing European youth organization, despite the resolution in which the young campers declared their "common will in founding on this site a permanent community of European Youth."[190]

11 "After so many years . . ." In this 1980 political cartoon by Swiss cartoonist Hans Geisen, French Marianne and German Michael no longer need encouragement to play together. Used with permission. © Collection Karikaturen & Cartoons, Cartoonmuseum Basel, Switzerland.

Gerhard Brunn and others assert that European integration has never been bolstered by a vast popular political movement; that the efforts in the 1950s to found a European youth movement to support federalism failed, as all such attempts have; and that there remains no European political consciousness.[191] This, however, is too narrow a view of political outcomes and EU institutions.

The organizers of Loreley intended for a set of cultural goals to reconcile the young generation of Western Europeans with young Germans through interpersonal interaction. Indeed, the programming was just as much about this kind of Europeanism as it was about promoting European federalism. There were social and cultural relations at play internationally in addition to the political and statist ones. This emphasis on youth travel and exchange, which began during the French occupation, coalesced within a Europeanist framework at Loreley, and vastly expanded through the bilateral FGYO, contributed to a larger cultural process of integration, one that helped make French and German youth more European without necessarily making them any less national.[192] As Tara Zahra has shown, restoring the young to national communities was a primary goal of the Allies immediately after the war and, through the nurture of families, was viewed as essential to postwar political stability.[193] The young French and Germans were never expected to shed their national identities. In some measure they were expected to embody these identities for their young counterparts in order for young Germans to "know" France and the French, and vice versa. Likewise, the fraternization of the young with the goal of generating new modes of belonging was meant ultimately to have a positive effect on the national audiences in France and West Germany. The 1988 political cartoon by Dutch cartoonist Fritz Behrendt in figure 12 captures this parallelism well by tracing, in tandem, rather hostile French and German historical archetypes, but with the final representation of each as benign, pleasant youth.[194]

Even the persistent trope of France and West Germany as "a couple" or "siblings" or "partners" in the context of Europe emphasizes the personal dimension of this diplomatic relationship.[195] The mobility of the young and the social integration of Europe were related cultural processes fundamental to one another as Europe, through the leadership of

12   "The Franco-German relationship." This 1988 political cartoon by Dutch cartoonist Fritz Behrendt shows reciprocal French and German historical archetypes, with the final representation of each as pleasant young men. Courtesy of *Frankfurter Allgemeine Zeitung*. Used with permission of Renate Behrendt © Fritz Behrendt heirs.

France and West Germany, sought to reconcile itself in ways that would promote peace and prosperity rather than war and conflict by building upon, rather than effacing, nationality. It is not a coincidence that the two countries most invested in such programs for the young and with vast mutual bilateral exchanges were also the two countries at the core of initiating the broader economic, political, and institutional integration process in the 1950s and 1960s.

THREE

Youth Movements

In the spring of 1968, twenty-two-year-old Richard Holmes had just completed a degree at Cambridge, and was living in a poor neighborhood of London near Paddington Station in a building full of young people who formed a kind of quasi-collective. He wrote:

It was a restless time. The window of my attic room overlooked the shunting yards of Paddington Station, and my dreams were shaken by the whistle and roar of departing trains. The sense of movement and change was everywhere. News of disturbances in Paris had been reported piecemeal in the English papers for weeks, but largely in terms of isolated disruptions by students at Nanterre, or *syndicalistes* at Renault. Then I began to get letters from friends already in the city, speaking in confused, rapturous terms of the long "sit-ins," the great marches and demonstrations, people coming from all over Europe—Berlin, Rome, Amsterdam—to celebrate the new spirit of *Liberté*, and take part in some huge, undefined *événement*. It was a carnival, they wrote, and a revolution too. The world would never be the same again, the authorities were cracking, the old order was in retreat.[1]

Holmes received a letter from his friend Françoise, who insisted he should come to Paris. He listened excitedly to live radio coverage, "and the noises seemed to fill my room. I could hear the huge crowds shouting, the crack of CRS gas-canisters, the brittle, thrilling sound of breaking glass, the sudden ragged bursts of cheering. And suddenly the idea of 'the Revolution' came to life in my head." This idea excited him as "something utterly new coming into being, some fresh, immense possibility of political life, a new community of hope."[2]

In Paris at the end of May, Holmes was leaving the Place de la Sorbonne with an armful of pamphlets and leaflets when he was caught up in a sudden police sweep. He found himself pinned against the iron fence of the Cluny monastery with the barrel of an automatic rifle pushed against his chest. "I felt lonely, unheroic and unrevolutionary," he wrote. Meekly, he whimpered, "Je suis anglais." The trooper paused, poked Holmes in the belly with his rifle, and responded in French, "Englishman, mind your own business, go home," and, with a roar, "Leave me the fuck alone!" Holmes saw this advice as a real challenge to his perspective: "If I were English, why indeed didn't I mind my own business and go home? I was a foreigner, an outsider." When confronted with the power of the state, he had sheepishly retreated behind his nationality rather than declare his international solidarity. Although challenged and chastened, Holmes stayed in Paris. Brooding on this encounter, he decided that he wanted to be there to make sense of what was happening among the young people who had gathered there; in particular he wanted to understand why this new French revolution appealed to young Europeans from other countries, just as its eighteenth-century predecessor had, and whether, perhaps, his nationality was not problematic at all.[3]

That year marked a significant moment in the cultural history of youth mobility. The events of 1968 were a turning point in the emergence of a cohort of young people who had come, through travel, to conceive of themselves not merely as members of a particular nation, but as a continent-wide, transnational social group.[4] It was a group based largely on age, and one that professed culturally internationalist sensibilities in addition to nationalist ones, as Holmes's experience makes clear. As young Europeans traveled between protest sites, they expressed this solidarity explicitly; some even demanded the abolition of national borders and the establishment of a united Europe with unhindered mobility. Thus, one aspect of the general internationalism of 1968 was specifically Europeanist and expressed within the context of ongoing European integration. The experience of travel within the emergent youth culture helped to shape a politicized European identity among the young protesters of 1968. The social encounters of postwar transnational travel found a political expression.

In the late 1960s, international youth movements, in the sense of both mobility and activism, crossed national borders repeatedly. Young people were increasingly viewing the world in international terms and participating in it in transnational ways. The iconic example is Che Guevara, the young Argentinean who fought for victory in Cuba before continuing the revolution in Bolivia. Rudi Dutschke was from East Germany but led the West German student movement; Daniel Cohn-Bendit, the face of the events of May in Paris, had West German citizenship; and Tariq Ali, the prominent organizer in Britain, was from Pakistan. Young activists did not feel constrained by nationality and, like the more general emerging travel culture, sought to cross European borders freely. By the end of the sixties, however, national governments in Western and Eastern Europe were taking measures to prevent the free movement of youth in response to such political activities. Most famously, in May 1968, France tried to deny Cohn-Bendit's return to France from West Germany, and later in June there was controversy in Britain, most prominently in Parliament, over his visit to appear on the BBC. Both events inspired further international protests by the young, who demanded free movement across national borders while expressing solidarity as a transnational age-based social group. These young people regarded themselves as a community with mutual interests and an interconnected well-being that was maintained through mobility.

As a cultural practice, travel had become fundamental to the internationalism of the postwar years, specifically for young Europeans. An alternative community was developing on the basis of informal interchanges and transnational cooperation. These international cultural relations were outside the framework of national diplomacy, although they had often been supported by intergovernmental cooperation and subsidy.[5] In 1968, young travelers sought, both intentionally and unintentionally, to use this cultural internationalism to reformulate the relationship of European states to each other and to their citizens. The transnational mobility of the young in this period stimulated the transformation of the Common Market into the European Community and its subsequent expansion as Europeanist politicians seized the initiative to justify further integration as a direct response to the events of 1968.

The Transnational Social Body of Youth

In the 1960s there was remarkable growth in mass tourism in general, not just that of the young, but it was the travel of the young that was particularly striking and noteworthy as a profound cultural phenomenon, something new and possibly troubling. Despite the wide variety of nationalities of the young who traveled to and through France in the 1960s, three-quarters of them were from Western Europe, and nearly half were German and British.[6] Thus, Western Europeans dominated the youth traveling culture there, though the phenomenon itself was more broadly international. In 1966, a French magazine article noted that "All the young people of the world have spontaneously found the same gestures, the same formulas"; it lamented the impossibility of preventing this emerging international youth culture from traveling across national borders. "Beatniks today flood across Europe and even onto the quais of the Seine. When someone tries to turn them back at the frontier, surprise, they spring up among us, right under our feet."[7] Roger Delagnes raised the issue in the French National Assembly, deploring the rapidly growing numbers of "dirty" and "ragged" young "international tramps" who had no resources and were threatening the French tourist industry, as well as endangering French youth through their bad example.[8] Indeed, that same year, sixteen-year-old Jean Solé, who later designed the iconic cover of the long-haired backpacker for the *Guide du routard* collection, encountered young travelers from Holland, England, Germany, and America congregated in the Square du Vert-Galant on the western tip of the Ile de la Cité. Solé had never encountered backpackers before, and the experience transformed his life. They seemed to him so free, so liberated, that he hit the road himself soon after, becoming a member of the late 1960s itinerant international community of traveling youth.[9]

Holmes characterized this form of independent travel by the young and the culture they carried as a "challenge to the conventions and structures of authority." He described the late 1960s traveling culture as marked by a "tone of confrontation, which took place daily, whether in the matter of clothes, art, sexual morality, religious piety or politics. Such confrontation was international: the counter-culture took to the road and passed all frontiers, entered all cities."[10] In the years leading to 1968, the emergent international youth culture, travel, and an attitude of oppositional rebellion converged.

Likewise, many 1968 activists developed a critical awareness of their societies through travel and interactions with foreign youth. British feminist Hilary Wainwright found that the time she spent in Portugal as a teenager in the mid-1960s had radicalized her sense of politics and her conceptualization of the world as being more than just Britain, in part through meeting and befriending Portuguese young people living under the dictatorship of António de Oliveira Salazar.[11] The young New Left activists in West Germany consistently attributed their development of a sense of *Weltoffenheit*, or openness to the world, to their travels and interpersonal transnational connections, believing that this contributed directly to their politicization in the 1960s.[12] Petr Uhl of Czechoslovakia

found that his travels in this period, especially through the semipermeable Iron Curtain, helped radicalize his politics.[13] As another observer proclaimed about the impact of youth travel on the politics of 1968, "More or
less spontaneously, youth had become an Internationale!"[14]

Joe Mack, an American college student who was hitchhiking through
Europe in the summer of 1968, said that in every youth hostel he visited,
"talking politics was what young people did." As Mack traveled around,
not only did people talk politics, but they also interrogated him on where
he had been, what he had seen, and what he had done. In August, while
hitchhiking in Sweden and Denmark, he was repeatedly questioned about
Prague, which he had visited in July. When he arrived in Copenhagen in
mid-August, the news, rumor, and gossip about the Soviet invasion of
Czechoslovakia was all that anybody wanted to talk about.[15] In letters to
his mother in Turin, twenty-year-old Paolo Ferro extolled the excitement
of leftist politics as he hitchhiked with like-minded people in Sweden and
joined crowds of protesters in attacking the American embassy in London.[16] For anyone who was young and traveling in Western Europe in
1968, it was hard to avoid politics, even outside the major centers of protest, because not only were young individuals being politicized through
travel, but the very places and practices of youth travel, such as hostels
and hitchhiking, had become politicized spaces and politicized activities.
Traveling developed as a way to share political news and political opinion,
even if not direct political participation. One didn't have to be a radical or
activist to experience it.

Toward the end of May 1968, the *Times* of London ran a series of
articles on the international youth rebellions. While the *Times* did not
find any evidence of an organized conspiracy, it did recognize a remarkable phenomenon at work: "National frontiers mean less than generational frontiers nowadays." This sense of collective identity and purpose
inspired a great deal of "cross-pollination" as young people visited each
other, swapped books and ideas, corresponded, and organized demonstrations of mutual support. The article noted the continual traffic in
exchange students over the 1960s as having particularly facilitated the
movement. It went on to point out the prominent role played by Germans in the Grosvenor Square demonstration in London on 17 March of
that year, the large numbers of British and German youth who had gone
to Paris in May, the Americans present throughout Western Europe, and
the efforts of Italian students to foster relations everywhere, with Italian
contingents having demonstrated in Berlin in April and in Paris in May.
"European student leaders now believe that international cooperation is
important. Contacts and visits are becoming steadily more frequent and

systematic," the *Times* noted with some concern.[17] These interpersonal political contacts were not only European, of course, but transatlantic, as many European activists had traveled westward and Americans eastward through the 1960s.[18]

Astounded by the scale of events in Paris, Americans Barbara and John Ehrenreich decided to leave graduate school in early May and cross the Atlantic to Paris to make sense of what was happening there. They continued their travels around Western Europe that summer, and wherever they went, they met other foreign young people—Americans, British, Dutch, French, Germans, and Italians—who were all seeking to experience, understand, and participate in this international movement of youth. According to the Ehrenreichs, a "migrant" youth culture developed in 1968 as the young people "traveled to Paris, Munich, Florence, or London, moving in the new underground of escaped students."[19]

The Ehrenreichs' description of these travels as a migration was indicative of the larger global migration into Europe at the time. Indeed, the massive influx of immigrants into Western Europe provided the backdrop against which the youth movements would be understood. The distinctions were important, however, because on the one hand there was the migration of mostly nonwhite non-European poor for economic reasons, and on the other there were the travels of mostly white Western European middle-class young people for social and political reasons. The economic boom, the interventionist welfare state, and the technological development of the knowledge society had led to a substantial broadening of the middle classes and an exponential increase in the number of university students in the 1960s. Meanwhile, the category of "youth" itself had become an ideological site of power and an object of political, economic, and cultural interest in the wake of the postwar baby boom. Young people, more numerous than ever before and now part of the social body of "youth," had been empowered.[20] Where the Ehrenreichs saw a "new underground" of mobility made up of "students" who had "escaped" the sedentary constriction of university life, others saw the emergence of a revolutionary and international social class.

Jerome Férrând specifically attributed the events of 1968 to the formation of "youth" as a new international social class, or as he described it, "the new Third Estate, who were nothing and became everything." He ascribed this development to the extension of transportation, travel, and communication, so that "behavior overflows frontiers and forms a specific civilization extending to millions of young people." He claimed that "their tastes and customs tend to unify them on a worldwide scale; young people today form a vast, coherent mass, which is definitively a social class." Moreover, this class was "conscious of having goals, a role to play, and an incontestable power."[21] Although Férrând—and many others like him—exaggerated the future role of youth as a revolutionary social class, the new Third Estate or Proletariat, he correctly identified that the formation of a new youth culture and its internationalist attitude had been facilitated by travel. In August 1968, a young Danish woman claimed that because young middle-class Europeans were now regularly visiting each other's countries, "Today, students feel more European than Danish, German, or French."[22]

State-led efforts to get the young of Western Europe to interact associated international travel with political citizenship. A 1960 intergovernmental study of exchange programs and travel by European youth had concluded that "the final goal of exchange programmes is a learning process, the learning of an international role, which should exist in addition to or perhaps above the national role. We must also realize that we live in a world of many cultures, in a world in which a revolutionary change in our way of life has occurred through technology and industry. International understanding therefore is a question of attitude, it is the result of an education to a pluralistic view of the world, to intercultural understanding."[23] Yet "we must ask ourselves more critically," it further concluded, "whether our aims with respect to 'international understanding' and the methods which we apply to this end produce a readiness to political action on the part of the participants. . . . The main goal should not be to educate to passive understanding, but to a readiness to take on political responsibility."[24] The report highlighted the importance of using the increased emphasis on travel by the young to do more than simply promote "international understanding"; young people should use this understanding for "political action" to make them responsible citizens in a plural Europe. However, the politicization and political action that resulted was not the benign citizenship these nation-states had envisioned.

Meet the Provos!

The Dutch Provo movement in many ways anticipated the cultural practices and political critiques that prevailed among the young protesters of 1968. From May 1965 to May 1967, a group of young people in Amsterdam who referred to themselves as Provos (derived from the Dutch word *provoceren*, "provoking") combined a novel mixture of art and politics with a dose of alternative youth culture to produce a political and cultural critique built on spectacle. The Provo movement began as simple acts of street theater at Spui Square and eventually grew into a full-blown political movement, with a newspaper that reached a circulation of twenty thousand. The Provos adopted white as their color of "provocation," wearing white clothes, issuing what they called "White Plans," and even proposing that central Amsterdam be closed to traffic, with white bicycles to be provided for free use. Most famously, in March 1966 they set off a series of white smoke bombs during the Dutch royal wedding cortege, creating a wild, chaotic scene. By June of that year, they even managed to get one of their leaders elected to the Amsterdam City Council.

Through the international publicity they generated with their outrageous stunts and the violent police crackdowns that often followed, the Provos became the darlings of European youth. The excitement and activity that surrounded them enthralled young nonconformists, and thousands of letters and visitors poured into Amsterdam from all over Western Europe and beyond. The young founded Provo groups across Western Europe, and in the United States, too (including future Yippie! Dana Beal's New York Provos), though Belgium was the only country outside the Netherlands in which they reached any significant numbers or managed to have an impact. Still, Daniel Cohn-Bendit has commented that without the example provided by the Dutch Provos to the young of other countries, Europe would have been a very different place in 1968.[25] Campus unrest in Turin, for example, included a series of *scioperi bianchi*, or "white strikes," protests designed as spectacle.[26]

As traveling to Amsterdam became characteristic of international youth culture generally, those who came had the opportunity to mingle not only with the Dutch Provos, but with each other as well. In fact, in the summer of 1966, the Dutch tourism board encouraged the rest of Europe to come to Amsterdam with a promotional campaign that proclaimed, "Meet the Provos!"[27] "Meet the Provos" offered a day-tour package for thirty guilders that departed each evening from Museumplein, visited a sixteenth-century tower in Enkhuizen, and provided aperitif, dinner, and a cruise on the Ijselmeer in the company of young Provos ready to answer questions.[28] By the spring of 1967, the number of young Europeans loitering in Amsterdam's Central Station led authorities to sweep through and close the main hall to all but "genuine" travelers.[29] Although there were only a few dozen core Provos, thousands of young European supporters floated in and out of Amsterdam, each staying an average of three weeks.[30] *Le Figaro littéraire* lamented that "there exists in Western Europe a new place of pilgrimage: Karthuizerstraat in Amsterdam. The pilgrims come from Scandinavia, Germany, England, France, and even the United States. They are angry young people who have come to learn the latest techniques and perspectives of a new type of subversion."[31] In the summer of 1966, many French young people, particularly in Paris and Strasbourg, had become fascinated by the Dutch Provos and their calls for an international "provotariat." A number of them went to Amsterdam to see, listen to, learn from, and experience an international youth movement that had declared itself to be revolutionary. A magazine article warned that young French people were going to Amsterdam out of a desire not just to see the Provos, but to identify with them, to become Provos themselves. The magazine described it as a "contagion" that was spreading to France through the mobility of the young.[32]

Returning to Paris from just such a trip, Danielle Bourgeois claimed that she intended to transform the Parisian beatniks into a provotariat. There was, to be sure, a brief flirtation between the young hippie youth in Paris and the Dutch Provos. [33] In 1966 and 1967, a handful of minor Provo demonstrations in the Latin Quarter resulted in skirmishes with police, arrests, and some expulsions, particularly of young Germans, Dutch, and Italians.[34] The Provos caught the attention of the Situationists from Strasbourg, who traveled to the Netherlands to meet them and discuss tactics, particularly at a Provo Congress held in Maastricht in November 1966, and the Provos featured prominently in Situationist literature. At the same time, other young people, among them Luisa Passerini and a group of Italians from Turin, came to Strasbourg to meet the Situationists who had taken over the Student Union and published their famous pamphlet on student misery.[35] Danish students began to visit Berlin and later Frankfurt, seeking ideas and looking for personal political connections.[36] In short, a circuit was developing in the late 1960s involving like-minded young people who were traveling and visiting one another within and through the larger network of youth mobility. Not simply inspired by one another, these political activists sought each other out by utilizing the cultural practices of travel at their disposal.

These travels included spontaneous adventures as well as planned meetings and congresses, of which there were far too many to note. Certainly the most significant was the International Vietnam Congress, held in West Berlin in February 1968. The West German SDS (Sozialistischer Deutscher Studentenbund) sponsored the event and invited antiwar activists from across the globe, but particularly from Europe. Thousands of students came from all over Western Europe to West Berlin, traveling along the narrow rail and roadway transit corridor through East Germany to reach the city. They attended workshops, speeches, and rallies, all with a radical leftist bent that emphasized international solidarity in an effort to protest and end the American war in Vietnam. In particular, the congress made Rudi Dutschke into something of an international star among radical youth; his speeches were the most effective and drew the greatest response from the crowds. Tariq Ali, Alain Krivine, and Daniel Cohn-Bendit, who would all become well known later in the year, attended as well. To conclude the congress, twenty thousand students marched through West Berlin with red banners and National Liberation Front flags and chanted their support for the Vietnamese. Ali described his participation at the Berlin Vietnam Congress as reinforcing his "internationalism as well as the desire for a world without frontiers."[37]

In the wake of the Berlin conference, the militant SDS of Germany became the focus of attention for other groups in Europe in the early spring of 1968. Dutschke visited Prague in April, speaking in Wenceslaus Square and meeting with young activists. A Czech student delegation then visited him and the SDS in Berlin. Despite their admiration for Dutschke and the SDS, the Czech students concluded that there was a distinct disagreement in their political visions: though they recognized an international solidarity that was partly based on age, they found their local conditions and personal understandings of socialism to be markedly different and incompatible.[38] Later in April, after the attempted assassination of Dutschke in front of his Berlin apartment, spontaneous protests broke out in Paris, New York, Berkeley, Toronto, London, Rome, Milan, Belgrade, and Prague, as well as all over West Germany. For the first time, an event specific to one country had led to widespread international student demonstrations[39] With the April assassination attempt and the extensive protests, people viewed West Germany as the place where student activism was the most promising, radical, volatile, and effective. France's March 22 Movement even looked to young Germans for inspiration by inviting Karl Dietrich Wolff, the leader of the German SDS, to speak at Nanterre in April.

The impression that France was comparatively "quiet" led a group of young French journalists who specialized in youth and the young to clamor to get to West Germany, where there was something significant going on. The FGYO, the Franco-German youth exchange program, finally organized a two-week tour of West Germany for them, and they left at the beginning of May. Ironically, while they were there, ostensibly to learn more about the viability of political activism among European youth and particularly the German SDS, Paris erupted. Stunned by the rapid escalation of events in France, the young journalists scrambled to make their way back, abandoning their German itinerary.[40] Paris became the destination of choice, including for young Germans. The French border police at Strasbourg turned away a vanload of Germans with radical leaflets on 7 May. At Orly Airport on 9 May, French police refused entry to two SDS members and treated them roughly before sending them back to West Germany, though they managed to get into France a couple of days later by car.[41] A week later, two other members of the German SDS rallied a large crowd at the Sorbonne.[42] Overall, a significant number of young Germans had made it to Paris. Some were hard-core revolutionaries from the SDS, but most had come out of curiosity once the events were underway.[43]

Young people from all over Europe—some activists, some not—gravitated to the events in Paris that spring, much as Europeans from abroad had been drawn to Paris during the French Revolution of the late eighteenth century. As a young William Wordsworth wrote after traveling to Paris in July 1790:

'Twas a time when Europe was rejoiced,
France standing at the top of golden hours
And human nature seeming born again.
Bliss was it in that dawn to be alive,
But to be young was very heaven![44]

A vanload of young Belgian radicals from Leuven came to Paris to share their recent experiences with how to deal with institutions and police.[45] Dozens of Roman students visited Nanterre and invited their French compatriots back to Rome.[46] In the middle of May, twenty-year-old Ron Hijman sat with four friends, one of them an attractive young nurse, drinking in a pub in Amsterdam. They were excitedly discussing the events in Paris, and "within an hour we decided, the five of us, to go that same night to Paris. Why? Thrilling senses; young and wild; all of us in love with the nurse?" They dashed home to get their passports and drove for hours through the night crammed into a small Renault, with Hijman strategically squeezed in the rear beside the warm body of the nurse. They managed to talk their way through the border control, arriving in Paris at dawn, where they stayed three days.[47] As the events in Paris had escalated, they wanted to join the other young Europeans who were already gathered there. Some, including Ika Meulman-Sorgdrager from Haarlem, simply happened to be in Paris as part of ongoing travels when the events broke out.[48] Western Europeans in general were very well represented. They had come to identify with other young people regardless of borders, emphasizing what the *Times* had called "generational frontiers" over the traditional "national frontiers."[49]

Thus, mutual efforts by young people characterized the movement back and forth between European protest sites throughout 1968. They hoped that they could help invigorate each other's local movements through transnational mobility—if not by participating fully, then at least by witnessing and expressing support. As travel had become a fundamental aspect of the new European youth culture, so it was fundamental to the youth political movements of 1968 and their transnational, even Europeanist, sensibility. Travel by middle-class youth in 1968 functioned as part of a collective identity across Western Europe based on age and politics. Young people were traveling specifically to meet one another rather than to visit a particular location; for this cohort, destinations were determined by activism more than tourism, or a combination thereof. The events of May–June inspired travel not only to Paris, but from it as well.

The Mobility of Daniel Cohn-Bendit

The cross-border mobility of one particular young man, Daniel Cohn-Bendit, became the concern of multiple governments and inspired transnational protests featuring thousands of young people. Because like-minded youth across Western Europe followed the events in Paris closely, and because Dany Cohn-Bendit had become the face of May, activists invited him to speak at several campuses and meetings around Western Europe. Feeling that he was at a bit of an impasse in Paris, Cohn-Bendit decided to accept these offers to explore the international solidarity of 1968, while also, he later admitted, indulging his new celebrity. His tour across the frontiers and borders of Western Europe proved problematic, as several governments considered free movement by the young to have become threatening, particularly when it involved someone such as Cohn-Bendit. Notably, both the radical youth and the nation-states of Western Europe recognized that the movements of 1968 were not contained within national borders; like the young themselves, the ideas of revolt and the sense of solidarity traveled freely.[50] Thus, governments sought to curtail such mobility through their prerogative to assert border controls more strictly. Cohn-Bendit's first scheduled destination was Brussels, but the Belgian government barred him from entering the country on 22 May, for fear that he might inspire further revolt there.[51]

Cohn-Bendit then traveled to Berlin instead, where he spoke to an enthusiastic crowd of a few thousand before heading to Amsterdam in the company of some members of the German SDS. After he had arrived in

Amsterdam, on 23 May, the French government announced that it now considered him an "undesirable" in France and would turn him back at the border if he tried to return.[52] That night, thousands of protesters in Paris demanded "Cohn-Bendit à Paris!" as they marched from the Latin Quarter to the National Assembly.[53] In Amsterdam, meanwhile, Cohn-Bendit announced that he was determined to return to France to continue the struggle, viewing it as his "duty."[54] He gave a speech in a large cinema, after which his audience swarmed the University of Amsterdam's campus and occupied several buildings—exactly the kind of behavior that government officials had feared he would inspire wherever he went.

French and German students gathered together at their shared border to protest France's refusal to let Cohn-Bendit return. His interdiction had united them in a way that enabled them to express their own sense of common identity. In fact, one coalition announced that it intended to march en masse and escort Cohn-Bendit across the Pont d'Europe connecting Kehl with Strasbourg; if necessary, they would "seize" the bridge.[55] Meanwhile, Cohn-Bendit announced his intention to cross the border the following day, Friday, 25 May. Members of the German SDS said they would accompany him, and Karl Dietrich Wolff, their leader, declared, "We will not let the friendship between French and German youth be hindered and destroyed by authoritarian governments and their means of power!"[56] He challenged the authority of nation-states to use their borders as a measure of inclusion and exclusion, particularly with regard to the young.

In the end, a thousand students from Saarbrücken University escorted Cohn-Bendit to the border at Forbach in the Saarland, where he officially presented himself at the Brême d'Or customs house with a bouquet of yellow forsythia and a battered West German passport. He was taken to the local prefect, who presented him with his official expulsion form, which he refused to sign.[57] He was in France for all of ninety minutes. The government tightened security by stationing riot police, mounted police, and canine patrols along the entire French border; groups of local veterans gathered to encourage their work and protest against Cohn-Bendit. In fact, the French government had already intensified border controls all along France's eastern frontier, with a stringent application of identity controls to prohibit entry into France of "provocateurs," who, unsurprisingly, they profiled primarily by age.[58]

Given the ease with which Cohn-Bendit later slipped into France clandestinely, his public display at Forbach seems an obviously symbolic act, intended to undermine the nation-state's emphasis of power and control over its borders and frontiers, as if a nation were a fortress.[59] After

13 "Cohn-Bendit Will Pass" suggests the inability of the Gaullist state to police its borders.

he had publicly presented himself at the border station to be officially rebuked by the state, his appearance days later in Paris heightened the artificiality of national borders and the inability of governments to maintain them effectively. Specifically, he mocked the Franco-German border, the very landscape where millions of French and Germans had died in the past century fighting for meager territorial gain along the most heavily fortified section of France's frontier. Cohn-Bendit's own Franco-German transnationality and personal history of moving freely between the two nations compounded the symbolism.[60]

Late in the evening of 28 May, a young man with dyed jet-black hair and dark sunglasses mounted the rostrum at the Sorbonne. He stood there for several moments with no reaction from the crowd. He removed his glasses, and "after a few seconds there was a tremendous ovation. People were standing and shouting 'Les frontiers on s'en fout!' " As the crowd gradually recognized Cohn-Bendit, a repeated chorus of "Fuck all frontiers!" grew in strength and volume.[61] He declared to them, "I am not a foreign agent, but I am an international revolutionary," emphasizing that being "international" was not the same as being "foreign."[62]

Soon after his triumphant, if brief, return to Paris, the BBC invited Cohn-Bendit to London to participate in a televised roundtable. To be entitled "Students in Revolt," it would include twelve student leaders from around the world. The program nearly did not air, as British immigration authorities attempted to keep the young radicals out. Cohn-Bendit arrived on 11 June, and the immigration office at Heathrow prepared to send him back to Frankfurt on the next plane. They also detained Lewis Cole from Columbia University for some time before releasing him.[63] British officials held both for several hours for detailed questioning. James Callaghan, the home secretary, interceded on behalf of the BBC and its invited guests. In the end, they granted Cohn-Bendit a two-week visa, which he used to travel in the UK and attend rallies at the London School of Economics (LSE) and other campuses.

As news of the upcoming program and the arrival of these young radicals became known, a great ruckus in the press decried the fact that the BBC, without government approval, had invited young agitators and revolutionaries to London, where many feared they might incite further revolt. Both the House of Commons and the House of Lords debated the problematic and dangerous situation of having such young extremists in London, especially "Dany the Red." The opposition Tories even submitted a motion condemning the BBC for inviting foreign students to the UK to take part in the broadcast. The BBC received 750 letters, postcards, and telegrams and 700 phone calls of protest during and after the program, with only 70 letters of appreciation.[64] The letter writers were outraged that the BBC had run the risk of importing revolution across national borders by facilitating the travel of these young people. Many letters referred to them as "parasites," as if the movements of 1968 constituted some kind of invasive species that ought to be quarantined at national frontiers. They often mentioned Cohn-Bendit specifically, which was not surprising since the BBC used his participation to promote the program as the best-known and most recognizable of all the participants.

Robert McKenzie moderated the program, which lasted forty minutes.

14   Daniel Cohn-Bendit at the BBC in June 1968 with Dragana Stavijel, Tariq Ali, and Alain Geismar. Keystone Pressedienst, Hamburg.

The participants expressed mutual sympathies and recognized certain commonalities, but they insisted on the local conditions and distinctiveness of their individual movements. Karl Dietrich Wolff did acknowledge a shared sense of solidarity and the emergence of a new kind of "Internationale." At the same time, Dragana Stavijel from Yugoslavia noted that this was the first time they had all met, and it was only because of the BBC. There was no conspiracy, she insisted, and no organized movement. In the end, the conversation was congenial, if a bit dull and dominated by the conventions of Marxist rhetoric. As the *Daily Telegraph* wrote after the program, "If this is revolution, one felt, it ought to be made of sterner stuff."[65]

Cohn-Bendit also appeared alone on the BBC interview program *24 Hours* with Michael Barratt. During the interview, he compared the situation in France to 1940, when de Gaulle was determined to fight the authoritarian fascism of Philippe Pétain, even from exile abroad. Barratt retorted, "But apart from the other obvious differences, there is one very crucial difference between de Gaulle and Dany, isn't there? He was a Frenchman. That's pretty crucial. And you are not." Cohn-Bendit responded, "Well, put it this way. I am born in France . . . I live in France, so I am in French politics. And I think the most important thing that we had in France in the last days, was the demonstration in the Gare de Lyon where sixty to seventy thousand young people chant[ed] 'We are all German Jews.'"[66]

This emphasis on Cohn-Bendit's nationality was revealing. The BBC itself had emphasized nationality in organizing the panel for "Students in Revolt," inviting one participant each from Belgium, Britain, Czechoslovakia, Italy, Japan, Spain, the United States, and Yugoslavia, and two each from France and West Germany. Noting this, one viewer wrote in to ask, "Were there any English students present? I do not regard Mr. Tarqui [sic] Ali as a representative English student."[67] Indeed, Ali's Pakistani nationality was problematic, like Cohn-Bendit's West German citizenship. Over the summer of 1968, as Ali became increasingly visible as a leader in England, the blatant racism of the tabloid press and various MPs inspired a large crowd at LSE to chant in support of him, "We are all foreign scum! We are all foreign scum!"[68]

In contrast to England, where Ali's foreignness was obvious because of his name, his accent, and his looks, in France the public could be excused for not realizing that Cohn-Bendit was technically German, since he came off as so, well, French, in his interviews and public appearances. When the government announced that it was prohibiting his return to France, *Le Monde* made sure to emphasize that his nationality was, in fact, West German, recognizing that the French public might be confused on this point.[69] Of course, Cohn-Bendit had spent the bulk of his life, all but three years, in France; he had grown up and gone to school there. His national citizenship was thus rather complicated.

Born in Montauban, France, in 1945, the son of German Jewish refugees, Cohn-Bendit described himself as having been for the most part "stateless" since birth, a fact that France's 1968 rejection had confirmed for him. Although his older brother had French citizenship, in 1959 Dany chose to adopt West German citizenship, an option open to him as the child of Jewish refugees, for the purpose of escaping mandatory French military service.[70] His decision to be "German" was a tactical rather than a nationalistic choice. As he said, he did not give "a damn about nationality."[71] He later wrote, "Neither French nor German, I am a bastard." This kind of wordplay typified Cohn-Bendit; the term *bâtard* means not only illegitimate but, importantly, ill-defined and hybrid as well. "I proclaim my transnationality with pride," he wrote.[72] His refusal to subscribe to a national identity placed him in marked contrast to those who wanted to emphasize it.

Indeed, others repeatedly insisted on his foreignness, his alien status, and his German nationality. On the left wing, Georges Marchais of the French Communist Party (PCF) famously called Cohn-Bendit a "German anarchist." The PCF denounced him as a foreigner and claimed that French workers did not need lessons from a "German Jew"—a double emphasis on his outsiderness and alien nature. They claimed that he was an agent of an international network and thus a threat to the French nation, ignoring the irony that the Communist Party was itself supposed to be both internationalist and revolutionary. The right wing, too, emphasized his Jewishness and Germanness. Whereas the student protesters demanded "Cohn-Bendit à Paris" after his expulsion, when the Gaullist right wing organized a mass rally on 30 May, chants of "Cohn-Bendit à Dachau" were heard from the more extreme participants, much to the chagrin of those who hoped to use the protest to showcase the respectable right. The nationalist politician Jean-Louis Tixier-Vignancour proclaimed that the French regime risked being "overwhelmed by a young German fanatic."[73] The press emphasized Cohn-Bendit's Germanness throughout its coverage in May. Even the *Times* of London usually referred to him as "Herr Cohn-Bendit" when readers were not reminded of his German nationality more explicitly.[74] The debate in the British Parliament on 13 June focused on Cohn-Bendit and his foreignness. MPs and Lords referred to him repeatedly as "this alien" or "this young foreigner" or "foreign student" or "German professional agitator." Yet while those in power used foreigners and outsiders to explain away the domestic upheavals of 1968, the young tended to embrace foreignness as an expression of their alienation from their own nation-states while also proclaiming solidarity with those being targeted by such attacks, specifically immigrants.

We Are All Foreigners!

While Parliament debated Cohn-Bendit's presence in the UK, French government officials announced three emergency measures on 12 June meant to curtail the ongoing events altogether, which in large part they did. In addition to announcing a ban on all demonstrations and outlawing leftist student organizations, the government announced publicly its intention to deport from France aliens who, it claimed, had disrupted public order, and who were, as Interior Minister Raymond Marcellin insisted, part of an international revolutionary conspiracy. In fact, Marcellin specifically claimed that among the thirty who had already been deported were twelve members of the German SDS.[75] By January 1969, the French government had deported more than one thousand people, although most of them were not young European radicals but rather young foreign residents who had come into France as immigrant labor.[76] The events had significant foreign participation, particularly as May 1968 provided a platform to critique governments around the world, and most aimed their protests at their countries of origin.[77]

Media coverage of the events varied, though it often clearly prioritized the presence of foreign nationals. *Le Figaro*, in particular, exhibited a strong streak of xenophobia, making consistent reference to the numbers of foreign nationals arrested on any given evening.[78] The proportion of foreigners detained was startling. During the events of May–June, foreign nationals made up more than 16 percent of those arrested.[79] Evidence suggested that the police targeted foreigners for arrest, so these numbers should not be taken as indicative of overall participation. Not surprisingly, the police continually blamed the events in Paris on a conspiracy of foreign revolutionaries, as did de Gaulle in his pivotal speech of 30 May.[80]

Emphasizing the sizable numbers of foreigners or nonstudents participating in demonstrations in France served as a means to delegitimize the movement altogether. The same was true elsewhere, including London, where press reports anticipated an invasion of young foreign revolutionaries, and a later government report ascribed considerable responsibility to young American "missionaries of student protest."[81] Czech students were turned away at the Polish border as agents of anti-state dissent.[82] In the wake of the Prague Spring, during the period known ominously as Normalization, a government narrative developed in Czechoslovakia that identified the whole episode as supposedly propagated by American hippies. The new regime depicted the political menace of the Prague Spring as "foreign" and "alien" and thus not native to Czechoslovakia. According to the authorities, this foreign insurrection had traveled to Czechoslovakia through western youth culture. This was a ruse, of course, for much of the initiative of the Prague Spring had come from within the Czechoslovak Communist Party itself; Alexander Dubček's government was a central actor in the reform movement.[83] Still, the new government put in place by the Soviets claimed that the whole episode had resulted partly from the mobility of the young. Over the course of 1968, young foreigners became suspect throughout Europe, East and West. In Yugoslavia, for example, following the invasion of Czechoslovakia, young travelers were harassed, arrested, and expelled.[84]

Peter Schneider's 1973 novella *Lenz*, which has become an iconic representation of the late-sixties student movement in West Germany, traces the emotional and political journey of a young, disillusioned Berlin activist over the second half of 1968. Discouraged by the lack of effective change, Lenz boards a train for Italy in the late summer: "He wanted only to ride, ride. . . . The train swept everything away." As he said, "I always felt more at home when I was underway than when I stayed somewhere and tried to settle down." After traveling a bit around Italy, he finds his way to Trento, where he gets involved with the joint struggles of students and workers, who welcome him, appreciate his attitude, and encourage him to stay. His Italian travels and activism thoroughly reinspire him politically. Soon, however, Lenz is picked up by the local police, shown his official expulsion order, and escorted to the border.[85] He had come to Trento as part of his ongoing travels, which were, to be sure, politically charged, but not part of any planned revolutionary scheme; still, the state considered his mobility a threat.

After the French Communist Party denounced Cohn-Bendit as a German Jew in early May, thousands of protesters proclaimed through marching, shouting, and posters that "We are all Jews and Germans!" When the government announced that Cohn-Bendit had been barred from reentering France for being an undesirable alien, tens of thousands of protesters resumed marching, chanting new slogans such as "We are all undesirables!," "We are all foreigners!," and "We are all aliens!"[86] Upon his clandestine return to Paris on 28 May, their new mantra became "Fuck all frontiers!" and "Frontiers = Repression."

These declarations—"We are all Jews and Germans," "We are all un-desirables," "We are all aliens," "We are all foreign scum," "Fuck all frontiers"—were not only proclamations of solidarity with those who were seen as being persecuted, including poor immigrants facing discrimination, but also a repudiation of nationality and the nation-state in favor of internationalism or transnationality. In West Germany, too, activists had come to identify with the non-Germans in their midst as a means to further protest, even making foreign concerns their own.[87] Meanwhile, the nation-state's stakeholders, the MPs, ministers, and party leaders, repeatedly emphasized nationality and the integrity of national borders precisely as a means of defense against the internationalism through which the young were clearly seeking to challenge national sovereignty. Border controls, expulsion, deportation, and xenophobic denunciation became the line of defense against international youth movements.[88]

This conflict over mobility, migration, and national borders took place in the highly charged context of massive immigration into Europe. Early iterations of integration had actually assumed that Africa would continue to be a resource for Europe; prior to decolonization, a vision of

15   "We Are All Jews and Germans," declares this poster featuring the gleeful face of Daniel Cohn-Bendit.

NOUS SOMMES TOUS INDÉSIRABLES

16   The same image with a new message, "We Are All Undesirables," following France's refusal to let Cohn-Bendit return.

a "Eurafrica" had been common, with colonial African labor, materials, and markets envisioned as prerequisite for the regeneration of Europe through integration. The French, in particular, were keen to see their African colonies included in the 1950s negotiations for integration among the Six. Creating Eurafrica might be a way for France to hold onto its old empire by making a new Europe.[89] To promote this, Jean Moreau's Office of International Meetings in the French Ministry of Foreign Affairs ensured that African students from French colonies had spots reserved specifically for them in organized youth exchanges with partner European countries.[90] Yet at the same time, the mobility of Algerian students in France became highly suspect due to the ongoing war in Algeria. In the end, France was unsuccessful either in convincing its European partners to include Africa (although the negotiations did result in the European Development Fund) or in holding on to its empire. Nevertheless, the push-and-pull factors of migration had brought significant numbers of people to France and elsewhere from the newly independent countries of Africa.

As a component of decolonization and the labor demands of the postwar economic boom of the 1960s, immigration was roiling Western Europe by the end of the decade. The newcomers arrived mostly from former colonies and the Mediterranean basin and were distinguishable by their racial, cultural, and religious backgrounds. Thus the nation-states of Western Europe were already dealing with the phenomenon of migration into and across Europe, which appeared to many to be beyond their control even if it was economically necessary. Enoch Powell, a conservative MP, became infamous for his anti-immigration politics in the UK, particularly his "rivers of blood" speech, which predicted oncoming racial conflict there. Significantly, this famous speech dates from April 1968. Another famously influential Powell speech, from 1970, identified the "enemy within" the UK as a combination of racial minorities, immigrants, and international student activists, all of whom, he said, had invaded Britain from abroad.[91] Hence, European youth were not in motion across a stagnant, immobile Europe. Rather, the challenge of their political mobility heightened the existing tensions over the sovereignty of nation-states to police and control their borders. Unsurprisingly, these nation-states often resorted to exclusions and expulsions as a means of response, while some in government, including Powell, advocated outright xenophobia. This global migration provided the vocabulary for talking about and dealing with the 1968 movements of youth; the borrowed formulations resonated.

In their consistent anxiety regarding young people and immigrants, the British state and public often conflated the two throughout the 1950s and 1960s.[92] In a special issue on "The Younger Generation" for the magazine *Encounter* in 1956, novelist Martha Gellhorn wrote what she described as a travelogue exploring the youth culture of London coffee bars. The racial overtones were clear as she talked of a sightseeing trip to a "foreign country," staring at "young natives" in their "strange, small chosen land." Her essay dripped with racial exoticism. She described lovely French girls "with black velvet eyes and hair," "drape-suited West Indian negroes" leaning against pinball machines, "a girl who might have been Spanish-Arab-Cuban," or another who was "impossible to place, a Chinese-Javanese-Siamese beauty," all interacting with and a part of the British scene. In this brief article, Gellhorn presented the youth culture of London as an imported racial amalgam, unrecognizable and incomprehensible. In her essay, the un-British and alien young of London drank Italian coffee and ate Spanish tortilla.[93]

In May 1968, Tariq Ali desperately wanted to go to Paris; he even had his bags packed when he received an anonymous phone call warning him that if he left the UK, he would jeopardize the status of his visa and be unable to return. Ali, of course, had been part of this immigration into Britain. Thus, he doubly stood out as an outsider and troublemaker. He balked at going to Paris, but remained uncertain whether that was the right decision: "To have missed Paris that spring was unforgivable." Likewise, he desperately wanted to get to Prague that summer, but the customs and controls of international borders and the status of his visa again prevented him. Many in the British government eagerly wished to deport Ali, but an easier gambit was simply to refuse him reentry, as the French did to Cohn-Bendit.[94]

The evolution of the concept and practice of the frontier was directly tied to the evolution of the sovereignty of the state.[95] While the frontier expressed the furthest limit of feudal power, in the modern period it became the linear demarcation of power and authority between nation-states. Thus "frontiers," as such, are weighted with history, an accumulation of past victories and defeats; they remain an expression in the present of past national struggles and serve as the legitimation of nation-state authority and power.[96] The multiplication and proliferation of national frontiers in twentieth-century Europe marked and resulted from the hypernationalism that had contributed to both world wars.

The fortified and articulated frontier was one of the most apparent products of the modern nation-state, with its notion of individual inclusion and exclusion in the national body. Border controls are funda-

LES FRONTIERES ON S'EN FOUT!

17   "Fuck All Frontiers!" The national border became a site and object of protest.

mentally nondemocratic, even for democratic states, as they are one of the central expressions of the state's discretionary power to discriminate.[97] Within both the western and eastern blocs, as well as across the Iron Curtain, we have the emphasis of those in power on "foreignness" and "undesirables" with the stricter application of border controls intended specifically to limit and contain the young. On the one hand, 1968 profoundly unsettled the national and Cold War boundaries of Europe; on the other hand, they were sanctioned anew in the response to youth mobility in the context of these movements. In the short term, cross-border mobility was curtailed as nation-states reaffirmed their sovereignty over territorial access. Yet in the long term, the modern European nation-state's use of territoriality as a powerful geographic strategy to control people and things by controlling area was unraveling.[98] The events of 1968 symbolically mark a moment when the privileging of the national community for personal identification and the territorial authority of the nation-state itself were both put in question by young protesters' demands for free mobility, which itself was often articulated through Europeanism.[99]

"The Student Revolution Will Be European or It Will Not Be"

Much has been made of the internationalism of the 1968 movements, with a primary focus on the "Third-Worldism" of the New Left activists in Europe and the United States, who looked to the developing world for inspiration amid postcolonial struggles and revolution.[100] Many considered Che Guevara, Ho Chi Minh, and Mao Zedong, among others, as heroic, while the war in Vietnam offered the most consistent target of protest.[101] Notably, internationalism and international solidarity between French and immigrant foreigners were the subject of two dozen posters in May and June 1968. When the French government made its 12 June announcement that it would deport foreign nationals, French students were preparing to hold the first of a number of planned protest rallies in support of immigrant workers, whom they viewed as being persecuted. However, another of the 12 June decrees, which made all demonstrations illegal, effectively shut down the rallies.[102] Still, we should not forget that for all the protests and rhetoric in support of the Third World or immigrant poor, 1968 remained predominantly Eurocentric.[103]

A distinctly European element pervaded much of this internationalism. Slogans of European solidarity, such as "Rome, Berlin, Warsaw, Paris," began to appear as early as 7 May. The radical newspaper *Black Dwarf* in London ran a cover story about Paris using the headline "We Shall Fight, We Will Win, Paris, London, Rome, Berlin," which indicated the underlying premise of solidarity across Western Europe, and a sense of collective endeavor and purpose among young European protesters.[104] Even the U.S. State Department concluded that the protests there were now "European in character" rather than nationally determined.[105] Parisian activists made plans in May to host a European summit for youth at the Sorbonne in July, where they could come to share experiences and coordinate action in their common struggle across the continent, though the events of June derailed these plans for a new Internationale.[106] Yet this was more than just an expression of transnational solidarity; many young activists demanded the abolition of borders and frontiers, a confrontation with the very concept of nationality and the nation-state, with an enthusiastic appeal for European integration.

How the protests of 1968 affected the ongoing process of European integration and were affected by it was on the minds of many, particularly regarding border controls. During the parliamentary debates about Cohn-Bendit and the other young radicals, MP Alfred Norris warned, "Speaking as one who is concerned for the future of Britain's application to join the Common Market, can my right honorable Friend give an assurance that any restriction on the free movement of our fellow West Europeans will not hurt our prospects as a prospective signatory of the Treaty of Rome?"[107] On Radio Luxembourg, Cohn-Bendit commented on his being barred from returning to France: "I don't see why today, when we speak of a Common Market, of international harmony, of peace, we expel someone from a country."[108] Likewise, Belgian students

FRONTIERES = REPRESSION

18   "Frontiers = Repression" emphasized the state's use of force to hinder mobility and, by extension, freedom.

used the European context to protest their government's decision to prohibit Cohn-Bendit by noting that "the Belgian bourgeoisie continues to construct a Europe that permits the free circulation of capital, of merchandise, of labor, yet it confirms its determination to oppose the free circulation of ideas."[109] The evolving European integration helped to frame the debates about Cohn-Bendit's travels.

When German and French students banded together to protest and escort Cohn-Bendit across the Franco-German border, they intentionally chose a stretch of territory that was heavily weighted with nationalist conflict: Alsace served as a "memory frontier" for both France and

Germany.[110] Additionally, France and West Germany had been leading the movement for European integration, and in 1953 had built the Pont d'Europe to acknowledge this endeavor and emphasize the connections and bonds between these formerly belligerent nations. In planning to seize the bridge for Cohn-Bendit's return, the young demonstrators were interested not only in defying the authority of nation-states to police their own borders, but also in expressing the transnational identity of their movement through a sense of common purpose and common identity across the Bridge of Europe.[111]

A week after the Strasbourg protests, the Action Committee for Franco-German Solidarity occupied the Parisian FGYO offices for two days. German activist Beate Klarsfeld led the group. She had earlier worked for the FGYO but was fired for her outspoken protest of West German chancellor Kurt Kiesinger's connections to Nazism. Her committee proclaimed the indispensable need for the young of both countries to expand their political connections and for French and German youth to work together to achieve their common aims. Further, they said, the Franco-German Youth Office should transform itself into the European Office of Youth and put its exchange and travel programs at the disposal of the political movement. The tract continued by proclaiming that the Youth Internationale had become a reality, and that the profound fraternity of the young would transform Europe into a new entity.[112]

A social psychology study begun in the early spring of 1968 was designed to ascertain Western European student attitudes toward integration. Campus unrest disrupted the extensive surveying of students at twelve universities in Belgium, France, Italy, West Germany, the Netherlands, and the UK. Once the study was completed, to the surprise of the authors, it showed that "the vast majority of the student test group was for or strongly for a United Europe." It found the test subjects to be well informed about European institutions, interested in seeing integration accelerated, and confident in its realization. The majority of students favored having all the Western European countries join, with the exception of Spain and Portugal because they were not democracies. Like the American political scientist Ronald Inglehart, the authors found the greatest difference in enthusiasm for integration between those students who had traveled abroad extensively and those who had done so rarely or not at all.[113]

Throughout the events of 1968 in Paris, some young protesters kept up the demand for European integration. In April, the Action Committee for the Independence of Europe issued a manifesto seeking a European climate of peace, cooperation, and independence from American and Soviet influence. Citing the ongoing events in Prague, it called for expanding the Common Market eastward, to unite all of Europe into a single integrated community, independent of the superpowers.[114] A tract from May, "What European Students Want," expressed solidarity with students in Tübingen, Heidelberg, Munich, Liège, Turin, and Rome and demanded the "definitive abolition of frontiers between European countries." Further, it stated a desire for a European parliament elected by direct suffrage, an increase in the powers of the Council of Ministers, and an expansion of the Common Market to include Great Britain and Scandinavia. Likewise, it said that students ought to be able to move freely between European universities in pursuit of their studies. In boldface type, it ended with the words "THE STUDENT REVOLUTION WILL BE EUROPEAN OR IT WILL NOT BE!"[115]

Even before Cohn-Bendit's widely publicized prohibition from reentering France, the Action Committee for Foreigners had issued a proclamation demanding the abolition of the Statute on Foreigners in France. Emphasizing that "[the] concept of nationality is profoundly reactionary," it asked for the dissolution of all visas, *cartes de séjour, cartes de travail,* and identity controls based upon nationality. The committee focused primarily on the thousands of immigrants who had come to France for work. But their claim that national differences were disappearing anyway, and that the whole notion of nationality was a thing of the past, posed a distinct challenge to the very conceptual apparatus of the nation-state.[116] They sought the freedom and mobility for individuals to live and work wherever they might choose.

In early June, the Action Committee for the Abolition of Frontiers formed to protest the closure of national borders to the young in response to the events of May. "This effort will not succeed, because the ideas of May 1968 cannot be stopped by a barrier or a cop. Young people cannot be stopped any more than ideas can," its young members responded, demanding the abolition of frontiers and border controls for the free movement of people and ideas across Europe.[117] In a second tract from later in June, they declared, "We are all European" and "the revolution of the twentieth century will be European." Advocating the formation of a federal Europe, they added the slogan "The revival of the university shows that Europe's time has come."[118] The rise of student activism across the continent, and the internationalist attitudes inherent to it, led them to hope for, and demand, a united Europe. To their mind, abolishing the frontiers and border controls inhibiting youth movements would be the first step toward this united Europe. Borders represented not only lines of division but thresholds of passage; the protesters regarded travel and mobility as fundamental to the Europe they envisioned. The Young European Federalists reinvigorated their activities, especially along the Austro-Italian border, where they installed road signs that read "You are staying in Europe" just after government road signs that read "You are leaving Austria" or "You are leaving Italy." They initiated more than fifty Alpine border actions in 1967–68 under the slogan "The frontiers will disappear—when WE want them to."[119]

Several other Parisian groups and action committees expressed similar ideas, including the European Federalist Students, the European Federalist Youth, and the more established European Federalist Movement, which in June called on the young to work toward an integrated Europe that would deny the lingering nationalism of the nation-state and the absurdity of borders.[120] The Committee for European University Federalism demanded a halt to French nationalism, the continued construction of Europe, the establishment of a United States of Europe, and France's ratification of the European Rights of Man.[121]

It is possible that some of these tracts emerged from the extreme right rather than the left. That is, young right-wingers saw 1968 as a revolutionary moment, like those on the New Left, and articulated this in terms that challenged the French state by demanding a united Europe of nationalist regimes. Groups such as Occident sought a revolutionary nationalist strategy to overthrow the Gaullist regime, but in the context of a broader, proto-fascist New Europe. Thus, the political articulation inherent to these tracts resonates to some degree with the discourse of right-wing 1968 revolutionaries, too.[122] Either way, whether left or right, these attitudes challenged the French nation-state in favor of a Europeanist paradigm.

In early July, a feature editorial published simultaneously in multiple European newspapers by the Italian diplomat Mario Toscano argued that the moment had come for the European project to move boldly *because* of events in France and beyond. The consistency of the 1968 crisis across Western Europe had shown how interconnected the nations of Europe had become since the Second World War. Asking to whom this revelation was owed, the author answered, "The young who look to each other across national borders." They reflected each other's subjective experiences despite nationality, "as if a single 'internationale' united them all." It would take European countries working together to solve problems jointly, to advance and progress. The events of 1968 showed how the problems extended beyond national borders. "The immediate construction of Europe," Toscano wrote, "has been revived, with no possibility of reversal, by the shake-up of these last weeks." He continued,

"The great crisis of 1968 has put the builders of Europe—the Europe of Six and the larger Europe—to their moment of truth."[123]

Indeed, the European project, as Toscano suggested, had stalled by 1968, yet it reemerged in 1969. The policies of de Gaulle in particular had helped to slow integration in the late sixties, so the young French Europeanists' demands helped reinvigorate the process that their own government had impeded. The renewed emphasis that followed came about particularly under the combined guidance of Georges Pompidou, who succeeded de Gaulle as president of France, and Willy Brandt, who succeeded Kiesinger as chancellor of West Germany. Just as the domestic turmoil of the late 1960s encouraged the world's leaders to work together for Cold War détente as a means to better focus on their internal problems, in the wake of 1968 the governments of the European Community adopted a frequent and regular summit schedule to coordinate better the domestic policies and concerns they held in common, leading to the optimistic "Spirit of the Hague" Europeanism that dominated the early 1970s.[124] In fact, it was at this moment that integrationists first began to discuss the need to develop "A People's Europe" and a European citizenship; culture and identity emerged for the first time as areas of policy in the economic and political aspirations of the European Commission.[125]

At the 1969 Hague Summit, Pierre Werner, the prime minister of Luxembourg, spoke about the disgruntled young and their "quarrels about issues which . . . can admittedly be regarded as a form of European collaboration."[126] The Italian prime minister, Mariano Rumor, urged his fellow heads of state to work toward further integration, "using all the energies of our countries and responding to the rightful and vigilant impatience of youth, which today thinks and acts with a European mind."[127] The final point of the official communiqué of the Hague Summit stated, "All the creative activities and the actions conducive to European growth decided upon here will be assured of a better future if the younger generation is closely associated with them; the governments are resolved to endorse this and the Communities will make provision for it."[128] The Council of Europe's Parliamentary Assembly and the European Economic Community's European Assembly both met in 1968 to discuss "the youth crisis" and reached similar conclusions.[129] Valéry Giscard d'Estaing, in the midst of the May crisis, made a speech in London in which he advocated a deepening and broadening of the European project, which seemed to him "to be the only way to give the troubled youth of our continent the modern and vast ambition allowing it to devote its fiery strength to a positive task."[130] The protests of 1968 allowed Europeanists to justify further integration and intergovernmental cooperation as a means of dealing with transnational problems, while at the same time they used the transnational nature of 1968 to declare an emergent European consciousness among the young, thus legitimizing their endeavors.

Meanwhile, the movement and protests of young Czechoslovaks active in the Prague Spring of 1968 helped make them a part of a larger international and specifically European movement. They sought to break away from the influence of the Soviet Union and looked to the "Europe" of the West. The sixth of the "Ten Commandments for a Young Czechoslovak Intellectual" read, "Don't think only as a Czech or a Slovak, think also like a European. . . . You live in Europe; you don't live in America or in the Soviet Union."[131] Caught between the Superpower East and West, young people in Czechoslovakia often emphasized a European particularity in the context of the Soviet-American Cold War; they strove for a sense of connection through Europeanness.

For Those under 30, Prague Was the Right Place to Be

Once Paris had calmed in June, young politically engaged travelers and student activists gravitated toward Prague. In the mid-1960s, the Czechoslovak government had begun encouraging tourism to and from Western Europe. Young people from the West took advantage of these policies and began to travel to Prague. When Tariq Ali passed through in January 1967, he found himself drinking in a beer hall with some young Berliners and discovered a sensibility among the young of Europe that crossed national frontiers. "Here were these Germans, like me in their early twenties," he said. "We talked long into the night and discovered that despite our varied political and cultural backgrounds we were affected in a very similar fashion by the same events." Interestingly, one of the Berliners complained about the political passivity of Czech students, who, he insisted, "were only interested in Western pop music and clothes."[132] Indeed, in the wake of the loosening of travel restrictions, a distinct exchange of people and ideas occurred as western books, newspapers, and music became accessible to Czechoslovaks. Perhaps the most visible byproduct of these policies (pursued for currency and economic reasons) was the development among young Czechs of a decidedly western youth culture, complete with music clubs, student activism, and a hippie counterculture.[133] Over the course of the 1960s, transnational mobility within the eastern bloc grew considerably as border controls between states were loosened and travel between the socialist states was encouraged, which meant that Poles or Bulgarians could encounter a little bit of the West if they came to Czechoslovakia. The scene in Prague shocked Soviet tourists on official trips there; meant to emphasize commonality, these official tourist trips instead pointed to political and cultural differences within the eastern bloc.[134] Notably, though the Czechoslovak government had relaxed travel restrictions for its citizens, the Prague City Council instituted a policy in 1966 that denied "unkempt youths" exit visas for travel abroad.[135] Thus, young Czechoslovaks who displayed an overt affinity for the West's youth culture were kept from traveling there. Significantly, the many liberal rights and reforms demanded in the Manifesto of Prague Youth in March 1968, such as freedom of the press and freedom of association, included the freedom to travel, as if this, too, constituted the most fundamental of political rights for the Prague Spring.[136]

While cross-border travel in 1968 was becoming more difficult for the young in Western Europe, in Czechoslovakia the borders were opened. With unrestricted travel now possible, thousands of young people packed their bags and went abroad. Despite the excitement of what was happening in Prague, they seized the new opportunity for unfettered mobility.[137] One Prague activist predicted that with so many young Czechoslovaks traveling westward that summer, they would gain "new experiences with the student struggle," which would inspire further reform and protest in the coming autumn. He expected Prague youth, through travel, to gain experience, develop ideas, interact with the broader western youth culture, and become part of it and its transnational movement for social change. The Soviet occupation of Czechoslovakia in August impeded such further efforts, and many of the young consequently opted to stay abroad rather than return home, knowing that the borders would soon be closed. Czech students had initially looked to western youth movements as models for their own politicization, but the more they learned about what was happening in West Germany, France, and elsewhere, and the more they encountered western youth, the more skeptical and less enamored they became about a common political project.[138]

Meanwhile, Prague was awash with young Europeans who had come in the summer of 1968 to express or experience an age-based solidarity that transcended national identity. In early August, the *New York Times* declared, "If you are under 30, Prague seems the place to be this summer," as the city was "thronged with young sympathizers from the West." Robert Engle, a Harvard law graduate who had been touring Europe on a skimpy budget since the previous fall, said that he hoped to "get a few ideas in Prague" about what kind of society he wanted to live in and what role he wanted to play. Monique Chaillot, a humanities student from the Sorbonne, had hitchhiked and taken trains across Europe with a girlfriend after de Gaulle's triumph in June. Disappointed with Paris, they had headed to Prague. "This is exactly what we wanted to do in Paris this spring," she enthused. She found herself "discussing endlessly with Czechoslovak students the various experiences each one [had] had during the last few months." Helmut Krone, a literature student from Hamburg, was excited about the youthful and international camaraderie he had found in Prague, where the young who had gathered there talked "about everything." The reporter noted how difficult it was to tell whether young people were Czech or foreign; clustered along the Charles Bridge with their long hair, beards, turtlenecks, and jeans, "they all look alike," he wrote. The only discernible way to differentiate their nationality, he found, was by language. Many young Prague residents could muddle through English, French, or German, but very few foreign visitors could speak any Czech. Not only had the international youth culture come to Prague, but so had international youth. The revolutionary graffiti covering the city's medieval walls that summer appeared in Czech, English, French, German, Spanish, and Italian.[139]

Young American Joe Mack hitchhiked there in July and "felt the exciting air of new freedoms" as he observed the nascent political culture of street speeches, posters, leaflets, debates, and demonstrations. The city was so overcrowded with young people that he couldn't find a place to stay and felt that "Prague was treading on the edges of public disorder."[140] Gérald Gassiot-Talabot, an art student, left Paris for Prague that summer, too. He took with him a collection of posters from the Beaux-Arts, which were eagerly snapped up by young Czech painters. Later that fall, one could see posters of protest against the Warsaw Pact invasion clearly inspired by those of Paris.[141] Susanne Müller even had her trip to Prague, which she described as "the center of the world," funded by her small town in the German Oberharz region, which sought to promote youth travel generally.[142] Even after the August crackdown, young Westerners continued their journey to Prague. Immediately after the military invasion, Peter Tautfest spontaneously left Berlin with three friends and headed to Prague, where they spent a few days distributing leaflets, confronting Russians, and conveying their support.[143] West German Sibylle Plogstedt returned to Prague after the invasion and had a prolonged affair with Petr Uhl—what she described as "socialism in one bed"—until they were both arrested in December 1969. She was later deported to West Germany.[144]

Young East Germans arrived in Prague in significant numbers through both official and unofficial channels. In total, there were fifty thousand East German trips to Czechoslovakia in 1967; in 1968 there were two hundred thousand.[145] The two countries ran numerous study exchange and holiday programs together, and these continued operating in the spring and summer of 1968, but with a considerable spike in the rate of participation. Private trips from East Germany to Czechoslovakia increased by 42 percent from May 1967 to May 1968, with the vast majority of these by the young. Young East Germans returned with German-language Czechoslovak material and talking about reform. This concerned the regime, which was worried about the potential subversive influence that contact with young Czechoslovaks and others in Prague was having on GDR youth. Nonetheless, few incidents of unrest took place in East Germany until the Warsaw Pact invasion. The Prague Spring only inspired protests by East German youth once it was being dismantled.[146] Still, in Prague, East Germans often found that contact with Westerners revealed significant differences in political perspective. When the Warsaw Pact forces invaded, Australian Brian Laver was in a park feverishly arguing politics with a group of East Germans. Earlier in the summer he had traveled to Bulgaria with a group of Czechoslovaks who found themselves harassed, arrested, and at odds with other socialist youth.[147]

While the confluence of eastern and western youth in Prague that year reflected a broad, diffuse sense of generational solidarity grounded in lifestyle and antiestablishment attitudes, it also revealed considerable disagreement when it came to the details of politics. Many left-wing Westerners were disappointed with the political program of the Prague Spring, seeing it as too much bourgeois liberalism, while Eastern Europeans often felt that the Westerners did not fully appreciate the difference between living in a socialist state and theorizing it.[148] Rudi Dutschke's visit to Prague in the spring of 1968 had revealed exactly this. An even better example was the Soviet-sponsored Ninth World Youth Festival, held in Sofia, Bulgaria, in July 1968. Eighteen thousand delegates from 130 nations met there amid considerable schism, tension, and tumult. Many Westerners were kept out altogether, and some who managed to get there, including Karl Dietrich Wolff, caused considerable disruption. Rather than fostering international solidarity, the event was marred by disharmony. Even young Czechoslovaks had trouble at the Bulgarian border and were criticized for their appearance, stripped of their leaflets, or denied admittance altogether.[149] Still, either before or after the meeting in Sofia, many delegates made it a point to visit Prague.

Michael Korda's experience in the 1956 Budapest uprising offers an important contrast to Prague in 1968. In late October 1956, Korda, then twenty-three, left England for Hungary, because "if you wanted to be where the action was, Budapest was the place, not Uxbridge or Oxford." He had been inspired by the young Hungarians who were at the forefront of the revolt there. He and two friends took off across Europe on a road trip to revolution in a rusty old Volkswagen convertible. Using a *Baedeker* as a guide, they roamed around Budapest during the Soviet crackdown, helping little but offering a bit of international solidarity as they joined the young revolutionaries on the barricades.[150] They did not encounter any other foreign youth who had crossed the open border to reach Budapest. This contrasted to the situation twelve years later in 1968, when the young of Western Europe rushed from protest to protest, including across the Iron Curtain to Prague. Something significant had changed in the span of a decade.

Revolutionary Tourists?

In 1964, Richard Holmes set off for adventure in Europe after ten years of English boarding schools. Dreams of "free thought, free travel, free love" inspired the eighteen-year-old's travel plans.[151] He associated mobility and travel with personal freedom, and this freedom lay within the emerging traveling culture of youth—the itinerant young who had begun to see themselves as a transnational social group. Excited by the events of Paris in 1968, and particularly by the fact that young people from all over Western Europe were gathering there, Holmes ventured to Paris seeking to discover "something utterly new coming into being," something he described as a "new community."[152] A British student activist similarly concluded that a search for community, a personal inclusion generated by activism, motivated the London protests.[153]

The ease and frequency with which middle-class young people in the 1960s traveled to cities such as Amsterdam, Berlin, London, Paris, and Prague created interpersonal solidarities that were crucial to the formation of movements that challenged national demarcations of power. More than mobilization, travel became the foundation for a youth identity that emphasized mobility and built a shared political culture across national boundaries. These qualities contested the frontiers of the dominant state powers, which were used to contain, segregate, and frequently close access for groups across societies. In this sense, through physical and ideological movements, young people in the late 1960s sought to create their own kind of interconnected European community.

The upheaval in May caused ordinary tourists to stay away from Paris in the spring and summer of 1968; at the same time, however, the number of young people traveling there reached a new record peak.[154] Relatedly, the number of young Americans studying abroad in France in the immediate wake of 1968 grew significantly.[155] Like Holmes, they were drawn rather than repelled by the political tensions there. Similarly, once Paris had calmed and Charles de Gaulle had successfully reasserted control, the young of Europe, including many from France, began traveling instead to Prague, which became the new destination for rebellious youthful camaraderie. They were all participating in a new cultural phenomenon, the mass mobility of Western European middle-class youth, which had emerged over the course of the 1960s and continued to grow well into the 1970s. Through public and private initiative, communities of young travelers contributed to the ethos of integration through their familiarity with one another and their interaction with foreign places, peoples, and cultures. Most importantly, they came to see themselves as belonging to a transnational community of youth, a sense of identity that they recognized in one another through their personal relationships and their cultural practices of travel.

A *New York Times* reporter in Prague described the confluence of European youth there as a "pilgrimage," a term that brings to mind the work of anthropologist Victor Turner.[156] The experience of pilgrimage, according to Turner, puts travelers in a liminal space, one that is anti-hierarchical, democratic, and full of potential for transformation; they are "betwixt and between." Once in this liminal space, the pilgrims or travelers experience *communitas*, an intense and spontaneous community spirit of equality, fraternity, and solidarity generated by their marginality and flux, however temporary and fleeting it may be. Significantly, Turner saw *communitas* as subversive, as a challenge to the structures of authority, because it makes a reordering of relations between ideas and people both possible and desirable.[157]

Holmes and the others were literally part of a mass movement as the young interacted with one another through travel and protest in the late 1960s. Although in experience and significance Holmes is quite different from Daniel Cohn-Bendit or the many other young activists who operated through radical networks, they all share something important—a sense of community based on age and premised on transnational mobility, which helped to shape the political worldview of millions of young

Europeans. As a figure of 1968, Cohn-Bendit traveled from Paris to Berlin to Amsterdam to Frankfurt to London and places in between to promote youth movements and mobility. As his supporters articulated, among their many goals they wanted reform of the border and frontier controls that were hindering their mobility.[158] Their sense of international identity emerged partially from transnational travel and a voluntary shared purpose that they experienced as a kind of transformative *communitas*. Meanwhile, those in power repeatedly emphasized nationality, foreignness, and the sanctity of borders and frontiers in response to the transnational aspirations of this young community. They rightly recognized that a reconfiguration of the nation-state underlay the demands and activities of 1968, even if there was no organized conspiracy of revolution, let alone consensus on a political program.

The U.S. government reached similar conclusions. In September 1968, a secret 250-page intelligence report entitled "Restless Youth" was presented to President Lyndon Johnson. It stated that the CIA had found no evidence of either a communist conspiracy or an organized international network of activists. While movement and contact existed between protest sites around the world, ease of travel and communication was the explanation, they wrote, not organized conspiracy. Interpersonal contact between activists had been irregular and of short duration. Still, because of increasing mobility, foreign exchanges, global telecommunication, and the like, students around the world increasingly recognized themselves "to be a community of interests."[159] A separate report by former ambassador George McGhee entitled "World Student Unrest" reached similar conclusions: while no command structure or formal organization existed, the young had mobility, communicated, and were able to "visit each other." Dissent spread through emulation and personal contact.[160] Another report, "An Overview of Student Unrest" by the Interagency Youth Committee, said something similar again: "Today's students, not just their leaders, are highly mobile; they travel within their own countries and abroad . . . and find that they share a common set of values and beliefs with their foreign counterparts. Declarations of mutual support or an identity of views among student dissidents from different countries should be considered from this perspective of commonly perceived values and not as evidence of common organization."[161]

Without the backing of an organized conspiracy, how can the breadth of transnational interaction in 1968 Europe be explained? The young of 1968 did not simply inspire one another. A cultural practice of travel in Europe undergirded a sense of solidarity, interactivity, common purpose, and common identity that facilitated revolt and collective action by the physical movement of young protesters from place to place, whether the destination was Amsterdam, Berlin, Paris, or Prague, demonstrating a fundamental interconnection between political and leisure practices.[162] This was despite the fact that they rarely agreed on the underlying ideological details or settled on a common program of activity. As Europe, and the world, became more integrated in the decades following the Second World War, it became more politically turbulent, too, in part as a consequence of this growing interaction and interdependence.[163] The physical movement of the young and their transnational activities, and particularly their desire for a more open and integrated Europe, helped reshape the European nation-states' relationship to each other.

We should be careful not to dismiss this phenomenon as "revolutionary tourism," a pejorative term that emerged in the era itself to dismiss as dilettantes those who came and went. Degrees of political commitment and militancy varied widely among the revolutionary youth of 1968. The mobility of informal political actors and their attendant polyvalent sympathies, in addition to the militant leftist vanguard, made these protest movements—in Paris or Prague or elsewhere—massive, involving millions of young people.[164] These youth movements do not explain 1968, of course, yet they are an important component that has remained unexplored. It resonates with the interrelated emergence of the transnational social body of youth, the cultural practice of youth travel, and a leftist cultural internationalism that was often expressed explicitly in terms of Europeanism. The internationalism of 1968 is usually viewed as at best ideological and at worst merely rhetorical, but the revolutionary exchange of young people across Europe shows that this internationalism was to some extent expressed as a communitarian cultural practice—one that would intersect with and anticipate the institutional efforts of European integration in the years to come.

When faced with the power of the French state, Holmes instinctively had retreated behind his British nationality. The French policeman thought Holmes should mind his own business and go home. Yet Holmes decided that what was happening in Paris was his business; he decided that he was not so much of an outsider as he had felt at that moment. Whether revolutionary tourist or not, he had come looking for a "new community," one with an "immense possibility of political life," and ostensibly, he found it.

FOUR

Continental Drifters

In June 1977, Larry Lipin, a twenty-one-year-old middle-class Californian, left his Los Angeles home with a *Let's Go* guidebook, a wad of American Express travelers cheques, a Eurail youth pass, a youth hostel card, and a variety of assorted items thrown at the last minute into his backpack. He went to the airport and boarded a charter flight headed to Paris. As he described it, he was "between first senior year and second senior year" at the University of California, Davis, and wanted a bit of adventure. He had taken some art history classes, and thought he would go explore the places and things he had read and heard about. Study abroad seemed too expensive, too restrictive, too much commitment, and kind of a hassle, while independent travel offered affordability, freedom, and simplicity that accommodated a lack of planning and forethought. Without any fixed itinerary for his three-month trip, he figured he would visit friends he knew were abroad in Paris and Gothenburg, go to Spain to practice his Spanish, see some art in Italy, and maybe visit relatives in London.[1]

His flight to Europe was itself kind of a party. The charter plane was full of other young Americans like himself, all very excited, talking about their plans for Europe, sharing ideas, and looking for travel partners. They were smoking and drinking, and the fervor of their excitement sustained them through the long flight. Lipin even made out with a couple of young women he met on the plane who were headed abroad together. In Europe, he stayed overnight in youth hostels when convenient, at the occasional pension

19 American Larry Lipin in Paris, June 1977. Photograph by Larry Lipin. Used with permission.

when possible, and in train stations as a last resort. At the Running of the Bulls in Pamplona, he slept on the sidewalk with others after many hours of drinking. On the trains he encountered "a conglomeration of Dutch, Germans, French, Brits, sometimes Italians and Spanish or Aussies and Kiwis," and of course other Americans, all of them gravitating toward or seeking out the rail compartments occupied by other young people. The typical compartment configuration of six seats facing each other created a communal atmosphere where food, wine, cigarettes, newspapers, card games, and conversation were shared among the cohort, with their gear piled both at their feet and on the racks above their heads. Membership in such small groups was in constant flux as young passengers got off and on the train with the ease and convenience afforded by rail passes.[2]

It was a profoundly social experience. Although Lipin was traveling by himself, he spent time with other young backpackers wherever he went. Whether in the beer halls in Munich or on the beach at Marbella, Spain, there were other young travelers to hang out with. In Paris he met a Nigerian fellow with whom he explored the city, even running into college acquaintances from Davis on the Left Bank. Though he was spending time with other American travelers, he wanted a foreign experience, whether with locals or other backpackers. For that reason, Marbella and the Swiss village of Grindelwald, both places where Anglophones would go to rest from the stress and strain of independent budget travel, were less interesting to him. Accordingly, he would often take local trains to remote villages, particularly in Spain, where he would be forced to communicate in Spanish. One of his favorite experiences was being picked up by a teeny car outside London while he was hitchhiking in the UK, where the Eurail pass was invalid. The driver turned out to be a communist, and they talked politics while driving north toward Edinburgh, taking a detour to see the cathedral at Durham at the insistence of the driver, and ending in Newcastle, where Lipin's new friend took him for drinks at a rather tired and dated working man's club.[3]

The freedom to do what he wanted was in part based on his position as a man. In Spain, a pretty, young hippie-esque woman invited him to travel with her through Morocco. He liked her, was attracted to her, and was tempted by the offer, but declined because he felt that his experience would be limited and determined by another to some degree, and he feared that a foray into Morocco would supplant his other plans for the summer. Though he messed around a bit, he avoided sexual encounters as something that might complicate his overall plans. He wanted to maintain his personal independence, a freedom he enjoyed in large part because of his gender. The women from the plane had also invited him to come along with them. Generally speaking, American women backpacking in Europe were interested to learn that he was American, too, and they probably felt safer and more comfortable with him along due to the risks for young women traveling on their own.[4]

In Spain, Lipin tried hashish for the first time as a hash cigarette was passed his way, and he later found it to be available with seeming regularity elsewhere, as the shared joint was a social convention of the time. Although he can't recall specifically smoking marijuana, because trying to remember if he smoked grass is like "trying to remember if I had lunch," he is confident that he did, but it was so unremarkable and unimportant to him that it left no memories; as at home in the United States, smoking weed for him was more about participating politely in a group ritual than it was about getting high. In fact, many of the habits and practices of his travel experience were things he did at home—hitchhiking, hopping trains, smoking marijuana, fooling around. In some ways, the rituals and norms of backpacking in Europe were unexceptional because they were part of the western youth culture more generally, or at least that of California. Even the practice of backpacking in Europe had, by 1977, become fairly common for his social class and milieu: "going to Europe was an extension of going to college. It wasn't a big deal; it was what you did." This hadn't always been the case; it had become so only in the decade prior to his trip.[5]

Lipin's experience exemplifies many aspects of the changes to independent youth travel in Europe that had taken place since the mid-1960s: the massive influx of Americans and other Westerners from outside Europe; the use of rail passes and hitchhiking for flexible, inexpensive mobility; the standardization of gear, methods, practices, routes, and destinations; the lasting influence of the sexual and cultural mores of the sixties counterculture; the sociability of the community of backpackers; and the gendered aspects that shaped the experience. While Lipin didn't set out with any grand scheme of self-discovery or intentions of marking a rite of passage, he found that the trip was a formative experience, shaping his adult life in all sorts of ways that he hadn't anticipated, and transforming his understanding of the United States, particularly of American cities.[6] He was participating in a new cultural model of independent youth travel, one that had developed over the course of the previous ten years and generated an anthropological structure of meaning out of the social practices of play.

A more nostalgic look back at the transformative experience of travel is seen in the 2003 hit Italian television miniseries *La meglio gioventù*, directed by Marco Tullio Giordana and released outside Italy as two three-hour films entitled *The Best of Youth*. The story follows four young men—two brothers, Nicola and Matteo, and their friends Carlo and Beto—through nearly forty years of Italian history, starting in the mid-1960s. The film begins with the four young Romans, in eager anticipation of completing their university exams, excitedly planning a trip to the opposite end of Europe at the Norwegian North Cape. Beto suggests that they take a car so they can pick up hitchhiking girls along the way. In the end, only Nicola ends up going, backpacking through West Germany up to Norway, where he befriends a young African American man avoiding Vietnam, hangs out with some hippie drifters who recite Beat poetry while bathing in waterfalls, and eventually settles for a time with a blonde Norwegian beauty who has a seaside cottage where he resides while working in a sawmill. His sojourn there is disrupted by news of the Arno flood, and he quickly returns to Italy to join his friends as Mud Angels doing relief work in Florence.[7]

As the center of the epic story, Nicola is used as a contrast to those who planned the trip but never embarked on it. He is the most complete, balanced, and well-adjusted character in the film. The significance of his travels as a young man becomes clear at the movie's end. Nicola never makes it to the North Cape of Norway, the ultimate goal of his prolonged travels. The film closes in 2003 with Matteo's son Andrea, the next generation, backpacking with his girlfriend, revisiting the same sites as Nicola, but in Andrea's case reaching the North Cape, completing the journey that his father and uncle failed to do of their own accord. The completion of the journey, the rite of passage, closes the story and reemphasizes the best of youth.[8]

Long-haul backpacking as a personal journey of self-discovery is a common trope. Importantly, though it emphasizes the internalized experience of the self, such personal development was accomplished in an increasingly ritualized social context. Through their habits of travel, the masses of backpacking youth drawn from within and without Europe were creating a community of practice from their social activity that spanned the western half of the continent and beyond. Though most of the young people who engaged in such endeavors were European, many were not, including the growing number of Canadians and Australians and the more than one million young Americans who traveled to Europe annually. Like most cultural forms and social practices, backpacking in Europe was something one learned to do from others through books, films, music, journalism, friends, relatives, or lived experience. In the decade and a half following the mid-sixties, youth travel in Europe was transformed into the iconic cultural form of backpacking that we understand it to be today. This chapter explores that development and considers the impact it had on the social group of youth as a community of practice.

Prescriptions and Representations

In 1963, Nicolas Bouvier published *L'Usage du monde* (translated into English as *The Way of the World*), a now classic travel narrative recounting the mid-1950s trip of two young Swiss men in a beat-up Fiat making their way across Turkey and Iran into Afghanistan. Over the course of the 1960s and 1970s, it was translated into many languages and became an underground sensation.[9] While the book narrates their adventurous ordeal of getting lost, having car trouble, and being broke, the thrust of Bouvier's story is philosophically introspective: "Travelling outgrows its motives," he wrote. "It soon proves sufficient in itself. You think you are making a trip, but soon it is making you—or unmaking you." Indeed, he saw it to be both literally and figuratively a rite of passage, as he concluded, "You perceive that travels may have a formative effect on youth, but they also make it pass."[10] Such travel becomes indicative of being young; as the journey concludes, so does one's youth. In this sense, being young is being mobile; being adult is being settled.

In contrast to Bouvier, the 1964 publication of *Ik, Jan Cremer* (*I, Jan Cremer*) was an immediate bestseller, second only to the Bible in Dutch publishing sales, and quickly translated into more than a dozen languages.[11] Subtitled *An Autobiographical Novel*, the book ostensibly details in episodic fashion the outrageous adventures of its obnoxious young rogue antihero as he rambles widely around Western Europe in the late fifties and early sixties. Cremer presents himself as a bad boy outlaw hustler on the make, and indeed, the book itself is something of a con, as his sexual, amoral, and criminal exploits bear an unmistakable artificiality. One admiring critic described Cremer as a "trans-European" who was "frankly absorbed in his own ego to the point of pathology."[12] In the Netherlands, the book was something of a wrecking ball, as Cremer knocked down polite Dutch facades and laid bare a framework of disreputable opinions and notorious behaviors. His scatological writing provoked prudish quietude with his forays into masturbation, defecation, and general misanthropic delinquency. In his tale, he crosses borders indiscriminately through a couple dozen countries, living the vagabond life, hitchhiking, sleeping rough, working odd jobs when he feels like it, stealing when necessary, carousing, drinking, smoking dope, doing speed and cocaine, and at times lashing out with violent cruelty and a crazed, vicious brutality. Intentionally offensive, Cremer set out to shock, and succeeded through his account of anarchistic freedom pursued through youthful mobility in a travel underground.

While the contrasting tone of Bouvier and Cremer cannot be overstated—one is ruminative exposition, the other risible braggadocio— they are both premised on the realization of the self through the freedom provided by youth mobility. Published nearly a decade and a half later but written in the late 1960s, the German novel-essay *Die Reise* (*The Trip*) by Bernward Vesper also relies on the master narrative of self-discovery and coming-of-age through travel. Vesper was the son of a Nazi poet, and his narrated trip unfolds in three parts: a set of adventures as he travels around Western Europe in the 1960s; a prolonged acid trip while hitchhiking through West Germany; and the journey to make sense of himself, his generation, his country, and his family's past.[13] Though by no means an international hit like the other two books, in his home country the 1977 posthumous publication of Vesper's *Die Reise* became an iconic bestseller as a legacy of the politics and culture of youth in 1960s West Germany. Importantly, Vesper was self-consciously autobiographical, both revealingly confessional like Cremer and subjectively aspirational like Bouvier.

Vesper had been influenced by reading Jack Kerouac, whose books *On the Road*, *Dharma Bums*, and *Lonesome Traveler* all celebrate the life of the young tramp.[14] Indeed, Kerouac's books had become a kind of canon for a western youth culture that prized mobility, particularly *On the Road* (1957), which continues to serve as the inspirational reference point par excellence for twenty-first-century backpackers.[15] It is difficult to measure the influence of *On the Road* in the development of backpacker travel in Western Europe, and yet references to it appear so frequently that it seems pervasive.[16] Kerouac portrays the erratic pursuit of self-discovery as enacted through a frugal, rambling existence that offers sex, drugs, parties, and adventure through the freedom of independent movement via road and rail networks. *On the Road*, in particular, stresses a relationship between spontaneous, erratic wandering and periodic serendipity. The novel helped inspire a passionate desire to travel, shaping the expectations for what life on the road might be like for a young man, and offering a rationale for why one ought to pursue it.[17]

The realization of the self through the wanderings and wonderings of a journey was not unique to the Beats and Kerouac, of course. It is a common trope of modern travel literature. One can point especially to the early-nineteenth-century poetic Romanticism of Lord Byron and Percy Bysshe Shelley, or even François-René de Chateaubriand's pilgrimage to Jerusalem as such travel literature. The popularity among the nineteenth-century bourgeoisie of the *bildungsroman*, the coming-of-age novel, tended toward similar themes. Above all, perhaps, the penurious wanderings of the young poets Arthur Rimbaud and Paul Verlaine in the mid-nineteenth century put such textual conceits into lived practice.[18]

How many dog-eared mass paperbacks of *On the Road* in whatever language may have journeyed around Europe in rucksacks is anyone's guess, but it belies the certain bookishness of youth travel there. With so much downtime while on trains, in stations, or along roadsides, there was considerable time to read en route. The novels of Hermann Hesse were popular, as were those of Ken Kesey. Reading material circulated among travelers. Novels, political treatises, and guidebooks, with select pages or whole chapters ripped out of them, were shared, traded, and passed along.

Guidebooks were fundamental in the prescriptive way that they set expectations, ordered experiences, and shaped behaviors for leisure travel. Tourist guidebooks had been serving this kind of function since the mid-nineteenth century with the mass embrace of *Murray's Handbooks for Travellers* in England and *Baedeker* guides in Germany. The latter emerged as the international paradigm for what a leisure travel guidebook ought to be, with recommendations on accommodations, food, and sightseeing.[19] Published guides reached a mass audience with Arthur Frommer's *Europe on $5 a Day*, a phenomenal success that emphasized useful tips for travel on the cheap, and which capitalized on the middle-class expansion of 1960s mass tourism.[20] The rise of mass backpacker tourism resulted in guidebooks, too. Several went on to become massive corporate publishing juggernauts, such as the American *Let's Go* guides, which began in the 1960s as mimeographed pamphlets handed out to students on charter flights to Europe; or the French *Guide du routard* from the early 1970s, originally constructed out of Michel Duval and Philippe Gloaguen's travel diaries; or the Anglo-Australian publication *Lonely Planet*, also originally from the early 1970s, which became the handbook for the hippie trail from Europe to Australia. Not surprisingly, established companies recognized the new market, too, including Fodor's, which came out with its *Europe Under 25* guide in 1972. But there were many other guidebooks that remained more underground; for example, Ken Welsh's *Hitch-hiker's Guide to Europe* (1972) and Ed Buryn's *Vagabonding in Europe and North Africa* (1971) never went mainstream yet went through multiple editions and many printings, selling tens of thousands of copies.

These guidebooks made all kinds of recommendations about where to go and where not to go, what to bring and what to leave behind, whom to seek out and whom to avoid, how to hitchhike, find drugs, and stay out of trouble, and, ultimately, why to bother traveling this way at all. As Ed Buryn opined in 1973, "The book tells you how to visit Europe as a way of blowing your mind and enriching your life. It says that tourism is bullshit unless you get involved. . . . Go as a wayfarer open to all experience; go as a courier over the map of Europe, bearing messages to your secret self. . . . This book is about doing it by and for yourself, as a free person, as a vagabond. Don't go just to see 'things,' but to encounter fellow humans and get your life messed with in the process. Go knowing that your travel style may cause you hassles, but in the end will get you closer to the miracle of Europe, of Europeans and of yourself. Can you dig it?"[21] Guidebooks provided detailed information on how and where to travel, literature offered prescriptions on why to do so, and films began to portray travel and mobility within the context of the emerging international youth culture.

The innocuous nature of the emergent youth tourism was depicted in Peter Yates's 1963 hit film *Summer Holiday*. The opening scene of a dreary English beach, with old folks shuffling about while a stodgy band plays, is an obvious contrast to the main subject of the film, as it shifts from cold black and white to warm, vibrant color, from brass band to pop, from rainy to sunny, from local to international, from old to young. In short, young British pop star Cliff Richard leads a group of lads in converting an old red double-decker London bus into a holiday transport and driving it to the sunny climes of the Mediterranean, having adventures along the way while periodically breaking into song. As the movie poster promised, "From first kiss in Paris . . . to last blush in Greece," the film is an innocent romp about finding love on the road, or as Richard sings, "every girl is a beautiful girl when you're a stranger in town."

A better and more sophisticated film—mature is perhaps the word for it—is *Two for the Road*, a 1967 romantic comedy starring Albert Finney and Audrey Hepburn. The two youngsters, Joanna and Mark, first meet in the late 1950s on a ferry to France as she helps him locate his passport amidst his rucksack, canteen, cook kit, sleeping bag, and other equipment strewn about the deck. They meet again not long after on the road in France, as he has hitched a ride with a farmer and she joins him, abandoning the young women's choir that she is traveling with. They ramble around France, sleep together, and fall in love. The movie becomes a chronicle of the ups and downs of their marriage as lived out in multiple trips to and through France, each with its own storyline, and between which the director, Stanley Donen, moves with abandon. As they age and mature, things become more complicated, but the foundation of their relationship remains that blissful moment of youthful discovery, of each other and of travel. Indeed, the film closes with them venturing into Italy for a new road trip in an effort to rediscover their youth and rekindle their marriage.

The idealization of youth travel was also depicted in the hit 1968 film from Mel Stuart *If It's Tuesday, This Must Be Belgium*. A comedy set within the mass tourism of the late 1960s, it follows a group of Americans on a package tour of nine countries in eighteen days. In a subplot storyline, Shelly, a teenager being dragged along by her parents, meets a young guy scamming for free samples of Gouda and Edam at the Alkmaar cheese market. He is a political activist riding around Europe on a motorcycle and handing out flyers to promote a demonstration. He and Shelly run into each other again in Switzerland. There he takes her to a youth hostel to, as he says, "meet some real people." The scene is more evocative of a coffeehouse in Greenwich Village than a hostel in the Swiss Alps with its smoky, candle-lit common room filled with young people lounging about as one fellow plays guitar beneath a wall poster of Che Guevara. This scene is intercut with another of the adult group suffering through "Fondue Fling Night," a tourist trap complete with yodelers in folk costume amid pots of molten cheese. Interestingly, the film uses this juxtaposition to satirize and ridicule the dynamic of the package tour phenomenon, but it doesn't do the same for the youth hostelers. Even though they are depicted stereotypically, the young people in the film are portrayed as having a sense of earnest authenticity, and their travel as being more genuine and less superficial than that of their elders.

Another film from 1969, a hit in Europe and still with quite a cult following, is Barbet Schroeder's first feature, *More*. It takes a different point of view on the transnational mobility of youth. Set primarily on the sun-drenched Spanish island of Ibiza, the film follows a rather staid young German student, Stefan, who hitchhikes from Munich to Paris for a break from his university studies. At a party in Paris, he meets a fast-living American named Estelle, whom he pursues and eventually follows to Ibiza. There they slowly begin a relationship, as Estelle introduces Stefan to many pleasures—namely, sex and drugs. Ultimately they become addicted to heroin, with tragic results. Viewed by many as a notorious exploitation film with its drug use, full frontal nudity, and Pink Floyd score, it isn't so much about travel as it is about the counterculture; still, it is noteworthy for its routine treatment of the transnational mobility of youth in Western Europe.

The freedom of travel posed risks as well as opportunities. Indeed, backpacking in Europe became the premise for all sorts of cautionary tales, including the spate of gory slasher films in the *Hostel* series and the now classic 1981 John Landis film *An American Werewolf in London*. In the latter movie, two young American men who are traveling through northern England stop one evening at a pub called the Slaughtered Lamb. Despite being warned by the patrons to "keep off the moors," they take an unwise shortcut and walk off into the darkness. As they hike through a cold rain with their colorful puffy down jackets and backpacks, thinking of their upcoming transcontinental journey to Rome and talking about girls and sex, a werewolf attacks, killing one of the young men, who becomes a hilariously sardonic decomposing zombie-ghost, and biting the other, who steadily transforms into the werewolf of the film's title, eventually meeting his own demise. By 1981 it was commonplace for young Americans to go backpacking in Europe, as the premise of the movie makes clear, because youth travel there had undergone a profound transformation in scope and practice. Backpacking in Europe had become a characteristic feature of the broader transnational youth culture of the West, intertwined with the social mores and cultural practices of the time.

Hippies, the Counterculture, and Moral Panic

The youth mobility of the 1960s and 1970s underwent a significant change not only in terms of scale but also in kind, particularly with the confluence of the independent youth traveler tourist and the itinerant countercultural hippie drifter. While open-ended drifterism was distinct from the defined episodic travel of the backpacker, there was tremendous overlap between the two and much fluidity from one to the other, as these young people would follow the same hitchhiking and rail routes, sleep in the same plazas and train stations, and gravitate toward the same destinations. They interacted socially as well, conversing, listening to music, hanging out, hooking up, and smoking dope. Some who began as backpackers ended up settling into transnational hippie communities, such as in the Matala caves on the southern shore of Crete, on the undeveloped northern shore of Ibiza, in the encampment of Barbonia City in Milan, and later in the Christiania enclave in Copenhagen.[22] Observers often failed to recognize any difference between the various sorts of youth mobility, as the trappings of the counterculture in style, manner, and behavior, if not always ideology, were adopted by the larger youth culture of travel. Long hair, beards, jeans, general unkemptness, living on the cheap, casual use of marijuana, disregard for adult authority, new sexual mores—all of these became pervasive if not standard. In Western Europe, the alternative milieu of the counterculture was premised on a transnational network of informal collectivity that operated in small units prizing individualization. The network was connected through alternative media and the mobility of the young, who moved between specific districts of cities such as Amsterdam, West Berlin, Copenhagen, and London.[23] Thus, the mobility of the counterculture was itself premised on the practice of independent youth travel.

The western counterculture of the late sixties and early seventies was a youthful affair that saw many young people, mostly from the middle

20   Backpackers in the 1960s often took on the trappings of the hip youth culture, such as these Britons at a German youth hostel. Photographer unknown. Used with permission of the Archiv beim DJH-Hauptverband, Detmold.

class, rejecting the social norms and cultural standards of their elders. It was a transnational phenomenon that initially developed in the United States and the United Kingdom and rapidly spread throughout North America and Western Europe and on into Eastern Europe and Latin America, taking on discrete local dimensions wherever it went.[24] The counterculture gave expression to a shared alienation from the dominant structures of Cold War conformity and technological change, but it did so in a host of ways. The social, cultural, and political movements associated with the counterculture are vast and varied, but the most consistent cultural representative was the hippie, a subcultural figure who embraced psychedelic music, recreational drugs, and the sexual revolution experienced within a communal environment, sometimes dropping out of mainstream society altogether to live alternatively for a time. Hippies embraced mobility, moving around with ease, if little money, by hitchhiking, tramping, or riding in the iconic painted minibus. They were "new gypsies who flow across the world; congealing in communal crash pads, caves, camping grounds, Youth Hostels, YMCAs and hotels," participating "in a turned-on league of nations," as one Australian adherent,

Richard Neville, described them at the time.[25] The hippie was thought to be immediately recognizable through personal affect—standard of dress, grooming, vocabulary and so on—that betrayed an ideological disposition. Yet who was or wasn't a hippie, and what his or her personal or political disposition might be, was never very clear.

A kind of moral panic emerged that equated hippiedom with youth mobility in general, whether in Europe or North America.[26] The political unease generated by the movement of young people between protest sites in 1968 was paralleled by a cultural unease about the effects of such mobility on the moral fiber of the young. Throughout the twentieth century, there had been a series of moral panics regarding juvenile delinquency, and to many the counterculture looked like delinquency on a mass scale. Without a doubt, the infrastructure, patterns, and habits of youth travel in Western Europe as it had developed since the war facilitated the spread and growth of the counterculture there, with each exerting a significant influence on the other.

The concern about young people's mobility revolved around questions of mass vagabondage. While youth travel had been promoted and championed by Western European states and societies, the more backpacking came to resemble vagrancy rather than tourism, the more troubling it became. Historically, the tourist was welcomed while the vagabond was expelled, doing much to define the West's understanding of mobility. The vagrant's mobility was by definition unstable, unpredictable, impoverished, and potentially threatening and destabilizing. In the late nineteenth century, vagrancy was criminalized and pathologized as something the modern state needed to control and regulate, helping to differentiate boundaries of inclusion and exclusion in the social body. French legal codes, in particular, had focused on youth vagabondage.[27]

In France, the top destination for 1960s international mass tourism, there was a largely unfavorable opinion of the "immense invasion" of "undesirable" youth. The "beatnik," a catchall term in France and elsewhere for a hippie, drifter, or young itinerant, had become the "number one enemy of tourism" in the mid- to late sixties. As early as the summer of 1964, hundreds of foreign youth were questioned by Parisian police for their "idleness," and many were expelled from the country, based on the nineteenth-century legal codes.[28] Whereas France saw the troublesome mobility of "beatnik" youth as being external and arriving there from beyond its borders, West Germany was worried about an internal dropout culture involving *die Gammler*, often considered the harbingers of the underground subcultural scenes that later developed in Munich, Frankfurt, Hamburg, and Berlin. *Der Spiegel* published a lengthy exposé on the *Gammler* phenomenon in September 1966, with a photograph on its cover of long-haired hippies hanging out and listening to music. The dropouts were males, roughly eighteen to twenty-five years old, of middle-class background. They hitchhiked to and from major European cities, "with a sleeping bag under the arm" and "a few coins in the pocket," riding "the stream of tourist convoys" and congregating in places such as Covent Garden in London, Vestergade in Copenhagen, and the Gedächtniskirche adjacent to Zoo Station in West Berlin. *Der Spiegel* claimed that there were about a thousand *Gammler* in West Germany and five thousand total in Western Europe. While it was a transnational phenomenon, it was seen to be particularly popular among young Germans, such as twenty-three-year-old Mick from Frankfurt, who for three years had been hitchhiking all over Western Europe living as an itinerant vagrant, or Petra and her friend Silke, both seventeen and from academic families, who were slowly making their way to Paris.[29]

In 1966–67, German journalist Margret Kosel set out to investigate and understand the new *Gammler* by traveling around Western Europe interviewing dropouts. She concluded that this mobile group who traveled "without money, without suitcases, without visas" was a transnational community of young Westerners who considered their itinerant lifestyle to be an ideological pursuit meant as a critique of bourgeois normality. Kosel pointed out that they were exploiting the public and private policies that had been promoting youth travel, and that this became a dilemma for governments that wanted to curtail their vagrancy. Many countries began to enforce minimum currency requirements or some other demonstration of means at border controls. While the numbers of such dropouts were, in fact, relatively small, the *Gammler* occupied a large space in the public imagination.[30] Much of the worry over this dropout culture was about drug use, which in the mid-1960s began to be conceived for the first time as distinctively a problem of youth.[31] In her study, Kosel observed the nascent countercultural movement in Western Europe and its relationship to the youth travel culture that was developing there.

In the summer of 1965, the first *capelloni* (long-hairs) began to appear in Italy, particularly in Rome, where young Western Europeans congregated at the Spanish Steps with an attitude described by one journalist as "Today Rome, Tomorrow Istanbul."[32] As in France, the phenomenon was seen to be an undesirable foreign import having an unwelcome influence on local youth. The first of many police actions to expel these hippies from the Spanish Steps took place in December 1966, but they kept returning, as portrayed in Federico Fellini's 1972 film *Roma*, which has an early scene of young foreign hippies sprawled about on the

Spanish Steps, sunning themselves, playing guitar and fife, washing in the fountains, but mostly making out.[33] The film's narrator describes them as "disenchanted youth," yet admires them for their comfortable and open sexuality. Toward the end of the film, Roman police come to clear the Piazza di Spagna of the throngs of young hippies, beating them and chasing them out of the piazza while older straight diners watch from their café tables. One bystander says, with a moral tone contradicting the earlier scene, "They've turned our piazzas and monuments into a garbage dump. All they think about is sex!"

For Italian hippies, the encampment known as "Barbonia City" (Vagabond City) around Via Ripamonti in Milan became the center of activity. Young people from all over Italy and abroad gathered there in 1966–67. Associated with a space used for happenings by the movement/magazine *Mondo Beat*, Barbonia City was a tent city of young hippies living in the surrounding streets and vacant lots. One of the leaders, Vittorio Di Russo, who had been involved with the Provos in Amsterdam, was arrested for creating a public disturbance. Interestingly, his sentence was a kind of internal exile meant to limit his mobility, as he was ordered to return to his home village and stay there. For his part, Di Russo declared that he didn't have or want a stable home because he was always on the move through different countries, and that it was his intention "to become a global citizen without any nationality."[34] This initial municipal crackdown on Barbonia City in November 1966 (which would continue throughout 1967 as Milan's primary newspaper, *Corriera della Sera*, led a press campaign detailing the depravity of the hippies there) coincided with the Arno flood, and many of the *capelloni* fled Milan for Florence to join the Mud Angels.[35] Reviled in Milan yet celebrated in Florence—devils in one place, angels in the other—mobile youth inspired a dichotomy of moral judgment.

As the routes of the European youth travel culture expanded into the Mediterranean peripheries and southern Asia, the counterculture did so as well. Eventually, as the numbers grew, there was a public backlash in each of these countries, with severe sentences for young Europeans who broke the law in Turkey, Iran, India, and Nepal. In the summer of 1968 in Yugoslavia, the Belgrade newspaper *Politika Ekspres* complained that "modern tourist nomads, boys and girls from all parts of the world, have become a menace to the city," and advocated running them out. In Turkey, the newspaper *Hurriyet* warned that Istanbul was being "stained by beatniks and hippies who have attached themselves to the city like ticks."[36] In Morocco, the moral panic about young European travelers centered on drug use and was led by the newspaper *L'Opinion*. Eventually governments took measures against these overlanders, restricting their mobility through border controls tied to financial solvency and personal grooming. In 1972, Tunisia, Libya, Uganda, Malawi, and Kenya introduced measures targeting the young, even requiring young men to shave and cut their hair at the border.[37]

A 1971 Bollywood film set in the hippie scene in Kathmandu, *Hare Rama Hare Krishna*, became an unexpected blockbuster hit in India. Dev Anand wrote, produced, directed, and starred in the film. It opens with shots of a map of Western Europe, young Hare Krishnas dancing in the streets there, and a pile of hippies smoking dope in Nepal. The plot revolves around a brother, Prashant (Anand), who is searching for his estranged and beautiful sister, Jasbir (played by Zeenat Aman, a former Miss India), who grew up in Canada but disappeared into the European counterculture. Prashant finds her in Kathmandu at the center of the hippies, getting stoned, dancing frenetically to psychedelic music, and calling herself Janice. As a hash pipe is passed around among the dancing hippies, she sings the popular song from the film, "Dum Maro Dum" ("Take Another Hit"). With an infectious the Doors-meet-Mumbai sound, the song was a massive success and is still familiar to fans of Bollywood. Jasbir/Janice has traveled through London, Paris, Istanbul, and Kabul to get to Kathmandu, which she describes as "a journey and no more." While the film treats the young Westerners more as decadent lost children than as a menace (the villains in the story are Indian artifact smugglers), it had the effect of introducing the phenomenon of the hippie trail to a mass Indian audience. Not long after, newspapers began to campaign against the young European travelers. The Pakistani *Rawalpindi Sun* wrote, "It is tragic indeed that our youth should indiscriminately try to ape Western values."[38]

There was practically a subgenre of autobiographical memoirs and novels in early 1970s France that recounted the adventures, often drug-riddled, of young French men and women in South Asia, usually to tragic effect.[39] The most famous, *The Road to Katmandu* (*Les chemins de Katmandou*), came out in 1969 as both a film and a novel. Set within the young overland travel scene, the novel was written by René Barjavel. The film was made by André Cayatte and starred Jane Birkin and Serge Gainsbourg, with a soundtrack by the latter. The movie bombed, but the book was a hit and went through three editions. The story follows Olivier (French) and Jane (British), who meet in Nepal after becoming disillusioned with Europe, particularly following the disappointments of 1968. Terrible things happen to the characters, including two who are raped and murdered by Afghan truck drivers. Toward the end, Jane kills herself during an LSD trip.

Deploying the persistent derogatory perception of young European travelers as migrants, the *Observer* in England wrote in 1967 with thinly veiled disgust of "the Migration of the Great Unwashed," as destitute, drugged-out young Europeans (it estimated ten thousand a year) moved back and forth through the network. It described how Vicky, a clerk from Liverpool, and her boyfriend, the son of a doctor, had both fallen into prostitution in Pakistan to support themselves, and how they suffered frequent violence as a consequence.[40] The *Guardian* expressed "alarm over British youths on drugs in Istanbul," describing penniless Britons high on dope taking up an increasing amount of consular time there as they passed through with the "swarm" of "young people from Scandinavia, Holland, and Germany."[41] A 1972 article in *Punch* most outrageously captures the concern as "a singular phenomenon of our erratically affluent age." Kenneth Allsop described "the new creed of international drop-outism, the waifs and strays of the mass-cult state, overlanders in an underground community, global villagers who scorn TV, the travellers whom the tourist industry doesn't want. It's largely a summer diaspora," he wrote, "when universities and techs pull out the vacation plug and the bottled-up young surge into the cosmopolitan plumbing system they've constructed for themselves." While he noted that some went farther abroad, Europe was "the main stamping ground of the bedraggled army, the Woodstock Nation in motion," whom he described as diseased beggars and hustlers, "Eurobums" out for a quick fix as "customers in a new Common Market [of drugs] not envisaged under the Treaty of Rome."[42] Despite such vitriolic reactions, youth travel continued to expand rapidly in this period. No doubt the fast growth of the phenomenon is part of what fueled the backlash. As an infrastructure and a practice, the travel culture of Western Europe's youth facilitated the transnational dimension of the counterculture there. As the habits, practices, and scale of youth travel in Western Europe developed and changed, even expanding its frontiers beyond the continent, the institutional infrastructure changed as well.

Hitchhiking and Hostels

In the 1960s and '70s, hitchhiking became a mass means of mobility for the young throughout the western world, North and South America included, but particularly so in Western Europe, where it was systemic and became vital to the youth travel culture. The *Let's Go* guidebooks added the thumbs-up hitchhiker symbol as their iconic logo in 1973. Hitchhiking gives the appearance of being a haphazard set of activities, but it

21   Hitchhiking backpackers in Utrecht, July 1974. Photograph by Bert Verhoeff. National
      Archives of the Netherlands/Anefo, license by CC-BY.

is a culturally constituted set of behaviors that involves a host of strategies related to getting rides, reaching a destination, and maintaining
personal safety. While it was a means of travel that rewarded improvisation and creativity, fundamentally it was a learned behavior of customs
and norms premised on sociability. It was also a predominantly male
world, as most of the hitchhikers lined up along the roads exiting cities
were men, as were the drivers who picked them up.[43] Matteo Guarnaccia
was taught to hitchhike at age fourteen by an American fellow traveler,
Gary, with whom he learned the ins and outs by tramping through Italy
before breaking out on his own and hitchhiking around Western Europe
at age fifteen.[44] In 1968, Prime Minister Pierre Trudeau urged the young
of Canada to hit the road and hitchhike in order to see and learn their
country and the world. He had adopted the ways and means of hitchhiking as a young man in Europe and the Middle East and heartily recommended it. With the opening of the Trans-Canada Highway, many
tens of thousands of young Canadians were doing just that each summer, moving back and forth across the continent and generating a public backlash in their wake.[45]

While it was utilitarian in its very low cost as a means of conveyance,
there was also something ideological about choosing to hitchhike—
namely, personal adventure, freedom, and a "vastly educational and personally rewarding way to discover Europe, Europeans, and yourself" that
manifested itself as a rejection of prepackaged mass tourism.[46] Ed Buryn

was something of a professional vagabond hitchhiking around Europe in the late 1960s and early 1970s. In 1969, he published *Hitch-hiking in Europe: An Informal Guidebook* to share his expertise. Hitchhiking there largely lacked the moral connotations it held in the United States, he maintained, where by the 1960s it was associated with deviancy. Unsurprisingly, as young Germans had developed a cultural mobility in the postwar period premised on the autostop, by 1970 West Germany was considered the easiest place to hitchhike, with England a close second, but those countries were also awash with hitchhikers competing with each other for rides. The farther south in Europe one went, the fewer the number of rides and the fewer the hitchhikers. In Northern Europe, highway ramps, rest stops, and gas stations could be occupied by dozens of young hitchhikers looking for a ride, particularly in the summer, when the weather was good and tourists were on the road. Buryn's main recommendation to beat the competition for rides, beyond not looking too much like a hippie, was to travel with a young woman. "What about a girl travelling alone?" he asked. "Not recommended for several reasons. But primarily due to unwanted sexual advances, if not sexual assault."[47]

Still, like men, young women also appreciated the adventure and autonomy offered by hitchhiking, even if it carried significant risk. Penelope Carstens learned to hitchhike with a friend in West Germany on her first trip abroad in 1965. As a seventeen-year-old, she was frightened by the speed of the autobahn, as well as by the intentions of one of the drivers who picked them up. Still, finding the experience exhilarating, at age nineteen she hitchhiked with a friend around northern France; they split up midtrip, and she picked up with a young Frenchman and continued on, with a final night spent in the cab of a truck, stopping for calvados and strong coffee before arriving at the Cherbourg ferry terminal. She later hitchhiked to the Pyrenees with her fiancé in 1970 and to Rome in 1971.[48] Chiara Albero traveled from Milan to Britain in the summer of 1980, when she was twenty-one. At a hostel in the Orkney Islands, she met a young Frenchman named Benoit, smoked some dope, had sex, and continued the liaison while hitchhiking around Scotland from hostel to hostel, with the duration of the love affair corresponding exactly with that of her trip.[49]

The International Youth Hostel Federation found that it needed to adjust to the changing attitudes and mores of youth budget travelers like Chiara. In the 1950s, there had been significant internal debate about whether or not hitchhikers represented the true hosteling spirit and if they should be welcomed.[50] Interestingly, the Canadian government's

1970 task force report on "Transient Youth" saw youth hostels as a solution to the potential social deviancy of hitchhiking and recommended a string of sex-segregated youth hostels to be opened in the summer along the Trans-Canada Highway to accommodate and monitor the young. By 1973, 120 youth hostels had been funded through the program.[51] While the IYHF's leaders had earlier reconciled themselves to hitchhiking and motorized transport, they had new concerns by the late 1960s. At their 1970 conference, they noted that the original hosteler of the interwar period had been a local countryside rambler, but now hostelers were typically international tourists, moving from city to city by rail or road, and their numbers were rapidly expanding. They recognized that the young wanted less spartan conditions, a relaxation of rules, and less authoritarian wardens; they saw that the recent student revolts, the growth of subcultures, and alternative lifestyles were having an impact well beyond the young people directly involved in each. "We should not be afraid of the hippies," they declared, and "modern dancing should not be opposed," but it was necessary to develop protocols and policies to deal with the increasing drug use, and sex was "already a major problem."[52] In his presidential address at the 1972 conference, Anton Grassl demonstrated an impressive sensitivity to what was going on: "It would be totally unjust to dismiss them all with a derogatory collective term as 'hoboes,' 'hippies,' or 'drop-outs.' It would also be unjust to link them as a matter of course with drugs. . . . No, the young people who come to our hostels want to discover the world, and they want to discover themselves. It may be that too little attention has been devoted so far to their need for self discovery."[53] Systemic change was slow to come about, however, as hostels were largely controlled by local or national authorities rather than the IYHF. A decade later, in 1982, the IYHF recognized that policies across the network were far too inconsistent, with many hostels remaining too rule bound in old-fashioned ways in a misbegotten attempt to preserve early-century hosteling, and that with increased competition to accommodate the explosion in youth travel, hosteling had missed an opportunity to expand its reach and influence.[54]

The Dutch were the first to engage proactively with the changing interests and demands of the youth hosteler. In 1966, the Dutch Youth Hostel Association began a multi-year study to consider how it might update its services to better fit the needs, expectations, and desires of the young. Noting that hippies "are not representative of the young tourist" and that they formed a minority of young international tourists, the 1970 report still recognized that the practice of youth travel was undergoing significant change. The study focused on Dutch youth and their expectations regarding travel. Its two main conclusions were that the most fundamental aspect of an ideal holiday for Dutch youth was to go abroad (in 1970, 800,000 Dutch youth did so) and be with people their own age, and that what they wanted to do while abroad was socialize: eat, drink, party, dance, make out, and have a fling. The study identified two main types of activities—the "erotic-adventurous" and the "cultural"—and found that these patterns corresponded to gender, male and female respectively, but were by no means mutually exclusive. Camping was the most popular type of accommodation, and getting around by car the ideal transport. Encountering foreigners was the most attractive aspect of youth hostels, while the least attractive aspect was that hostel rules and regulations were considered too restrictive. The critical respondents didn't like gender-segregated dormitories, curfews, rules against smoking, drinking, and dancing, or the authority of strict old-fogey hostel wardens. In short, what Dutch youth sought from their ideal holiday was freedom and autonomy exercised within a transnational peer group.[55] In the wake of this study, the Dutch Youth Hostel Association made some minor changes—namely, serving beer and loosening curfews—which the IYHF later credited for the favorability that hostels in the Netherlands enjoyed among international youth hostelers.[56]

Faced with a declining share of hostelers among total youth travelers, the IYHF produced a similar but much more expansive study in 1977. International youth tourism, especially in Europe, had grown very rapidly in the previous ten years, but hosteling had expanded more slowly in comparison. In 1977 there had still been 3.5 million foreign overnights in hostels by Western Europeans, but total world foreign overnights had peaked in 1972. In addition to the oil crisis and the global recession, which of course were beyond the IYHF's control, the increasing cost of hosteling and the desire for greater freedom in relation to leisure activities were seen to be inhibiting growth. England, France, and West Germany were selected as the main target for the survey because members from those three countries accounted for half the world's hostel overnights, while the hostels in those countries attracted half the world's overnights.[57]

The nearly three thousand youth surveyed were both hostelers and non-hostelers, of evenly mixed gender, between the ages of eighteen and twenty-five, with half identifying as students, a quarter as clerical workers, and a quarter as manual workers. In total, they were remarkably well traveled, with over 90 percent of the Germans, nearly 70 percent of the British, and 60 percent of the French having been abroad. Among these groups, the French manual workers were the least likely to have been abroad, and the German students the most likely. Hostel members were drawn largely from the middle classes, regardless of their national origin. North Americans and Australians were well informed about youth hostels before coming to Europe, but few had been members prior to their trip.[58]

In short, the IYHF concluded that less paternalism in hostel rules and regulations and greater encouragement of autonomy among hostelers were the primary shifts required to attract and serve the young better. Flexibility in travel arrangements (the preferred means of travel were train, automobile, and hitchhiking), freedom from rules and regulations (especially regarding curfews and hours of operation), meeting people their own age, and keeping the cost of the holiday to the absolute minimum were the most important factors for planning trips abroad among both those who utilized hostels and those who did not. Norway, Sweden, Denmark, and the Netherlands were considered to have the best hostels in terms of both facilities and atmosphere, and this was true by reputation even among non-hostelers. The study concluded that this was in part due to size, as Scandinavian hostels tended to be smaller and more intimate, and also, importantly, more flexible in terms of booking policies, self-catering cooking, and the freedom for people to come and go as they pleased, with no fixed curfew. Still, the IYHF found no great clamoring for mixed dormitories—in fact, it found the opposite. Nor was there any great demand for alcohol, and the traditional requirement of chores and duties was viewed quite positively. The IYHF recognized that independent youth travelers had a growing number of options for accommodations—a large number of independent hostels had opened, for example—and the federation felt that those who wanted mixed dormitories or a bar or a more freewheeling party scene (Bob's Youth Hostel in Amsterdam comes to mind) would tend to self-select.[59] Nevertheless, from their roots as shelters for young hikers rambling in the rural areas of their own country, hostels had evolved considerably over the last half century. Hosteling was now primarily about foreign travel by a highly mobile middle-class social body whose members were seeking, above all, to interact with one another, while doing so as cheaply as possible.

Unsurprisingly, hostels played an important part in the development of youth travel practice. Youth hostels had become spaces of intentional intercultural encounter. One of the primary motives for staying in a hostel was to meet other young people, ideally from elsewhere in the world. Youth hostels thus became cosmopolitan spaces that mixed local culture with the ways of itinerant residents. Those who sought them out demonstrated an inclination toward an interactive communal environment where they might find travel or touring partners, play card games, give and receive recommendations and warnings, trade information, books, cassette tapes, or gear, cook and eat together, and learn about other people and other parts of the world without even visiting them.[60] The youth hostel was as fundamental to backpacking in Western Europe as were hitchhiking and rail passes.

An American Invasion

First offered in 1959, the Eurail pass was created to offer a united Europe for an American tourist market, with the goal of luring U.S. dollars into the European economy through extended travel and tourism. It was a cooperative arrangement among thirteen Western European national rail companies, which took turns administering the program. The Eurail pass was not available to Europeans themselves, and though it was designed for wealthy adult Americans, it was available throughout the (primarily) western world—including North and South America, Japan, and Australia—though the United States accounted for roughly 90 percent of annual sales during the 1960s. It entitled the holder to unlimited first-class rail travel at any time on virtually every train within and between participating countries for a period of three weeks to three months.[61]

The Eurail pass was a quick success, not least because of the growing numbers of young Americans coming to travel in Europe over the course of the 1960s. In 1960 there were ten thousand Eurail passengers; by 1970 that number had risen to over one hundred thousand.[62] It is not hard to see why an easy-to-use prepaid pass allowing unlimited mileage through virtually all of continental Western Europe for a prolonged period of time without a preplanned itinerary was so appealing to the young. By the end of the decade, middle-class American youth were crowding the first-class rail cars of Western Europe, particularly during the summer months. Other first-class passengers—business travelers and tourists alike—were not pleased.[63] As Helen Tyrrell complained in a letter to the editor of the *New York Times* in 1971, "In Europe—first-class, reserved accommodations notwithstanding—travel on railroad and ship has been made unbearable by the hippie invasion. They are like locusts, strewing litter and bad manners everywhere, cluttering up aisles of trains, lying over the decks of ships."[64] Indeed, first class-cabins crowded with guitar-playing, smoking, drinking youngsters who were living on the cheap, sleeping in odd configurations, and often letting their standards of personal hygiene slide created a backlash. Recognizing a market demand, in 1971 the Eurail consortium introduced the student pass, good for unlimited second-class rail travel for two months at the very affordable cost of $125, compared to $330 for the traditional first-class pass.[65]

The Eurail student pass (later that decade renamed the Eurail youth pass) combined with a drop in the cost of airfare to expand significantly the numbers of young Americans who could afford to undertake prolonged travel in Europe. By the mid-1970s, more than a million a year were doing so. In the major cities of Europe, the streets and sidewalks around American Express offices became unofficial flea markets where young Americans bought and sold items to raise money and gear up for more travel.[66] These offices were an ideal place to meet other young travelers; in addition to its well-known cable service for receiving wired money when funds ran low, American Express offered a mail service through which letters and parcels could be forwarded from one office to another, bouncing around the continent in pursuit of the itinerant recipient.[67] "Every Monday we get 3,000 pieces of mail in our clients' mail service; half of them for kids under 21. We don't mind. You'd be surprised how many carry credit cards," said Nils Thorbjornsen of the Copenhagen office.[68] With the drop in transport costs, such travel became an option open to the vast American middle class, a journey undertaken either prior to or after college or during the summer between terms. It was an inexpensive and exciting way to travel, for some by necessity, for others by choice.

The backpacker circuit could also be a convenient place for a young man to avoid his local draft board. Nineteen-year-old Crawford Dunnett got a letter in 1970 asking him to report for a physical. "I knew everybody was going to Canada, and I wanted to be different, so I decided to go to Europe." Letters from his draft board followed Dunnett around European American Express offices for months. Eventually he moved south into and through Africa, returning to the United States in 1973. Gary Isringhaus was drafted and went to Stockholm because Sweden offered asylum to American servicemen and draft dodgers. He continued on to West Germany and moved around Western Europe until he ran out of money and was forced to return home.[69] Young Portuguese men also avoided conscription by traveling in Europe; a significant number could be found in Paris during the events of May 1968.[70] Arthur Goldhammer, on the other hand, returned to the U.S. in 1968 from his summer travels between terms at MIT to discover that his draft board considered his European trip to be indicative that he was no longer a student and was therefore eligible to serve. Despite his appeal, he was inducted into the army in November.[71]

Crossing the Atlantic had long been the impediment to European travel for Americans. In 1960, 1.3 million U.S. citizens flew to Europe; in 1974, the number was 6.5 million. Meanwhile, the profile of the American traveler had changed considerably, not only in social class but in terms of average age, which had dropped precipitously as the proportion of youth in overall travel rose markedly. It continued to do so even during the worldwide economic downturn in the mid-1970s, when youth travel was the only tourism sector to continue seeing substantial growth.[72]

The boom in transatlantic air travel was in large part due to the youth market. To fill empty seats, airlines began offering last-minute fares to qualifying students in the late 1960s. One airline, Icelandic, became known as "the hippie airline" because of all the young people who took advantage of its fares, which were typically 15 percent cheaper than the industry standard. Soon all the major airlines were offering promotional student fares for transatlantic flights in an effort to compete with the booming trade in charter travel, which was becoming a big business, as several companies—including Trans International, World, and Overseas International—operated exclusively on a charter basis, bringing planeloads of young Americans to Europe.[73] At the time, Bill Bryson set out on a charter flight for his first trip to Europe: "Everyone on the plane was a hippie, except the crew and two herring-factory executives in first class. It was rather like being on a Greyhound bus on the way to a folk-singers' convention."[74] To compete, in 1971 Pan Am offered a $220 student fare for round-trip travel from the United States to Europe, hoping to get a share of the 750,000 American college students traveling there that summer. A tightening economy in the 1970s meant that summer jobs were few and paid poorly, while the rise in discounted airfares and charter flights combined with discounted rail passes made an extended stay in Europe affordable. For someone on the East Coast, it was cheaper, for example, to spend spring break in Paris than in Denver. This also fit in neatly with the growing trend for independent travel among young Americans, as it was much less costly than the packaged group tours they had relied on previously. Independent itineraries tended to be spur of the moment rather than rigidly preplanned, and there was the important benefit of freedom from the adult supervision of formal programs.[75]

The number of young Americans studying abroad doubled between 1965 and 1975 and continued to expand thereafter. Such programs grew in number and global diversity, yet in the mid-1980s, 80 percent of all Americans studying abroad were still opting for programs in Western Europe. By the 1970s, study abroad was no longer the purview of private liberal arts colleges but included many state universities and even two-year institutions.[76] In some cases, consortia of state universities worked together to provide opportunities for their students through multiple programs. The Kentucky Institute for European Studies, for example, recognizing that backpacking was a fundamental appeal of study abroad, organized its programs on four-day-a-week schedules so that students had three-day weekends for independent travel, and the cost of the program included a Eurail pass to boot.[77]

Meanwhile, charter flights and rail passes became available to young Europeans and other Westerners as well. Between 1961 and 1971, international departures for Australians aged twenty to twenty-four increased more than sixfold.[78] In the summer of 1971 alone, the International Student Travel Confederation offered five thousand intra-European charter flights between fifty-six cities.[79] Interrail was set up in 1972 to establish a rail pass for European youth. Again the national rail companies cooperated, and a ticket allowing unlimited second-class travel for one month was made available to young Europeans up to twenty-one years of age for £27.50. (At this time the UK participated in Interrail, but not Eurail.) In 1973, the age limit for the Interrail pass was raised to twenty-three, and in 1979 to twenty-six.[80] In 1972, its first year, there were 88,000 Interrail passengers, and in 1979, 229,000.[81] From the early 1970s, then, youth from within Western Europe had the Interrail pass available, and those from outside Europe had the Eurail youth pass, giving the young tremendous flexibility to move about nearly all of Western Europe by rail cheaply. The subjects of a study looking at youth rail travel in the mid-1980s found that those who used these passes traveled an average of six thousand kilometers to twelve destinations, whereas those traveling without Eurail or Interrail averaged twenty-seven hundred kilometers and seven destinations. The mere possibility of free movement across the European rail network reinforced and encouraged the restless mobility of the young travelers, even if that made for a more stressful travel experience.[82]

It is worth considering how the advent of these rail passes shaped the practice of youth travel in Europe. As no reservations were required, one could hop on and off at will; it was a kind of legal riding-the-rails tramping, even if it initially took place in first class. Because the ticket was prepaid and didn't impact one's daily budget, these frugal travelers quickly learned to sleep on trains to save money. One could explore two areas of Europe at the same time by alternating daily between them, sleeping at night on the long train ride in between.[83] As two Americans described, "We were young adventurers . . . and we valued the very things that

22   Three Eurailing Americans resting on Norway's Oslo-Bergen line, July 1970. Photograph by
Carlo Bavagnoli. The Life Picture Collection/Getty Images.

the Eurailpass not only made possible but also celebrated: thrift, spontaneity, simplicity, a sense of camaraderie with other travelers and the opportunity for contact with local people. The Eurailpass went with Icelandic Airlines, backpacks, guitar cases, youth hostels, hitchhiking, bed-and-breakfast inns, and daily picnics of French bread and cheese and rough red wine."[84]

Though American students were accustomed to middle-class comforts at home, they happily put up with cramped accommodations without plumbing, the vagaries of hitchhiking, warm beer, and unfamiliar food. For most, this was necessary budgeting for a prolonged journey, while for those who could afford otherwise, it was all part of the adventure, because this was how it was done and thus an essential component of the experience. Importantly, the practice of penurious youth travel had been established two decades earlier by those whose childhood and youth had been marked by an era of intense privation, a pattern of behavior that persisted among the young, who at this point had access to much greater prosperity.

Young Americans backpacking in Europe became newsworthy in the 1970s, and press coverage was common. No doubt many learned the ins and outs of drifter tourism by reading the newspaper. Articles abounded in the United States about the large and growing number of young travelers, the appeal and danger of drugs, the problem of looking like a hippie, how to hitchhike, how to use a Eurail pass or the hostel system, what to bring, how to budget, the "it" destinations, and the metaphysical meaning of it all. Some journalists managed to do all of the above; in a syndicated series of articles entitled "Rucksack Summer '72," which was picked up by papers across the country, June Goodwin detailed her travels through the Western European backpacker circuit, explaining the phenomenon to readers at home through her weekly dispatches.[85] A *New York Times* writer concluded, "If European travel has not yet become an accepted part of life for the American masses, it has for their children."[86]

Anxious about the rapidly growing number of young backpackers in the early 1970s, American and otherwise, cities sought to increase the number of cheap beds available in the summer by utilizing space in churches, youth centers, community halls, and schools. Western Europeans between the ages of sixteen and twenty-four were 34 percent of all tourists to the UK in 1970, and 45 percent of all tourists to London in 1975.[87] The number of young summer visitors to Britain grew from 2.2 million in 1970 to 3 million in 1971. In London, an information center was set up near Victoria Station in an attempt to get the

23   Beds were in high demand as backpackers queued outside the Carter Lane Youth Hostel in London, July 1971. Associated Newspapers/Rex/Shutterstock.

young efficiently distributed throughout the available beds, as the city had been inundated each summer since the late sixties, with the lack of beds forcing the young visitors to sleep in the parks, plazas, and train stations. One of the largest London hostels in Kensington had to establish a maximum stay of only four nights to encourage turnover.[88] The *Economist* recommended that London find ways to welcome and accommodate these budget travelers, as "today's penny-pinchers could be tomorrow's big-spenders."[89] Even if young backpackers didn't spend much individually, in the aggregate they did.[90] In 1971, the British Tourist Authority concluded that youth tourism accounted for a quarter of the industry's total revenues in the UK.[91] Even if the services provided by a city came at the expense of taxpayers, it was considered a good investment. The mayor of Copenhagen, Urban Hansen, insisted that similar "good publicity would have cost us $40 million."[92] This was a common attitude among tourist and municipal officials in several cities, perhaps most evident in Amsterdam and Copenhagen, as the considerable growth in tourism receipts grew largely due to the mass influx of young travelers. Indeed, more than anywhere else in Europe, these two cities came to be associated with the young backpacker phenomenon of the early 1970s. After extensive travels, Steven Anderson, an eighteen-year-old from Long Beach, California, stood in the London American Express office and declared with exhausted determination, "I'm washed out. I'm going home. But first, I'm off to Amsterdam and then Copenhagen."[93]

The Magical Center of Vacation Hippies

By the end of the 1960s, Magical Amsterdam had replaced Swinging London as a must-visit destination on many young travelers' European itineraries. Amsterdam was cheap, beautiful, and tolerant of the emerging youth counterculture and its emphasis on personal freedom, particularly regarding sex and drugs. By 1970, it had become such a focal point for backpackers that the small city struggled to accommodate the annual summer crush of hundreds of thousands of itinerant young people. It became known as "the Magical Center of Europe," a reputation it has never quite shaken, as young backpackers still visit there in throngs, hoping to experience, or at least witness, a bit of the wild life denied them in their daily lives at home. As Ed Buryn put it in 1973, Amsterdam "is the freak capital of Europe. Every type of young vagabond traveler crosses through here. The crush is terrific, but so is the level of excitement."[94]

Amsterdam underwent a remarkable transformation from a quaint provincial capital of quiet canals—the very definition of a backwater— to the party center of Europe in less than a decade. As a port city, it had long had a gritty reputation owing to its famous red-light district of quasi-legal prostitution. Still, at the end of the 1950s, no one would have thought that staid, traditional Amsterdam would become infamous as the new "International Babylon" a decade later. The city was already, by the early 1960s, drawing a considerable number of Dutch youth from the provinces, and this concentration of young people helped spur the Provo, Kabouter, and student movements there throughout the decade. Thus, Amsterdam was in many ways already under the influence of the young before the arrival of masses of foreign backpackers; indeed, the international celebrity of Dutch youth movements helped draw the others there.[95] But importantly, though these young foreign travelers individually stayed in Amsterdam for short durations, together they contributed to the rapid transformation of the city.

Dutch political culture had changed significantly in the postwar period, accommodating a pragmatic internationalism that opened the Netherlands to the rest of Europe. The neutrality and isolationism of the Dutch had not served them well in the face of Nazi aggression. This pragmatic approach to politics extended to the municipal governance of Amsterdam as well, where the city leadership responded to change cautiously, adopting myriad policies that appeared progressive to outsiders, but to insiders seemed rational and technocratic—an approach for accommodating change in an effort to manage it. These Dutch authorities approached governance with a knack for problem solving rather than a zeal for ideology, becoming a tolerant, if paternalistic, officialdom.[96]

In the mid-1960s, Amsterdam scored lowest on the cost index of Western European cities.[97] Arthur Frommer, famous for his budget travel guidebooks, used the title *Surprising Amsterdam* for his 1965 guide to the city because it had so much to offer at so little cost. Amsterdam beckoned to the budget traveler, or as Fabio Treves, a young Italian, put it, "Amsterdam was the London of the poor."[98] Meanwhile, the antics of the Provos raised the international profile of Amsterdam among European youth, who started showing up in large numbers in 1967.[99] This mass of young travelers looking to spend as little money as possible while desiring to congregate in Amsterdam created a unique kind of housing crisis for the city. In general, Amsterdammers sought to welcome and accommodate their young guests, but the lack of cheap places to stay and the number of people sleeping in the streets, plazas, and parks became a problem.

This was nowhere more evident than in Dam Square, a short walk's distance down the Damrak from Central Station, with the Royal Palace on one side and the National Monument commemorating the victims of the Nazi occupation on the other. Amsterdam lacked sufficient low-cost lodging to house the thousands of young people who showed up daily. The city's tourist infrastructure was designed to accommodate older, more affluent tourists; there were few youth hostels or budget hotels. The summers in Holland in the late sixties were unusually warm and dry. As early as 1967, an impromptu multinational encampment had emerged on and around the National Monument at the eastern end of Dam Square. During the rest of the year it continued to serve as a gathering place, but in the summers, the wide stone platform at the base of the monument became known colloquially as "the international mattress."[100]

By the summer of 1969, this had clearly become a problem.[101] Hundreds of young people were encamped nightly in Dam Square, causing sanitation and public health problems, disrupting traffic, and, perhaps most grievously, offending many older Dutch with what they saw as the abuse of the National Monument as the young people hung out, played music, smoked marijuana, and generally loitered about. Newspapers in the Dutch provinces began to pay attention to the *Damslapers* (Dam sleepers), and municipal politicians began getting resentful letters from all over the country. Indeed, the young were even becoming a tourist attraction themselves as older tourists came by just to observe them from a distance.[102] Police periodically moved the young away from the monument so it could be cleaned, and flower boxes were put in place to try to define space so as to maintain free access to the memorial.

By October 1969, the members of the city council had begun to consider an official ban on *Damslapen*, but they were reluctant to do so for a variety of reasons, mainly because they didn't want to do anything to disrupt the growing international tourism to their city.[103] Instead, they set up a work group to study the problem, which recommended that the city act as a tolerant host and find a way to accommodate these young tourists by providing budget lodging. For the summer of 1970, the city set up cheap sleeping accommodations in three vacant sites in the city center. Called "sleep-ins," they featured long rows of foam rubber mats on the floors of two empty factories and a sports hall. Backpackers were also encouraged to use a nearby city park as a place where they could sleep, make music, and gather without disturbing anyone.[104] Although these measures achieved some success—in the summer of 1970, the sleep-ins accommodated seventy-five thousand overnights, and the numbers congregating in Vondelpark grew significantly—an encampment remained at Dam Square.[105]

An estimated quarter million young people passed through the city in the summer of 1970. In early August, 75 percent of the hundreds of young people on Dam Square were between the ages of seventeen and twenty-one, with a three-to-one male-to-female gender ratio. They were 85 percent Western European (including Dutch) and 10 percent American. Germans were by far the most numerous, accounting for 27 percent of the total. Just more than half identified themselves as students, and a quarter as workers. A little less than half had slept outdoors the night before.[106] From the point of view of the city, the international throng there had become a public nuisance.

On 21 August, the mayor and city council voted officially to prohibit sleeping on Dam Square. A skirmish with police the following Monday, which reportedly began when police sent away an ice cream vendor lacking a permit, escalated into a small riot. The following day, 25 August, dozens of Dutch sailors from Den Helder came into town spoiling for a fight, attacking more than a thousand foreign youth at Dam Square with the police caught in between.[107] On the third day, the several hundred remaining young foreigners armed themselves with sticks, paving stones, and even Molotov cocktails in preparation for another attack. They were joined by scores of young Dutch who came to fight beside

24   *Damslapers* during the daytime at the National Monument, Dam Square, Amsterdam, 25 August 1970. The attack by Dutch sailors and the subsequent rioting would begin that night. Photographer unknown. National Archive of the Netherlands/Spaarnestad/NFP.

them in solidarity.[108] The sailors returned, many in street clothes this time, and the third day of rioting spilled out into the adjacent neighborhoods, but by the end of the night, the police had regained control. After three days of rioting, there had been seventy-seven reported injuries and forty-two arrests in total. Interestingly, the city report on the incident was rather lenient with respect to both the police and the foreign *Damslapers*, but harsh on the sailors, whom the city viewed as responsible for the violence, property damage, and prolongation of the affair.[109] As Mayor Ivo Samkalden stated emphatically, "I want to stress that these difficulties were *not* caused by young foreign tourists."[110] He insisted that young foreigners would continue to be welcomed by the city, but by September 1970, the *Damslapers* would have to find somewhere else to spend the night.[111] The Dam remained a youthful international meeting place and hangout, if not a mattress; one young Italian referred to the square as "a de facto area of extraterritoriality."[112]

The following summer, the multinational encampment moved westward to Vondelpark, the largest green space in the center of the city, composed of wooded glens, grassy lawns, and a winding series of ponds and pools. Located in an affluent neighborhood near the Rijksmuseum just west of Leidseplein, a prominent nightlife area of bars and clubs, Vondelpark was already in the process of becoming the regular spot for local youth to sit on the grass or lie in the sun, smoke hash, and play music. The foreign travelers, with city encouragement, followed. The city set up a baggage depot, information center, first-aid station, and recreation center at the entrance to the park, with temporary bathrooms and showers added throughout. Still, the facilities could not keep up with demand, as those who slept elsewhere often spent their days in the park, too.

In the summer of 1971, the three city sleep-ins accommodated roughly one hundred thousand overnights, while a municipal camping site provided another thirty thousand.[113] For Vondelpark, the numbers were more

25   Backpackers sleeping in Vondelpark, Amsterdam, July 1971. Photograph by Rob C. Croes. National Archives of the Netherlands/Anefo, license by CC-BY.

guesswork, based on a daily police headcount, but were estimated to have been about fifty thousand total overnights. Ninety percent of those staying in Vondelpark were from EEC countries, the UK, or the United States, and 92 percent were between sixteen and twenty-five years of age. Tens of thousands of other overnights were spent in squats, youth hostels, and cheap hotels. Around one-third of the total visitors were female. Germans and Italians were more frequently found in the sleep-ins, French in the park, and Americans in youth hostels. Socioeconomically, just over half were students, and just under a quarter identified as industrial or clerical workers. The backpackers spent much less money but stayed longer than typical tourists.[114]

Congestion, litter, and sanitation again became a problem, as Vondelpark was covered with tents and sleeping bags, with thousands of young people hanging out there daily. By the end of the summer, a neighborhood association, "Save the Park," had formed to express support for the experiment while also advocating policy changes to remedy the problems. The nearby residents were particularly concerned with the damage being done to the park landscape.[115] In 1972, the city established a series of sleeping zones within the park to try to contain the backpackers and limit the number of overnights. Tents, carpets, and plastic were also prohibited in an attempt to preserve the grass.[116] Within a couple of years, however, the Vondelpark experiment had ended. The city's tourist infrastructure now had more beds available to the young, and the number of overnights in the park had already decreased significantly as criminal activity there had surged. In 1974, the city prohibited sleeping in the park, though young travelers continued to congregate there during the day.[117]

Backpacker activities were not centered on Amsterdam; rather, the city was mostly used as a tolerant context, not as something interesting in itself, despite the wonderful art museums and historical sites.[118] The remarkably friendly relationship among the young tourists who congregated in small groups was based on a number of criteria: the short-term visitors, which described most of them, clustered together according to nationality and language; those who stayed for a longer duration tended toward a more transnational social life, with greater differentiation in nationality but less in lifestyle and activity, which might include a focus on playing and listening to music or games and conversation, or eating and drinking or smoking hashish and marijuana.[119] Ninety percent of the young tourists who came to Vondelpark in 1972 had used drugs prior to their arrival, so on the one hand they were self-selecting as a specific drug-using cohort, but on the other hand they were overwhelmingly casual in their use, smoking grass or hash temporarily for recreation. One study called them "vacation hippies"; another said they were "playing a hippie game."[120]

Cannabis, as hash or marijuana, was common across the backpacker circuit in this era, and police and border controls responded with search, seizure, and arrest. Not only amateurs, but professional drug-trade operations used the existing youth travel network to move goods across international borders.[121] Many countries, like Greece, blamed the spread of marijuana among their youth on the young vagabond tourists (*alitotouristes*) from Western Europe who visited there.[122] Guidebooks and news articles warned travelers that being young and foreign, having beards and long hair, dressing in blue jeans, and carrying a backpack would make them suspicious and a target for police attention. A 1970 cover story in *Life* magazine declared a "fair warning to American amateurs abroad" by profiling young Americans serving time in European jails for drug offenses. Most had been arrested at borders for smuggling a bit of hash, as was the case for a midwestern couple, both twenty-one, who were serving a six-year jail term in Cadiz; others were dealt with even more harshly, such as Max Belsen, a twenty-one-year-old Canadian who fainted when a London court sentenced him to ten years in prison for possession of cannabis.[123]

The U.S. State Department was alarmed by the rising number of young Americans being held abroad on drug charges. In 1969 the number was 142, but it exceeded 1,000 by 1973. Nearly all of those arrested were under thirty years of age. The department issued a notice, "Drug Arrests Abroad," and a booklet, *Youth Travel Abroad: What to Know before You Go,* in the early 1970s in an effort to engage with "young Americans who are now traveling widely and in larger numbers than ever before." Millions of these notices and brochures were published and distributed throughout the 1970s to universities, travel agencies, libraries, consulates, passport agencies, and the like. American Express reprinted five hundred thousand for their own free distribution.[124] While it wasn't difficult to find and consume cannabis elsewhere, Amsterdam gained the reputation of being a safe and convenient place to do so. The city understood this. City councilman Huib Riethof argued favorably for Dutch tolerance: "Amsterdam is gradually becoming an oasis for youth who seek refuge from the increasingly intolerant atmosphere in the lands around us." Even the police officer in charge of Vondelpark, Evert Jagerman, was largely untroubled: "The Americans behave very well. Our problem," he said, is with those "who are not interested in the subcultural aspect but

are existing on a criminal level—thieves and pushers and other parasites. Most often these are Dutch."[125]

In the late 1960s, youth recreational centers opened through generous municipal subsidy to provide gathering places for Amsterdam youth.
Clubs such as Paradiso, Melkweg, and Kosmos, set up in a former church,
warehouse, and mansion respectively, offered programming such as concerts, films, plays, light shows, dances, and political forums, as well as bars
and cafés. Between 1965 and 1968, marijuana use among the general
Dutch population doubled every year. In 1968, the government appointed
a commission, led by the city's chief inspector of mental health, Pieter
Baan, to investigate drug use and suggest policy reform. By this point, the
Amsterdam youth centers were making no effort to curb soft drug use by
their young clientele. The Baan Commission concluded that soft drugs,
such as hashish and marijuana, posed no significant threat, but that
hard drugs, such as opiates, amphetamines, and cocaine, did, and that
it was important to treat them separately. While soft drugs were never
fully legalized, they were effectively decriminalized through lack of enforcement, or became what the Dutch call *gedogen*, illegal but officially
tolerated.[126]

By the middle of the 1970s, the open sale of soft drugs had moved out
from the youth centers to more commercial operations—the famous Amsterdam "coffee shops." Historically, cafés were licensed to sell alcohol,
necessitating official police regulation, whereas coffee shops merely sold
coffee and food, and had no such police oversight. In 1980, there were
a couple dozen "coffee shops" in Amsterdam where hash and marijuana
were on sale; by 1990 there were several hundred throughout the city,
with most concentrated in the tourist areas around Leidseplein, Central
Station, and the red-light district. Their clientele consisted mostly of
young backpackers, who explored the varieties of hash and grass on the
menus while Pink Floyd and Bob Marley wafted from stereo speakers.
As Rick, a young man from Boston, said at the time, "It's best to save
Amsterdam for the last. If you start with Amsterdam, you might not get
around to seeing the rest of Europe."[127]

A team of American academics went to Amsterdam in 1970 to study
drug abuse, and found, to their surprise, that with respect to hard drugs,
the Dutch had far lower usage, addiction, and overdose rates than did
the United States. They found little hard drug use among Americans
there, but a considerable number of young hashish smokers who were
passing through, including Beth, a Phi Beta Kappa and third-year medi-
cal student. Along the banks of the canals, young Americans sat smok-

ing hashish, often with young people from elsewhere in Europe. As one said, "It's a sin to be in Amsterdam and not get stoned every night of the week."[128] The authors cautioned that although many of the young had long hair or beards, dressed colorfully, and maybe needed a bath, they were not hippies per se, and were much more likely to be conducting an experiment in self-discovery than an ideological pursuit. They enjoyed "enthusiastic citizenship in the disreputable nation of the happy turned-on," the authors wrote.[129] Psychedelic drugs such as acid and mushrooms straddled the soft/hard drug binary and were not difficult to find, but were much less prevalent than cannabis. Still, pamphlets, brochures, flyers, and magazines such as *Freeway Amsterdam*, *Together*, *Aloha*, and *Use It Weekly* offered a mix of advice and warnings about where to procure such things and how much to pay, the best parks in the city for tripping, recipes for muesli, and so on.[130] The goal was to live and travel as cheaply as possible, and Amsterdam had cheap and accessible hash, free beer on the Heineken brewery tour, canal-side herring carts, paper cones of delicious fries, and the bonus of sleeping outside for free. Magical Center, indeed.

Though niche guidebooks such as *Amsterdam after Dark* and *Mankoff's Lusty Europe* described the city in terms of a lurid, if not debauched, sexual fantasy—"wild, weird, and way out" was one catchphrase—this wasn't quite the experience of young backpackers.[131] The studies being done showed that there was less sexual interest and activity than expected among them, and certainly less than the city's reputation as a center of the sexual revolution seemed to warrant.[132] Though the city's sex industry expanded at this time, with the addition of sex shows and sex clubs for a mostly tourist clientele, the cost of such activities was prohibitive for backpackers, who found it much more in line with their meager budgets to roam about the red-light district gawking at the prostitutes behind glass.[133] The city sleep-ins were not segregated according to gender as hostels were, and though Vondelpark became known to some as "Fondle Park" because of the occasional love-in, there was clear dissatisfaction with the gender ratio there, with men tending to outnumber women three to one.[134] Nevertheless, Amsterdam was undergoing significant change as both heterosexual and homosexual norms were liberalized, and, as elsewhere, this was particularly so among the young.[135] The city became a destination for young tourists seeking casual sex with other young tourists, such as Matteo Guarnaccia, who at age fifteen hitchhiked there from Milan to "enjoy my own personal summer of love."[136] Noticeably, this was true for homosexual activity as well.

Oscar Moore described a visit to Amsterdam when he was sixteen. He met someone there from Paris, and "I was startled that he held my hand as we walked down the street. I wasn't comfortable with it because I'm not into public displays of affection—typically British—but I still got a thrill out of it, just from the sheer novelty of being able to do it. That was the first inkling I had that these things were possible. But they didn't feel possible in London."[137] Amsterdam had a unique reputation as "Europe's Gayest Capital," where young gay men could not only find sexual partners, but be conspicuous about doing so.[138]

The allure of Amsterdam was more than just sex and drugs; it was also the collection of young people themselves, the "foreign summer colony" of youth.[139] Away from their parents, friends, school, work, and home country, these young people dressed differently, lived differently, and behaved differently than they did at home, distinguishing themselves from the local population and other tourists, and they sought to do so in like company. The use of soft drugs was seen to be a subcultural phenomenon rather than a stepping-stone to hard drugs and addiction.[140] That is, hash smoking in Amsterdam was considered to be a cultural behavior arising out of social relations reflecting the values, norms, and attitudes within this cohort of young travelers.[141] The circulating joint symbolized this sense of community through participation; the shared experience was central to the socially integrating function of the ritual. Still, the social bonds and attachments remained loose and temporary as the young in question sought to live free, independent, highly individualized lives. As one twenty-one-year-old put it, "I can be free here, no paranoia about it. You don't feel that you are doing anything wrong when you turn on."[142]

Despite this emphasis on personalized freedom, however, there was considerable similarity, if not outright conformity, in behavior and outlook, and this freedom was exercised through social activity. As one field study concluded, "the young came especially to Amsterdam because it offered, or seemed to offer, a certain freedom from external restraint and repression, a certain tolerance for deviant forms [of behavior] and some possibilities to live alternatively," and, importantly, this took place among like-minded peers through social encounter.[143] Another study described these weak yet fundamental social relations among the young in Vondelpark as being "together alone."[144] Richard Neville described Amsterdam in 1970 as "a seething European Headopolis where countless wanderers celebrate their exile, smoke pot freely in the clubs Kosmos and Fantasio and, joining forces with the gentle locals, fruitfully multiply into a new community."[145]

In his memoir, Matteo Guarnaccia valued traveling to Amsterdam as an essential personal experience that was "both a pleasure and an obligation. It was a kind of collective initiation," one where you might encounter other young people you had already met in Paris or Rome or Ibiza. But even if it was "a way to discover your own personal myth," it was given meaning only by others. He described Amsterdam alternately as "the holy city of world hippiedom," an "official site in the grand circuit of modern pilgrimage," a "twentieth-century children's crusade," an "enchanted labyrinth," a "frontier space," and a "hippie popular democracy."[146] In his view, the experience was sacred, spiritual, and transcendent, premised on the self but realized in the collective; it was individually liberating, yet socially ritualized.

Two other young Italians give us a somewhat more prosaic perspective. Alberto Camerini and Eugenio Finardi, eighteen and nineteen respectively, did some traveling together around Western Europe in 1970 before heading to the Isle of Wight for a music festival at the end of August. It was important to them to spend some time "in the wonderful and mythic Amsterdam, a city full of hippies, head freaks, and the modern capital of freedom." They stayed in the Rosengracht Sleep-In, where Camerini coupled with a Dutch girl and Finardi a Swedish one, with whom they smoked hash at Dam Square and a few days later tripped on acid while wandering the canals. Camerini wrote of the experience, "we were part of a new nation, as big as the planet earth, without borders, without written laws, inhabiting an invisible state, all equal, all different, all colors, all beautiful, with a thousand foreign tongues but speaking the same language. There was a strong solidarity among those who dressed, lived, traveled and dreamed the same way, we all belonged to Hippie Nation."[147]

Copenhagen soon became an additional destination for this itinerant social group, an alternative to the terrific crush of Amsterdam—something that the Danish city encouraged. With young people starting to show up in large numbers in the summer of 1970, hanging out on the pedestrian Stroeget, overflowing the hostels and sleeping in streets and parks, the Danes quickly set up a working group to study the sleep-ins and evolving policies in the Netherlands. For the summer of 1971, the city offered new arrivals a combination newspaper-map crammed with survival facts, set up sleep-ins in a former warehouse, a school, and a tramway office, and added the Green Camp on the edge of town, a compound of two dozen army tents with twenty-five mattresses packed into each. There, for eighty cents, one could get a bed, a sheet and blanket, gear storage, and a communal hot breakfast served outdoors on long wooden tables.[148] Ali Sahafi, a New Yorker who had come to Europe via Icelandic Airlines, sat at a picnic table among German, French, and Japanese travelers and enthused, "It's starting to happen here: a lot of beautiful people are grooving this way." He had found the permissive attitude to pot, sex, and long hair to his liking. The Green Camp and sleep-ins had no gender segregation; indeed, young men and women often shared not just the same tents, but the same sleeping bags.[149]

In 1970 the Copenhagen youth hostels had hosted 175,000 overnights, but in 1971 the number decreased to 152,000. The municipal sleep-ins hosted an additional 60,000 overnights from May to September, with 35,000 total guests, more than a third of whom stayed at the Green Camp. The guests in the four sleep-ins tended to stay no more than two days on average and came from 116 different countries. Of the total, 22,500 were from Europe, with the top countries of origin being the United States, with 7,300, and West Germany, with 6,000. While the age distribution was wide, the majority were between fifteen and twenty-five, with the older guests coming from the more distant parts of the world, and with the European visitors particularly young, especially those from Scandinavia and West Germany.[150] The city considered the sleep-ins to have been a great success and added a fifth one for the summer of 1972.

Thus in the early 1970s, Copenhagen positioned itself as a friendly rival to Amsterdam as the "It Destination," "Youth Capital," and "Eden to the Love Generation." As in Amsterdam, over the 1970s a dense urban infrastructure developed in Copenhagen of pubs, clubs, shops, and media to serve the growing community of itinerant young people. Much of it took on a political dimension, such as the alternative quasi-commune Freetown Christiania or the "Travelling University," an alternative education model that valued travel as both a source of practical knowledge and a crucial component of personal development.[151] Some were simply passing through to somewhere else, and knew Copenhagen by reputation to be a place worth spending a little time, like Larry Lipin, who stopped on his way to Gothenburg, and fondly recalled the delicious *wienerbrød*, the famous Danish pastry. Even if Copenhagen couldn't compete with Amsterdam's abundant supply of cannabis, it remained a place where "long-haired backpackers" convened, "in large part to meet each other and smoke pot," as the *Hartford Courant* said. The backpackers who gathered there did so because they wanted to be together and because they were made welcome. Sahafi said as much: "We're not running away from anything. We're going toward something, toward a spirit of international language and communication that may bring about a community of peace everywhere."[152]

Sex and Gender

The expansion of mass backpacker tourism in Europe corresponded with what has come to be known as the sexual revolution. The changes in public attitudes that took place in western sexual culture over the 1960s, particularly in the latter half of the decade, were profound. These changes happened earlier in some places, like Sweden, and later in others, like Spain.[153] Still, by the mid-1970s there had been a liberalization of sexual legal codes throughout Western Europe, a pronounced sexualization of pop culture and consumerist advertising, sociological study of sexual norms and the popularization of sexual knowledge, politicization of sex and sexuality as a human right, exponential growth in commercial pornography in the wake of liberalized obscenity laws, and expanded access to contraception, particularly the birth control pill, the reliability of which gave women potential sexual freedom. As access to the pill expanded, young women had the highest usage rates of all. By 1975, for example, nearly 80 percent of West German women under age twenty were on the pill.[154]

The sexual revolution is often associated with the young, and while rates of premarital sex had been on the rise throughout the West since the Second World War, in the 1960s this change in behavior and attitude accelerated and became much more public as young people insisted on their right to sexual expression and sexual practice.[155] The young were often, though not always, central actors in the sexual liberalization of the 1960s. The sexual liberalism of Sweden, for example, has been characterized as a "revolt of heterosexual youth."[156] Already by the mid-1960s, there was considerable demonstrable change in sexual activity by the young. Separate studies of teens in the UK and Italy found that premarital sex was common and that many were not ashamed to admit it. Asked in 1964, "Is it moral to have premarital sex?" Laura, a seventeen-year-old Italian, answered, "Yes," and added, "I don't consider myself immoral: I've done it, perhaps because everybody else does it and perhaps because I believe it's something one ought to do."[157] A late-sixties study of West German twenty- and twenty-one-year-olds found similar results across class and gender: premarital sex was accepted and practiced.[158] Studies in the UK showed the same thing.[159] The average age of first intercourse began to drop rapidly, too, with many young people having sex several years earlier than even their own siblings had. By the early 1970s in West Germany, a third of youth reported having intercourse by age sixteen, and over two-thirds by age twenty.[160]

The practical circumstances of travel have long been a spur to sexual activity, and the association of travel with sexual freedom is long-standing (as the commerce of contemporary sex tourism makes clear). Traveling for sex—male or female, homosexual or heterosexual—has been around as long as travel, it seems. Being abroad presents opportunities for sexual liaisons not readily available or acceptable at home. Indeed, the instructive function of the eighteenth-century Grand Tour for young men was as much sexual initiation as cultural enlightenment. As much as travel might be a rite of passage for the young, extended travel was a way to avoid adulthood and prolong youth, as sex was for pleasure and self-discovery rather than the procreative efforts to build a family. Richard Neville depicted the hippie trail in *Play Power* as a self-indulgent hedonism of sexual experience.[161] In the Soviet Union of the time, "tourist hike" was a euphemism used by young people who were going camping for the weekend in order to have sex.[162] As attitudes changed in 1970s Greece, summer came to be recognized as an acceptable season to deviate from traditional sexual norms; such practice was understood to be an import from foreign tourists.[163] Socio-psychological studies have shown that young people on holiday display situational disinhibition toward sexual activity. That is, they tend to be more willing to engage in casual sexual behavior while away than when at home.[164] As Tony Whitehead from Yorkshire described, "one holiday in about 1968 I met this guy on a train and one thing led incredibly to another, and that's where I lost my virginity." Or Kitty Gadding: "I do like the idea of a zipless fuck. Perfect casual sex. When I was abroad I began to feel: Well, perhaps I can never be faithful to anybody. New bodies, after all, are exciting."[165]

Of course, people had short-term consensual affairs while on holiday prior to the sexual revolution as well. One can anecdotally point out that much of it was transnational in nature, whether on an Austrian ski holiday or a Spanish beach vacation.[166] Françoise Jeannot traveled to Spain in the mid-1950s, when she was in her early twenties, and was smitten with a young Andalusian there, Antonio, with whom she had a love affair. When he later visited her in Paris, she found herself disappointed. She had been very excited for his visit, but was surprised to find that outside the context of being abroad, she was much less interested in him.[167] In 1952, eighteen-year-old Giorgio Lamberti left Orvieto, Italy, and traveled on his own through Scandinavia. In 1947, when Lamberti was thirteen, he had taken part in a Red Cross exchange program that had placed him on a farm near Copenhagen. He returned to visit his Danish "family" in 1952, and then continued his travel independently. His journal betrays a lively, spontaneous spirit who befriended people easily, particularly those his own age. He recorded meeting and making out with numerous young women, like Bente in Denmark, with whom he shared a kiss while riding bicycles, only to end up in a tangled pile on the roadway, or another young woman with whom he frolicked naked in the Norwegian woods.[168] Lamberti's journal brims with a youthful exuberance born of the independent adventure and sexual excitement of self-discovery afforded by mobility. A pop cultural, and much more benign, example of such romantic trysts can be found in the first episode of *The Likely Lads,* a popular BBC sitcom from the mid-1960s that featured two young working-class protagonists returning to their flat in Newcastle-upon-Tyne after their first trip abroad to Spain. As Bob and Terry reminisce about all the girls they met there and the fun they had, they learn that a French girl, Louise, has followed them back to England—although it turns out that she is not quite what she seems.[169]

A 1963 study of young lower-middle-class Germans on vacation in Catania, Sicily, described their holiday as swinging wildly between lazily "bumming around" and an ardent "Carnival" where immediate gratification was the rule. They talked openly of sex, and they seemingly coupled with abandon.[170] The study created quite a response in West German pedagogical circles, where the educational value of travel for the young had been championed for years. There was considerable outrage at the hedonism described, and many suggested that independent, unchaperoned travel by the young should no longer be encouraged.[171]

In 1967, a journalist at Barbonia City was interviewing a young Italian woman when she saw a young man and ran to give him a hug and kiss. She returned saying, "He is English. He slept in my tent last night. I had never seen him before, and I won't meet him again, but it's been wonderful." A nineteen-year-old young man from Bologna described meeting Carmen, "a blonde, lovely good figure, the type I fancy. She's exquisite. We were necking all day and got totally turned on. So in the evening we went out into the fields to make love."[172] In the early 1980s, a twenty-two-year-old German who was climbing into the sleeping bag of a young woman in Sweden put it this way: "with so many strangers to sleep with in such a short time, travel enables contact."[173]

European travel was increasingly being represented and understood to be an opportunity for sex. Expectations were often high. As Bill Bryson recounted about his first trip to Europe as a young man in 1972, "In the long, exciting weeks preceding the flight I had sustained myself, I confess, with a series of bedroom-ceiling fantasies that generally involved finding myself seated next to a panting young beauty being sent by her father against her wishes to the Lausanne Institute for Nymphomaniacal

Disorders, who would turn to me somewhere over [the] mid-Atlantic and say, 'Forgive me, but would it be all right if I sat on your face for a while?' "[174] Alice Kaplan recalled that freedom, or *liberté*, while studying abroad "meant liberty to have sex, and life in France without sex was inconceivable to me."[175] A 1972 *Harper's Magazine* article found the whole thing to be a process of democratization: "It's no accident that Arthur Frommer, the Pill, and the credit card are simultaneous phenomena. Everybody deserves everything. . . . Screwing for everybody and Europe for everybody too. This is the egalitarian key to a proper understanding of *Europe on $5 a Day*," it said.[176] In the 1968 movie *If It's Tuesday, This Must Be Belgium*, Bert and Steve have a friendly exchange as they imagine their upcoming trip: "Let's say that I hook up with one chick in each country. Just one. Ah, I hope I have enough stamina." "Bert, baby, you don't even score in this country." "This is Europe, Steve, *everybody* scores in Europe!"[177] In the UK, Matthew Russell recalled this about the sixties: "one day you're at public school then suddenly there are all these American chicks who would fuck you."[178] In Spain, twenty-three-year old Pedro Nuñez said, "Foreign girls are easy, they come here for a good time and they'll do anything."[179] As such sentiment makes clear, European youth travel had become a space of male sexual privilege, as the complaints of Paul Cuneo from Los Angeles also show: "three episodes of wopping prick-teasing (even in bed) with American females, and I'd had it. Then I met Lucie and things changed. But she was Swiss, which made a considerable difference."[180] American men eroticized European women, while European men did the same to American women. Dutch men saw France—especially Paris—as a place of erotic opportunity; for the British, it was Italy, and for the Italians, Scandinavia. And so it goes. Such sexual imaginings of foreign travel shaped expectations and structured experiences, and, of course, gendered them as well, though certainly sexual fantasy and experience was not limited to men.[181]

Ed Buryn felt that he needed to temper expectations a bit in his underground guidebook: "This is for men. Getting laid in Europe by a genuine European lass is not going to be easy." However, he pointed out that it would be easier to accomplish in Northern Europe than in the south; and importantly, there was "another outlet." Despite Paul Cuneo's experience, Buryn recommended that "sexual success is much likelier if you stick to the American girls traveling in Europe. Like you, they are eager to spice their European adventure with the salt of sex, and the resultant action is heavy." For women he had different advice: "American women traveling in Europe have the reputation of being easy lays and of having money," he said, so they should be careful and be wary.

Nevertheless, he insisted, "part of the excitement of travel and vaga-bonding is unquestionably a sexual excitement, so don't try to repress it out of existence."[182] As Buryn's advice suggests, young women were told to avoid behavior and activities that might attract sexual predators but also not to be so frigid as to foreclose the possibility of sexual encounter. Women travelers in Greece might be subjected to the practice of *kamaki*, whereby local young men in coastal and island resort areas would ag-gressively flirt with the "liberated" women of Northern Europe in pur-suit of sexual encounter that the men envisaged as a predatory conquest of the poor over the rich.[183]

This was a difficult route for young women to navigate. Delly Kauf-mann from New York found that she could make the aggressive atten-tion work in her favor. She found getting rides while hitchhiking in Southern Europe much easier than in the north, since "the men are really trying to make American and N. European women, because there is a myth about their sexual liberality."[184] Yet this doesn't discount the very real danger of sexual assault to young women, such as the case of a young Brazilian hitchhiker who was brutally raped in Belgium in 1976.[185] There was also the famous incident in which two young Belgian women were raped by three local young men while encamped near Mar-seilles in August 1974. The case became a *cause célèbre* in France, where it was central to a feminist campaign highlighting the unjust cultural acceptability of rape, the inadequate legal codes, and the lack of pros-ecutorial zeal with regard to rapists.[186]

The case highlights the ways in which youth travel had been sexu-alized and gendered with a patriarchal heteronormativity that sought to challenge and constrain the freedom and mobility of young women. Having done some traveling in Spain, the two Belgians, a lesbian couple, were headed to a nudist colony. The defense lawyer for the men por-trayed two worlds coming into conflict: that of the young, macho Medi-terranean and that of the independent, liberated women of the north accustomed to the freedom to hitchhike, travel, and camp on their own without male companionship. The young men, he said, had simply mis-interpreted this liberation as consent, while the young women knew that their freedom came with significant risk.[187] What is particularly interest-ing about the case is that the fact that the young women were indepen-dent travelers was used both to defend and condemn the young men. The defense attorney dismissed the whole affair as an understandable, if regrettable, "vacation prank," while one of the victims testified that one rapist had declared with male authority, "Two girls alone on vacation need to spend [it] with men."[188] In Canada, judges were known to dismiss sexual assault charges involving drivers and female hitchhikers along the Trans-Canada Highway; one emphasized explicitly that he did so because young women invited molestation by the very act of hitchhiking.[189]

Given the history of underreporting for rape, it is likely impossible to know how many similar cases there may have been. It seems safe to assume, given the scale of youth travel and the way in which it had been sexualized, that there were many more. Nor can we measure or quantify the consensual sexual activity. Despite the anecdotal evidence presented in this chapter (and much that is not included), certainly not everyone was having sex while traveling, even among those who desired it. Still, sexual desire and agency gave meaning to the practices of independent travel, helping to further gender mobility. Think, for example, of the gendered moral geography implied by the term "tramp," which for men carried suspect class connotations but for women entailed a sexualized reproach. Historically, vagrancy legal codes defined tramps explicitly as men, whereas women's equivalent mobility was associated with sexual impropriety, legally defining them as prostitutes.[190]

The association of the freedom of travel with young men's sexual liberality was evident in the novels *Philip and the Others*, *Out of the Shelter*, *Absolute Beginners*, and *On the Road*, as well as the travelogues *I, Jan Cremer* and *Play Power*, and the films *Summer Holiday*, *More*, and *Going Places*. Directed by Bertrand Blier, *Going Places* is reminiscent of the debased machismo depicted by Jan Cremer in his autobiographical novel. The 1974 hit film, which made Gérard Depardieu a star, is a black comedy about two young sociopaths on the loose in France. While the main characters are not backpackers, the film portrays masculine youthful mobility as a sexual menace for women—old or young, willing or unwilling. Kenneth Allsop, in his 1972 denunciation of youth travel in *Punch*, emphasized the implicit sexual danger posed by men, both homosexual and heterosexual, when he quoted "a couple of ex-Eurobums in their early twenties" as saying that young male backpackers should anticipate "having to fight off queers with flick-knives" (switchblades), and that young women needed to avoid "realistic bad scenes . . . like being mauled by a lorry driver at 60 mph and then dumped in the middle of nowhere."[191]

While independent youth travel was gendered male, study abroad, by contrast, had a strong female cast; over the twentieth century, increasingly more young women than men participated in its structured configuration of foreign experience, which, accordingly, had been designed with specific gendered protocols.[192] Throughout the second half of the century, young women studying abroad outnumbered men by nearly two to one, and this remains true today.[193] Thus, by the 1970s, conventional wisdom suggested that girls studied abroad and boys back-packed. Still, the gendering of independent youth travel probably resulted less from the greater numbers of young men than women who traveled in such fashion, and more from the extent to which a masculine normative framework defined this form of travel. This was true even though drifter backpacking was in many ways a rejection of traditionally respectable masculinity. European backpacker travel offered not only a physical space within which young men, unattached and away from home, could fulfill their desire for romantic, heroic adventure, but also a cultural space within which young, rugged masculinity could be elaborated, sexual and otherwise.[194] The numerical advantage of men to women was maintained, no doubt in part, by the threat of sexual danger that men posed to young women. This was clearly evident in guide-books that gave specific warnings to young women about the risks of independent travel. The gendered dimensions were part of the experience for women, as Vicki Hedtke wrote in a letter to Ed Buryn: "There was such a definite male slant to your book. . . . interesting but I had to take it with a grain of salt. You couldn't possibly know how deeply this gap separates the experiences of a guy on the road alone and a girl trying to get along the same way on her own."[195] Being on one's own, the autonomous individual detached from home and family, living and moving about independently, denoted different meanings and experiences depending on gender.

Still, the self-empowering, liberating effect of travel worked on young women, too, who often cited precisely this rationale for backpacking around Europe. The androgyny of the gear, grittiness, and demeanor was a self-conscious form of emancipation, as young women considered mobility through backpacking or hitchhiking to be a declaration of independence from stay-at-home domesticity.[196] As one young American woman stated simply, "I feel more confident in Europe."[197] Particularly since traveling without a man would mean there was no male authority to take charge, make decisions, and determine outcomes, backpacking in Europe was seen as a training ground for adult autonomy; it was its own form of women's liberation. In a 1972 article for the *Boston Globe* entitled "For the Single Girl, the Best Way to See Europe Is Alone," Carol Orsborn pointed out that "going the hitching-hostelling route assures the single girl of a deluge of companions, partners and would-be lovers." Over three months, Orsborn traveled with twelve different people, mostly men, whom she had met along the way. She claimed to have "met an incredible number of girls whose main topic of conversation was 'which country's males make love better,' " though she found her own sex life "much more conservative abroad than at home," despite, or perhaps because of, the frequent harassment of catcalls and pinches, particularly in Spain and Italy. Ultimately, she recommended traveling alone because "there is no place in the world . . . you can go to escape yourself. If you take this guide's advice, walking the tightrope without fear of the hard times and slip ups, you will return home with a great deal more knowledge and understanding of the world, and of yourself."[198]

Narrativity of Self and Rites of Passage

By the mid-twentieth century, vacation time had come to mean a time apart, a time away in a space where patterns of behavior were disrupted, where fantasy and desire could be expressed through a consumerist culture of distraction during a delimited, often quite brief, period of time.[199] Independent youth travel was a step beyond a beach holiday or family vacation in duration, itinerary, and motivation. The prolonged improvisational nature of independent youth travel helped to emphasize the continuity of self amid the ongoing contextual flux of people and place. As Cees Nooteboom observed, "Traveling . . . is something you have to learn. It is a constant transaction with others in the course of which you are simultaneously alone."[200] The individual trajectory of arrivals and departures, of movements and passages, of circulations and flows, of encounters and exchanges, produced individualized narratives generated within a loose associative collective. Novelties, souvenirs, photographs, journals, diaries, postcards, and patches or national flags on backpacks all convey personal narratives while emphasizing the social position of the traveler. An individual's vacation narratives serve to legitimize and make sense of experience and define the self.[201] Such individual understandings of experience interact with the prescriptive narratives of novels, memoirs, guidebooks, journalism, films, and music that did so much to set the terms that had defined youth travel. Though backpackers might move toward or with the crowd, their experiences were mediated individually. Backpacking was a means of detachment and attachment; it created individuals as it created communities.

As Orsborn indicated in her 1972 article, telling stories about one's travels, which might include sexual experiences, was common. For all the ways in which this form of travel was about the self, it was premised on sociability, on sharing the experience, however temporarily, with others. Very often this sharing with others took the form of autobiographical storytelling in hostels, in cars, on trains, or while waiting for transport, when one might share where one had been and what one had done, or make recommendations and issue warnings. Such storytelling is most directly demonstrated by the published work of Jack Kerouac, Nicolas Bouvier, Jan Cremer, Bernward Vesper, Philippe Gloaguen, Matteo Guarnaccia, Richard Neville, and Cees Nooteboom, American, Swiss, Dutch, German, French, Italian, and Anglo-Australian men. The lack of published female equivalents from the era speaks to how the story of independent youth travel, if western and transnational, was gendered male.

The narrativity of self has been studied among contemporary Israeli backpackers and in how they envision their treks—before, during, and after—as personal development negotiated within gendered norms. Among middle-class Israelis, backpacking to Asia or South America has become a self-imposed and socially sanctioned rite of passage following obligatory military service for both men and women. One of the main motivations for Israeli backpacking is to play with identity construction, to test and perhaps transform the self through personal experience, before returning home as an adult, ready for work and family.[202] The completion of the journey is associated with the completion of the self.

Likewise, in the late 1960s and 1970s, backpacking in Europe was often considered a self-imposed, if communally sanctioned, rite of passage. European youth travel was a chance for personal growth and a search for personal meaning offered by the dislocation of being away from friends, family, home, school, work, and social and institutional obligations. An exercise in autonomy, this form of travel was consciously imagined as a means by which an independent transformation of the self could be performed and narrated. A young British tramp of the 1960s had this to say about the revelatory nature of such dislocation: "It gave me a clue to the insubstantiality of identity. . . . I learned to distinguish self from identity. If you like, to distinguish what I more or less always am from all the things I am temporarily said to be."[203]

Rites of passage are traditionally highly formalized rituals defining an individual or group's change in social status. They most often have ceremonial aspects, as defined and required by the community, and they nearly always have gendered dimensions. The most common rites of passage mark the transition from youth to adulthood and are meant to empower the individual through challenging personal development leading toward adult responsibility and status. The classic formulation of this socialization as defined by Arnold van Gennep includes three stages: separation, liminality, and incorporation. In the first stage, separation, the individual is detached from his or her fixed social position and set adrift outside the formal social hierarchy. The second stage is the period of transition, when the individual's social position is in flux on the margins. The third stage is the return, when the individual reenters society with a new social position. Clearly, we can see these elements present in how young people and others viewed their international travel experience through Europe as it developed in the late 1960s and 1970s. Importantly, however, it was an informal, independent, highly individualized experience. Those who participated did so voluntarily, attributing this meaning to their travels on their own, without the necessary approval, requirement, or sanction of the larger society. Indeed, many in Europe disapproved of this experience and condemned those undertaking it, though as we have seen, there also had been considerable promotion of the personal benefits of international travel for the young since the Second World War, and many millions had done it.

The scale of participation in what seemed to be a new mass phenomenon attracted sociological attention. One of the first and more influential essays was by Erik Cohen, who saw the new drifter tourist as "predominantly a child of affluence on a prolonged moratorium from adult, middle-class responsibility, seeking spontaneous experiences in the excitement of complete strangeness."[204] Cohen pointed out that it was an overwhelmingly European phenomenon with a growing number of Americans, Canadians, and Australians, while the trajectories of drifter tourism were expanding far beyond Western Europe, and the number of working-class drifters was on the rise, too. Cohen emphasized this drifter tourism as an expression of alienation with strong connections to the counterculture and drugs. In his view, the young were running away or escaping from something.

Jay Vogt responded by arguing something more benign, that the main motivation among young "wanderers" was the quest for personal growth "achieved through autonomy in decision-making, stimulation in daily life, learning through exposure and detachment, and transient yet intense personal relationships."[205] Others explicitly referred to this arduous, self-testing tourism as a voluntary rite of passage, taken up in part because modern society offered so few satisfactory rites to mark major life changes.[206] Reflecting on the personal impact of their travels from more than a decade earlier, Americans Alexandra Marshall and James Carroll noted approvingly, "As our ticket—our pass—to the great monuments of Europe, Eurail made possible a hip, democratic version of that classic initiation rite, the grand tour."[207] The eighteenth-century Grand Tour was often invoked in both the popular press and academic journalism, where it was noted that the contemporary practice of travel for self-improvement marked a democratization of the Grand Tour from the aristocracy to the middle class—a sort of trickle-down tourism.[208]

Judith Adler persuasively argued that instead of being viewed as a democratized elite tradition, the contemporary road culture of youth travel ought to be seen as an upwardly rather than downwardly mobile cultural form. That is, tramping was a well-established, institutionalized form of travel for the young working class. Historically, it took the form of the journeyman's *tour de France* or *Wanderjahr,* and though structured as a Western European system of labor and occupational advancement, it was also a ritual separation from home and family, offering young men an opportunity for travel, adventure, and education as they worked their way through the labor circuit—living on the cheap, drifting from place to place, sometimes alone, sometimes with others, sometimes hitching rides, sometimes taking trains, while finding lodging and food in hostels established for them along the most traveled routes.[209]

The independent youth travel of the 1970s had its roots in both the aristocratic gentleman's Grand Tour and the working-class journeyman's tour. On the one hand, as with the Grand Tour, the impulse was self-improvement through long-term mobile leisure and sociability with others, while on the other hand it took the form of minimalist self-deprivation, living and traveling as cheaply as possible. Carrying all one's material goods in a rucksack, hitchhiking, and sleeping in the rough— these practices resonate with the working-class tramping of the eighteenth and nineteenth centuries. The social dislocation as a rite of passage marking the transition to adulthood through European travel, by coming of age sexually and otherwise, was redolent of both traditions that formalized class-specific and gendered transitions in social status from youth to adult.

In the mid-1980s, psychologist Rainer Schönhammer led studies of youth backpacker tourism that sought to explore it as a transitional stage on the way to adulthood. The researchers, who interviewed and surveyed a few hundred young people from a dozen countries in hostels and railway stations as they passed through Bavaria, concluded that these young travelers were in part motivated by a need to expand their "region of free movement" and widen their "life space" beyond adult control and supervision. Youth travel provided them with independent mobility beyond the boundaries of their life space into unknown and unfamiliar spaces, which offered freedom but posed risks. As such, they constituted a "tremendous international peer group which provides a feeling of familiarity among a world of strangers." Their feelings of solidarity or mutual empathy were understood to be a way of coping "with the ambivalence of free movement in a strange space."[210] That is, this communal sociability was a fundamental component in defining and enabling the experience.

The first of Schönhammer's studies, in 1984, conducted in youth hostels, asked participants to narrate their personal experiences with foreign peoples and cultures by writing compositions. One young British man wrote, "Although traveling alone, I have never spent one minute without companionship of some kind: in trains, buses, ships, railway and bus stations; but above all, youth hostels have provided me with friends and conversation from all corners of the world. Youth hostels have matured my mind, they have shown me many nationalities operating together under one roof." A young Canadian woman wrote, "Whether traveling alone or with friends, there is nothing more special than sharing a part of your journey with a new friend. After all, it is not only the countries that we want to see when we travel, it is especially the people." The foreign people that these young people encountered and interacted with the most were other young tourists from elsewhere rather than people from the host country.[211]

Despite the language differences, which could create social barriers, one young British man wrote, "what did 'bind' us together was a common interest in travel, seeing different places and meeting different people. . . . it has surprised me how easily people from so many nations can come together and communicate."[212] A young British woman wrote that always "there is a rapport between fellow travelers that allows me to strike up a conversation with other young people: far more easily perhaps than one could in one's own country. Some days nearly all the people you meet seem to be 'inter-railing' their way around Europe. It's not only interesting but also very useful to be able to exchange tips and information or swap experiences with other people. There's almost a feeling of solidarity—'We are all in this together: for better or for worse.' But although informative and educational, the conversation is almost always purely factual, which means at the end of an hour or two one still scarcely knows them any better."[213] Fluent conversations between travelers with different native languages were rare. Instead, a multilingual pidgin was often employed, as groups would converse through limited vocabularies of several languages.[214]

Eurobarometer focused two studies on Young Europeans in 1987 and 1990. They found that for the young, a fear of language difficulty was the primary obstacle to foreign travel, even more so than adequate funding, yet over 70 percent of all European Community youth between the ages of fifteen and twenty-four had traveled abroad. Ninety percent had studied a foreign language. Sixty-six percent of the EC young had studied English as a foreign language, as compared to 33 percent of adults; 42 percent of the young had studied French, as compared to 24 percent of adults; German and Spanish were the third and fourth most studied foreign languages. Among the young, roughly 40 percent could carry on a conversation in English, 20 percent in French, and 10 percent in German. Young women learned more languages than young men; Northern European youth learned more languages than Southern European youth; and the affluent learned more languages than the poor. The number of foreign languages that young people could speak was highly correlated with the number of months spent abroad; yet regardless of where they traveled, the primary foreign language spoken by young travelers was English. The studies concluded that although there was a strong correlation between foreign travel and competency in a foreign language, there was no clear correlation between the actual countries visited by young people and their linguistic prowess.[215]

In Amsterdam, alternative newspapers such as *Together* and *Use It Weekly* initially published in four languages, but by the mid-1970s, they began to publish only in English, because "it was the spoken language among young people who visit Amsterdam."[216] Ed Buryn recommended that young Americans brush up on their high school French, German, or Spanish before heading to Europe. Any little bit of foreign language would be helpful, he wrote, but one could usually expect to find young Europeans who knew some English. He also said that the best foreign language to know was German, since young Germans could be found in the travel network all over Europe.[217] Still, English fell short of being a lingua franca for the backpacker circuit. Though it was the most commonly used language among young travelers, only half could speak it, and their levels of proficiency varied widely. Language wasn't merely an instrument of communication, but rather a system of crossed usages at multiple levels; stumbling through language barriers was part of the practice of travel as translation. Even though language was the primary factor of exclusion in small group encounters in hostels or trains, Schönhammer concluded that the struggle to overcome language barriers itself contributed to young travelers' consciousness of being a peer group. Exchanging contact information was a common practice to solidify communal feeling, but because actually maintaining contact was so rare, it was also indicative of just how weak such bonds were, particularly if they involved a foreign language.[218] A 1983 study of European youth exchange programs revealed, for example, that correspondence exchanged after visits tended to be between young people from the same country rather than across linguistic barriers.[219]

Sometimes, however, the correspondence might be maintained for several years, as was the case with Michael Hai Young Chiang. After graduating from Singapore University in 1979, Chiang spent three months backpacking in Europe, using his brother's apartment in Bonn as a kind of base camp: "From Germany, I used a Eurail pass, just as everybody else does, to catch a train, go to as many places as possible, and stay in as cheap accommodation as I could find." Using *Europe on $10 a Day*, he "obediently" went to see the recommended sights. He traveled up through Scandinavia and down through Italy to Greece, then over to France and the United Kingdom. Although he was by himself, "it was exhilarating for me to suddenly be out there, doing this trip that I'd been aching to do for so many years." He found it easy to meet people, especially other backpackers, with whom he would travel for a day or two. He said, "It was quite a nice feeling to feel that there were quite a lot of like-minded people and [that] you had a lot in common with them." He remained in contact with a couple from Australia and a young woman from New York for several years afterward.[220]

For all the ways in which this travel was independent, it was a learned social practice with ritualized forms of activity and meaning defined by the sociability of group membership. While Erik Cohen described the drifters' "escapism" as "hedonistic and often anarchistic," he acknowledged that there remained a strong camaraderie among them.[221] Jay Vogt, who otherwise largely disagreed with Cohen, pointed out that "among the most significant patterns in wandering . . . is the tendency to establish gathering and resting places."[222] Backpacker tourism was a communal activity, and as such had the markings of a loose, associational community of practice.

The term "community" tends to evoke self-identified groups of rich emotional ties within a bounded space of local connectedness, physical proximity, and common language, characteristics that these backpackers did not really share. In the last decade, "communities of practice" has been used as a conceptual tool to examine the process of globalization, particularly regarding business, economics, governance, and learning. A concept popularized by Etienne Wenger, communities of practice are defined as informal communities of individuals with a collective identity that emerges from practical activities and recognition of shared interests, which may or may not translate into strong cognitive or affective ties. Indeed, communities of practice tend to have a weak sense of belonging; the community arises out of common routine more than self-identification. Though full consensus among community members is not necessary, there should be a shared "we" consciousness that transcends differences of one kind or another. Transnational communities of practice remain fluid, relational constructs that are mobile and in flux as members are bound across borders through their shared practices. Moreover, associational membership within a community of practice is often of limited duration; it doesn't imply or require equal involvement or investment, and, at the same time, members remain embedded and rooted in other, more stable, communities.[223]

Communities of practice have highly dispersed memberships, with the social glue holding them together consisting of a repertoire of shared practices, routines, behaviors, and discourses. There is a sense of joint enterprise even if motivations and goals may differ. They are open to outsiders, who become part of the community through the development of knowledge and practical skill sets.[224] As with Benedict Anderson's "imagined communities," the sense of belonging and the associated meaning can vary significantly between members. While a French hostel warden described the young Americans who passed through his hostel as individual rather than group travelers—"adventuresome wanderers in search of something they have not yet found"—European backpackers held two complementary judgments about the effect the large number of young Americans had had on the international peer group of travelers.[225] On the one hand, the sociability of the "easygoing American" was a catalyst for the formation of group feeling and togetherness, while on the other hand, the perceived "superficiality" of Americans was thought to prevent a deeper affective engagement from developing.[226]

Others, like journalist Fabrizio Abbate, were amazed by the European and American youth who gathered in and around Rome in the 1970s. Abbate found their ability to associate with one another in impermanent and transitory ways to be one of their most interesting and distinguishing characteristics. He admired their communal "plasticity," the way they could easily join together and dissolve according to social activity and personal regard.[227] The fusionable and fissionable quality of such group dynamics was one of its primary characteristics. As Eric Leed has written, "the force of mobility is a source of both solidarity and detachment, a cement and a solvent of human association."[228]

In Amsterdam, some among the Dutch saw the arrival of masses of foreign young as a harbinger of change. In the mid-1960s, Dutch artist Constant Nieuwenhuys advocated a "New Babylon," a utopian city for a new, nomadic man, a *homo ludens*, where humankind would free itself from labor and devote itself to travel, adventure, and creativity, or, in short, to play. To Nieuwenhuys, the arrival of the young in Amsterdam in the late sixties and early seventies signaled that they might be the ones to lead such a play-filled society. They had come, he felt, to pursue "communal initiatives" and "collective endeavors . . . for it is not silence and solitude that the young are after, but encounters with others in a social environment."[229] Gerard Haas referred to them as an invading army seeking the "international center of the magical sixties."[230] *Use It Weekly* said, "Amsterdam can only be compared to a kind of place of pilgrimage. Like Lourdes, with Vondelpark and Paradiso as sacred places, and dope as a kind of miraculous water."[231] Former Provo Simon Vinkenoog felt that Amsterdam had become "a cosmopolitan village" for the young; it was "an asylum, a place of refuge" for European youth seeking freedom. The city should welcome them because they were putting Amsterdam at the center of "a new European renaissance."[232]

Indeed, though we see here enthusiastic hyperbole, there is no question that the young travelers flocking to Amsterdam like "migratory birds" were having an effect on the cultural ecosystem.[233] This helped change Amsterdam in significant ways—the growth of tourism, the fame and reputation of the city, the drug commerce—for decades to come. The number of young backpackers grew exponentially and helped set the city on a new course, one that altered the urban experience, as immigration and popular democracy political movements and globalized capitalism have also done. Similarly, we can imagine the impact these young travelers had on Western Europe as a whole.

At the same time that the formal structure of political and economic integration (ECSC, EEC, Euratom) was deepened following its 1967 transformation into the European Communities (EC) and broadened with the addition of new member states in the 1970s (Denmark, Ireland, the UK), each year a growing number of young independent travelers, joined by millions of Americans, set their own agendas and moved at their own pace, often without plans or intentions, outside the structured experiences of cultural exchange but within a highly gendered context that was framed by a paradigm of self-discovery through travel adventure.[234] The young backpacker with a Eurail or Interrail pass or hitchhiking along the roadways had emerged as a discernible cultural phenomenon. This kind of travel was a learned behavior premised on particular activities, methods, and motives, and these young people, wittingly or not, became members of a community of practice that transcended the national boundaries across Western Europe, even beyond those of the EC, through their adopted habits of travel. As such, they created common patterns throughout Western Europe through their mobility and social activity as they participated in a kind of rite of passage of their own design. Distributed throughout Western Europe, from Scandinavia to the Mediterranean, young backpackers, drawn together through common routine, had created their own community interconnecting the western half of the continent and supported by an integrated infrastructure of hostel systems, rail passes, and social practices.

FIVE

East of the Wall, South of the Sea

I arrived in Berlin with my 1990 summer traveling companion, Mike Quinn, using our Eurail youth passes to cross through what was, for only a short while longer, East Germany. I'm still not sure whether we paid a legitimate surcharge or a bribe to a rail conductor who visited our cabin in the middle of the night to check passports and tickets; I think the latter since we got no receipt in return. We spent three days in Berlin, exploring the east side and the west side, even renting sledgehammers by the minute to break off pieces of the Berlin Wall, much of it already gone, to bring home. We had come to Berlin after visiting Prague, and Budapest before that. This was the first summer season of backpacking since Eastern Europe had opened up to travelers after the extraordinary events of 1989. Budapest, Prague, and Berlin were struggling to accommodate the new summer influx of young western travelers, and in each city we ended up finding accommodations with locals who solicited arriving backpackers at the main train stations.

The contrast between East and West in these cities was still clear, of course, but from our vantage point, the infrastructure in place to accommodate budget travelers like us was perhaps most noticeable: the daily grind of finding lodging, food, local transport, tourist sites, rail tickets, and visas for the next destination (still required in these countries), with little English available in print or in person, proved to be noticeably more difficult. Also noticeable was how cheap everything was, especially the great beer in Prague. Still, the

26   About 350,000 attended Roger Waters's performance of *The Wall* in Potsdamer Platz, Berlin, 21 July 1990. The dilapidated Reichstag can be seen behind. Bundesarchiv, Bild 183-1990-0722-402/photo: Robert Roeske.

lack of a full-scale tourist infrastructure gave these cities a charm that was lacking in the West, while the sense of revolutionary change underway gave them a charged excitement. Mike and I were nearing the end of our two-month summer travels, and to conclude the trip, after Berlin, we had plans to meet two friends with whom we had traveled earlier in the summer, Larissa and Natalie, for some beachfront rest and relaxation at the Pink Palace in Corfu, Greece, a renowned party spot we had heard about repeatedly along the backpacker circuit.

What had brought us to Berlin at this exact time was a rock concert. Roger Waters of Pink Floyd was going to be performing his magnum opus *The Wall* in its entirety. We had heard of the show from other backpackers and bought our concert tickets in June at a record store in Bregenz, Austria. *The Wall* had not been performed in nearly a decade, and only twenty-nine times in total. Since then Waters had left Pink Floyd and once declared that he would mount the show again only if and when the Berlin Wall came down. Pink Floyd's *The Wall* was one of the best-selling albums of all time (by 1990 it had sold nearly twenty million copies, and by 2015 some thirty million). The 1979 double album had been followed by a trippy 1982 film directed by Alan Parker and starring Bob Geldof as Pink, a lonely and tormented rock star who eventually summons the will to break down the psychological wall he has built between himself, his audience, and the world. With fascistic overtones, the rock opera resonates with oppression and liberation, though without any sort of specific commentary on, or connection to, the Cold War or Berlin. Yet over the 1980s, Pink Floyd's *The Wall* had become a pop culture marker conflating Cold War allegory and western youth culture; Waters played on these symbolic forms in the concert itself.

For one night only, on 21 July 1990, a mere nine months after the fall of the Berlin Wall, Roger Waters staged a performance of *The Wall* to a crowd of about 350,000 people in what had been Potsdamer Platz. Prior to the Second World War, Potsdamer Platz had been the nerve center of the Berlin metropolis, where roadways and railways intersected to form a large square in the middle of the city. Allied bombing obliterated the area, and the Cold War division of Berlin bisected the wasteland. It became a no-man's-land of barbed wire and minefields later bifurcated by the Berlin Wall. Thus *The Wall* was performed in the very center of Berlin, in what had been the heart of the unified city but was now a vast empty space that could accommodate a large production while symbolically straddling the former pathway of the Berlin Wall. It took more than two months to prepare the site and build the set. Upon arrival, concertgoers could see a large pile of World War II–era bombs, rocket launchers, grenades, mines, and a hundred thousand rounds of ammunition, all dug out of the ground to clear the area and make it safe for passage. This created a wide, flat swath of dirt, and with a few hundred thousand people milling about for a few hours in the dry July heat, a dust cloud enveloped and clung to us all.[1]

Reportedly one of the biggest stages ever built, the massive structure was six hundred feet long and sixty feet high, consisting of a wall made of twenty-five hundred large plastic foam bricks, which was completed as the show progressed, obscuring the musicians behind it. Flanking each side of the stage were two six-story-high stacks of loudspeakers. The colossal production had a cast of over three hundred, including the Marching Band of the Combined Soviet Forces and the East Berlin Rundfunk Symphony Orchestra, a flyover by military helicopters, and massive tower cranes hoisting fifty-foot-high inflatable pig and schoolmaster puppets. The gargantuan spectacle featured at one point dozens of commandos rappelling down the facade of the wall, a convoy of armored personnel carriers, and marching soldiers carrying banners in a mock fascist rally.

Without Pink Floyd, Waters invited a host of musicians to help perform the songs, including the Scorpions, Sinead O'Connor, Joni Mitchell, Bryan Adams, Cyndi Lauper, and Van Morrison, the last of whom gave a stirring rendition of "Comfortably Numb." As the show reached its climax, artistic graffiti from the Berlin Wall was projected onto the vast expanse of the white stage wall, with the crowd surging forward, chanting, "Tear down the wall! Tear down the wall!" as the large foam bricks tumbled and cascaded down into a massive pile of rubble, revealing the musicians behind.

The windows and rooftops of nearby buildings teemed with people as every available space seemed to be jammed with spectators. The concert was broadcast live on television to thirty-five countries, with a purported audience of nearly one billion. The event was sold out at 250,000 tickets, but the crowds outside the security fence became so large that the producers opened the gates to them, too. They had come from all over Europe and beyond. Thousands had pitched tents and camped out near the concert site. Angelika Arnold, a thirty-year-old East German, commented that she used to watch concerts like this on West German television, and that the fall of the wall had made not only the concert possible, but, more importantly, her ability to attend it. Rimas Vaitaitis, a young American of Lithuanian lineage, had come from Denver and saw the concert as a fitting culmination to his summer backpacking tour of Eastern Europe.[2] By 1990, youth, travel, and rock music had a long association in Europe. Indeed, they seemed to be mutually constitutive.

The celebrated Spanish filmmaker Pedro Almodóvar recalled in an interview that when the young foreign tourists began to arrive in the early 1970s, all kinds of cultural products from abroad began to arrive in Spain with them. "You can't imagine how important the music was to us. . . . For a Spanish boy in the '70s, London meant freedom," he said. "It came in a very surreptitious way . . . it started seeping in, from Paris and London. During the last five years of the dictator's life [1970–75], we started to be a part of Europe."[3] Backpackers like American Larry Lipin, who were drawn to Spain in part because of the excitement of a perceived liberation underway, found that Spain was already incorporated into the larger western youth culture of mobility and music. As was the case elsewhere in Western Europe, "music was the cultural capital that everyone shared. Wherever you went, music was a kind of lingua franca, always in the background, always in the bars, like a soundtrack."[4] For Ian Coburn from Edinburgh, his first significant independent travel was to London as a teenager for the sole purpose of visiting the Rough Trade record shop, where rare and imported albums could be procured in the late seventies. This, in turn, led to travel to festivals and concerts, which eventually gave him the confidence to travel abroad on the continent.[5] There were Deadheads, fans who made a ritual of following the Grateful Dead around on their European tours, the first of which resulted in what many consider to be their best live album, *Europe '72*. In Italy, rock 'n' roll was initially known as *musica urlato,* or "scream music," and blue jeans as "transatlantic trousers"; one of the first of the Italian youth movies was *I ragazzi dei juke-box* (The jukebox boys).[6] A couple of decades later, Italian Fabio Maggioni found that he could quickly make friends and find travel companions by talking about Bruce Springsteen as he moved from hostel to hostel through Ireland in the 1980s.[7]

This was true in Eastern Europe, too. Some former young activists from the 1968 era have conceded that their attraction to the materials of western consumer society—jeans, parkas, records, magazines, literature—was as important in the long run to generating feelings of commonality and solidarity across the Iron Curtain as were reformist political programs.[8] The Russian playwright David Gurevich recalled, "Rock & roll was the battering ram that the West drove into our collective psyche. Then everything else rushed in: art, fashion, books, and, sometimes, politics."[9] In May 1974, fifteen-year-old Andrei Vadimov wrote in his diary about a class trip to the city of L'viv in western Ukraine, where foreign travelers were welcome. He came from the closed city of Dnipropetrovsk, where they were not. The highlights of his trip to L'viv were meeting Canadian and American tourists "speaking real English, my favorite language, the tongue of the Beatles, the Rolling Stones, and Deep Purple," and going to the local black market, where he bought a new record, the rock opera *Jesus Christ Superstar,* from some Polish tourists.[10] By the end of the 1980s, the profitable and extensive black market economy in the Eastern European states was driven largely by youth demand for cassettes, books, comics, and other such commodities.[11]

Popular mass media, through radio, magazines, albums, and cassette tapes, functioned as an intermediary between national youth cultures, promoting a kind of cultural exchange that encouraged an internationalization of the young, even if within national markets. Austrian Peter Krauss and Sicilian Salvatore Adamo became stars in France, while Françoise Hardy, Sylvie Vartan, and Johnny Hallyday had hits in the Netherlands and West Germany.[12] An early sixties French duo known as Les Travellers had hits playing covers of Elvis Presley and Jerry Lee Lewis. Meanwhile, the Mods, who originated in London, were arguably the first transnational youth subculture, and one premised on consumption and the cultural transfer of style—Italian gear was their favorite—combined with geographic mobility via Lambretta and Vespa scooters. An early Mod dance craze was called "the hitchhiker." In the mid-1960s, internationalist Mods with a shared sense of style and musical taste could be found in London, Hamburg, Stockholm, Milan, Prague, New York, Tokyo, and places in between.[13] In the 1970s and 1980s, backpacker itineraries would often incorporate a visit to and photo of the zebra crosswalk at Abbey Road in London or the grave of Jim Morrison in Paris.

Music, probably more than anything else, was central in establishing local, national, and international youth cultures after the Second World War.[14] For the young, personal identity and social community were reorganized around leisure and consumption, and this was a remarkably transnational process that permeated both the European Cold War East and West.[15] Even if it was a local, situated practice, the styles, habits, symbols, and sounds crossed national borders. From Sweden to Greece, Spain to Ukraine, the consumption of music led to an internationalization and Europeanization of youth in the 1960s and 1970s that oriented them toward a peer group defined by its generational difference locally as well as transnationally.[16] Thus, youth culture provided a means of age cohort identification across geopolitical, linguistic, and cultural boundaries. Western youth culture provided a common reference point for Eastern European youth.[17] For the young who saw themselves as isolated on the periphery, music and youth culture was a way to participate in the mainstream, to be part of the larger world beyond, whether they were in Portugal or East Germany.

This chapter explores the centrality of music to youth travel and how the geopolitical limits of the Cold War circumscribed both, but also, importantly, how youth culture and youth travel expanded the social space of transnational youth activity into the eastern and southern peripheries of Western Europe. Notably, it was the music and travel culture of the young that in many ways was most successful at traversing the Cold War division of Europe, with considerable attention focused on Berlin as a kind of unruly frontier space of cultural transfer. Moreover, rock music of the late sixties and early seventies, in particular, made a virtue of mobility, while the young themselves traveled across borders to congregate in large numbers for music festivals and concerts. The New Age Travellers, for example, a subculture of young nomads of the 1970s and 1980s, adopted a lifestyle of illegal trespass out of their peregrinations between music festivals and spread out from Britain to continental Europe, adopting a near stateless existence as they rambled in seeming perpetuity across the continent attending raves and music festivals. Music was also central to the overland experience along the hippie trail. Rock music, like travel, served as a core social phenomenon binding the young together as a perceived cohort or community that transcended not only national boundaries, but ideological ones as well.

Cold War Mobility

The selective border crossings of the Iron Curtain's semipermeable membrane were highly regulated but not fully controlled.[18] As those who write about borderlands have amply demonstrated, borders are sites and symbols of power—most usually state power—and as such they are both institutions and processes. What counted as Western Europe was often determined by borders that served to limit the trajectories of mobility and youth travel. These boundaries were also dynamic, undergoing constant revision by the human activity along and through them. Edith Sheffer's history of the border between East and West Germany demonstrates that while the geopolitics of the Cold War superpowers may have determined the physical boundary between East and West, it was largely the Germans who lived along the border who gave it shape, definition, and meaning. Their daily choices implemented and sustained the formidable barrier. Sheffer also shows that the most persistent transgressors of this frontier, before, during, and after its fortification, were the young.[19] Peter Schneider, in his celebrated collection of stories *The Wall Jumper*, set in 1980s Berlin, opens each chapter with an image of border crossing: by plane, by train, by automobile, by foot, some approved, others surreptitious, some planned, others impetuous. These little snapshots of daily life in Berlin were premised on mobility of one kind or another, even if that mobility was often thwarted and stifled. The border, the wall, shapes the characters' lives just as, in turn, they shape it. It is a dynamic zone of activity.[20]

Official territorial configurations marked by the borders of nation-states, membership in the European Community, the Eurail and Interrail systems, and especially the Cold War division of Europe along the Iron Curtain created bounded spaces within which and through which youth mobility was enacted. The circumscribed peripheries were also perforated by transnational youth travel and international youth culture. That is, the activity of the young challenged such limits and helped expand the space that counted as western and European, particularly to the east and south. By exceeding the limits of rail passes or Cold War borders, they extended the range of their influence, including, to a smaller degree, south of the Mediterranean and east of the Bosporus. In the early seventies, Ed Buryn, the iconic vagabonder, wrote, "I've been searched at only three borders: East Germany, Greece, and Spain. Regarding the first mentioned search, you can expect a hard time from some of the East European border people." Still, he highly recommended Eastern Europe as a "whole different world," a place of adventure at a bargain price, even with the "suspicious and hard-nosed people at the bureaucratic and official levels."[21] Youth travel over the 1970s and 1980s continued to grow in exactly those places, even becoming commonplace. Travel expanded not only to those places, but from them as well, as young Spaniards, Greeks, and East Germans adopted the practices of youth travel. By the early 1990s, those boundaries were no longer able to contain or curtail youth travel, as the space of that activity had expanded, pushing the peripheries farther east and south. Still, the efforts to control movement across borders were one of the key ways that young people experienced the Cold War.

Even the international counterculture of the 1960s and '70s was both a product of the Cold War and an agent in its transformation. The social and political history of the youth counterculture and the Cold War are deeply intertwined, as the young participants in both the West and the East (there was a significant if much smaller hippie movement in the eastern bloc and Soviet Union) responded with dissatisfaction to the conformity of the Cold War status quo. The transnational and trans–Cold War geographic breadth of the counterculture is one of its most salient features even if it lacks a consistent coherence across countries and blocs or continents.[22] The counterculture was able to cross borders via the networks of youth mobility that enabled cultural transfer.[23]

In Berlin, internal Stasi reports indicated that the young East German *Grenzgänger* had been prone to transgressing more than just the border; they were embracing western consumption rather than building eastern socialism. Searches of young deserters' homes revealed audiotapes and records of western rock 'n' roll, letters and magazines from West Germany, and in one case, photographs of Elvis Presley all over the bedroom wall.[24] The East German officials who built the Berlin Wall sought not only to halt the drain of young workers, which was hurting the GDR's economy, but also to stop the influx of West European and especially American cultural products, as young East Germans could freely cross the Berlin border in search of entertainment and amusement. In 1959, in separate incidents in Leipzig and Dresden, groups of adolescents marched through the streets denouncing the regime and shouting "Long live Elvis Presley!" and "We want rock 'n' roll!" The U.S. State Department, for its part, began to consider how western youth culture, specifically rock 'n' roll transmitted through radio broadcasts, could be used as a tool in the Cold War.[25]

The GDR went back and forth on its policies regarding the influence and influx of rock 'n' roll. Efforts to either co-opt it or quash it failed. After the wall was built, the East German police, with the help of the

Freie Deutsche Jugend, went around taking down or redirecting radio and television antennas that seemed oriented toward western stations. Yet contraband smuggled by West German relatives continued to come through. When travel restrictions for the elderly were eased, grandparents became one of the major conduits for the latest records and tapes from West Germany. Attempts to limit the influence of western culture on East German youth were ineffective, so in 1963 the regime sought to reset its relationship with young people by reviewing its policies and adopting a more open, liberalized approach.

This new attitude culminated in the 1964 *Deutschlandtreffen*, or Germany Meeting, a gigantic international youth festival held in East Berlin that focused on bilateral relations between East and West German youth. Rather than boring political speeches or parades, the 1964 Germany Meeting was meant to promote better relationships between the young of the two regimes through unobstructed interaction during three days of concerts, dances, films, and sports. The contrast to the 1951 Berlin World Youth Festival was striking. More than half a million young Germans from East and West attended the 1964 gathering. To convey the new liberalized attitude, the West German newsmagazine *Der Spiegel* described the event as "sun, sex, and socialism." The GDR even set up its own radio station for the festival, DT-64, which played lots of western rock music. The station survived until 1989, though its programming was frequently interfered with by the state as it waffled on what it considered appropriate music.[26] The Germany Meeting was considered a great success, and in the following months the regime not only tolerated but encouraged young music making through guitar groups modeled on the Beatles, whose records were made available for purchase.[27] For a little more than a year, the regime sponsored beat festivals and competitions. It quickly found it very difficult to manage, regulate, or monitor Beatlemania and the speed with which it was sweeping through East German youth culture. Hundreds of amateur beat bands were formed, with Leipzig's the Butlers being the most popular and most highly regarded; and the state found that it couldn't effectively control or monitor the situation, as there was always a basement or some other space where it was possible to listen to or play the Beatles or Rolling Stones independent of state scrutiny. For a state obsessed with surveillance and conformity, this made the rock 'n' roll youth culture in East Germany a political issue for the regime, if not necessarily for the young themselves.[28]

The Butlers and other bands began to find themselves subjected to petty harassment. A moral panic campaign was orchestrated in the media, connecting rock 'n' roll with delinquency, which peaked with the depiction of a police skirmish at a Rolling Stones concert in West Berlin as an out-of-control riot by young hooligans. In late October 1965, the regime officially banned beat music, and a protest by beat fans in Leipzig led to an outright street battle with the police. Hundreds of young people were arrested, and some were sent to camps for reeducation. Western rock music moved underground, but remained a potent force in East German youth culture.[29]

Music and the Mobility of Youth Culture

The cultural transfer of rock 'n' roll through the continent was itself a process of Europeanization as Europe developed a shared language of pop music. Though local contexts shaped the styles and tastes of performers and fans, there was a convergence driven by emulation, first of Americans, then of the British: Pim Maas was the Dutch Elvis, Ib Jensen the Danish Elvis; the Rattles were the West German Beatles, the Butlers the East German Beatles; and so on. The Beatles themselves had developed their signature Anglo-American musical style through a prolonged gig in Hamburg, while their haircuts and black turtlenecks were an imitation of Left Bank Paris.[30] The Beatles and the music of the 1960s developed and moved through preexisting networks of youth cultural contact, amplifying and augmenting the sensibility of a common cultural platform. Beatlemania, then, was in part a point of convergence.

It would be difficult to overstate the impact of the Beatles and the extraordinary rapidity with which Beatlemania swept the continent in the mid-sixties. In their wake, British bands of all kinds, most particularly the Rolling Stones, came to dominate the record charts on the continent and in Scandinavia just as they did in the "British Invasion" of the United States. Driven by the proximity of contact and prolific cultural transfer, "Swinging London" became the focus of European youth culture as well as the center of the European, if not world, music industry.[31] In 1968, the Beatles performed their new single "All You Need Is Love" in Abbey Road Studios on a live television special, simulcast through newly interconnected communication satellites. Reaching an unprecedented audience of hundreds of millions, it was the first global television event.[32] That same year, one music critic claimed that "the closest Western Civilization has come to unity since the Congress of Vienna in 1815 was the week the *Sgt. Pepper* album was released. In every city in Europe and America the stereo systems and the radio played, 'What would you think if I sang out of tune' . . . and everyone listened.

203

For a brief while the irreparably fragmented consciousness of the West was unified, at least in the minds of the young."[33] If the world seemed to be flying apart in different directions, he suggested that the cultural practice of the young was one of the few things continuing to hold it together.

Youth music culture was one of the primary conduits channeling the political internationalism of the 1968 era stimulating transnational connections, even if imaginary, across Cold War borders, whether Berlin or Prague.[34] With the ambiguity of its form and content, music could be loaded with political meanings, but more important was the sociocultural process that enabled its use as a democratic form of expression and shared participation. Rock music was the soundtrack of 1968 because musical taste was the symbolic anchor point for the transnational youth culture, not the other way around.[35] It could also overtly engage politics, of course. In 1967 there were two pop singles about the Dutch Provo white bicycles, one British, the other Italian, exemplifying the intra-European crossovers of music, politics, and youth culture.[36]

Radio programming was essential to the rapid spread of youth music culture in the mid-1960s. Dozens of so-called pirate radio stations proliferated in the early and middle years of the decade off the coasts of Northern Europe, targeting the UK, the Netherlands, Denmark, Norway, Sweden, and West Germany. These stations not only defied national broadcasting regulations by operating on ships anchored outside legal jurisdiction, but they revolutionized radio programming as well by adopting a top-forty American-style format. They played current pop and rock while personality DJs provided commentary and information. Radio Caroline and Radio London each had over one million listeners in the UK by 1966, while Radio Veronica had similar success in the Netherlands and Belgium, as did Radio Mercur in Denmark. Through such competition, pirate radio forced state and commercial radio stations to respond; both the BBC and Radio Luxembourg quickly adopted a similar format, as did West German stations.[37] Cheap transistor radios meant that the young could access such stations from nearly anywhere, including across the Iron Curtain. Even East Berlin, in 1964, launched a radio station aimed at the young by playing western beat music at the same time that Moscow launched its own youth-oriented rock station, Beacon (Maiak). Quite literally, the radio transmission of rock moved across borders and boundaries of all sorts.

Radio programming of pop music shifted to English-language songs earlier in West Germany than elsewhere.[38] In Italy, foreign-language pop songs were recorded in Italian by local bands, and the listening public often had no idea that they were listening to music that had originated elsewhere. This was true in other Southern European countries as well, with the cover record serving as a cross-cultural instrument that put foreign music into local languages connecting disparate national and linguistic communities through the same songs. The advent of rock music, however, did not lend itself so well to the cover format, with audiences preferring to buy original versions of hit rock songs.[39] Increasingly, English became the predominant language of pop and rock, helping the language to spread through youth culture.[40] Still, even within a transnational music culture and economic market, nationality continued to have its place, as popular music frequently became a forum for debates about national identity and its place in a globalizing world.[41]

The association of freedom with mobility in rock and pop songs was overt and pervasive, particularly in the late 1960s and early 1970s. One could be born to run, or a ramblin' man who needed to ramble on like a rolling stone. The Beatles sang about having a ticket to ride and magical mystery tours, long and winding roads, and being back in the USSR. Vanity Fair sang, "Ride, ride, ride, hitchin' a ride"; Iron Maiden's first hit was "Running Free." Whether it was taking off or getting away on big old jet airliners or being a rocket man, metaphorical mobility was an ethos of independence and autonomy even if it was often also associated with shared hardship in the course of a journey: Simon and Garfunkel looked for America though eventually they, too, were homeward bound; Carole King in "So Far Away" sang with wistful world-weariness of "one more song about moving along the highway," asking, "doesn't anybody stay in one place anymore?" The impulse to identify with songs as collective representations suggests these pervasive tropes as some kind of symbolic fiction, almost a folklore of youth culture that idealized mobility as ontological aspiration.

Given how central it was to international youth culture, it is no surprise that European backpacking appeared in numerous songs. In 1971, on her classic album *Blue*, Joni Mitchell sang, "Maybe I'll go to Amsterdam, maybe I'll go to Rome" in one song, while in another she sang of sitting in a park in Paris, hanging out on a Greek isle, and attending a party in Spain, but all the while she was lonely traveling among strangers and homesick for California. That same year, Bob Dylan sang about the crowded Spanish Steps in Rome and Belgian girls eating mussels in Brussels in "When I Paint My Masterpiece." On *Who's Next*, Pete Townshend sang of "going mobile" as a "hippy gypsy." A couple of years earlier, Crosby, Stills, and Nash had sung of adventures in Morocco aboard the Marrakesh Express. One of Bob Seger's first hits was about getting away to Kathmandu. A little later, in 1977, even the Sex Pistols would sing of "Holidays in the Sun," imagining a rough-and-tumble trip to the Berlin Wall, and Iggy Pop sang that same year of being "the passenger" traveling through East Berlin on the S-Bahn. I Nomadi, perhaps the most famous Italian group from the era, and whose name was the original Italian term for backpackers, sang in their huge hit "Io vagabondo" of being a young traveling drifter. Another Italian band, Dik Dik—the name itself a reference to the sound of a Vespa—released the hit song "Viaggio di un poeta" about a penurious twenty-year-old traveling around to different countries and cities. Dik Dik had another big hit, "L'isola di Wight," about a young couple traveling together, spending their youth attending festivals and concerts, culminating at the 1970 Isle of Wight Festival.[42]

The European youth travel culture and music festivals were mutually constitutive, as the young developed and utilized their travel practices in the process of attending festivals, and vice versa. Half a million West German youth attended pop and rock festivals in 1970.[43] In addition to the Dutch youth clubs, pop festivals proliferated in the Netherlands in the late 1960s as the primary gathering site of like-minded youth. Starting with Amsterdam's "Hai in de Rai" festival in 1967, these events became increasingly international, peaking with the 1970 Holland Pop Festival near Rotterdam in Kralingse Bos, a forested park with meadows and cobbled lanes.[44] Also known as Stomping Ground or Kralingen, the 1970 festival was intentionally imagined as a European Woodstock with such popular acts as the Byrds, Jefferson Airplane, Canned Heat, and Pink Floyd playing in continuous succession before a crowd of about a hundred thousand over a three-day weekend in late June.[45] Though the *Nieuwe Rotterdamse Courant* reported that local politicians were worried about unruly youth and the potential for disturbances to public order, the *Times* reported that Rotterdam's chief inspector of police had said it was the best-behaved large crowd he had ever heard of, let alone handled.[46] As a precaution, the local government had teams of social workers there wearing matching T-shirts that said, in English, WE HELP YOU.[47] They observed that most attendees smoked hash, several thousand took LSD, and young women were more likely than young men to have brought, and insisted on the use of, condoms. The median age of the attendees was twenty, with a third of the total female. The crowd was 80 percent Dutch and 15 percent Western European, including a considerable number of American soldiers from bases in West Germany.[48]

That summer, eighteen-year-old Alberto Camerini and his nineteen-year-old friend Eugenio Finardi left Milan like "two Easy Riders" on motorcycles, one of which belonged to Camerini's older brother, who was traveling overland to India. Their ultimate destination was the Isle of Wight Festival at the end of August, but in between they planned to travel around Europe, attending Kralingen and some other pop festivals and spending some time in Amsterdam. They stayed longer in Amsterdam than intended, which was not uncommon, and had to rush to the Isle of Wight. There was a terrific crush of traffic moving toward Portsmouth to catch the ferry there. Camerini likened it to an invasion.[49]

Just getting to the Isle of Wight was part of the experience, as hundreds of thousands of young people carrying rucksacks and bedrolls gathered in very long lines to board buses and trains that would take them to ports to catch ferries to the normally sedate island off the southern coast of England. The only way onto the Isle of Wight was by boat, and according to British Rail, more than six hundred thousand festivalgoers made the trip via their ferries.[50] In fact, young people had been arriving from across Western Europe for several weeks, and as the festival neared, seemingly every conceivable space was occupied. Sherri Segel, a twenty-one-year-old Californian, said, "The Isle of Wight is something you had to be at if you're in Europe and you're young," while Jane Lawrence of Iowa said, "We were in Italy and everyone was going to the Isle of Wight. Here we are. I'm confused. I'm a little scared. I hope it doesn't rain."[51]

This was actually the third Isle of Wight Festival and was meant to be the last (it was revived thirty years later), and it was by far the largest. The festival accepted a host of national currencies, while more than a dozen different national flags flew above the massive crowd gathered on the two-hundred-acre site. Rod Allen, a young American photographer, commented on "the number, the huge number, of Europeans who made the trek to come to the Isle of Wight. There's got to be something good about that. Announcements were made from the stage in French, German, and Italian, and I personally was surrounded by foreign people all the time I was there. I don't know if you can derive any philosophical conclusion from all that, but you can dig it."[52]

They had come to see a remarkable lineup of nearly five days of continuous music, which featured the debut of Emerson, Lake and Palmer and one of the final performances by Jimi Hendrix. Miles Davis played a bewitching show at sunset on Saturday, later followed by a brooding, dark, and powerful midnight performance by the Doors, then a blistering two-and-a-half-hour set by the Who in the early morning hours of Sunday, and a joyful Sly and the Family Stone celebration as the sun came up. Other performers included Joan Baez, Joni Mitchell, Leonard Cohen, Procol Harum, Jethro Tull, and the Moody Blues. And yet despite the great music, the weekend was infected by a rather sour mood. Though

27   The crowd at the Isle of Wight Festival, August 1970. Half a million attended, many without
     paying, such as those along "Desolation Row" on the hillside beyond the fence. Photograph
     by Robert Bush. iStock/Getty Images.

the sound and lighting systems were plagued by technical difficulties
and there were widespread complaints about the three-pound cost of the
ticket, and the overpriced hot dog and hamburger stands, the main cause
of the attendees' unhappiness was a conflict that originated outside the
grounds.

East Afton Farm, where the festival was held, was a large natural bowl
ringed by hillsides. Although the site itself was fenced off and patrolled
by guards with dogs, perhaps as many as fifty thousand young people set
up on the hillside overlooking the concert grounds in an encampment
that became known as "Desolation Row." Among them were free festival
activists, who not only refused to pay the entry fee, but demanded access to the site anyway, protested against the promoters, and attacked
the fence, likening it to the Berlin Wall. They wrestled with security
guards in a scrum on Friday. On Saturday morning, one activist got up
on stage and interrupted Joni Mitchell's set, inspiring the increasingly
rowdy crowd to throw bottles and cans. In frustration, Mitchell made a
heartfelt speech, pleading with the crowd to behave and stop "acting like
tourists." Tensions continued to build over the weekend, and on Sunday
the promoters resigned themselves to taking a significant financial loss
and declared Wight to be a free festival. The gates were opened, and part

of the fence came down.[53] On Monday, the rain arrived and the young departed, weary and disenchanted, leaving a prodigious mess in their wake. Mary Drysdale, a nineteen-year-old from Washington, shook her head: "Don't tell me there was any kindness or sharing or love at this festival. It was cold, man, cold and I didn't like it one bit."[54] Others took it more in stride: "Most people got a little bored with the French anarchists from the hill who kept beating on the fences," said Rod Allen. But "I find it rather nice to know that the spirit of revolution, which last flared seriously in May 1968, is still alive in the young French. So it was good to see all the Europeans, and especially the French, getting it together at the Isle of Wight [because] music crosses national barriers."[55] Another attendee reflected that "perhaps Afton was a kind of precursor to the EC," not only due to the Western European community gathered there, but also because of the conflicts and squabbling.[56]

New Age Travellers as Transitory Europeans

Although the muddled disorder and financial loss and a resulting act of Parliament restricting the size of future gatherings on the island ensured that there was no Isle of Wight Festival there the following year, the Glastonbury Fair of 1971 picked up where it had left off, if on a much smaller scale, and the free festival movement, especially the Windsor Free Festivals of music, arts, and cultural activities, carried forward the association of youth, travel, and music in the 1970s UK. The New Age Travellers emerged out of the 1960s counterculture and the English free festivals of the 1970s. Though the phenomenon lacks a clear point of origin, it began as part of a circuit of transit between the various annual summer music festivals of the early 1970s, including the Stonehenge, Windsor, and Glastonbury festivals and some smaller rural carnivals. By the mid-1970s, young people were spending their summers traveling in caravans around the English countryside to and from the various free festivals. By the early 1980s, many had adopted the lifestyle as a year-round pursuit. This traveling culture developed as a community. One young Traveller described the early years as "a spontaneous experiment in human trust and co-operation. . . . to live an alternative without the state."[57] This way of living was reminiscent of hippie communes, whose members shared labor and resources in an effort to maintain self-sufficiency outside the usual paradigm of job, home, and welfare state. Importantly, though, this nomadic communal existence remained in perpetual flux in terms of place, space, and persons.

28   A New Age Traveller couple in their bus, part of a convoy, in Britain, summer 1987. The New Age Travellers adopted a lifestyle of mobile passage. Associated Newspapers/ Rex/Shutterstock.

Successive waves of young people became New Age Travellers, so that the phenomenon never lost its association with youth and youth culture or music, even as many of its practitioners aged and the music changed. In the early 1980s, the hippie tone began to shift to something more punkish and anarchist; by the early 1990s, the New Age Travellers were the primary force behind the rave culture of techno music. Traveller collectives, such as the Spiral Tribe and Circus Warp, would set up their sound systems to host impromptu all-night parties with pounding electronic music in vacant warehouses or forest clearings. Importantly, the New Age Travellers were a heterogeneous group, and many of them would disagree that they were a group at all. Even the name is a contentious one. Though it is the terminology that has endured, most who live this way prefer to be known simply as Travellers.

The New Age Travellers attracted widespread public attention in the mid-1980s with what the media dubbed the "Peace Convoy," a collection of a few hundred converted and colorfully painted vehicles that traveled around England between festivals and the women's peace camp at the Greenham Common airbase. In 1985, several hundred police officers confronted and attacked the convoy in a brutal ambush as it made its way toward Stonehenge to celebrate the summer solstice. The public questioned why young people in Britain would adopt such a rootless and seemingly amoral existence, and Parliament even held hearings and passed legislation meant to discourage their activity through criminalization. The Battle of the Beanfield, as the Peace Convoy incident has become known, was the beginning of a sustained campaign of harassment, marginalization, and criminalization of the New Age Traveller lifestyle in Britain. Margaret Thatcher is famous for having threatened to "make their lives as difficult as possible," while her successor, John Major, in his address to the 1992 Conservative Party Conference, declared, "New age travellers? Not in this age. Not in any age."[58] Specifically, the 1986 Public Order Act and the 1994 Criminal Justice and Public Order Act included provisions to empower local authorities to contest, evict, and arrest Travellers. The 1994 act outlawed raves, which were defined, rather ridiculously, as gatherings of more than twenty people listening to amplified music "characterised by the emission of a succession of repetitive beats."[59] For the members of Parliament, the intimate association of music with youth culture was clear, and in order to attack the latter, it was necessary to outlaw the former.

In the wake of the 1985 Battle of the Beanfield, New Age Travellers no longer moved around in large convoys, but dispersed into much smaller units. With continued harassment and criminalization, many Travellers left England altogether in the late 1980s and early 1990s to pursue their chosen itinerant lifestyle as a diaspora outside Britain. As one said, "Every Traveller who's got his head screwed on is heading out now."[60] No one is certain how many people have been involved in this community, though it is clear that in total there have been tens of thousands of New Age Travellers, many of whom were and continue to be outside Britain or were not themselves British.

Em, who was in her twenties, spent much time traveling independently around Europe in the early 1990s, returning for several summers to southern Crete. She described living in a community of young Travellers this way: "We are a large, unwieldy troupe, my group of friends, eleven in all. We drifted together randomly like flotsam and jetsam. We gain and we lose momentum; dispersing, dissolving, and regrouping. Shifting sands; budding, burgeoning, blossoming and collapsing relationships." Though the individual interpersonal relationships of this community may have been impermanent—in fact, they were premised on impermanence—Em gives us a sense of a larger collective exercise of community based on people coming and going at will. "What bonds tie me to these beautiful strangers?" she asked rhetorically. "There is no personal space in our camp; everyone is lumped together in a jumbled, fluid community. . . .

There are no rules, we are free. There are no boundaries, no perimeter fences."[61] Shannon explained how her sense of belonging extended beyond her immediate companions at any given moment. "This has been my scene and my family, a world-wide tribe," she wrote. "It's completely international, although some of the British people were once Travellers in Britain—there's German, French, American, Australian, Dutch, Italians."[62] Bruce put it this way: "I have known it in the tens of thousands of decent, caring, suffering, unpublicised people worldwide who struggle in their different ways toward a new kind of world community into which the old nationalisms do not fit. The framework for that new unity and the terms of our trusteeship we have yet to understand. But there is a new country."[63] While he was unable to define or name this "new country," clearly it was a kind of imagined community, though importantly one decidedly non-nationalist, and as Em emphasized, one without boundaries or perimeter fences—this simply wasn't geopolitical.

Miranda left England in a Dodge van. "When I first started travelling in Europe," she wrote, "the horizons seemed to expand alarmingly. Where was it safe to park up? How to make money? Where were the festivals? Then I started to make connections. Gradually I became aware of overlapping scenes, an ever-expanding family, circulating between various safe havens, beautiful remote places and industrial chaos zones. Now as the continent starts to feel more like home, I am excited by places I don't know, rather than intimidated." Miranda appealed for "the free flow of people and ideas between Britain and the rest of Europe," and she advocated that Travellers were the way to accomplish this, because "a kind of post-colonial arrogance we get taught in school makes us think that we don't need to connect with anywhere else." She continued, "For me, being a Traveller is about side-stepping the boundaries that the state tries to fence us in with. Some of these boundaries are obvious, like national borders, but others are implanted in our heads, encouraging us to be narrow-minded about the unfamiliar. Britain is where I come from, but the whole world is home."[64]

Like the Roma and Sinti, the New Age Travellers exemplified or at least proclaimed a largely stateless identity, but unlike traditional populations, they had adopted this lifestyle of nomadism from a sedentary existence, and they were not a distinct ethnic or racial group, but instead a community based within a youth culture. For the New Age Travellers, this was a way out of the world that surrounded them. The practice of travel with no intended return or destination was a practice that enabled them, in their words, to escape society, to live without the state, to adopt a life of exile or refugee status. Though they traveled perpetually, they were never away from home; thus, there was no need for return. Travel became a state in itself, one without national borders.

In the early 1990s, Lizzy Bean traced a large figure eight, or sign of infinity, through Europe in a converted bus she called the Phoebus @pollo. Without a set final destination, she had left England to pursue an itinerant existence of undetermined duration. Her initial destination was Hostimice, south of Prague in the Czech Republic, where she and seven young passengers she described as "English, Irish, Scottish, German, Israeli, and Unknown" headed to the Teknival, a recurring techno-carnival, or rave, that drew thousands of nomadic youth from across the continent to what she described as "a wicked party."[65] Lizzy Bean, and other young people like her, had embraced travel not for mere edification or a holiday, but as a nomadic lifestyle that offered an alternative to the fixed sessility of modern nation-states. In a poem, she wrote:

WE ARE THE NEW TRUE AMBASSADORS OF THE E.C.
WE ARE THE QUALITY CONTROLLERS OF THE NEW EUROP@
WE TEST THE ROADS, THE POLICE, THE PARKING, THE SHOPPING,
THE CULTURE, THE FOOD
OUR POCKETS ARE ALREADY FULL WITH PFENNIGS & PESETAS
WE'VE GOT OUR OWN E.C.U.
WE HAVE NO LAWS & NO LIMITS IN OUR SEARCH
FOR FREEDOM OF MOVEMENT
WE VOW TO LIVE FOR THE MOMENT
TOTAL RESISTANCE TO THE ALIEN-NATION.[66]

"We are the new true ambassadors of the E.C.," she proclaimed, as well as the "quality controllers" testing the limits of "the New Europ@." Importantly, she juxtaposed this role with a "total resistance to the alien-nation," implying an opposition to the alienating nation-state and the embrace of an identity based on something other than nationality or territoriality. Her poem suggests the problematic nature of this chosen lifestyle and identity for European nation-states as she, in some ways, denied their geopolitical legitimacy. Further, she insisted that the New Age Travellers, through the cultural practice of nomadic travel, were the ones interconnecting a "New Europ@" through the "freedom of movement" that challenged and "test[ed]" the national order in terms of "the roads, the police," culture, food, and so on. It was a "search" with "no laws" and "no limits."

In addition to her lyrical paean to the "New Europ@," Lizzy Bean offered a list of "EC highs," delighting in particular beers, dollar stores, sound systems, festivals, and the like. When she wrote that in Berlin "I see the old east and the new west. Now it's the new east and the old west," she placed herself at the intersection of the past and future Europe, the old and the new, the west and the east. As we know, Berlin in particular exemplified the modern nation-state's preoccupation with territorial borders to control the movements of those within and without. In contrast, Lizzy Bean imagined her travels as a "Moebius road-trip," an ongoing circuit of freedom that would extend beyond the old and the new, through the east and the west, helping to stitch together the territorial fragments of Europe, the east and the west converging at Berlin, through the cultural practice of travel between music festivals.[67]

Today Rome, Tomorrow Istanbul

The itineracy of the counterculture was perhaps best exemplified by the "hippie trail," which became famous in the 1970s as a loosely conceived overland itinerary from Europe to India, with major hubs in Marrakesh, Istanbul, Tabriz, Kabul, Kathmandu, and Goa. Most of those who ventured along the hippie trail to "Freak Street" in Kathmandu, or later Bangkok, had first developed their travel skills in Europe, even if they were American or Australian.[68] Parisian Philippe Gloaguen described the youth scene in late-sixties London as "a new world" of longer hair, shorter skirts, and rowdier music. "It's the whole planet [the young] roam in the Chinese, Pakistani, and Indian neighborhoods," he wrote. "London, it's Asia, America, and Africa mixed together with England," giving "the desire to go further, see more." In 1970, to fulfill an old promise to his parents, Gloaguen canceled his plan to hitchhike around Europe in order to focus on improving his English. As a compromise, he arranged for a kind of internship in the UK by working at the Isle of Wight Festival. If he could accommodate his parents in this way and pass his exams in English, the avid young traveler intended to take off the next summer on the overland route to India. He did so, and later turned the journals from that trip into the first *Guide du Routard*, which was initially entitled *La Route des Zindes*.[69] Eva Douglas was a young Swede who had made her way to London and became part of the King's Road scene in the late 1960s. "People were listening to Ravi Shankar, sitting on cushions, and burning incense," she wrote. "The music, the Indian ambience, Timothy Leary, the Beatles meeting the Maharishi Mahesh Yogi: all this said to us that India was where the magic, the mystic, that *something else*, might be found." Douglas first spent time in Greece, then Morocco. "Greece had been the first step to the East, but Morocco *was* Eastern. . . . This going from Sweden to London to Greece to Morocco and finally to India was a gradual undoing of my upbringing. India was to finish off this undoing process and then introduce a whole new way of life, a whole new set of perceptions."[70]

Like Eva, most young travelers moved initially into the Mediterranean peripheries on the edge of Europe. Morocco and Turkey especially became included as destinations in backpacking itineraries of Europe. Some would later move across Iran and Afghanistan to Nepal and India. Robin Brown described "little try-out runs to Morocco," while Carmel Lyons noted that "few people I knew in Amsterdam had been to India, though many had been to Morocco, and India was the stage after that, the next stage in the journey." Harry Deissing was a *Gammler* in Munich, where he met others who had been to Istanbul, which made him want to go. Once there, he went farther.[71]

In his 1971 guidebook *Vagabonding in Europe and North Africa*, Ed Buryn singled out the Mediterranean—Turkey, Israel, Tunisia, Algeria, Morocco—as a suitable stretch of contiguous territory for the practice of youthful European vagabonding. He described Algeria as "the most European of the North African countries," but also warned that it was not a tourist country due to its recent war for independence from France. Yet hitchhiking was very easy there, especially for someone without long hair. This was true across North Africa, where the Arab population would give people rides more than the Europeans did. English-language skills wouldn't get one very far, but French or Arabic would. At the time there was a backlash against hippie travelers in Morocco, and Buryn was stern about not inviting trouble through appearance and behavior. Be careful of the dope, he warned; you could get in trouble quickly, but it was cheap and plentiful in Marrakesh. Turkey was similar, "where east meets west," and a wonderful place to visit, but it was important to be careful of the "fuzz and informers everywhere." He described Israel as "a young people's country—modern and swinging," and possibly "the best hitchhiking country of all," with youth hostels as "the place to stay" and individual as "the way to be."[72] Over the 1970s, guidebooks in general expanded their geographical understanding of what counted as European travel. By the 1980s, the coverage of *Let's Go Europe*, for example, had extended south and east to include Israel, Morocco, Turkey, and the Soviet Union. The European Interrail pass included Morocco and Turkey and destinations as far east as Romania.

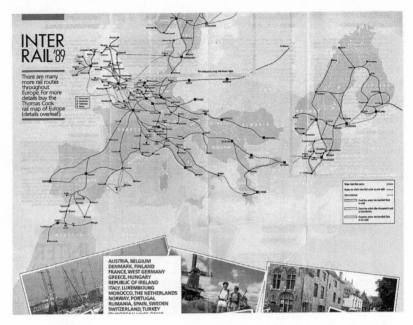

29   By the 1980s, the area reachable with an Interrail pass had expanded south and east to include Morocco and Turkey, and deep into the eastern bloc as far as Romania. © Eurail Group G. I. E.

Such travel was stimulated by the events of 1968. Lieschen Müller recalled, "you either stayed at home and got into politics, the French Revolution of '68, the Vietnam demonstrations, Red Rudi Dutschke in Berlin, or you went East. A lot of people stayed for the politics, got disillusioned and *then* went East." Carlo di Paoli was involved in the political struggle in Italy: "my focus had moved from seeking a perfect society to seeking a perfect state of inner being. . . . [My friends] told me I was betraying the struggle. I said, 'No, going to India is part of it.'" Frenchman Christian Mottet recalled that "it was all too depressing. We wanted to breathe fresh air. I think that's why I wanted to go to India: for the freedom. The spiritual aspect didn't figure particularly, because India was quite new to me, quite unknown. Perhaps it had more influence in England, because the Beatles had inspired this guru thing with their visit to the Maharishi. In France we weren't so inspired by the Beatles. We were more interested in India as a place where we could be free." Briton Robin Brown noted, "I think that the first time a lot of people were on the road was after the French riots of '68. That's when suddenly tons of Frenchmen appeared."[73]

Although the association of the hippie trail with 1968 is strong, especially among the French, overland travel across South Asia predated
the youth movements of 1968.[74] The Indian government estimated that
there were already more than ten thousand young foreigners in the
country in 1967. By 1970, the young were a majority of all foreign nationals there. In 1972, ten thousand foreigners crossed into India from
Pakistan at the Wagah border in a single week. In 1973, the French embassy estimated that there were 250,000 French nationals in India, and
that the majority of them were young.[75] No one really knows how many
young overlanders there were in total between the mid-1960s and 1979,
but "hundreds of thousands" seems as accurate as is possible.[76]

By the end of the 1960s, entrepreneurial tour operators offered cheap
passage aboard a fleet of decrepit buses that would often begin in London, Amsterdam, or elsewhere in Europe. Rudy, a driver who worked the
route for more than ten years, would start by collecting passengers at
Victoria Station in London. He next stopped in Amsterdam, then typically at youth hostels in Munich and Salzburg, and then at the Pudding
Shop in Istanbul, before heading out toward Kathmandu. People would
get on and off, joining for partial or full passage. Magic Bus had an office
on Dam Square in Amsterdam, operating as an agency booking passage

30   Aboard the "Intercontinental Express" bus from London to New Delhi, somewhere in
Afghanistan, October 1975. Photograph by Deena Atlas. Used with permission.

on a variety of buses.[77] American Deena Atlas took the "Intercontinental Express" from London to New Delhi in 1975. The bus was half full until Istanbul, where it filled with others for the overland trip.[78] The hippie trail lasted until 1979, when Afghanistan collapsed into war and Iran into revolution, effectively shutting off the overland route. *Le Monde* in 1980 declared the *routard*, the French term for independent travelers and often associated with the hippie trail, to be "dead."[79]

Rudy said that "the stereo system was the first thing every driver arranged."[80] Drivers would trade tapes along the route to try to vary the monotony. Pauline Hyland was thankful that the bus she took along the hippie trail—like most, a wheezing, ramshackle contraption—had a speaker system. "All seventeen of us murmured thanks for the heaven-sent mercy of a functioning sound system. Heating may have been an optional extra, but music was a life support."[81] In Istanbul, Ersin Kalkan, a young Turk, would seek out the European backpackers because he was interested in what books they were reading and what music they were listening to; the young travelers moving along the hippie trail were his conduit to western youth culture, as they were for young Iranian Nazzer Poor, who was inspired to grow "Elvis Presley sideburns" and make his way to Europe, even spending time in a commune in Yorkshire.[82]

When in Asia, the overlanders sought each other out in drifter enclaves of expatriates such as Gülhane Park in Istanbul, Chicken Street in Kabul, and Freak Street in Kathmandu. Within these enclaves, western youth culture, especially its music, predominated in the guesthouses and bars, though materially it incorporated local panache like Nehru jackets and Afghan coats, which were in turn brought back to the West. Angelika Bergmann's travel diary from India is full of her encounters with other Europeans, especially fellow Germans, and their conversations about European life and politics.[83] While European travel culture was broadening its geographic reach, the privilege of participating in such independent travel was not readily available to young people from those places. The powerful standards of in-group behavior and the practice of western youth travel remained strong in the youthful enclaves stretching across North Africa, the Middle East, and South Asia. This postcolonial youth travel very often relied upon the patterns and privileges accorded to former imperial networks, thus reinscribing its distinguishing European character, even if it was not fully limited to European youth or Europe.[84]

Travel, tourism, and circulation through colonial networks had been a fundamental component of imperialism. For the French and British, colonial tourism often served as a means to assert hegemony and to develop an imperial consciousness that relied on hierarchies of difference determining who could travel where.[85] Still, the colonized sometimes circulated as well, especially the young, as maritime or other labor or as students to the metropole, although of course hierarchies of mobility still applied.[86] Even after decolonization, mass tourism outside the continent continued to follow well-established colonial routes and destinations.[87] Among the earliest enclaves of the hippie trail were the former hill stations of Manali and Dharamsala in India and the Cameron Highlands in Malaysia.[88]

The overland route across Asia relied on the infrastructure and patterns of imperial travel cultures, whether or not it offered opportunities for Kiplingesque adventure.[89] The overlanders certainly didn't think of themselves as occupying a privileged position or engaging in colonialist behaviors. If anything, they sought a precolonial ideal informed by Orientalist notions of authenticity that had been stimulated by the end of empire. Australian Pauline Hyland, who took a bus from London to Kathmandu in 1977, unwittingly articulated this when she wrote, "Only places in such quick, uneven transition could satisfy two backpacker demands: that a place still be wildly exotic and that it also be reasonably accessible to Westerners. And places like this, moving from the fifteenth century into the twenty-first, were likely candidates for upheaval."[90] Young Westerners gathered in their allotted spaces, from which they observed and toured the local cultures.[91] As much as their travel was based on self-discovery, it relied upon difference from the other. The mobility of young Westerners was a defining contrast to that of the young in former colonies or in the Soviet bloc.

Eastern Europe, East Germany, and East Berlin

Though independent travel was far less common, there were those who managed during the Cold War to travel through Eastern Europe and the Soviet Union while avoiding the prescribed routes, and even hitchhiking along the way.[92] The Soviet Union even had its own version of a 1970s hippie trail, stretching from the Baltic states across the steppes of Central Asia.[93] This kind of independent travel had been discouraged within the USSR itself, especially for the young, because it was considered bourgeois individualism. Tourism and travel, like everything else, ought to be collective and serve the interests of building socialism. Thus, the tourist and holiday infrastructures were taken over and organized by the state throughout Eastern Europe, hostel systems and holiday centers included. Independent travel, as such, was considered vagrancy and illegal, while the young were considered especially vulnerable to the seductions of foreign travel, especially to the West.[94] Yet in the interests of state building, the young were encouraged to travel in official ways, with a "Young Tourist" badge, awarded to Pioneers, or a "Tourist of the USSR" badge for those older than thirteen.[95]

Like so much else after Stalin, the ability to travel, especially abroad, marked the cultural thaw of the Khrushchev era. Gradually, there was an increasingly transnational circulation of people within the eastern bloc, and beyond it, too. Tourists to capitalist countries were seen as envoys who could help normalize relations through personal encounter, even if this was heavily managed by official oversight. The young were seen to be a liability on such trips, as they too often admired life abroad. Western youth culture was already making inroads into the Soviet Union and was seen as potentially subversive. Importantly, part of the rationale for the growing number and frequency of trips abroad to Western Europe was the opportunity to convey an image of the Soviet Union as fundamentally European, by emphasizing a shared history and heritage that excluded the United States.[96] Meanwhile, the promise of western currency meant that eastern bloc countries were negotiating ever larger visa quotas, allowing more western tourists to travel east.[97] In the mid-1960s, the large numbers of western tourists on the Black Sea coast were drawing young Bulgarians and other Easterners there for potential sexual escapades. Young men and women sought out sexual partners who might buy them material goods or even take them out of Bulgaria. This, in turn, drew more western tourists, who would plan their trip for the peak season.[98] Similarly, the 1957 Moscow Youth Festival came to be known for sexually active Soviet girls wantonly having sex with foreign guests. The ensuing hoopla revealed anxieties about not only adolescent female sexuality but the influence of western youth culture as well.[99] As in the West, travel away from home came to be associated with opportunities for sexual exploration. As hitchhiking became increasingly common in the 1970s GDR, so did casual premarital sex, on the road and away from home.[100]

The growing mobility in the eastern bloc facilitated the spread of music and youth culture there. After 1972, for example, East Germans could travel to most eastern bloc countries without a visa. Both within the Soviet bloc and beyond it, the growing circulation of people facilitated the circulation of goods. The apparatchik elite, even the KGB, brought their children records and magazines from trips abroad. Black markets such as the "Broadway" stretch of Karl Marx Avenue in Dnipropetrovsk sold contraband commodities from western tourists. East Germans traveled to Hungary to buy western albums, and so on. In the wake of rock music came other pop cultural goods, so that in the 1970s the young throughout the Soviet bloc experienced a kind of Westernization that was spearheaded by music but driven by local tastes and demands, such as the enormous popularity of Deep Purple among young Ukrainians. The East had a proliferation of tourist rallies and music festivals, too; singing and songwriting there were tied to the habits of travel and tourism. This democratization of daily life came about largely through the cultural exchange of mobility. This wasn't simply Americanization; it was a complex process of cultural transfer enabled by the movement of people and goods, which was both facilitated by the state and in direct defiance of it as well.[101]

In the early 1970s, the Social Democratic chancellor of West Germany, Willy Brandt, sought to normalize relations with East Germany against the backdrop of Richard Nixon and Leonid Brezhnev's superpower détente. Brandt's policy of *Ostpolitik* was a decided turn from Adenauer and the Christian Democrats' *Westpolitik*, which had dominated official foreign policy since the establishment of the Federal Republic. *Westpolitik* had emphasized a westward orientation for West Germany, and a stern denial of the legitimacy of the East German regime as well as a refusal to deal with those states that did recognize it—namely, the eastern bloc. Brandt, a former mayor of West Berlin, was particularly sensitive to the rupture that the division of Germany had caused for the German people. Moreover, by seeking to normalize relations with the GDR, and officially recognizing the postwar changes to geopolitical borders throughout Eastern Europe, the Federal Republic of Germany (FRG) would be able to open diplomacy and trade with the entirety of the Soviet bloc; in fact, the rapidly growing trade with Eastern Europe that resulted from *Ostpolitik* considerably tempered the 1970s economic downturn in West Germany.[102]

Official mutual recognition of state sovereignty was not quite established between the two Germanies. *Ostpolitik* instead emphasized a multitude of diplomatic, institutional, and human contacts between them. Among Germans themselves, contact and communication grew extraordinarily in the late seventies and early eighties; through telephone calls and letters, television and radio broadcasts, and public ceremonies and private visits, regular interaction was restored between the peoples of East and West Germany. Partnerships between East and West German cities flourished, with sports competitions, cultural exchanges, school trips, trade shows, and church conferences. With the success of such official, formal exchange programs, slowly liberalized travel restrictions enabled 1.5 million East Germans to travel to the West in 1981, and 5 million in 1987. Meanwhile, millions of West Germans—7 million in 1979 alone—traveled with relative ease to the East. This proliferation of human networking and contact through personal encounter did much to Westernize the isolated population of the GDR in the 1980s.[103] The demand and desire for cross-border travel slowly undermined the republic's credibility and power over the course of the decade. Détente and *Ostpolitik* had brought about a greater appreciation of the West, and the East suffered by comparison.[104]

As it had done with France and Israel, West Germany quickly sought to set up robust youth exchange programs with East Germany and Poland as part of a deliberate effort to normalize relations with those countries with which it had a troubled past.[105] Youth exchanges had also been one of the ways in which West Germany had responded to the building of the Berlin Wall. Between 1966 and 1970, concerns about the isolation of West Berlin led the FRG to establish an exchange program specifically for young people in the western half of the city in an effort to anchor them better within Western Europe. In total, it brought a few thousand young people from around Western Europe to Berlin while sending young West Berliners abroad. Some trips were bilateral group meetings; for example, ten British and eleven West Berlin youth spent a week together at a hostel in Uelsen, West Germany.[106] With *Ostpolitik*, the emphasis on exchange shifted further. For their parts, both Poland and East Germany had fully developed youth hostel systems to accommodate group travel into and around their countries, making them well positioned and open to such exchange programs. The Freie Deutsche Jugend in East Germany had many holiday centers, and even its own youth travel agency, Jugendtourist, created in 1975, which had a history of coordinating and arranging group travel, often abroad to other eastern bloc countries.[107] Through such programs, young East and West Germans began to grasp the drastic differences between their two countries—indeed, closer contact often had the effect of greater estrangement and alienation—but they also often recognized their common Germanness, that in fact they shared a heritage and a nationality if not a state.[108] In 1988, at age seventeen, Christiane Schildt from Nürtigen took a week-long student trip to the GDR. While she wrote in her diary about the boring discos and grim apartment blocks, she also described a long conversation her group had had with East German youth in a Weimar hostel, where they openly discussed the merits and faults of each system and speculated on what a united Germany might look like. The conversation seemed premised on the assumption that there would be a new Germany.[109] Meanwhile, by traveling to the West through these group exchanges, young East Germans gained direct access to the material goods of the western youth culture with which so many of them were enamored.

Even after the building of the wall and the official ban on beat music, enthusiasm for western rock continued to build among East German youth. Berlin became a zone of exchange for youth culture. American cultural products were readily available in the western half of the city, and bringing these goods in by illegal channels wasn't difficult. Illegal record clubs smuggled in and shared contraband Bob Dylan and Jimi Hendrix albums, taped them, and circulated them into the provinces. One could publicly express one's affinity with the international youth culture through a personal style of shaggy hair and blue jeans, though looking like a hippie could get one arrested for intent to flee.[110] Because of the tremendous pressure for political and social conformity, trivial matters such as hair length and clothing had political significance for the highest levels of the party. To the East German regime, if not the young themselves, the music and fashion of western youth culture were indicative of a more general, if diffused and unfocused, dissent.[111] For example, Ulrich Plenzdorf's *The New Sufferings of Young W.* became one of the most popular novels in East Germany. It was first a short story, then a radio drama, then a stage play, then a novel. Published in 1973, the book was meant to both honor and parody Goethe's Young Werther, with a heavy dose of Holden Caulfield. The central character, Edgar Wibeau, is a charming seventeen-year-old who gets fed up with being the model GDR boy and simply drops out, running away to East Berlin, where he lives a ramshackle existence in the youth culture. In a famous passage, Wibeau waxes philosophical about the allure, appeal, and all-around awesomeness of blue jeans and their association with the West, the young, and music. Wibeau wants to be part of the international youth culture. He identifies with it, particularly the ways it crosses borders, and he wants to escape East Germany to see the world.[112]

An amusing example of the GDR's attempts to address the conflation of music and travel in youth culture was the hit film *Heißer Sommer* (Hot Summer), directed by Joachim Hasler. Released in August 1968, it offered an escapist movie experience with catchy pop songs at the time of the Warsaw Pact invasion of Czechoslovakia. Starring the pop celebrity couple Chris Doerk and Frank Schöbel, *Heißer Sommer* was the first GDR film in many years designed to appeal to youth. As difficult as it is to imagine, the film was a state-sanctioned East German socialist equivalent of the fluffy teen musical *Summer Holiday*. A group of eleven young women from Berlin and ten young men from Leipzig encounter each other while hitchhiking toward a beach holiday on the Baltic coast. They compete for rides as rivals, eventually arriving at the same destination with a host of rather chaste hijinks and pranks along the way, and lots of singing and dancing. The main song, which reprises throughout the film and became a hit, has the ensemble singing, "Today I want to embark into the world for some adventure. I want to see things I don't get to see any old day. I want adventures, more adventures. I want to act like a child. I want to go wild. Let's do things we don't do just any old day." A sense of group collective overrides individual prerogative: Brit, who is the most sexually open, finds herself rebuked by the group because of it; and when Wolf declares his intention to flee after a prank goes wrong and involves the police, another boy chastises him as cowardly, referring, of course, to *Republikflucht*. The film depicted, then, a youthful freedom to travel under spontaneous circumstances, but not as an individual, and only within the GDR. Still, the content, premise, and success of *Heißer Sommer* demonstrate that young people on the eastern side of the wall were in step with the larger transnational youth culture of the time.

A 1971 GDR study indicated that over 90 percent of young people had access to radio and/or television, and that 93 percent of them listened to and watched western media.[113] Unlike their peers elsewhere in the eastern bloc, young East Germans could easily consume western pop culture in their native language. Having failed to stamp out rock music with its 1965 ban, the GDR politburo reversed course in 1972, recognizing "youth dance music" as a legitimate cultural activity worthy of support and promotion by the state, while also permitting the public to watch western television without risk of repercussions. The regime sought in this way to reintegrate the disenchanted young while exerting social and political control over which music and bands would be officially promoted. Most famously, the regime expelled musician Wolf Biermann in the mid-1970s due to his increasingly overt political criticism and popularity among the young. From 1982 to 1987, the state sponsored the annual "Rock for Peace" music festival in the Palace of the Republic itself, where, over three days, thousands of rock music fans listened to dozens of approved GDR bands. Over the decade, an increasingly pluralistic youth culture developed in East Germany, with some genres of music, like GDR rock, getting official support, while others, such as punk, were actively and explicitly repressed.[114] In the second half of the 1980s, as local bands became bolder in their political criticism, the GDR tried to undermine their popularity by flooding East Germany with bootleg copies of western rock music. Thus the regime was actually producing and distributing western rock albums in an effort to curtail the popularity of GDR bands that the regime had itself initially sponsored but now considered suspect.[115]

West Berlin became a center of music and youth culture for young West Germans while international travel to and from the city grew substantially. Annual transit traffic into and out of West Berlin climbed to twenty million trips in 1982, not only because of *Ostpolitik* but also because East Germany accepted the Interrail youth pass for travel through its territory on limited routes.[116] The vibrant youth culture scene drew David Bowie and Iggy Pop to relocate there to record albums, as U2 would do a decade later. By the 1980s, West Berlin had a raw, frontier-town quality, particularly in the Kreuzberg neighborhood, with its thriving punk scene and anarchistic squats. The East and West Berlin punk scenes interacted frequently, with bands slipping across the border to play illegal gigs, and grannies visiting grungy record stores in the West at the request of their grandkids in the East.[117] Though critical attitudes toward the U.S. government remained the norm in Kreuzberg, western pop and rock still ruled in the bars, clubs, and concert scene. As Uwe Goltz related, "There is no hate between Germans and Americans. People may complain about Reagan, but they still drink Coca-Cola, wear jeans and listen to Springsteen." Goltz continued, "Pop music helped the cultures mix so much that it's hard to talk about the strict American culture or European culture anymore." Hans Schneider stressed that music "crosses borders in ways that politicians never could. It's the same in East Berlin. To people my age there, Lennon is a more important influence in their lives than Lenin."[118]

A week before Ronald Reagan's famous June 1987 speech near the Brandenburg Gate, in which he urged "Mr. Gorbachev" to "tear down this wall," David Bowie, the Eurythmics, and Genesis performed on successive nights in front of the nearby dilapidated Reichstag building and adjacent to the Berlin Wall. Bowie's performance of "Heroes," a song written about Berlin, had a special emotional resonance that night. During his show, a few hundred meters away along the Unter den Linden Avenue on the eastern side of the Berlin Wall, crowds of young people clashed with East German police as they gathered to listen to the music. Riots ensued, with the young crowd battling police and shouting, "The Wall Must Go" and "We Want Gorbachev." Even more young people returned the next night. Again the police attacked, dragging hundreds of the six thousand off to security vans. The same thing happened on the third night when Phil Collins of Genesis sent his greetings from the stage to "all Berliners, East and West."[119]

The *Guardian* reported that the young were frustrated by their inability to attend the concerts, and that, among other things, the riots "should be seen as an expression of youthful frustration over travel restrictions." Indeed, one young East German pointedly asked a police officer, "Why don't you let us travel west?"[120] A year later, in June 1988, the state sought to avoid a repeat of such conflict. In order to placate music fans who wouldn't be able to cross to West Berlin to see megastar Michael Jackson perform, the GDR scheduled a simultaneous concert in East Berlin featuring Bryan Adams and Big Country and hosted by figure-skating celebrity Katarina Witt. While the show was a success, about three thousand East German fans still gathered at the wall to hear but not see Michael Jackson. "Michael Jackson is a lot better," a sixteen-year-old explained. "We should break down the wall." A nineteen-year-old stated more plainly, "This is our chance to show a little our opposition to the government."[121] The GDR again concluded that in order to counter the appeal of western rock music, it had to try to harness it. Thus it sponsored a performance by Bruce Springsteen and the E Street Band in late July 1988, which, with three hundred thousand in attendance and millions of others watching via a live broadcast, was the largest concert in GDR history. The state's various attempts to placate or accommodate young East German rock music fans had a history of mixed results, and this time was no different, as even the Stasi concluded that Springsteen's concert had actually hastened the spirit of rebellion there rather than assuaged it.[122] When David Bowie died in early 2016, the German Foreign Ministry tweeted, "Goodbye, David Bowie. You are now among #Heroes. Thank you for helping to bring down the #wall."[123]

Youth riots at rock concerts and protests about the availability of music were arguably the most consistent form of popular dissent against the regime, spanning each decade of its existence. In October 1977, a crowd of nearly ten thousand young people on East Berlin's Alexanderplatz rioted when a rock concert by the local group Express was interrupted by state officials. In the ensuing battle, two hundred young people were wounded, seven hundred were detained, and three people died, including two policemen.[124] In October 1969, a false rumor spread in East Berlin that the Rolling Stones were going to play a concert atop the Springer Press building overlooking the wall from the western side. Though there was no concert, several thousand fans showed up on the eastern side of the wall and fought with police, whose presence politicized the scene. Young would-be concertgoers began shouting, "Long live Dubček!" Nearly four hundred of them were arrested.[125] In 1968, the Stasi pointed out that many of those it arrested for protesting the invasion of Czechoslovakia were young people in possession of western youth cultural contraband.[126] Of course, there had been the 1965 street battles in Leipzig following the ban on beat music, and the even earlier 1959 Leipzig and Dresden protests. However, the vast majority of young people in East Germany did not engage in protest and conflict with the regime. The mundane activities and experiences of daily life for millions of young people continued to take place in state-sponsored youth clubs. Even there, internal studies by the regime pointed to a worryingly accelerating process of individualization among young people in the 1980s.[127] More importantly, western youth culture and rock music in the GDR was a political phenomenon because of actions taken by the regime more so than by the young. State efforts to disrupt and interfere with this cultural phenomenon had overtly politicized it again and again.

As demonstrated by the young East German music fans who listened to concerts in West Berlin without being able to attend them, GDR citizens most resented the state's restrictions on mobility. By the end of the 1980s, studies revealed an incredibly pent-up demand for independent youth travel abroad. While there was considerable group travel into the eastern bloc and increasing group travel into the West, East German youth really desired independent travel to and through Western Europe.[128] Over the 1980s, the increasing frequency of travel between the two Germanies had led to an erosion of the strict border regime. The more East Germans traveled, the more they demanded to do so, and with greater frequency. Far from relieving tensions, the increased mobility of the young (and old) aggravated their discontent.[129]

The opening of the Hungarian border with Austria in the summer of 1989 permitted a mass flight from East Germany through Czechoslovakia, Hungary, and Austria into West Germany. In June and July alone, more than five hundred thousand GDR citizens made their way to the FRG, and in keeping with the historical pattern, they were disproportionately young.[130] In response to the large numbers of young East Germans who were fleeing the country via Hungary in September, over a thousand of the GDR's most popular rock musicians signed a declaration in support of democracy, open political activism, and the reform of travel restrictions. In October, the petition circulated through the music community and was read aloud at rock concerts, which rapidly turned into political rallies.[131] Once East Germany's external borders were circumvented, the state began to lose control. Because the suppression of travel and mobility had been the touchstone of the regime's authority, its seeming incapacity to maintain that authority in the summer and fall of 1989 led to emboldened critiques and transgressions by its citizens, with hundreds of thousands marching and protesting by late October.[132] The 9 November opening of the Berlin Wall itself was the result of a botched press conference announcing a loosening of travel restrictions. When asked when the new regulations would be implemented, the GDR spokesman responded on live television, without clear information to the contrary, "it's now, immediately, without delay." And so it was.

The comedic premise of Peter Timm's 1986 film *Meier* is mobility, or the lack thereof. An East German wallpaper hanger inherits a considerable sum of money and is allowed to cross over to West Berlin to claim it, but before returning home, he seizes the opportunity to embark on an around-the-world trip. Upon his return, he spends the remainder of his money on a West Berlin identity card and travel documents so that he will be able to go back and forth between East and West Berlin with ease. Asked at one point whether he is East or West German, Meier responds, "Gesamtdeutsch," or "all-German," using the term for the on-again, off-again exchange and contact programs between the two regimes. Timm also made the 1991 box-office smash hit *Go Trabi Go*, in which the members of an East German family, now able to travel without restriction, have a series of misadventures with their unreliable two-cylinder disaster of a car as they pollute their way south to vacation in and through Italy.

The film that best captures youth, immobility, and music in East Berlin is *Sonnenallee* (Sun Avenue). Directed by Leander Haussmann, the 1999 hit and multiple award winner is about a group of East Berlin youth circa 1980. The opening credits pan through seventeen-year-old Micha's room, showing posters of the Beatles, drawings of rock bands, stacks of cassettes, stolen street signs, and pictures of the Who and Batman torn out of magazines and tacked to the wall. Micha is using a reel-to-reel tape recorder to record a song off West Berlin radio and onto a bootleg cassette. He wears sneakers and a T-shirt that says "Rock & Pop." He and his friends from the neighborhood hangout along Sonnenallee, a street that dead-ends into the Berlin Wall. They have a "dealer" who trades in contraband: *Bravo* and other rock magazines, cassettes, even albums. One of Micha's friends, Wuschel, is obsessed with getting a pristine copy of the Rolling Stones' *Exile on Main Street*. The film traces the group of adolescents through a series of innocuous goings-on amid the daily life of the neighborhood in close proximity to the wall, which dynamically shapes their existence. The closing credits feature the Box Tops' "The Letter," a song about freedom, travel, and mobility, over a fantasy sequence of the people of the neighborhood dancing slowly, inexorably down the street, toward the wall, and beyond it. *Sonnenallee*, like the later *Goodbye, Lenin*, is a melancholy comedy about the former GDR, inspiring a sense of nostalgia (*Ostalgie*) for its distinct culture and social relations. It shows Micha's family and friends outwardly conforming to the system while maintaining a degree of opposition at the personal level. Western rock music and an interest in girls provide the group of boys with their shared identity, a sense of purpose, and two topics of conversation. The film shows how rock 'n' roll played an imaginative role for the young in their limited interactions with the West, giving them a sense of participating in the larger youth culture.[133]

While studying abroad in France in the 1990s, Leipziger Jana Hensel felt a bit isolated from her fellow students from Spain, Italy, France, Germany, and Austria because she didn't know the pop cultural references of their western childhoods. She was unfamiliar with the Smurfs, hadn't seen the same movies or read the same books. Yet music remained the one cultural reference that made her feel a part of international youth culture due to her familiarity with the Pet Shop Boys, the Cure, and Depeche Mode. Hensel's bestselling memoir, *After the Wall: Confessions from an East German Childhood and the Life That Came Next*, is another example of the millennial *Ostalgie* that captured the German public's imagination. Born in 1976, Hensel sets out to insist that things weren't so terrible in the GDR, and that she had a rich and worthwhile childhood, with her only complaint being limited mobility: "I wanted to travel, and I needed some Western money. Otherwise, I was basically satisfied with the way my life had been." Speaking for people her age, she says, "The only type of change we know is departure," referencing the term *die Wende* (the "change" or "turn"), which has come to signify the transition from two German states to one.[134] A 1991 study of German backpackers showed that since 1989, young West Germans had been flocking to Eastern Europe, and East Germans to Western Europe.[135]

At the end of the 1980s, Hensel participated in a series of group travel exchange programs with West Germany, but immediately after the wall came down, they no longer visited partner cities like Hamburg or Schweinfurt, but instead took class trips all over Western Europe: her Latin class went to Italy, her French class to Paris, her English class to London. It was through travel abroad in Western Europe and in the company of other young Europeans that she came to see herself as both German and European. Because of her age and her travel, she says, "I began to consider myself a citizen of Europe before most of my fellow East Germans did." The more adventurous of her friends bought Interrail tickets to explore Western Europe thoroughly and independently, many of them going as far away from East Germany as Interrail would take them, such as Ireland, but especially to the warm beaches of Portugal and Spain, directly connecting the opposed peripheries of Western Europe.[136]

Southern European Periphery

Over the 1960s, Western European travel to Spain grew exponentially. By the mid-1970s, foreign visitors to Spain numbered thirty-five million annually. The masses of Western Europeans frequenting the inexpensive and accessible resorts of the Spanish Mediterranean brought with them the norms, habits, and behaviors of their own societies, often challenging the conservative and hierarchical ways of more traditional Spain. Foreign tourists didn't simply invade Spain and bring liberalization with them; rather, they were invited to come. Hosteling was one of many policies the government pursued in this endeavor. Others included loosening border controls, participating in Eurail and Interrail, investing in infrastructure, reforming commercial policy and regulations, devaluing the peseta, and, not least, tolerating the more liberal social mores of the tourists. Economic development cast within the idea of a European Spain animated this state-led endeavor and served as the primary agent of modernization leading up to the formal democratization following Franco's death in the mid-1970s.[137]

The correlation between tourism and sexual permissiveness was strong, even inspiring a subgenre of Spanish cinema. Various states of undress, particularly the bikini, became common along the Costa del Sol, and eventually among young Spanish women, too. The term *sueca*, meaning Swedish woman, referred metonymically to any woman—initially blonde foreigners, but later brunette locals as well—who projected a liberated attitude and behavior toward sexual and gender norms.[138] In the early 1970s, Ronald Fraser documented the transformation of Tajos, a mountain village above the Costa del Sol. He noted that foreign influence in Tajos was most evident among the young, particularly regarding norms of gender and sexuality. Twenty-seven-year-old Lazaro Rodriguez said that "the tourists have brought more freedom." Twenty-one-year-old Josefa Alarcon recognized that "the foreign girls are freer than us." "It would be nice to have a bit more freedom," she said, something she associated with going abroad: "I'd like to travel, go to Portugal, London, Paris." While Pedro Nuñez, twenty-three, claimed that "foreign girls are easy," Teresa Gamez, twenty-one, pointed out that "it's the same boys who go with the foreign girls who say they would never want a village girl to carry on like the foreigners. The boys want it both ways—that's why we don't know what to do anymore. The girls are going to have to change."[139]

James Michener set *The Drifters*, his epic 1971 bestselling novel about youth travel, primarily on the Costa del Sol, in Torremolinos. By 1975 it had sold over two million copies; it was ultimately translated into a dozen languages. The book focuses on a group of western youth who have ended up in southern Spain by various circumstances, including an American draft dodger, a Norwegian beauty escaping a dull home life, a dangerously rebellious daughter of a British imperialist, an African American radical, and an Israeli war hero. Torremolinos is described as "the capital of the world" for youth, and the dozens of primary and secondary characters come from all over the western world, but primarily Europe and North America. They display a positive communal attitude by sharing resources and projecting a flexible inclusivity, though there are also hustlers, dropouts, and charlatans. The young in Torremolinos come and go, hanging out on the beach and in the clubs and bars, where "at any table of six you might find four nationalities." They spend the off-season there before being pushed out by the Spanish police in preparation for the high tourist season of summer. They then hit the road as "the riffraff of Europe, in shaggy hairdo and tattered dress," some taking trains, others hitchhiking, and one group heading out in a yellow pop-top minibus.[140]

The book's narrator is George Fairbanks, an older businessman who tries to look out for the young in an avuncular fashion. He relates the story, provides commentary, and generally sympathizes with the young characters. Michener uses Fairbanks as a device to try to explain this new transnational youth culture to his adult readers. Each main character highlights some particular issue associated with the young of the era, such as sexual liberation, political activism, generational rebellion, communal living, or escapist drug consumption. Though the book is rather heavy-handed, Michener manages to put these issues into relief and touches on several others as well, including the threat of nuclear war, the scourge of South African apartheid, the rejection of nationality, and the prolongation of youth. Fairbanks, for his part, clearly envies the easy sexuality of the young, among whom a chap could "find himself any number of lively young ladies prepared to make love in Belgian, Dutch, Italian or Danish." Though he also sees the perils of rampantly wanton promiscuity, Fairbanks is most concerned with the drug taking. Marijuana is common in the book, with one character used as a cautionary tale as she quickly moves from pot to acid to heroin, the last of which kills her.[141] On the one hand, the book is typical in the way the adult gaze makes a moral typology of the young; on the other hand, it sketches out several prominent aspects of the new transnational youth culture of mobility and travel, even if those features are overdrawn.

According to Fairbanks, the primary cultural glue holding this multinational community of young people together is music: "Regardless of which nation the young people had grown up in, they accepted this throbbing music as an integral part of their culture and were at home with it." Some, like the young Englishwoman Monica, "seemed to need music." Fairbanks recognized "how little I know of the music," yet "what a powerful influence it was having upon this generation." He determined that if he were to discover "the world which the young people around me were inhabiting," then their music would be "a passport to a terra incognita." Gretchen, an aspiring folk singer, tells Fairbanks, "you see, Uncle George, this music really is international . . . as we are international." A secondary character, Clive, circulates through Western Europe carrying the latest albums in a purple carpetbag. He is a kind of proto-DJ, hitting all the young hot spots with the newest records from London, keeping the international youth enclaves tuned in and up to date. Clive is an agent working along what he describes as "Torremolinos and Ibiza and the endless road of music that [is] uniting us all."[142]

The Balearic Islands of Ibiza and Formentera off the northeastern coast of Spain were renowned for having an itinerant and international population of young people. The islands became well known in the late 1960s for the hippie community there, as portrayed in Barbet Schroeder's 1969 film *More*. The young Dutchman Jan Cremer spent a couple of years there while bouncing back and forth between other destinations. It was in Ibiza where Cremer began to develop his talents as an artist while living in the bohemian enclave, where "instead of a dish of candy on the table, we had a big jar of pot and cigarette papers. It was all so cool, so relaxed, that I could feel the aggression flow out of me like semen. I laughed and sunbathed, fucked and smoked."[143] Ibiza and Formentera became famous as a sensual and utopian endpoint on the Europe-Asia hippie trail. Young Spaniards like Juan Aranzadi went there to be with the young foreign travelers and learn from them.[144] For several weeks in the summer of 1969, foreign youth actually outnumbered Spaniards on Formentera, testing the locals' patience with their appearance and behavior, particularly their nudity and drugs.[145] In July 1971, Spanish police moved in force on the hippies in Ibiza, leading to dozens of arrests of foreign youth, with some reportedly hiding in caves along the northern coast, and an exodus of others who declared their intention to relocate to Amsterdam.[146]

Nevertheless, foreign youth continued to be drawn there largely because of each other, with some settling there permanently or semi-permanently. Indeed, they formed their own community, distinct from that of the locals. Several weekly "hippie markets" that were scattered across Ibiza selling trinkets and handmade tchotchkes became tourist destinations themselves. This marginal tourist culture was eventually embraced by the establishment, with backpackers and hippies appearing in official promotional materials. In the early 1980s, the Ibiza and Formentera tourist board adopted the slogan "Islands of Youth" and began to promote the islands as a tolerant beach paradise with a long-standing and unique gravitational power that drew in the young of the world. By the end of the decade, some 650,000 foreign travelers and tourists were passing through Ibiza annually.[147]

Many of those visitors had come to dance. In the late eighties, Ibiza became famous for electronic music superclubs, where the young would take ecstasy and other recreational drugs and stay up all night dancing to the repetitive rhythms of remix DJs before spilling out onto the beaches at sunrise. The industry transformed the island into a resort destination of massive dance clubs, as fans of house and techno music in its various forms—Ambient, Jungle, Rave, Trance, and the like—would follow their favorite DJs to Ibiza to dance in mountains of foam. Ibiza became the world's top destination for fans of dance music generally, and it is credited with being the source of the explosive dance music scene in the UK and elsewhere, with the London-Ibiza "Second Summer of Love" in 1988 considered the moment that raving came out from the illegal underground of warehouse parties and started to go mainstream in dance clubs and on radio.[148] Even if there was a very strong British contingent, as UK club owners in particular began to promote package tours, the scene was built on the long tradition of Ibiza and Formentera as transnational spaces of mobility interconnected within a circuit of youth travel.[149]

Spain is the best example of how the spread of travel and tourism into the Mediterranean peripheries of Western Europe contributed to a process of Europeanization, anticipating, in some places, formal accession into the European Community. The Portuguese and Greek hostel associations both joined the International Youth Hostel Federation in 1959 as the governments began to pursue policies similar to those in Spain to draw in foreign tourists, though on a less comprehensive and smaller scale. Greece struggled to keep up with the demand for hostel space, with the number of foreign overnights jumping from 17,000 in 1960 to 105,000 by 1966, and with domestic overnights growing equally fast.[150] Yugoslavia joined

31   In the 1970s, Eurail and Interrail offered free passage aboard ferries, bringing Greece and
      its archipelago into the backpacker circuit. Undated. Agentur Garp/Keystone Pressedienst,
      Hamburg.

the IYHF in 1968 and Interrail in 1972, and it already had an established youth travel culture with a network of forty youth hostels and two hundred thousand members.[151] In the 1960s, its Youth Labor Action program was itself undergoing a dramatic shift away from voluntary physical hard labor to holiday making, so that by the 1970s the emphasis was on youth leisure, making friends, touring, and being away from home rather than building socialism.[152] Yugoslavia was in an interesting position, drawing large numbers of tourists from both Western and Eastern Europe. Those from the West saw the country as a glimpse of the communist East, while those from the East saw it as offering a taste of the capitalist West. Yugoslavia could become an interesting contact zone for those on holiday during the Cold War.[153] There could also be a backlash, however, as in Belgrade, where there was a reported war on foreign hippies and efforts to cut their hair in the summer of 1968.[154]

Over the 1970s, Western European mass tourism into these Mediterranean countries grew significantly, creating an interdependent economic model of multinational development.[155] The Pink Palace on Corfu, for example, was easily reachable by an overnight ferry with Eurail and Interrail passes, making it a destination for beachfront hedonism. In the late 1960s, the new youth spaces of *boîtes* and discotheques in the Plaka neighborhood of Athens were understood to be imports from Western Europe, drawing foreign tourists and local youth.[156] The same era saw considerable growth in the number of students from the Mediterranean participating in study abroad programs in Northern Europe as well. Greek, Portuguese, and Spanish youth in particular began studying in significant numbers in France, the United Kingdom, and West Germany, with the latter eventually surpassing the United States as the host to the largest number of European foreign exchange students.[157] In the late 1970s, the Council of Europe began sponsoring binational youth exchange programs organized around the premise of Europeanism between northern countries, especially Ireland and the United Kingdom, and southern ones such as Greece, Italy, Portugal, and Spain.[158] Meanwhile, Greece, Portugal, and Spain underwent a transition from authoritarian to democratic regimes over the same decade. Greece was admitted to the European Community in 1981, and Portugal and Spain in 1986. International tourism has been credited with having a democratizing effect in each of these countries during the 1970s.[159]

Greek youth studying in West Germany also learned to hitchhike and Interrail there. Initially, the only travel these students undertook consisted of going home to Greece for a visit, but they soon began exploring other parts of their home country, often at the invitation of friends who were visiting from West Germany. In the 1970s, young Greeks began traveling on holiday with their peers rather than their families, adopting the frugal practices of backpacking by riding on the decks of boats to reach remote islands, sleeping on the beach or camping while there. Their mobility subsequently expanded throughout Western Europe, becoming a part of their sense of self and sociability as middle-class students. On his way to visit a pen pal in London, Grigoris Parakampos encountered West German backpackers and soon adopted the travel practice himself. As a resident of West Germany, Yorgos Kallidromitis developed an attachment for Spain, where he felt a strong Mediterranean affinity, which helped to foster a sense of regional difference for him between Northern and Southern Europe. Greek youth travel intertwined and overlapped with Greek migrant travel, though the two practices of mobility remained distinct. Young Greek migrant laborers in West Germany returned home regularly to visit and help their families in the 1960s and 1970s. They tended not to travel beyond Greece, however, either for personal edification or with non-Greek peers. This was distinct from the sociability of the Greek students who were Interrailing and hitchhiking within the circuit of independent youth travel. Indeed, hitchhiking in particular was seen by both students and workers to be a distinguishing feature of class, embraced by one group and rejected by the other as a legitimate means of travel and social distinction.[160]

From the late 1950s to the mid-1970s, millions of Greek, Portuguese, and Spanish laborers migrated north, while millions of British, French, and German tourists traveled south in an interconnected, interwoven, and entangled network of foreign workers and tourists. Greece, like Portugal and Spain, had been involved in massive labor recruitment programs established in the late 1950s and early 1960s by Northern European countries. For example, West Germany negotiated bilateral treaties to bring in large numbers of young men from all around the Mediterranean basin to labor as "guest workers." Similar programs across northwestern Europe did the same as the booming economy suffered from underemployment.

There was considerable overlap between migrant labor and tourists. To accelerate labor recruitment into the French economy, for example, industry, with the sanction of the state, circumvented official protocols and encouraged potential laborers from the Mediterranean basin to enter France as tourists in order to find work. By using this channel to come into the country, workers could avoid the cumbersome visa requirements, which even the French state viewed as being too slow to keep up with the demand for labor. This held true as a means of entry not only for Southern Europeans, but for North Africans as well. By 1968, 80 percent of the immigrant workforce in France had entered the country as tourists without a visa.[161]

Importantly, these programs were conceptualized as circulatory: once workers had completed the terms of their contract, they would presumably return to their home countries rather than settle permanently in their host countries. In fact, their patterns of mobility were circulatory, although not in the ways imagined by European states. Immigrants with valid residency visas returned regularly to their countries of origin for holiday and familial visits, especially women and children, despite the risk of discriminatory border controls.[162] In response to the oil embargo and the resulting sharp economic downturn, governments ended these labor recruitment programs and replaced them in 1973 and 1974 with strict border controls for entry and immigration. By the middle of the decade, with immigrants having become a growing target for hostility and with immigration now heavily curtailed across Western Europe (even for family reunification), such migrants were condemned as "false tourists" (*faux tourists* or *falsche Touristen*). Tourist visas were now required to enter Europe, and they were not easy to obtain for Algerians, Moroccans, and Turks. The interconnected migration and tourist systems linking Europe with non-Europeans was increasingly disrupted.

Significantly, the application of stricter border controls in the 1970s was designed to identify and keep out such "false tourists." Determining people's motives and intent became a paramount means of border control, even for those with the appropriate visas: were they real tourists or false ones? In effect, this produced racial profiling, as North Africans in particular fell under suspicion of false tourism and were denied entry even as they undertook legitimate holidays. In practice, therefore, tourist mobility within Europe was becoming increasingly a kind of white European privilege, in particular because of its entanglement with the mobility of immigration.[163]

In November 1983, three young French Foreign Legion recruits harassed, attacked, beat, and stabbed Habib Grimzi, a twenty-six-year-old Algerian, and threw him from a train to his death. Grimzi was not an immigrant but a tourist who had been traveling around France visiting friends. On his way home to Oran, he was contentedly listening to his Walkman on the Bordeaux-Vintimille express headed for Marseilles. His drunken tormenters harassed him and pursued him through the train even after a conductor had relocated him into a locked compartment for his protection. Other than this rail conductor, no one intervened on Grimzi's behalf through his prolonged ordeal. The murderers blamed their actions on alcohol, but there is no denying the racism involved, as reported by witnesses and as evident in statements made by the defendants themselves. It was clear the young Legionnaires viewed Grimzi as an interloper, as someone who didn't belong, and they felt provoked by his presence whether they assumed him to be an immigrant or not. Young activists, meanwhile, made use of the tourist-immigrant conflation by rallying around his murder in their ongoing efforts to highlight the violence and racism to which they, as Franco-Maghrebi immigrants, were subject in France.[164] As a young Algerian traveling in France, Habib Grimzi didn't have access to the same expanding freedom of movement accorded to Western Europeans or North Americans, especially white ones.

In the mid-1980s, twenty-five-year-old West Indian Briton Caryl Phillips left Oxford University and set out to explore his European and British identity through a prolonged journey across the continent. He sought to reconcile how he, as a black man, felt to be both of Europe and not of Europe. Tellingly, he began his year-long exploration of Europeanness in Morocco before traveling through Spain, France, Italy, the Netherlands, Ireland, Norway, West and East Germany, Poland, and the Soviet Union. In Morocco he felt targeted as a rich northerner being hustled by streetwise young men. In Venice he identified with Othello and Shylock, in Amsterdam with Anne Frank. Wherever he traveled, he felt he was viewed with suspicion, even when his British nationality was known. Although he held a UK passport, he suffered the petty bigotries of border, immigration, and customs controls, nowhere more so than in Oslo, where he was harassed and aggressively interrogated about his financial status, permanent residency, and itinerary, indicating that the officials were concerned about the legitimacy of his visit there, and that he might be a false tourist. Phillips had gone to Norway specifically "to test [his] own sense of negritude." In many ways, that is what he was doing throughout his trip. In his travelogue book of personal essays *The European Tribe*, published in 1987, Phillips described a European community united in bigotry toward the nonwhite other, an attitude that he found crossed the national and Cold War divisions of the continent. While his trip did not resolve the contradictory feeling of being a British European while also being told, subtly and not so subtly, that he didn't belong, it did help him to define the parameters of his dilemma and to see in it a different kind of shared Europeanization, a white tribal one, as the continent continued its struggle to accommodate the mobility and residency of minority populations.[165]

About the same time, frustrated with the slow negotiations on the Single European Act (SEA), which structurally overhauled the Common Market in preparation for developing the European Union, the governments of France, Germany, and the Benelux states (five of the ten members of the EC) signed the Schengen Agreement in 1985. The signatory governments agreed gradually to remove all controls at their common borders. The terms were implemented over the following decade, and by the mid-1990s the "Schengenland" signatories had expanded to include practically all of Western Europe, with the exception of Ireland and the UK. Although initially independent of the European Union, Schengen was formally incorporated into it in 1999.[166]

Western Europe achieved the internal borderless mobility that so many had demanded, but it did so only by hardening controls at new external borders as determined by the agreement, especially toward the south. Initially, Southern European countries were reluctant to participate in Schengen because of worries about illegal immigration. The accession of Greece, Portugal, and Spain into the EC in the 1980s had an immediate impact on the Mediterranean as a region, because long-standing social formations of trade and mobility traversing the Mediterranean were disrupted between the new EC members and countries on the southern and eastern shores as a consequence of this membership. Morocco and Turkey both expressed interest in joining the EC as a measure to restore regional integrity.[167] Their participation in Interrail reflected this. In 1989, for example, the two countries together sold more than four thousand Interrail youth passes.[168] Prior to decolonization, the Mediterranean had been a threshold of passage rather than a barrier to it. The combined effect of decolonization and European integration rendered the Mediterranean a frontier zone, with the term "Mediterranean" often used in contradistinction to "European."[169] The internal freedom of movement achieved within Western Europe and its expanding boundaries was defined by the external restrictions on entry, creating a "Fortress Europe." This Europeanization was premised on excluding specific non-Europeans. This shift is also telling in that the initial goals for freedom of movement as outlined in the 1957 Treaty of Rome had been for goods, capital, and labor. No longer seen as a mere economic opportunity, transnational mobility had become a political right. Freedom of movement was no longer based on one's economic activity in the market but instead was tied to one's political capacity as a citizen in the European Union. By the time of the European Union, those who were making the most of this unhindered mobility were tourists, especially young ones.

Youth Tourism and Europeanization

In the late 1980s, tourists accounted for three-quarters of all cross-border traffic in Western Europe. In this region more than any other in the world, massive movements of foreign tourists dwarfed all other kinds of population movements.[170] Two-thirds of all global international travel was to member states of the European Community, and the majority of this international tourism came from within the EC itself. Intra-EC tourism was 70 percent of global international tourism in 1989. European mass tourism had grown tremendously since the postwar period and had resulted in a significant transfer of wealth from north to south, from the wealthier EC members to the poorer ones. The European Commission came to recognize that tourism served not only the economic goals of the European Community, but also the political principles of integration. Throughout the 1980s, the commission took measures to standardize and harmonize tourist facilities, transport, and services, even declaring 1988 the European Year of Tourism.[171] That same year, the Council of Europe declared the Camino de Santiago as the "First European Cultural Itinerary" just two years after Spain's admission into the EC. More than just spiritual pilgrimage, the Camino came to be celebrated for the transnational European consciousness it inspired.[172]

Youth travel continued to increase at a more rapid rate than international tourist travel overall. From 1980 to 1990, the proportion of young tourists among international arrivals rose from 15 to 20 percent.[173] A 1990 market study of youth tourism in the UK found that 70 percent of those between the ages of fifteen and thirty-four had been abroad, with Europe as the most popular destination and independent travel as the preferred mode. Not only were the young the most likely to travel independently, but the study predicted that this trend was likely to become even more pronounced as Britain became more integrated with the rest of the continent through the imminent European Union. Those who chose independent travel over inclusive package holidays were overwhelmingly likely to be young and to choose Europe; and the young who chose independent travel farther afield had first developed a taste and skill for independent travel in Western Europe. Among those who traveled to Europe in 1988, 77 percent of young independent travelers visited EC countries. The largest statistical difference between independent and inclusive holidays was in non-EC Europe, where the percentage of young travelers on inclusive tours was double the number of those traveling independently, inverting the trend within EC countries. On the continent, therefore, independent youth travel was overwhelmingly associated with Western Europe specifically.[174] Similarly, a 1990 study in Italy found that young Italians traveled more than all other Italian demographic groups, and that they did so to get to know Europe, its people, and themselves.[175] When young Italians first began to travel in significant numbers in the 1960s, they were referred to with the general term *nomadi*, but as their numbers grew and practices evolved, and as they became integrated into the larger culture of youth travel, by the 1980s they were being called *saccopelisti* (sleeping bags), the Italian equivalent of backpackers.[176]

A 1990 Eurobarometer statistical survey of young people from EC member states revealed considerable data about travel. Of the seventy-six hundred respondents, who were between the ages of fifteen and twenty-four, more than two-thirds had traveled abroad, and nearly half had spent more than a month abroad. There was no important breakdown by gender in terms of number of countries visited or time spent abroad, but young women were more likely than young men to have gone as part of organized exchanges. The more affluent and educated had done more foreign travel of longer duration. France and Spain were the two preferred destinations, visited by nearly half of the respondents;

Italy was a more distant third. Tellingly, young people from Benelux and Scandinavia had visited the most EC countries, averaging more than four, while young people from the Mediterranean member states had visited the fewest, averaging less than two. Furthermore, over 70 percent of young Greeks had not been abroad at all, compared to less than 2 percent of young Danes.[177]

In the mid-1980s, Copenhagen opened an Interrail Centre beneath its central railway station, offering showers, lockers, a place to rest and cook, information services, and free condoms seventeen hours a day. The facility was open to the young, who needed only to show their Interrail or Eurail pass to achieve entry. In the peak summer months, five hundred people a day would pass through, with a total of more than fifty thousand for the season. The stationmaster was delighted with the young visitors. "The Interrailers are the most positive and pleasant customers we have," he said. Though the number of Italians and Britons was significant, the largest number of those passing through came from Scandinavia, as Copenhagen was the narrow conduit through which young Norwegians or Swedes would flow to and from the continent.[178]

The debate about Swedish membership in the EC (Sweden joined the EU in 1995) often revolved around youth travel. Compared to their older counterparts, the young were overwhelmingly in favor of the Europeanization of Sweden. In 1990, 65 percent of Swedes between the ages of seventeen and twenty-four traveled independently in Europe, while 50 percent of all international travel into Sweden was by people under age thirty. Compared to other forms of consumption, foreign travel was the preferred target of spending by young Swedes. Once Sweden began to consider membership seriously, it intensified state-sponsored youth travel and exchanges with EC member states to foster relations, as the UK had done earlier. More than any official program, however, the Interrail pass spurred the Europeanization of Swedish youth. When it was introduced in 1972, young Swedes bought two thousand tickets. In 1989 they purchased nearly fifty thousand tickets, putting Sweden at the top of all member countries. Independent foreign travel had become a rite of passage for Swedish youth, while package tours and charter travel continued to characterize Swedish adult travel abroad.[179]

This connection between transnational travel and Europeanization underlay a large study of young backpackers conducted in the mid-1980s through the West German Institute for Tourism in Starnberg. Researchers designed the study as an essay contest, asking young Germans aged twelve to twenty-five to narrate their experiences on the theme of traveling and becoming familiar with Europe. The contest generated more

than a thousand responses, which were edited and published as two thematic reports by Birgitte Gayler.[180] In one essay, Friedrich Burschel, age
twenty, described rolling out his sleeping bag on the wide open forecourt
of the Venice train station facing the Grand Canal, sharing cheap wine
with his community of fellow backpackers amidst "a babble of voices
from all over the place, here an American, there a Portuguese, a Japanese, Danes, English, Germans, French, Irish, Austrians, Italians." During "these warm summer nights," Burschel wrote, this concentration of
young travelers settled in at the Venice train station "is Europe, is the
world," conflating the two.[181]

What Burschel had described so warmly was not so warmly welcomed
by the leaders of Venice. As the city became overwhelmed by an influx
of tourists in the mid-1980s, young backpackers were seen as particularly
problematic. While the young had access to Venice across the causeway
via their rail passes, they couldn't afford the expensive tourist infrastructure designed for an affluent clientele, and thousands began to sleep and
hang out in the open plazas of the city, much as they had done in Amsterdam more than a decade earlier. Piazza San Marco became a kind of
bivouac for mostly young European *saccopelisti*, where they would gather
under the arcades to seek shelter from the heat, or sit in circles sharing
food and cheap wine, or roll out sleeping bags for a nap, or blare music
from portable tape players. In July 1986 the city posted notices in four
languages that picnicking, playing music, and singing were now prohibited in Piazza San Marco, and requiring visitors to wear more than a bathing suit while touring the city.[182] The city opened a new youth hostel,
expanded another one, and set up an officially sanctioned camping area
on another Venetian island, while at the train station it used water can-
nons regularly to wash away the backpackers from the outside terrace.
These new policies had, on the whole, the desired effect, yet the general
crush of tourism in Venice remains unabated with the current dilemma
of cruise-ship day-trippers.[183]

Nevertheless, statistical and anecdotal evidence from the late seventies through the eighties seemed to confirm Ronald Inglehart's studies
of the sixties related to youth attitudes toward Europe. An extensive poll
from 1977 conducted in the UK, France, and West Germany revealed
that young people in all three countries felt an overwhelming solidarity
with one another, and the pollsters concluded that the young already
expressed the values and met the criteria to qualify as European, even if
they didn't articulate it as such. As the headline read, "The Europe of the
Young Is Already Here."[184] In a pro-European editorial published in *Le
Monde* in 1978, a French student, Xavier Allouis, wrote, "Our generation

was born with the Europe of the Treaty of Rome," and that this "communitarian generation" didn't "understand the reason for borders. The youth of Europe travel today more than ever before" as "Europe narrows to the dimensions of a single country."[185] An editorial from 1983 noted that, because of the transnational youth culture, exchanges, travel, and hitchhiking, the young took Europe for granted, even in the face of harsh socioeconomic realities.[186] In a pro-integration polemic called *Generation Europe*, two young French authors pointed to the June 1987 concert by David Bowie and Genesis, and the large numbers of East German youth who had gathered on their side of the wall to listen to it, even fighting with police to do so, as indicative of young people's desire for unfettered mobility connected to a united Europe. The authors celebrated the removal of border controls, and suggested that just as youth had been central to Franco-German reconciliation, so the young might also reconcile the Cold War East and West. Indeed, the authors suggested that the young already recognized themselves as having shared interests through music and youth culture.[187]

Importantly, these examples emphasized a cultural affinity for being European rather than a pronounced political disposition. This was confirmed in a 1990 Eurobarometer study showing that four-fifths of youth in EC member states were in favor of efforts to unify and integrate Western Europe, yet lacked any great passion or general rationale for these views.[188] Later in the 1990s, however, pollsters found that the opinions of the young about integration were coming closer to those of their elders when social factors such as wealth and education were considered, and that in the context of the fervent and polarized debate about the Maastricht Treaty in the early and mid-1990s, statistical evidence showed that the enthusiasm of the young, though still greater than that of their adult counterparts, was falling just as the EU began earnestly to implement policies designed specifically for them.[189]

The Cold War Circulations of Youth Culture

With the fall of the Berlin Wall in late 1989 and the dissolution of the Soviet Union in 1992, the Cold War seemingly came to end. Former eastern bloc states sought and secured membership in the European Union, which had redefined political and economic integration with the 1992 Treaty of Maastricht. Youth rail pass networks were extended farther east and southeast to the borders of the former Soviet Union. Youth hostel membership in the IYHF network (now known as Hostelling

International) expanded even further and included Russia. What is western and what is European continues to be in flux, as are the habits, practices, destinations, and itineraries of youth travel.

In the summer of 1990, where I, as a Eurailing American, might travel and what I might do had expanded considerably with the easier accessibility of central and Eastern Europe. *Who* was able to travel underwent profound change as well, because tens of thousands of youth from Eastern Europe, particularly young East Germans, began to join their western compatriots in the transnational culture of youth travel. In early July, Mike, Larissa, and Natalie went to Spain for the Running of the Bulls in Pamplona, while I went to Belgium for the Rock Torhout festival featuring De La Soul, Sinead O'Connor, Lenny Kravitz, Midnight Oil, Bob Dylan, and the Cure. It was a very wet, muddy day for the sixty thousand of us gathered in an open field. I spent some time with a couple of young East Germans who had generously offered to let me huddle beneath some plastic sheeting with them. Like me, they had come because of the great lineup; unlike me, they were exercising a new freedom to travel. I don't recall their names or where else they had been or planned to go—in fact, we didn't communicate very well—yet their independent mobility and love of live rock music had intersected with my own. While wholly unintended, this shared mutuality made us participants in something bigger than ourselves.

Without doubt, a principal concern of the Cold War rivalry between the superpower blocs focused on the young. The policies toward youth and youth culture in the two Germanies, for example, made this clear. While the political dissidence of rock music in the eastern bloc countries has been overstated (not least by the regimes themselves), what hasn't been fully considered is the connection between the cultural exchange of music and the movement of people: East Germans went to Hungary to buy albums, young Soviets consumed Polish media, and young Czechoslovak musicians came to East Germany to hear their favorite GDR-approved rock bands.[190] The interconnectedness of the youth music culture and youth mobility characterized both sides of the Iron Curtain and was, arguably, one of the things that moved most frequently across it, though not really in both directions. Overwhelmingly, western youth and western youth culture moved east rather than the other way around. Yet the continuities of rock 'n' roll crossing the Iron Curtain, from the public attitudes of the state to the private practices of individuals, were remarkably consistent on both sides. As Jonathyne Briggs has argued, the portability and ubiquity of rock music helped to create a community of listeners as a fundamental component of the community of youth, and the shared patterns across the Cold War should be considered as compelling as the idiosyncratic differences.[191] The intertwined frequency of youth travel and the spread of youth culture enabled connections between periphery and center, expanding who, where, and what integrated to varying degrees. The integrating effect of the transnational youth culture had a strong emphasis on the mobility of music as well as the young.

Social scientific studies have suggested that human musicality evolved in the service of group living. Individual responses to music have been identified as primarily social phenomena binding humans together into groups. Human musicality, then, is a special form of social cognition that supports group cohesion, in both communicative and affective terms, and served over time as a tool for social living, creating interconnected communities. Importantly, members of the group do not need to know one another interpersonally, as music enables group cohesion over considerable distance and time.[192] An early essay by Stuart Hall and Paddy Whannel, "The Young Audience" (1964), made a similar point: young music fans formed a community wherein a common set of symbols and meanings provided an expressive field for them socially to work through being young together.[193] The capacity of music to foster participation in fluid and plastic ways enabled the formation of a wide variety of communities, whether generational or gendered, national or transnational, subcultural or mainstream.[194] The simultaneity of the transnational rock 'n' roll and travel cultures permitted new possibilities for interaction within social networks of the young, each helping to expand the reach of the other. In the time and place studied here, a process of Europeanization unfolded, expanding boundaries and drawing in peripheries.

Examining the phenomenon of the New Age Travellers throws into sharp relief the relationship between youth, music, travel, and the state. These young people rejected the institutional frameworks intended for the short-term travel of the young within a structured, governmentally promoted paradigm. Their vagabond lifestyle proliferated outward from Britain, as others joined this nearly stateless group of young people in their peregrinations across the continent. Suddenly a trans-European identity became problematic for the nation-states that had once so actively promoted such an attitude via youth travel in hostel and exchange systems. New Age Travellers constantly refused to accept the boundaries of identity based on a sedentary existence or national or Cold War frontiers. They adhered to being a kind of stateless tribe in flux, roaming through the European Community or Union and beyond. Their struggle wasn't solely for the right to be on the move; it was an expression of identity that proclaimed new ways of community membership that were defined in a manner outside geopolitical territory and based instead on the cultural practice of travel. A struggle for autonomy took place in the interstitial spaces of the continent, whether in rural park-ups in the Pyrenees or in the Christiania enclave of Copenhagen. With an emphasis on local configurations of alternative daily life, the Travellers rejected the EC/EU as an alienating European superpower.[195]

Still, does this make them European? Perhaps they were transitory Europeans in both senses of the term. They moved about Europe in perpetual transit, but their European identity itself was transitory and unfixed. While they may have in many ways rejected the modern nation-state, that does not by necessity mean they embraced a post-nation-state, supranational entity such as the European Union. Instead, their "New Europ@" was based on the interpersonal interaction of being in movement that congregated and dispersed across the continent and beyond. Perhaps these communities of young travelers contributed to the ethos of integration through their familiarity with one another and their interaction with foreign places, peoples, and cultures. In particular, they came to see themselves as forming a transnational community of traveling youth, a sense of identity that they recognized in one another through the personal relationships and cultural practices of travel. The process itself was political and democratic, if only via cultural practice.

The political philosopher Etienne Balibar sees the project of European citizenship as fraught with complications of many kinds—structural, racial, and national, among others. He believes that the way forward must be both voluntarist and fundamentally democratic. That is, it is up to the people of Europe to devise a new way of being through the development of a new political process that is "neither the clauses of a treaty nor the program of a party or a government; it is rather a program to 'think Europe' . . . through worksites constituted by transnational initiatives."[196] Balibar identifies several possible "worksites of democracy" as potentially fruitful for "collective political practice, collective access to citizenship, 'always in the making.'" One of these "worksites" is the "democratization of borders," where Europe might develop a "universal right of circulation and residency" amid a "shared construction of citizenship." He insists that "we must think of the means to change the historical relation between territory and population in order to free it from schemas of property (including state property)."[197] The 1989 collapse of the Cold War border regimes was one example of such a process, though of course the nation-state continues to be the primary means of organizing polities.

Those backpacking in Europe were, of their own accord, doing some of this voluntarist democratization of the borders of Europe through their circuitous travels and interpersonal interaction, though in ways well outside the federalist European project. Their sense of community was exactly one of a shared construction that denied the fundamental relationship of people to territory or property. While this may not be indicative of political unification, there was a process of integration underway as new places and peoples were incorporated into this flexing and fluxing community of travelers, a community that developed at the intersection of youth travel and youth music.

The expanding circulations of youth helped to spread the integrating effect of a transnational youth culture into and beyond the peripheries of Western Europe. Neither Eurail nor Interrail was a program of the European Community. These rail passes were not a part of official integration; instead, they contributed to its development. Indeed, youth rail passes preceded, anticipated, and enabled the expansion of membership in the EC (and after 1992, the EU) into Northern Europe (Denmark, Ireland, Sweden, and the United Kingdom), Southern Europe (Greece, Portugal, and Spain), and Eastern Europe (East Germany, Hungary, Poland, and Romania)—all of which were members of one or both rail networks prior to joining the EC or EU. What it meant to backpack in Europe continued to evolve, particularly in terms of where it took place. The large unified area of Schengenland produced an image of internal coherence for Western Europe, where population movements were fluid and free. Yet such internal coherence was premised on the application of increasingly rigid discriminatory controls at Europe's external borders.

Intercultural encounters outside of Europe helped generate feelings of European belonging, too, as we saw with the hippie trail. National particularities within Europe often seemed minor in comparison, whether they were generated through imperialism, migration, or travel.[198] Decolonization and the extra-European encounter shaped the postwar "European" consciousness as well. In 1945 France, the question of how to differentiate citizenship along race for inhabitants of what would become the French Union of overseas territories settled on the coded language of "European" and "autochtone."[199] Through a series of influential books, anthropologists such as Claude Lévi-Strauss began the systematic comparison of western and non-western cultures, helping to differentiate the European and non-European. In 1955 in *Tristes tropiques*, Lévi-Strauss even directly compared the cross-cultural explorations and journeys of youth, noting the "renewed vogue" for travel among adolescent Europeans as an example of their "quest for power" in the context of rites of passage.[200] A 1979 ethnographic exhibition in Switzerland entitled "Being Nomadic Today" included young European travelers in South Asia beside pastoral herders in sub-Saharan Africa, the equine communities of the Central Asian steppes, the seabound Inuit of North America, and the Touareg caravans of the Sahara.[201] Postcolonial ethnography in Western Europe emphasized a universal humanity while also reinscribing hierarchies of otherness.[202] Thus, where to include the overlanders of the hippie trail was problematic. On the one hand, young Europeans backpacking outside Europe in the 1970s generated a contrast of inclusion and exclusion along racial and ethnic lines. But on the other hand, their practice of travel was considered to be liminal, transgressing accepted patterns of behavior distinguishing the West from the rest, especially when it resembled vagabondage or became entangled with migration.

Rights of Passage

In September 2010, a thirty-three-year-old Dutchman named Wijnand Boon set out to walk across Europe. He used Internet technology to document his trip, but also to demonstrate how he could use social media to plan his itinerary, arrange lodging, get help, and, most important of all, connect with others and build community. He was inspired by the previous year's Christmas speech by the Netherlands' Queen Beatrix, in which she lamented that personal technologies had led to a social atomization and fragmentation of community. Carrying a guitar, an iPhone, and a backpack with an attached two-wheeled cart, Boon wanted to show how technology could help create transnational social relations among strangers, and he relied upon the tradition of independent travel for his experiment. A musician, Boon brought his guitar along as a social strategy, and many of his online posts included videos of him playing and singing with others he had met en route. He set up a website, a blog, a Twitter feed, a Facebook page, a Pinterest page, a YouTube channel, and an e-mail account to document his trip and make improvisational arrangements along the way. He relied on the altruism of others to volunteer as hosts, give advice, and help connect him with people farther down the road. He initially set out for Santiago de Compostela, but then extended his trip across Southern Europe to Istanbul, which he reached three years later, in September 2013, opting to go no farther because of the war in Syria. Across the nearly ten thousand kilometers, he improvised his route, found places to sleep, got counsel, received donations, and made friends through social media. He used no guide-books, no hostels, no rail passes.[1]

The practice of backpacking and travel has changed significantly in the last twenty-five years, not least because of technological efficiencies: the widespread availability of ATMs allows for easy access to personal bank accounts and foreign currency; the expansion of high-speed rail and the rise of discount airlines, particularly in Europe, offer cheap and quick means to reach distant destinations for spontaneous short-term excursions; cellphones, smartphones, and Internet cafés make it possible to maintain daily contact with friends and family as well as make detailed travel arrangements. The most frequent use of the Internet by Europeans has been to book travel and holiday accommodations.[2] Even as the numbers of travelers and trips within Europe has grown considerably, the annual sales of Eurail and Interrail passes peaked in 1990 and 1991 respectively, with Interrail in particular experiencing a precipitous decline over the 1990s.[3] Backpackers have proliferated outside the continent, and there, too, their interconnected hypermobility flows as much across the Internet and telecommunications as they do across the world in overlapping mobile networks.[4]

A variety of mobilities are increasingly defining the social lives of people around the world. John Urry and Tim Cresswell insist that in the last twenty-five years we have experienced a "mobility turn," as different forms of travel, transport, and communication have come to define the interconnective and interactive social experiences of the early twenty-first century. Such mobility is supported by overlapping and interdependent systems of circulation, the networks of which are increasingly decentralized. This mobility is maintained and articulated through social practice. As the largest industry in Europe and the world, contemporary travel and tourism represents an unprecedented voluntary movement of people.[5] Such transnational circulation remains most prevalent in Europe. In 2007, for example, 90 percent of the more than 450 million tourists in Europe were Europeans themselves.[6]

As we have seen, the young acted as vanguards for the European right of passage across open borders: European states reduced or eliminated visa, passport, and currency restrictions to enable and promote youth travel and social interaction as a privileged priority; the young were at the forefront of political activity, demanding the opening of borders, as demonstrated by the 1950s European Movement and the 1968 student protests; the mass practice of cross-border travel through Eurail and Interrail often rendered national frontiers increasingly inconsequential, while this mobility acted as a conduit of cultural transfer, even across the ideological divide of the Cold War. The traceable history and geography of their movements—the patterns, representations, and practices—generated social relations with long-term political effects.[7]

During the 1992 debates about the Maastricht Treaty and the creation of the European Union, Dutch novelist Cees Nooteboom wrote an editorial that was published simultaneously in the *Guardian* and *Süddeutsche Zeitung*, in which he celebrated what he saw as the diversity of Europe in terms of landscape, language, religion, and tradition, asking "How does one become a European?" In his case, he concluded that it wasn't through a treaty, but rather through his travels as a young man, which had enabled him to know Europe and become European. At twenty he wrote his first novel, *Philip and the Others* (1954), based on his earlier hitchhiking adventures. The "others" of the title was meant to refer to the diverse people he encountered while traveling.[8] Nooteboom later put it this way: "One fine day, and I know how romantic and old-fashioned that sounds, but it is what happened in my case, I packed a rucksack, took leave of my mother, and caught the train to Breda. An hour later—you know how small the Netherlands is—I was standing at the side of the road on the Belgian border sticking my thumb in the air, and I have never really stopped since. At that time any meditative thought, any metaphysical pretension was foreign to me, those sorts of things only come later . . . with the movement preceding the thought."[9] Like East German Jana Hensel in the 1990s, or Swedish youth of the 1980s, he found his Europeanness through his youth travel rather than the other way around.[10] Nor was this the result of efforts by the European Community.

It was only at the end of the 1980s that the formal institutions of Europe began to promote programs of youth mobility. In tandem with YES for Europe (an exchange program modeled on the Franco-German Youth Office, later renamed Youth for Europe), the EC approved the more famous Erasmus program (European Community Action Scheme for the Mobility of University Students), intended to significantly increase university student mobility across member states. Erasmus was seen as essential to establishing the practice of mobility beyond the mere right of it through foreign study. As with American study abroad, female students remain everywhere in Europe more mobile for foreign study than male students.[11] Importantly, the impulse behind Erasmus was more than just student exchange; it was also a measure to get European institutions of higher education to harmonize curriculums, policies, and standards while also emphasizing to the European public the human dimension of integration beyond bureaucratic regulation. That is, the EC's interest in Erasmus was largely related to how students studying abroad could facilitate the interests of integration rather than the other way around.[12] By 1995, more than three hundred thousand university students had participated in Erasmus (and a couple of million since then). On the whole, they found the experience worthwhile in furthering their educational, professional, and linguistic goals, as well as enabling them to become acquainted with foreign people and places. The European Commission was pleased to find that the program stimulated institutional cooperation and harmonization among universities and enjoyed a positive reputation among the European public.[13] Erasmus represents an institutionalization of individual youth mobility by the EU for the purpose of Europeanization. Or as Xavier, the protagonist of Cédric Klapisch's hit 2002 film *L'auberge espagnole* sums up his Erasmus experience in Barcelona, "I'm French, Spanish, English, Danish. I'm not one, but many. I'm like Europe. I'm all that. I'm a real mess."

The EU continues to try to understand how to make youth mobility work in its favor. It recognizes that youth travel has had an integrating effect on Europe, but that this has not necessarily translated into support for the political institutions of the European Union. Thus it sees youth mobility as being too "spontaneous" and as needing to be organized in a systematic way that would serve the interests of the EU.[14] Throughout the twentieth century, European ideologues imbued their Europeanism with the regenerative and rejuvenating metaphor of youth. These appeals were most often mere rhetorical posture rather than practical policy initiatives in the interests of the young. The European Youth Campaign of the 1950s, for example, faded away due to a lack of support and funding. In the wake of 1968, the young became the object of European policy in the 1970s, with concrete proposals for youth travel developed in the 1980s, followed by Article 127 of the 1992 Maastricht Treaty, which explicitly promoted youth mobility. Ironically, just as the European Union began to take the young seriously as a matter of policy, enthusiasm among them for the European project waned to a kind of lukewarm consent, so that today the young are only marginally more enthusiastic about the EU than any other group. Age is no longer as significant an indicator of Europeanism as it once was, but foreign travel continues to be.[15]

Statistically, at the turn of the twenty-first century, of all people worldwide, Western European youth had the greatest propensity for foreign travel. Their travel remained primarily intra-European, with fifty-three million trips in 2000. That same year there were four million trips to Europe by young people from other continents, including the American folk punk duo Ghost Mice, whose 2006 album *Europe* contains songs written about and named for each country they traveled through on their extended road trip of bad weather and poor funding. Meanwhile, seven million young Europeans traveled to other continents. Those who engaged in long-distance backpacking in Asia, South America, or elsewhere had already developed their foreign travel skills in Europe.[16] Independent travel and tourism outside Europe continued to be associated with the young, as adult tourists opted for package tours and inclusive resort holidays in those same regions.[17]

Because the popular activity of backpacking was premised on crossing national frontiers, the social process that developed out of it was transnational in character. The expanding boundaries of backpacker practice—who participates, what they do, and where they go—reveals the expanding dimensions of backpacking across the globe. While this community of practice is heterogeneous and in constant flux, evolving and interacting within new contexts and through new people, it reveals how this cultural form of global mobility, while by no means universal, has spread across the globe from its European origins and reached an extraordinary scale and scope, having powerful political, economic, social, and cultural effects, as we have seen. What were initially locally scaled activities and conditions have been articulated through a fluid global dynamic to create an interconnected continuity of practice.[18]

Within independent youth travel, there is a significantly larger percentage of participation by lower social classes, and a smaller percentage of participation by higher social classes, as compared with tourism generally.[19] Some studies have shown that twice as many backpackers came from a working-class background as had working-class occupations or identified as working class, suggesting that, like higher education, backpacking was a way to become middle class. Its deep association with the postwar broadening of the European middle class turned it into a practice used to enhance social position through the acquisition of social and cultural capital.[20] If one thought of oneself as middle class or aspired to be middle class, foreign travel was seen as a central element in that social distinction.

This was most evident in the emergence of the gap year, which became especially popular in the 1990s and was increasingly seen to be a good professional career move by demonstrating individual autonomy and worldly experience. The affluence of the 1990s gave people confidence that they could quit a job, take a year or more off from participating in the local labor force, and find another position without difficulty upon their return. Since the global economic crisis of 2008, however, the difficulty of funding such a trip combined with the fear of possibly missing out on viable employment forced many young people to abandon their plans for such long-term, long-haul travel.[21] Nevertheless, gap years were especially popular among young Anglophones from the UK, Canada, Hong Kong, Ireland, Australia, and New Zealand. The "overseas experience" (commonly known in New Zealand as the "Big OE") was both tourism and temporary migration, as the young would uproot for a few months to a couple of years, taking advantage of the legacy of imperial networks and the privileges of membership in the British Commonwealth, which enabled them to find temporary legal employment along the way through working holiday visas.[22] Europe became one site in a prolonged, often globe-spanning journey that would focus on multiple continents or regions.

Over the 1950s and '60s, the youth hostel movement made a concerted effort to expand beyond Europe and North America. As had been the case in the 1920s, the idea spread to other countries and continents primarily through the enthusiasm of those who had taken advantage of European youth hostels and hoped to develop their own associations at home. In Latin America, especially, hostels were the result of efforts by the young people themselves who had traveled to Europe or the United States. Elsewhere, such efforts were aided by unofficial IYHF ambassadors such as Jack Catchpool, who, upon retiring as president of the IYHF, took it upon himself to advocate for hosteling associations overseas. His first visit was to India and Pakistan in 1951–52, where he helped to arrange student exchanges across the disputed Kashmiri frontier. In the course of his return overland to England, he traveled through Afghanistan, Iran, Iraq, Syria, and Lebanon, in the hope of making a youth hostel route from Europe to India, and he later published a booklet entitled *The Overland Route*, with lists of hospitable institutions, though not formal hostels. In 1956 he visited Africa, meeting with hostel enthusiasts in South Africa, Rhodesia, and Kenya. The imperial framework of Catchpool's efforts is clear, as he focused on territories of the British Empire and Commonwealth.[23] Indeed, the global landscapes of backpacking, the enclaves of inclusion and exclusion, and their gendered and racial practices have relied upon a corpus of colonial knowledge, policies, frameworks, infrastructures, hierarchies, and power relations that work to western benefit as an enduring legacy of imperial tourism and travel.[24]

By the 1960s, India and Pakistan had viable, if small, hostel associations, but the real success stories were in Japan and Israel. Japanese hosteling took off at an extraordinary rate. Between 1955 and 1960, membership grew tenfold, and by 1963, Japanese hostels were second only to West Germany's in the number of total overnights. In Israel, most of the youth hostelers came from the *kibbutzim,* where hostels were often located. Like their predecessors, these new associations were focused on utilizing youth hostels for national consolidation. Only Israeli hostels, at this point, had any significant foreign usage, as European backpackers explored the Mediterranean basin.[25] Importantly, though, the success of fostering a domestic hosteling culture among Japanese and Israeli youth would lay the groundwork for later international travel abroad. In 1964, the Japanese government deregulated overseas travel by Japanese nationals. By 1970, more than three thousand Japanese hostelers had recorded more than one hundred thousand total overnights in Western Europe, with those numbers growing significantly in the following decade.[26]

With revolution in Iran, war in Afghanistan, and renewed Cold War tension between the superpowers, the "hippie trail" was effectively shut down by 1980. Consequently, by the 1990s, the focus of long-haul backpacker travel had shifted from the overland route of Central Asia to the beaches of Southeast Asia, Thailand and Bali most famously, but also Central and Latin America. Young Germans and Scandinavians in particular began expanding the radius of long-distance independent youth travel in the 1980s, with a commercial tourist infrastructure rapidly developing to accommodate them.[27] The majority of these backpackers remained young, white, male, middle class, single, and European even as backpacking as a whole was becoming more diverse. For them, such independent, budget-conscious travel abroad had been normalized. Most were at a life juncture, having just completed a university degree or pausing between jobs or anticipating settling down soon into marriage and a career. As had been the case in Europe, Western Europeans were the majority of such backpackers, with a fair share of Australians and New Zealanders, but Americans were decidedly underrepresented. While a couple of months spent backpacking in Europe was certainly acceptable, such long-term long-distance travel was socially frowned upon in the United States as being reckless and irresponsible.[28]

By the twenty-first century, Europe had been decentered as the concentrated locale of backpacking, and Europeans were no longer the overwhelming majority of backpackers. Thus the European character of backpacking has been diluted, and its association with Europe has weakened. In each year since 1981, for example, more Australians have traveled to Asia than to Europe, a reversal from the earlier pattern. In the previous decade and a half, the many thousands of young Australians who traveled to Asia had primarily done so as a component of going to or coming from Europe, taking several weeks or months or even years to make the trip. Asia became the primary destination itself rather than being passed through en route as long-haul backpacker travel became more mainstream and less associated with hippie subculture.[29] At the same time, young Israelis became avid backpackers in mass numbers, with their prolonged travels often marking the end of required military service for young men and women. Israeli backpacking has focused on Asia and Central and South America, where it is common to find information in Hebrew in backpacker enclaves.[30] Collectively, backpackers have had a tremendous economic impact on these regions, because their economic outlay tends to stay within the local economy, supporting the entrepreneurs who operate as hosts, restaurateurs, and tour brokers, in contrast to the multinational corporate holiday resorts that siphon off tourism profits to global shareholders.[31]

The increasing numbers of young Asian backpackers have demonstrated a more individualist sociability, in contrast to the traditional collectivist ethos, as they gradually adopt the habits and behaviors of hosteling around the world.[32] Japanese youth were the first to begin taking up such practices in the 1960s and '70s and in large numbers in the 1980s, as the practice of backpacking in Europe became more socially acceptable and affordable with growing Japanese wealth. Some backpackers were referred to as "datsu-sara," or those who were escaping or abandoning the salaryman life of their fathers.[33] While Europe was the initial focus of Japanese backpackers, that is no longer the case, as interest has shifted to exploring the East Asian region. They have been joined by growing numbers of Chinese, Korean, Malaysian, and Singaporean backpackers. Their activity is helping to decenter the western orientation of backpacking. For example, businesses along Khao San Road in Bangkok developed to cater to the western backpacker, with guesthouses, restaurants, and services designed to appeal to western tastes and interests, to the exclusion of non-western backpackers. Businesses on the adjacent Thanon Rambuttri, however, cater to the growing Asian backpacker clientele, which in turn is having an impact on Khao San as local businesses compete for customers of different linguistic and cultural backgrounds.[34]

Because of continued government restrictions on individual travel, Chinese students find it easier to be independent travelers by officially studying abroad. They often choose their university based not on academics, but on proximity to tourist destinations and travel infrastructure. Consequently, there has been a surge of Chinese students in London, who describe travel in Europe as their primary reason for being there and education as secondary.[35] As Chinese wealth and power has expanded, so has Chinese tourism to and through Europe. Since 2000, there has been a democratization of travel in China as more and more Chinese of varying means are able to travel abroad. This is almost en-

32   Young tourists on Khao San Road, Bangkok, Thailand, February 2012. Photograph by Akabei.
      iStock/Getty Images.

tirely through government-sanctioned travel agencies and with highly
regulated group package tours. Still, independent backpacker travel is
spreading among young, wealthy, and educated Chinese, even within
China, as the government continues to rapidly expand the youth hostel
system there. Chinese youth understand backpacking to be a foreign
practice, with much of its legitimacy derived from its association with
western modernity. By participating, they demonstrate China's own modernity. In an article for the Shanghai newspaper *Travel Times*, a young
Chinese backpacker expressed her joy over the freedom and independence of such travel, but also the sense of international camaraderie she
experienced among the backpacker community in India. "The backpacker tribe," she wrote, "is best able to embody a nation's economic
strength and its national quality. The fact that Japanese backpackers are
found in every corner of the earth is inseparable from Japan's enormous
economic strength." Thus, traveling abroad on equal terms with Japanese and western youth belies the view of international travel as quintes-
sentially modern not only in its western individualism, but also as an
expression of economic and national power.[36]

Much has been made of Arjun Appadurai's notion of "scapes" as el-
ementary frameworks of contemporary global cultural flows, such as the
mediascape of visual culture or the ethnoscape of popular mobility.[37]

Young people are integral to all five of Appadurai's categories (the other three are ideoscape, financescape, and technoscape), and their role in globalization, particularly historically, remains underappreciated. The notion of a "youthscape" as an application of Appadurai's ideas highlights the globalizing effect of youth practice in its social, political, economic, and cultural effects.[38] The practice of backpacking, for example, has been embedded within and integral to some of the most significant historical developments of the last half century in both obvious and unexpected ways. As backpackers built a transnational network of mobility, their interactivity incorporated growing numbers of young people into a transnational youth culture, thus having an integrating effect on youth as a social body around the world. Youth and young people have too often been studied from the perspective of deviance or subculture and not been appreciated as historical actors shaping the world in their own right; at best they have been considered tangential or illustrative. But taking their activity seriously leads us to reconsider major historical events, including the social and cultural integration of Europe in the second half of the twentieth century.

The practice of transnational youth travel in the decades after the Second World War eventually became a kind of mediation between the national and the global as it moved beyond the boundaries of Europe. While initially it was Eurocentric, interconnecting the national territories of Western Europe, it steadily transgressed its Europeanism as growing numbers of non-Europeans participated and as their routes and destinations expanded, becoming intercontinental rather than merely international. This was true already in the late 1960s in Canada, Mexico, and Argentina, for example.[39] It is a mobility of mass cultural practice spanning the globe, but it remains a privileged one.

The 2004 film *Exils*, directed by Tony Gatlif, follows the French son of *pied-noirs*, Zano, and his Franco-Maghrebi girlfriend, Naima, along a meandering journey from Paris to Algiers in search of their distinct Algerian roots. They follow a typical drifter itinerary, hopping on trains, sleeping in the rough, and hitchhiking as they make their way slowly through France, Spain, Morocco, and Algeria, engaging in whatever activity suits their mood and finances. In Spain they encounter Said and Leila, Algerian siblings a decade younger, who are illegally making their way north in search of better opportunity. A lorry picks them up along the road. The driver asks Naima if she and Zano are looking for work, too. "No, we're traveling," she responds laconically. Later, in southern Spain, Naima and Zano work a bit with migrant laborers picking fruit. They stay overnight with the North Africans in a ruined farm compound, which is raided by police in the morning. While their hosts are arrested, Zano and Naima are protected by their citizenship. Due to Naima's obvious ethnicity, a Spanish officer scrutinizes her passport closely, inspiring her to retort, "I'm French, shithead." Another scene depicts Zano and Naima moving along a crowded roadway against a mighty flow of refugees displaced by an earthquake in North Africa. Zano and Naima's journey is not enforced by circumstance, but is circuitous, impulsive, and touristic. They risk little with their cross-border mobility compared to their young counterparts moving in the opposite direction.[40]

The neoliberal globalization unleashed in the post–Cold War era consisted primarily of an elite internationalization without popular participation. It was bureaucratic, financial, and corporate. One significant exception is mass mobility and the historical entanglement of travel and migration. The freedom of movement within Europe as a circulatory regime has activated a complex interplay between various transnational flows. The EU itself can be viewed as an elaborate circulatory system designed to facilitate the flows of goods, capital, finance, labor, and people. The networks of youth mobility overlap and intermingle with others, especially tourism and migration, as we have seen. The guest worker programs of the 1960s were premised on circulation rather than immigration and utilized tourist and travel networks, yet they resulted in a European diaspora of new resident ethnic communities that have continued to grow. In the 1990s, immigrant communities themselves turned to supranational institutions in the New Europe to secure cultural and linguistic rights in a transnationalization of cultural politics that benefited from the possibilities of mobility provided by the European Union.[41] The reordering of cross-border flows and globalization of the 1990s created conditions for a diversification, expansion, and increase of migration, which added to the permanent ethnic minority communities already in Europe, further complicating the question of who counted as European.[42]

Mobility has become a primary point of tension within the European Union, even as the EU articulated the freedom of movement as one of its defining principles. The Maastricht Treaty, which transformed the European Community into the European Union, affirmed the concept of EU citizenship for nationals of all member states, giving them the right to move, live, and work anywhere in the European Union, although only 2 percent of EU citizens have actually established residency in other member states.[43] Overwhelmingly, the primary form of cross-border mobility remains individual travel and tourism. The borderless territory of Schengenland has been expanded and incorporated as an institutional framework for the EU, although not all EU members are in Schengen, nor are all the Schengen countries members of the EU. The inability of European states to strictly control access to their own territory, because of EU reciprocity or Schengen or both, has reshaped debates over immigration and had a major impact on EU expansion into Eastern Europe.

The sociopolitical context of intra-European mobility changed dramatically in the early 1990s through the combined effects of the end of the Cold War and the establishment of the European Union. The Cold War had stabilized postwar Europe as armed wars took place elsewhere. It managed conflict in Europe by enabling states to reorganize their governments around peace rather than war.[44] The end of the Cold War had a destabilizing effect, most tragically in the dissolution of Yugoslavia. It also reconfigured what was "Europe" from having been contiguous with the western half of the continent to a new boundary that moved successively eastward. Vaclav Havel spoke of the East's "return to Europe" as if it had somehow been somewhere else during the Cold War.[45] This reconstitution of Europe was expressed partly in mobility, as we saw in the East German case. Czech visits to other European destinations grew nearly tenfold between 1988 and 1994. Eastern Europe generally experienced incredible growth in tourist activity in the 1990s, and the EU quickly recognized tourism to and from there as having an integrating effect, as it had in Southern Europe, and encouraged it as a prelude to accession for new member states.[46] The entanglement of mobility as migration and tourism was central to British debates regarding the 2004 enlargement of the European Union from fifteen to twenty-five member states. Opponents bemoaned the potential influx of cheap labor, or were alarmed at the prospect of unrestricted migrants taking advantage of the UK's generous welfare state. Others countered that visits to the UK from new members would be routinely temporary, and would generate substantial tourist revenues, while Britons could anticipate cheap holidays abroad in "Europe's New Playground," maybe even with second-home ownership in Poland or the Baltic states.[47]

Hostility toward mobility, even from within the EU, drives much of the populist politics in member countries, from Enoch Powell circa 1970 to Marine Le Pen circa 2015. In 2001, when Denmark joined the Schengen zone, the right-wing Danish People's Party bought a decommissioned guardhouse at the German border, vowing to one day put it to use again.[48] Indeed, there are currently efforts across the Schengen zone to reinstitute national border controls to slow the movement of immigrants, who have grown in number and visibility in the last decade as conditions of daily life have deteriorated on the southern and eastern peripheries of

Europe. EU member states across this region are overwhelmed with African, Asian, and Middle Eastern immigrants desperate to escape the current economic and political turmoil in their home countries. The walls, fences, and barrier controls intended to stifle mobility on the exterior European borders have been strengthened as people who are considered to be economic, cultural, or security threats have themselves become more mobile. The EU's eastern boundary with Russia, Belarus, and Ukraine and its southern border with Serbia, Turkey, and Morocco have been substantially fortified in an attempt to create a Fortress Europe. At the same time, the exponential growth of intra-European cross-border traffic compels governments to continue to accommodate it. In the mid-1960s, for example, British subjects made five million visits to continental Europe every year; by 1990 that number was twenty-five million, and by 2015 it had reached nearly fifty million.[49] Who has freedom of movement, and how to accommodate it for some but not others, is a question that bedevils current policymakers.

As one measure to deal with the ongoing massive influx of refugees fleeing the civil war in Syria, the EU negotiated a provisional deal with Turkey to help stave the flow in exchange for visa-free travel to the EU for Turkish citizens. Thus, Turkey used the mass migration of Syrians as leverage to achieve for Turks better access to the free mobility system of Europe. In the weeks prior to the 23 June 2016 national referendum on Britain's EU membership (Brexit), the EU deal with Turkey seemed to exacerbate fears in Britain and bolster the Leave side, who depicted waves of Turks overwhelming the UK. The Vote Leave campaign focused intently on open borders, national security, and Muslim refugee immigrants, and misrepresented Turkey's accession to the EU as being imminent.[50]

Britain, in fact, is not a member of the Schengen zone (nor the Eurozone) and, technically, border controls remain in place. But because it is an EU member, citizens from other member countries are free to travel, work, and live in the UK, which is reciprocated to the British. A majority of Britons voted in the Brexit referendum to leave the European Union. Polling data showed that it was the older age cohorts who voted to leave, and that immigration was their primary concern, while younger cohorts voted overwhelmingly to remain, and did so to maintain their mobility to travel, study, and work in the EU. The data also revealed that the strongest correlations of votes to remain or leave were based on age, educational level, social class, and whether or not someone held a passport. Those who were younger, had more education, were of a higher social class, and had a valid passport voted to remain. The opposite trends were true for those who voted to leave.[51]

Although 75 percent of British voters under age twenty-five voted to stay in the EU, their turnout numbers were low compared to those over age sixty-five, of whom 60 percent voted to leave.[52] The difference in opinion according to age was clear prior to the vote. Rhiannon Lucy Cosslett published an impassioned opinion piece in the *Guardian* in the days leading up to the referendum, urging her fellow young people to vote and condemning the older generation of Britons for narrow-mindedly clinging to "a nostalgic fantasy of a Britain that no longer exists": a place "where the ginger beer is flowing, girls are all called Fanny, and foreigners are viewed with suspicion." She emphasized that European integration had stabilized the continent, and above all brought peace as well as prosperity to the UK. She concluded, "People from all classes have benefited from freedom of movement—we are not only the best-travelled generation to ever have lived, with the unprecedented freedom to live, work and study abroad (more than 15,000 of us did Erasmus last year) but Europeans are our colleagues, our friends and flatmates, our doctors and nurses, the people we kiss, live with, marry and have children with. You are young, and you have the whole of Europe at your feet. It is a privilege. Do not throw it away."[53]

After the referendum, the *New York Times* ran a story entitled "Among Young Britons, Fear and Despair over Vote to Leave E.U."[54] The *Daily Mail* described crowds of young protesters with the headline "Millennials vent fury at baby boomers for voting Britain OUT of the EU." In the days following the vote to leave, hundreds of young Britons marched and demonstrated throughout London. Wearing face paint and carrying lighted flares, they held signs and large banners that declared "I am not leaving," "I am not British I am European," and "No Borders! No Boris!" While the latter shows a rejection of the mayor of London, Boris Johnson, a leader of the Leave campaign, it reveals yet again young people's political protest against borders and their association of the freedom of mobility with Europan integration.[55]

How the UK's departure from the politico-economic European Union will affect its sociocultural integration with Europe is unclear. As I have tried to show in this book, the EU and European integration are not precisely the same thing. Britain is already not a part of Schengen; nor does it use the Euro. Certainly Brexit will result in a retrenchment of some kind, the details of which will be the subject of intense negotiation, but the young who were so keen to remain will soon rise to positions of power and influence and will have some impact on this future. While the UK is leaving the EU, that doesn't mean that it is leaving Europe.

In fall 2016, a German MEP proposed that the EU award an Interrail ticket to all EU citizens on their eighteenth birthday. The European Parliament responded positively, and the European Commission has taken it under consideration for a full review. In the wake of Brexit and the declining support among the young for the EU, the goal is to build enthusiasm for the European Union through intra-European youth travel. While the evidence herein demonstrates that such travel fosters Europeanism, it is questionable whether this expensive proposal would achieve the intended effect if the EU does not also address underlying structural and economic problems, including prolonged unemployment for the young. Still, as the protests by young Britons have reminded us, and as the proposed "Interrail at 18" intends, the transnational mobility of youth may well remain an impetus for integration.

The European Union delineates mobility rights of inclusion and exclusion, and this right to freedom of movement is seen as foundational and central to other rights. The Delphic priests of ancient Greece considered the right to come and go to be one of the four fundamental elements of freedom.[56] Entangled mobility networks of travel and migration have interconnected Europe with its southern and eastern peripheries for many decades, in both intra-European and extra-European ways. Such travel and migration helped to bring Southern and Eastern European countries into closer contact with Northern and Western ones.[57] Repeated surveys show that among citizens of the European Union, an absolute majority view freedom of movement across borders as the most positive consequence of membership—even more than peace among member states. When asked what the EU has meant to them personally on an individual level, the freedom to travel is the top response among citizens. These sentiments are strongest among the newest member states, those of the former Soviet bloc. In the UK, too, ease of travel is the top vote-getter, with the reduction of border controls and cheaper flights as the top two responses regarding the personal benefits of EU membership.[58] As internal border controls are reintroduced within Europe to stem the flow of migrants, refugees, and security threats, it is ironic that while free mobility was used as a means to achieve stability and national security in the decades after the Second World War, it is now seen as a threat to those achievements. If rights of passage, the freedom of movement, were to be curtailed and the open borders closed, what effect this would have on European integration, already under stress, is unclear. Still, the transnational mobility of youth may remain an impetus for integration, as the protests by young Britons have reminded us.

Acknowledgments

In 1990, I spent the summer between my junior and senior years of college backpacking in Europe. I was a history major at Murray State University, and my parents were keen for me to go to law school, but I wasn't so enthusiastic. After my summer ramblings, I was determined to go to graduate school and earn my doctorate so that, I hoped, I might be able to return to Europe regularly for work. To my surprise, and that of my parents especially, it has worked out that way. So, first, I want to acknowledge and thank my parents, Sid and Loretta Jobs, for their support of a young historian with a penchant for travel. I'd also like to recognize and thank some of my early travel companions, including Mike Quinn, Larissa Wardeiner, Natalie Black, Emily Satterwhite, Mark Henderson, and Ari Kellner.

It was clear that researching *Backpack Ambassadors* would require a truly transnational methodological approach, necessitating that I spend time in a variety of cities and countries following the archival trail wherever it might lead, hence satisfying the original rationale of the project to enable my personal travel. A few years ago, while based at the European University Institute (EUI) in Fiesole, Italy, to conduct research for this project, I met with Federico Romero, an EUI faculty member and respected historian of European integration and postwar transnational history. He was intrigued by my project and quite supportive, in part because he had himself backpacked around Europe as a young man. He understood what I was getting at, yet he was also puzzled. With a look of amiable concern, he asked, "But what about sources? How will you be able to research this?" Given that historians place great

32 The author as a Eurailing backpacker, Austria, 1990.

emphasis on substantial primary evidence as the standard of scholarship, studying the transnational history of youth poses the significant practical challenge of locating and accessing primary materials.

Historians of childhood and youth are often confronted with this challenge, particularly if one wants to portray the agency of the young as historical actors. Simply put, the young don't leave much of an archival paper trail. My dilemma was compounded by the one that faces those who do transnational history: archival systems, whether governmental or not, remain overwhelmingly organized within and through the nation-state. Indeed, for this project, there was no centralized collection where I could immerse myself, no single archive where I might take up residence for an extended period of time. Instead, I have conducted research at roughly forty archives, libraries, and institutes in eight countries and five languages. There are considerable state sources related to these sorts of programs intended to promote travel and exchange, in addition to the national and international hostel associations and other private groups, but still the materials are spread out over several countries.

Methodologically, I have sought to combine the rigor of archival research on the institutional framework of cultural integration through youth travel with the drama of young people's personal travel experiences. That is, I wanted young independent voices in addition to adult institutional ones. Diaries, memoirs, journals, newspapers, magazines, reports, and interviews allow their voices to articulate the experience of travel—the adventures and pitfalls, the adrenaline and exhaustion—and the activities, interests, and experiences of the young within these broader historical transformations. I have tapped into various autobiographical libraries and archives that have been collecting "life stories" from the twentieth century to complement and humanize my use of the programs and policies from traditional archives and libraries. Belgium, France, Germany, Italy, and the Netherlands each have a private depository where unpublished journals, memoirs, letters, and the like are collected and cataloged, while the UK has the Mass Observation Archive, with its personal narrative responses to survey prompts. These collections offer a lot to historians of childhood and youth because so many of the documents were produced while the authors were young, and others, such as unpublished memoirs, can provide a reflective commentary on being young from the perspective of adulthood, or even old age.

Finally, this book would have been impossible a decade ago, as it benefits from the remarkable productivity of other researchers into its various thematic lines of inquiry. *Backpack Ambassadors* has a significant synthetic quality, as I have relied on the recently published work of others who, in mostly but not exclusively national contexts, have written on the history of youth and young people, European integration, the postwar era, the Cold War, decolonization and immigration, travel and tourism, and youth culture. There are also considerable interdisciplinary dimensions; my notes will guide the interested reader toward some of this rich material. This secondary source base has been essential in a book of such scale and scope, giving it a survey quality to complement its more narrowly defined premise.

This research was supported with funding from the National Endowment for the Humanities, the Fulbright Commission, the Arnold L. and Lois S. Graves Award, the American Philosophical Society, and Pacific University. Herrick Chapman, John Gillis, James Kennedy, Susan Kingsley Kent, and Whitney Walton all wrote letters in support of the project at one point or another, and I appreciate their endorsement. I benefited from skilled research assistants who accompanied me at different moments, making my archival visits much more productive and efficient. I thank Irene Fattaciu, Carla MacDougall, Katherine Spingarn, and Frank Verburg for their good work on my behalf. I was given special guidance at particular archives by Philippe Lejeune, Alison Margrave, Rachel Morton-Young, and Hasso Spode. Others helped give me direction, passed along citations, shared research, facilitated introductions, or answered questions, such as Bartolomé Yun Casallila, Tamara Chaplin, Stephen Harp, Dagmar Herzog, Rick Keller, Lisa Leff, Max Likin, Emily Marker, Christina Norwig, Roxanne Panchasi, Nick Rutter, Sandrine Sanos, Todd Shepard, Paul Silverstein, and Jialin Christina Wu. Yahn Jeannot continues to be a good friend, hosting me when possible in Paris. At Pacific University, my department and college accommodated me in a number of ways that enabled me to complete this project; I especially thank Larry Lipin, Martha Rampton, Sarah Phillips, David Friedman, Jules Boykoff, Jeff Seward, Loreley French, John Hayes, Lisa Carstens, and Virginia Adams.

Several people read portions of the book while it was in progress. I thank Jonathyne Briggs, Belinda Davis, Cheleen Mahar, Pat McDevitt, and Chris Wilkes, the latter of whom helped edit the manuscript entirely. I thank the publishers' readers, Detlef Siegfried, Tara Zahra, and my anonymous reader, for their remarkably enthusiastic response and very helpful feedback. They paid me the compliment of thinking with me, riffing on a variety of potentialities and possibilities, and spinning out creative ideas for elaboration in ways that helped me clarify my arguments and, I think, take the book to another level of erudition.

For a decade Bonnie Smith has encouraged the project, raised questions about it, helped me talk to the right people, and directed me toward funding. Most recently, she read the completed manuscript and gave helpful feedback. She continues to mentor me, though I long ago completed my doctorate under her direction at Rutgers University. David Pomfret has been exceptionally supportive of the project since its inception and a good friend willing to share a pint or two when our paths cross. Together we have thought through similar historical questions and sharpened each other's thinking and writing. I am glad to have him as a friend and colleague. Doug Mitchell, my editor at the University of Chicago Press, has been an enthusiast since we first discussed the book. His encouragement has been essential to facilitating my vision. Finally, I benefited from Jane Lyle's incredible diligence as a copy editor and fact-checker. I am very grateful for her work on my behalf.

Living with me has meant living with *Backpack Ambassadors*, and so I dedicate the book to Kim, Greta, and Ezra and thank them for indulging my love of history and travel. Greta and Ezra have lived with this project their entire lives, accompanying me on multiple research trips abroad and attending professional conferences in the United States, Canada, and Sweden. They are delightful travelers in their own right, and have profoundly enriched this experience with their joyful enthusiasm and unbelievable patience. More than anyone else, Kim has shouldered the heaviest load to enable this ambitious project (especially due to the aforementioned Greta and Ezra). At home or at work, she is the gravitational center that holds it all together. Nor will she let me have it any other way.

Archives and Libraries Consulted

Belgium

Association pour l'autobiographie et le patrimoine belgique, Brussels
European Commission Historical Archives, Brussels
European Commission Library, Brussels (ECL)

France

Archives de l'Occupation françaises en Allemagne et en Autriche, Colmar (AOFAA)
Archives nationales de France, Paris (ANF)
Association pour l'autobiographie et le patrimoine, Ambérieu (APA)
Bibliothèque nationale de France, Paris
Centre des archives contemporaines, Fontainebleau (CAC)
UNESCO Archives, Paris

Germany

Archiv der Jugendkulturen, Berlin (AJK)
Bundesarchiv, Koblenz (BAK)
Deutschen Gesellschaft für Auswärtige Politik, Berlin
Deutsches Tagebucharchiv, Emmendingen (DTA)
Historisches Archiv zum Tourismus, Berlin
Institut für Auslandsbeziehungen, Stuttgart
Leibniz-Institut für Sozialwissenschaften, Cologne
Staatsbibliothek zu Berlin

Italy

Archivio diaristico nazionale, Pieve Santo Stefano (ADN)
Archivio storico capitolino, Rome
Biblioteca del viaggio in Italia, Moncalieri
European University Institute Library, Fiesole
Historical Archives of the European Union, Fiesole (HAEU)

Netherlands

Eurail Group, Utrecht
International Institute for Social History, Amsterdam (IISG)
International Student Travel Confederation, Amsterdam (ISTC)
Stadsarchief Amsterdam (SAA)
Universiteit van Amsterdam

Singapore

National Archives of Singapore

United Kingdom

BBC Written Archives Center, Reading (BBC WAC)
British Library, London
Hostelling International Archive, Welwyn Garden City (HIA)
Mass Observation Archive, Sussex (MOA)
United Kingdom National Archives, Kew (UKNA)

United States

Georgetown University Library Special Collections, Washington, DC
Library of Congress, Washington, DC
Lyndon Baines Johnson Library, Austin, TX
National Archives and Records Administration, College Park, MD (NARA)

Notes

BACKPACK AMBASSADORS

1. Horak and Weber, "Youth Tourism in Europe."
2. See chapter 4.
3. Iriye, *Cultural Internationalism*; Iriye, *Global Community*.
4. See Honeck and Rosenberg, "Transnational Generations"; and Norwig, *Die erste europäische Generation*.
5. For example, Schildt and Siegfried, *Between Marx and Coca-Cola*; Risch, *Youth and Rock in the Soviet Bloc*; Briggs, *Sounds French*.
6. See Jobs and Pomfret, *Transnational Histories of Youth*.
7. See, for example, Lawrence Grossberg, "The Political Status of Youth and Youth Culture," in Epstein, *Adolescents and Their Music*, 25–46; Bucholtz, "Youth and Cultural Practice"; and Richard Ivan Jobs and David M. Pomfret, "The Transnationality of Youth," in *Transnational Histories of Youth*, 1–19.
8. Bucholtz, "Youth and Cultural Practice."
9. Endy, *Cold War Holidays*; Pack, *Tourism and Dictatorship*; Gorsuch and Koenker, *Turizm*; Gorsuch, *All This Is Your World*; Zuelow, *Touring beyond the Nation*; Walton, "Travel as a Force of Historical Change,"; Harp, *Au Naturel*; Sobocinska, *Visiting the Neighbours*.
10. See, for example, Koshar, *German Travel Cultures*; Koshar, *Histories of Leisure*; Gorsuch and Koenker, *Turizm*; Thomas Mergel, "Europe as Leisure Time Communication: Tourism and Transnational Interaction since 1945," in Jarausch and Lindenberger, *Conflicted Memories*, 133–53; Rosemary Wakeman, "Veblen Redivivus: Leisure and Excess in Europe," in Stone, *The Oxford Handbook of Postwar European History*, 423–42; and Papadogiannis and Siegfried, "Between Leisure, Work and Study."

11. Löfgren, *On Holiday*; Baranowski and Furlough, *Being Elsewhere*; Walton, *Internationalism, National Identities, and Study Abroad*.

12. Richards and Wilson, *The Global Nomad*; Richards, *Youth Travel Matters*; Hannam and Ateljevic, *Backpacker Tourism*.

13. Ngai, "Promises and Perils of Transnational History."

14. See, for example, Balibar, *We, the People of Europe?*; Urry, *Mobilities*; Verstraete, *Tracking Europe*; Greenblatt, *Cultural Mobility*; Saunier, *Transnational History*.

15. Urry, *Mobilities*.

16. Among the several books on this subject, the main one is Bauman, *Liquid Modernity*.

17. These are terms set out recently by Stephen Greenblatt in his "Mobility Studies Manifesto." Greenblatt, "A Mobility Studies Manifesto," in *Cultural Mobility*, 250–53.

18. On the history of the idea of travel, see the marvelous book by Eric J. Leed, *The Mind of the Traveler*.

19. See Casson, *Travel in the Ancient World*.

20. Leed, *The Mind of the Traveler*.

21. See, for example, Solnit, *Wanderlust*.

22. Towner, "The Grand Tour."

23. Löfgren, *On Holiday*, 271.

24. See, for example, Wallace, "Rescue or Retreat?"; Wolfram Kaiser, "From State to Society? The Historiography of European Integration," in Cini and Bourne, *Palgrave Advances in European Union Studies*, 190–208; and Loth, "Explaining European Integration."

25. Patel, "Provincialising European Union"; see also Kaiser and Starie, *Transnational European Union*; Konrad H. Jarausch and Thomas Lindenberger, "Contours of a Critical History of Contemporary Europe: A Transnational Agenda," in *Conflicted Memories*, 1–20.

26. Conway and Patel, *Europeanization*. See also Wolfram Kaiser, "Transnational Western Europe since 1945," in Kaiser and Starie, *Transnational European Union*, 17–35.

27. For example, Misa and Schot, "Inventing Europe"; Schipper, *Driving Europe*; Badenoch and Fickers, *Materializing Europe*; Högselius, *Red Gas*.

28. For example, Shore, *Building Europe*; Demossier, *The European Puzzle*; Gostmann and Schatilow, *Europa unterwegs*.

CHAPTER ONE

1. As quoted in Mack and Humphries, *London at War*, 161.

2. Anne O'Hare McCormick, "Abroad: The Dark Alternatives to Big Three Agreement," *New York Times*, May 11, 1946, 22.

3. This is the subject of Tara Zahra's excellent book *The Lost Children*.

4. Indeed, there was a tremendous amount of internationalist activity in the interwar period. See, for example, Reis, "Cultural Internationalism at the Cité Universitaire"; and Laqua, *Internationalism Reconfigured*.

5. On the transnationality of interwar internationalism see Laqua, *Internationalism Reconfigured*.

6. See Barbara Stambolis, "Aufbrüche: Jugend um 1900 unterwegs," in Reulecke and Stambolis, *100 Jahre Jugendherbergen*, 29–41. There is a vast German literature on the *wandervögel*. The classic English-language text is Laqueur, *Young Germany*; a more recent treatment is included in Williams, *Turning to Nature in Germany*.

7. See Heinrich Ulrich Seidel, "Der Weg zur estern Jugendherberge im westfälischen Altena," in Reulecke and Stambolis, *100 Jahre Jugendherbergen*, 43–56; Stefanie Hanke, "Die Anfänge des Jugendherbergswerks," ibid., 69–75; and Grassl and Heath, *The Magic Triangle*, 13–16.

8. See Stefanie Hanke, "Reorganisation und Ausbau der Jugendherbergen nach 1918," in Reulecke and Stambolis, *100 Jahre Jugendherbergen*, 99–110; and Heath, *The International Youth Hostel Manual*, 13.

9. See Jürgen Reulecke, "Horizonte und Organisationenen: Jugend und junge Generation in den zwanziger Jahren im Umfeld des Jugendherbergswerks," in Reulecke and Stambolis, *100 Jahre Jugendherbergen*, 83–97; Eike Stiller, " 'Zur Freunde aller . . .': Das Verhältnis der Arbeitersportsbewegung zum deutschen Jugendherbergswesen 1920–1933," ibid., 127–35.

10. See Stefanie Hanke, "Die Anfänge des internationalen Jugendherbergswesens," ibid., 151–58.

11. Grassl and Heath, *The Magic Triangle*, 30–49.

12. Reulecke, "Horizonte und Organisationenen," 94–95.

13. Grassl and Heath, *The Magic Triangle*, 32.

14. Ibid., 35.

15. As quoted in Orvar Löfgren, "Know Your Country: A Comparative Perspective on Tourism and Nation Building in Sweden," in Baranowski and Furlough, *Being Elsewhere*, 146.

16. Per Lundin, "Coping with Cars, Families, and Foreigners: Swedish Postwar Tourism," in Lundin and Kaiserfeld, *The Making of European Consumption*, 209–14.

17. Eva Kraus, "Jugendherbergswerk und Nationalsozialismus," in Reulecke and Stambolis, *100 Jahre Jugendherbergen*, 175–85.

18. See Biesanz, "Nazi Influence"; see also Jürgen Reulecke, "Vergungen und ideologische Vereinnahmungen: Zur Nutzung der Jugendherbergen durch das NS-Regime," in Reulecke and Stambolis, *100 Jahre Jugendherbergen*, 195–207. For the ways that the Nazis used group travel and tourism for nationalist purposes, see Shelley Baranowski, "Strength through Joy: Tourism and National Integration in the Third Reich," in Baranowski and Furlough, *Being Elsewhere*, 213–36.

19. Guérin, *The Brown Plague*, 48–52, 50, 89–91.
20. See Leo Meilink, "The International Youth Hostel Federation," in Heath, *The International Youth Hostel Manual*, 24–34.
21. See Barbara Stambolis, "Jugendherbergen als Jugendbegegnungsstätten: Grenzüberschreitend," in Reulecke and Stambolis, *100 Jahre Jugendherbergen*, 159–67.
22. For a succinct history of cultural internationalism, see Iriye, *Cultural Internationalism*; Iriye, *Global Community*; and Sluga, *Internationalism in the Age of Nationalism*.
23. Frevert, "Europeanizing Germany's Twentieth Century."
24. As quoted in Coburn, *Youth Hostel Story*, 168–69.
25. As quoted in Grassl and Heath, *The Magic Triangle*, 91–92.
26. "Report of the Meeting of the Committee of the International Youth Hostels Association," Paris, 3–4 February 1946, 2, Hostelling International Archive, Welwyn Garden City, UK [hereafter HIA].
27. Hartvig Frisch, "Address to the International Conference in Krogerup," from "Report of the Eleventh Conference of the International Youth Hostel Federation," August 1949, 1, HIA.
28. As quoted in Röling, *Idealisme en toerisme*, 27.
29. John Catchpool, "Presidential Address," from "Report of the Tenth Conference of the International Youth Hostel Federation," September 1948, 9, HIA.
30. John Catchpool, "Presidential Address," from "Report of the Eleventh Conference of the International Youth Hostel Federation," August 1949, 2, HIA.
31. Ibid., 5.
32. "Constitution of the International Youth Hostel Federation," from "Report of the Twelfth Conference of the International Youth Hostel Federation," August 1950, 65, HIA.
33. "Working Paper for the Commission on 'How Can the Youth Hostels Movement Serve Humanity?,'" from "Documents for the Nineteenth International Youth Hostel Federation Conference," August 1958, 82–83, HIA.
34. For more on the reconstruction and humanitarian efforts to restore democracy through liberal individualism, see Zahra, *The Lost Children*.
35. Martin Conway and Volker Depkat, "Towards a European History of the Discourse of Democracy: Discussing Democracy in Western Europe, 1945–1960," in Conway and Patel, *Europeanization*, 132–56.
36. Catchpool, "Presidential Address," 1949, 3–4.
37. Catchpool, "Presidential Address," 1948, 8.
38. The constitution also insisted that there would *not* be a compulsory uniform for its membership. "Constitution of the International Youth Hostel Federation," from "Report of the Twelfth Conference of the International Youth Hostel Federation," August 1950, 65–66, HIA.
39. "Minutes of the First Post-War Conference of the International Youth Hostel Federation," Loch Lomond, 4–6 September 1946, 4, HIA.

40. "Minutes of the Ninth Conference of the International Youth Hostel Federation," September 1947, 5, HIA.

41. Cline, "Youth Hosteling," 252, 255.

42. Biesanz, "Nazi Influence," 554, 555.

43. Biesanz and Biesanz, "Social Distance in the Youth Hostel Movement," 241, 242.

44. Debates about the pedagogical uses of travel, tourism, and hosteling expanded in the 1950s and 1960s. See Benno Hafeneger, "Bewegte Jugend: Pädagogik des Reisens und Wanderns in den fünfziger und sechziger Jahren," in Reulecke and Stambolis, 100 Jahre Jugendherbergen, 255–63.

45. "Minutes of the First Post-War Conference of the International Youth Hostel Federation," 1–7.

46. Grassl and Heath, The Magic Triangle, 78–81.

47. "Statistical Report 1946 & 1947," HIA.

48. Grassl and Heath, The Magic Triangle, 89.

49. As quoted in Coburn, Youth Hostel Story, 173.

50. Francis Bolen, "A Song for Ameland," UNESCO Courier 3, no. 6–7 (July–August 1950): 12; "A Song for Ameland," Impetus 4, no. 5 (May 1950): 12–13, UNESCO Archives, Paris [hereafter UNESCO].

51. "Youth Service Camps," Reconstruction and Rehabilitation Newsletter 1, no. 3 (March 1947): 1–2, UNESCO REC & REH/01.

52. "Les rencontres de jeunesses organisée par la Direction de l'education publique," 12 February 1948, 5, Archives de l'Occupation françaises en Allemagne et en Autriche, Colmar [hereafter AOFAA] AC 69/2a.

53. "Travail de jeunes volontaires allemands en France," 24 July 1947, AOFAA AC 69/2b.

54. "T.I.C.E.R.: What It Is, How It Works, What It Does," UNESCO Publication 182, UNESCO 361.9 A01 TICER; "Youth Service Camp Committee of TICER," 19 April 1948, UNESCO 361.9 A01 TICER 369.4 A 075/02.

55. "Youth Joins in Building the Peace," Reconstruction and Rehabilitation Newsletter 2, no. 6 (June 1948): 2–7, UNESCO REC & REH/02.

56. "Work Camps: Agencies List Projects for 1949," Reconstruction and Rehabilitation Newsletter 3, no. 6 (June 1949): 8–10, UNESCO REC & REH/03; for the difficulty of arranging "East-West" camps, see Dorothy Guiborat, "International Voluntary Work Camps," in papers from the UNESCO conference "Educational Youth Travel," 27 October 1961, 26–30, UNESCO, http://unesdoc.unesco.org/images/0012/001280/128002EB.pdf.

57. Fieldston, "Little Cold Warriors."

58. "World Youth Festival in Prague," Reconstruction and Rehabilitation Newsletter 1, no. 8–9 (August–September 1947): 2, UNESCO REC & REH/01.

59. See the pamphlet "Our Feat" (Yugoslavia, 1947), International Institute of Social History, Amsterdam [hereafter IISG].

60. The Samac-Sarajevo Youth Railway, n.p., n.d., British Library; "Yugoslav Youth Railway," Manchester Guardian, 3 July 1947, 4.

61. See Rory Yeomans, "From Comrades to Consumers: Holidays, Leisure Time, and Ideology in Communist Yugoslavia," in Grandits and Taylor, *Yugoslavia's Sunny Side*, 69–105; and Dragan Popović, "Youth Labor Action (*Omlandinska radna akcija, ORA*) as Ideological Holiday-Making," ibid., 279–302.

62. Thompson, *The Railway*, 23–24, 26; for more on the ways Yugoslavia combined its youth labor projects with tourism, see Popović, "Youth Labor Action."

63. Lesley Caldwell, "The Family in the Fifties: A Notion in Conflict with Reality," in Duggan and Wagstaff, *Italy in the Cold War*, 149–58; Sassoon, *Contemporary Italy*, 115–25; Ginsborg, *A History of Contemporary Italy*, 242–49.

64. "Minutes of the First Post-War Conference of the International Youth Hostel Federation," 6.

65. Grassl and Heath, *The Magic Triangle*, 101.

66. Ibid., 129–30.

67. "Documents for the Twentieth International Youth Hostel Federation Conference," August 1959, 16, HIA.

68. "Annual Report of the International Youth Hostel Federation for 1968," appendix, HIA.

69. Judt, *Postwar*, 343.

70. Pack, *Tourism and Dictatorship*.

71. Aldo Pessina, "Italian Youth Hostels Association Report," from "Report of the Tenth Conference of the International Youth Hostel Federation," September 1948, 1, HIA.

72. Grassl and Heath, *The Magic Triangle*, 96, 144.

73. Ibid., 102–3.

74. See Sinika Stubbe, "Der Wiederbeginn des Jugendherbergswesens nach 1945," in Reulecke and Stambolis, *100 Jahre Jugendherbergen*, 223–37.

75. "Report of the Meeting of the Committee of the International Youth Hostels Association," February 1946, 4.

76. "Minutes of the First Post-War Conference of the International Youth Hostel Federation," 4. See also Sinika Stubbe, "Die internationale Arbeit des Jugendherbergswerks in der frühen Nachkriegszeit," in Reulecke and Stambolis, *100 Jahre Jugendherbergen*, 241–50.

77. See John Catchpool and Leo Meilink, "A L'Allied Control Council: Mémoire concernant l'activité international des Auberges de la jeunesse et la renaissance de l'activité des A.J. en Allemagne," 1946, AOFAA AC 347/4; and "Rapport sur la rencontre Interalliée des officiers de jeunesse à Dusseldorf, les 30 et 31 Janvier 1949," AOFAA AC 69/3.

78. As quoted in Grassl and Heath, *The Magic Triangle*, 103.

79. Catchpool, "Presidential Address," 1948, 3.

80. "Minutes of the Meeting of the Executive Committee of the International Youth Hostel Federation," Stockholm, 15–16 May 1947, 1, HIA.

81. "Report of the Meeting of the Committee of the International Youth Hostels Association," February 1946, 2.
82. "Report on the German Hostels 1948," from "Report of the Tenth Conference of the International Youth Hostel Association," September 1948, HIA.
83. There is a large file full of these inspection forms in AOFAA 347/4.
84. See chapter 2.
85. Grassl and Heath, *The Magic Triangle*, 104.
86. Röling, *Idealisme en toerisme*, 27.
87. Ibid. The young Dutch were staunch Europeanists. See Goudsblom, *De nieuwe volwassenen*.
88. "Report on the German Hostels 1948," from "Report of the Tenth Conference of the International Youth Hostel Association," September 1948, HIA.
89. Graham Heath, "The Growth of the Youth Hostel Movement," in *International Youth Hostel Manual*, 16.
90. "Report of the Meeting of the Committee of the International Youth Hostels Association," 2.
91. However, with the outbreak of the Korean War in the summer of 1950, the U.S. government requisitioned all chartered planes and ships. Grassl and Heath, *The Magic Triangle*, 97–98. Another example of the ways in which American hosteling was focused on Europe was a program in the late forties at which the American Youth Hostel Association invited select hostelers from each European association to participate in an all-expenses-paid leadership training course in the United States, while in turn sponsoring ten American hostelers to go back with each European in order to tour their home country. See Coburn, *Youth Hostel Story*, 161.
92. "Preliminary Report on the Problem of Tourism for Young People," 19 June 1949, Historical Archives of the European Union [hereafter HAEU] OEEC-1300.
93. Eric G. E. Zuelow, "The Necessity of Touring beyond the Nation: An Introduction," in *Touring beyond the Nation*, 1–16; see also Adri A. Albert de la Bruhèze, "Confronting the Lure of American Tourism: Modern Accommodation in the Netherlands," in Lundin and Kaiserfeld, *The Making of European Consumption*, 157–77.
94. Endy, *Cold War Holidays*, 131. For a history of American study abroad, see Walton, *Internationalism, National Identities, and Study Abroad*.
95. Grassl and Heath, *The Magic Triangle*, 20.
96. Ibid., 140–41.
97. "International Youth Cities," 22 June 1951, UNESCO 369.4 A 031; "Centre International de la jeunesse," 12 March 1954, ibid.
98. The possibility for hostels to function in this way was recognized early on in the 1920s, though they did not really achieve that until the 1950s. See Stambolis, "Jugendherbergen als Jugendbegegnungsstätten."

99. "Documents for the Twentieth Conference of the International Youth Hostel Federation," August 1959, 9, HIA.

100. "Exposé des motifs FNAJ," 1954, Archives Nationales de France, Paris [hereafter ANF], F44/105/art.4.

101. Shinkfield, *A Student's Travel Guide to the Netherlands*.

102. Grassl and Heath, *The Magic Triangle*, 100–1.

103. A. F. Pessina, "Italian Youth Hostels Association Report," from "Report of the Tenth Conference of the International Youth Hostel Federation," September 1948, 1, HIA.

104. Berrino, *Storia del turismo in Italia*, 239–75.

105. Clipping from *Capitolium*, May 1964, 248–264, Archivio storico capitolino [hereafter ASC], file: 39_1964_05_039–070.

106. "Il turismo scolastico negli ostelli delle gioventù," *Giovane Europa* 2, no. 14 (24 June 1955): 6, HAEU ME-126.

107. "Total Worldwide Figures," spreadsheet, HIA.

108. Grassl and Heath, *The Magic Triangle*, 133–34.

109. Alon Confino, "Traveling as a Culture of Remembrance: Traces of National Socialism in West Germany, 1945–1960," in *Germany as a Culture of Remembrance*, 235–54; Sonja Levsen, "Kontrollierte Grenzüberschreitungen: Jungendreisen als Friedenserziehung nach 1945—Konzepte und Ambivalenzen in deutsch-französischer Perspektive," in Kössler and Schwitanski, *Frieden lernen*, 181–200; and Julia Wagner, "German Tourists in Europe and Reminders of a Disturbing Past," in Bird et al., *Reverberations of Nazi Violence*, 199–214.

110. Confino, "Traveling as a Culture of Remembrance," 245–46, 253.

111. Baumann, "Die Stellung Deutschlands im internationalen Reiseverkehr," 4.

112. Grassl and Heath, *The Magic Triangle*, 134.

113. Anton Grassl, "Working Paper for the Commission on 'Training of Wardens for Their International Function,'" from "Documents for the Nineteenth International Youth Hostel Federation Conference," August 1958, 85, HIA.

114. "Report of the Executive Committee for 1956/57," ibid., 9–10.

115. Rudy Koshar, "Fodor's Germany," in *German Travel Cultures*, 172, 174.

116. Jarausch, *After Hitler*, 105, 110.

117. Glaser, *The Rubble Years*, 34; see also Sheffer, *Burned Bridge*, 34–41.

118. For essays about postwar German mass tourism see Schäfer, *Endlich Urlaub!* For a brief survey of German travel in the modern era, see Spode, *Wie die Deutschen "Reiseweltmeister" wurden*.

119. Belinda Davis, "A Whole World Opening Up: Transcultural Contact, Difference, and the Politicization of 'New Left' Activists," in Davis et al., *Changing the World, Changing Oneself*, 261.

120. See particularly chapter 1 in Fisher, *Disciplining Germany*.

121. Borchert, *The Man Outside*, 40.

122. Ibid., 38.

123. Jürgen Reulecke, "Rückkehr in die Ferne: Statt eines Vorworts," in *Rückkehr in die Ferne*, 7–8.

124. "Dokumente: Fahrtensommer 1947," ibid., 188.

125. Luitweiler, *The Seeds of Servas*, 10.

126. Norbert Schwarte and Jürgen Reulecke, "Fernweh und Großfahrten in der Bündischen Jugend der Nachkriegszeit," in Reulecke, *Rückkehr in die Ferne*, 151–68, quotation from 162.

127. Günther Birkenfeld, "Was wir wollen," *Horizont*, 9 December 1945.

128. "Zeitzeugenbericht: Dieter Danckwortt, Bonn," in Reulecke, *Rückkehr in die Ferne*, 59–62.

129. Press clipping from *Rhein-Zeitung*, 7 August 1948, and *Der Westen*, 7 August 1948, AOFAA AC 364/16.

130. "Zeitzeugenbericht: Doris Ackermann, Düsseldorf," in Reulecke, *Rückkehr in die Ferne*, 37–44.

131. Rainer Schönhammer, "Unabhängiger Jugendtourismus in der Nachkriegszeit," in Spode, *Goldstrand und Teutonengrill*, 117–28.

132. Confino, "Traveling as a Culture of Remembrance," 250.

133. Ibid.

134. Schlink, *The Reader*, 149, 157.

135. Hans Magnus Enzensberger, "Bin ich ein Deutscher?," *Die Zeit*, 12 June 1964, 9.

136. See Jarausch, "Die postnationale Nation"; and Schissler, "Postnationality."

137. Roger Alain, "Jeunesse allemande—jeunesse européenne (les suites d'une enquête)," n.d., AOFAA AC 42/3.

138. As quoted in Judt, *Postwar*, 275.

139. Frevert, "Europeanizing Germany's Twentieth Century."

140. Sheffer, *Burned Bridge*, 149–52.

141. McDougall, *Youth Politics in East Germany*, 110–32.

142. Sheffer, *Burned Bridge*, 142.

143. Poiger, *Jazz, Rock, and Rebels*, 131–32.

144. Patrick Major, "Going West: The Open Border and the Problem of *Republikflucht*," in Major and Osmond, *The Workers' and Peasants' State*, 204; McDougall, *Youth Politics in East Germany*, 122.

145. Taylor, *The Berlin Wall*, 239–40, 256–59, 290, 296–305, 315, 322–23. On the youthfulness of the escapee cohort, see also Kleindienst, *Mauer-Passagen*.

146. Sheffer, *Burned Bridge*, 199–202, 215.

147. See Zahra, *The Great Departure*.

148. Creswell and Trachtenberg, "France and the German Question."

149. Schwabe, "The Cold War and European Integration."

150. Antonio Varsori, "Italy's Policy towards European Integration (1947–1958)," in Duggan and Wagstaff, *Italy in the Cold War*, 47–66.

151. Deutsch, *Political Community and the North Atlantic Area*, 53, 151–54, 170.

152. Cold War politics of course shaped youth organizations as they reoriented

along ideological lines, often in a kind of parallel formation, with the Scouting and Young Pioneer movements being the most famous, or the Anglo-American-sponsored World Assembly of Youth (WAY) and Soviet-sponsored World Federation of Democratic Youth (WFDY) and a host of others. Within this Cold War paradigm, organizing the young into international and transnational movements within their respective blocs became paramount as a means of consolidating one side in a charged distinction from the other. See Honeck and Rosenberg, "Transnational Generations"; see also several of the chapters in Jobs and Pomfret, *Transnational Histories of Youth*.

153. Western European Union, *Youth in the Western European Union Countries*, 48.

154. Christina Norwig, "'Unser Paß ist die Europa-Fahne': Junge Reisende und europäische Integration in den 1950er Jahren," in Bösch, Brill, and Greiner, *Europabilder im 20. Jahrhundert*, 216–36.

155. For more on the European Youth Campaign, particularly its rationale, see Norwig, "A First European Generation?"; and Norwig, *Die erste europäische Generation*.

156. Eigel Steinmetz, "Les pays scandinaves abolissent les passeports," *Jeune Europe*, no. 6 (August 1952): 1, HAEU PD-10; "Quand L'Europe sera faite 1954–1964," *Jeune Europe*, no. 23 (April 1954): 3, HAEU ME-1369; Sylvette Mauduy and Gérard Badel, "Et vous, Madame Dupont qu'en pensez-vous?," *Jeune Europe*, no. 11 (5 September 1953): 8, HAEU ME-1369.

157. "Campaign de l'amitié internationale," HAEU UEF-175; "Concours d'été organize par la CEJ," HAEU ME-1370. See also François-Xavier Lafféach, "An *Avant-garde* for Europe: The Young European Federalists and the Emergence of a European Consciousness, 1948–1972," in Rasmussen and Knudsen, *The Road to a United Europe*, 39–51.

158. Flyer, *Föderalistichen Jugend Europas*, 1954, HAEU ME-200.

159. Lafféach, "An *Avant-garde* for Europe"; Palayret, "Eduquer les jeunes a l'Union." For details on how the CIA funded the movement, see chapter 16 in Aldrich, *The Hidden Hand*, 342–70.

160. "Le movement européen a brulé un Poteau symbolique à la frontière de Menton," *Le Figaro*, 29 December 1952, 4.

161. "Students Burn Frontier Post," *Manchester Guardian*, 7 August 1950, 5.

162. "Wissembourg: Le Bourg Blanc," HAEU UEF-176; "Grenzen Weg," clipping from *Het Parool*, 14 January 1952, Archief Hendrika Scheffer, IISG; "Stages, Camps, Manifestation et Autres Activités Politiques," HAEU ME-1357; "5.000 jeunes à la Haye," *Jeune Europe*, no. 13 (20 October 1953): 8, HAEU PD-10. See also Daniela Preda, "La jeunesse fédéralistes européennes," in Pistone, *I movimenti per l'unità europea*, 229–59.

163. Norwig, "'Unser Paß ist die Europa-Fahne,'" 224.

164. "Activités de l'Assemblée européen des jeunesse politiques crée sous l'égide de la CEJ," October 1952, 39, HAEU ME-105.

165. See Furlough, "Making Mass Vacations," especially 265–73 on social tourism.

166. "Centre d'information des chemins de fer européens et Commission international des voyages de la jeunesse," May 1955, HAEU ME-1373.

167. For details on the origins of the identity card, see "International Student Identity Card," International Student Travel Confederation, Archives Amsterdam, 6 AGM 1955.

168. Council of Europe, "European Agreement on Travel by Young Persons on Collective Passports between Member Countries of the Council of Europe," European Treaty Series, no. 37 (1962).

169. Winfried Böll, "Rummelplatz Europa," *Jugend Europas*, no. 7 (November 1953): 6, HAEU ME-1417.

170. "Strangled Woman Tourist, French Tramp Admits," *Chicago Daily Tribune*, 12 January 1956, 1.

171. Herzog, "'Pleasure, Sex, and Politics Belong Together,'" 397, 412.

172. Heineman, *Before Porn Was Legal*, 81.

173. Ruff, *The Wayward Flock*, 63.

174. Levsen, "Kontrollierte Grenzüberschreitungen."

175. Grassl and Heath, *The Magic Triangle*, 134–35.

176. "Politik des Reisens?" For the 1960s moral concern for youth travel, see chapter 4.

177. Per Lundin, "Coping with Cars, Families, and Foreigners: Swedish Postwar Tourism," in Lundin and Kaiserfeld, *The Making of European Consumption*, 216–20.

178. Grassl and Heath, *The Magic Triangle*, 113.

179. Both quoted in Rainer Schönhammer, "Unabhängiger Jugendtourismus," in Spode, *Goldstrand und Teutonengrill*, 120, 123.

180. "Julie Thomas" is a pseudonym. MO P2175, Summer 2000 Directive: Travelling, Mass Observation Archive, Sussex [hereafter MOA].

181. Mahood, "Thumb Wars."

182. TEO Eng Seng, Oral History Interview, reel 2 of 6, transcript 36–49, Accession Number 003351, National Archives of Singapore.

183. Levenstein, *We'll Always Have Paris*, 120–23.

184. Endy, *Cold War Holidays*, 131.

185. Walton, *Internationalism, National Identities, and Study Abroad*.

186. Hoffa, *A History of US Study Abroad*, 122–23, 200–7, 228–33.

187. See chapter 3 in Bailkin, *The Afterlife of Empire*; and chapter 5 in Perraton, *A History of Foreign Students in Britain*. For France see Marker, "France between Europe and Africa."

188. Timothy Nicholson, "East African Students in a (Post-)Imperial World," in Robinson and Sleight, *Children, Childhood and Youth in the British World*, 109–26.

189. See chapter 1 in Lyons, *The Civilizing Mission in the Metropole*.

190. Walton, *Internationalism, National Identities, and Study Abroad*, 94, 134.

191. Tim Cresswell and Tanu Priya Uteng, "Gendered Mobilities: Towards an Holistic Understanding," in Uteng and Cresswell, *Gendered Mobilities*, 1–12.

192. Dr. Danckwortt, "International Exchange Programs for Young People: Social Science Methods of Inquiry and Results," in UNESCO Institute for Youth, *An Analysis of the Impact of International Travel and Exchange Programmes on Young People*, November 1960, 4.

193. "Report from Nederlandse Jeugherberg Centrale on Research Work," from the Annual Report of the International Youth Hostel Federation for 1967, 25, HIA.

194. "Report on Student Hostels in Copenhagen Run by the Danish International Student Committee," 3 November 1952, 2, UNESCO 369.4 A 031.

195. Georg Beez, "Jugend und Jugendherberge," from the Annual Report of the International Youth Hostel Federation for 1967, 26–27, HIA.

196. Axel Schildt, "Across the Border: West German Youth Travel to Western Europe," in Schildt and Siegfried, *Between Marx and Coca-Cola*, 152.

197. Cees Nooteboom, "Birth of a New Nation?," *Guardian*, 8 May 1992, 23.

198. Nooteboom, *Philip and the Others*.

199. Lodge, *Out of the Shelter*, x.

200. Colin MacInnes, "Pop Songs and Teenagers," originally published in *The Twentieth Century*, February 1958, reprinted in *England, Half English*, 57.

201. MacInnes, *Absolute Beginners*, 75, 220.

202. Inglehart, "The New Europeans."

203. Inglehart, "An End to European Integration?," 92, 93.

204. Inglehart, "Changing Value Priorities and European Integration," 27–28, 34.

205. The best English-language book on the flood is Clark, *Dark Water*. Jack Fox, "Art Lovers Go to Florence's Aid," *Boston Globe*, 14 May 1967, 69.

206. D'Angelis, *Angeli del fango*, 202.

207. Clark, *Dark Water*; see also Taylor, *Diary of a Florence Flood*.

208. Taken from testimonies in D'Angelis, *Angeli del fango*, 164, 204, 156, 158, 206.

209. "Ignacio Serrano Garcia" and "Riccardo Lanza," from www.angelidelfango .it, a website of testimony marking the fortieth anniversary of the flood, produced by a collaboration of various Tuscan institutions. Accessed 5 October 2011.

210. Honeck and Rosenberg, "Transnational Generations," 233–39.

211. Patel, "Provicialising European Union."

212. Conway and Patel, *Europeanization*.

213. Ibid.; Frevert, "Europeanizing Germany's Twentieth Century"; Kaiser, "Transnational Western Europe since 1945."

214. Trevor L. Christie, "Tourism and the Common Market," *ASTA Travel News* 33 (February 1963): 56–57.

215. "Working Parties of the Tourism Committee: Youth Tourism," HAEU OECD-1487.

216. Diethard Beck is a pseudonym. "Balkan '62: Reisetagbuch 1962," Deutsches Tagebucharchiv, Emmendingen [hereafter DTA] 1681.

217. Nugent, *The Grand Tour*.

218. Wolff, *Inventing Eastern Europe*.

219. Böröcz, "Travel-Capitalism."

220. "Minutes of the Conference: Planning of Student Travels 1950s," Copenhagen International Student Travel Confederation.

221. Luitweiler, *The Seeds of Servas*, 20.

222. Saunier, *Transnational History*.

223. Lefebvre, *The Production of Space*.

224. See David M. Pomfret, "'Colonial Circulations': Vietnamese Youth, Travel, and Empire, 1919–1940," in Jobs and Pomfret, *Transnational Histories of Youth*, 115–43.

225. Ludger Pries, "The Approach of Transnational Social Spaces: Responding to New Configurations of the Social and the Spatial," in *New Transnational Social Spaces*, 3–33.

226. Thomas Faist, "The Border-Crossing Expansion of Social Space: Concepts, Questions and Topics," in Faist and Özveren, *Transnational Social Spaces*, 1–34.

227. For more on the varieties of Europeanization, see Conway and Patel, *Europeanization*.

228. Frank Schimmelfennig, "Transnational Socialization: Community-Building in an Integrated Europe," in Kaiser and Starie, *Transnational European Union*, 61–82.

229. For more on the interrelationship between internationalism and transnationalism, see Laqua, *Internationalism Reconfigured*.

230. "Mitch Perko" is a pseudonym. MO D944, Spring 2000 Directive: Travelling, MOA.

CHAPTER TWO

1. Günther et al., *Tourismusforschung in Bayern*, 29–32.

2. Hahn, *Internationaler Jugendtourismus*, 11, 26–27.

3. Helmut Kentler, "Die Entwicklung des Jugendtourismus in Europa," ibid., 17.

4. Standard works on the history of Franco-German relations include Farquharson and Holt, *Europe from Below*; Picht and Wessels, *Motor für Europa?*; Friend, *The Linchpin*; Jurt, *Von der Besatzungszeit*; Ménudier, *Le couple franco-allemand en Europe*; Sauder and Schild, *Handeln für Europa*; Leblond, *Le couple franco-allemand depuis 1945*; Calleo and Staal, *Europe's Franco-German Engine*; Cole, *Franco-German Relations*; Hendriks and Morgan, *The Franco-German Axis in European Integration*; and Germond and Türk, *A History of Franco-German Relations in Europe*.

5. Michael Sutton makes a strong case that the "geopolitical imperative" to ensure French national security was the primary impetus for integration across regimes in France. Sutton, *France and the Construction of Europe*.

6. For an overview of recent work, see Christian Kleinschmidt's review essay "Infrastructure, Networks, (Large) Technical Systems." See also Badenoch and Fickers, *Materializing Europe*.

7. Office of Military Government for Germany (U.S.), "Youth Activities: Report on German Youth, Second Year of Occupation," 31 March 1947, 1–2, United Kingdom National Archives [hereafter UKNA], FO 1050/1086. This kind of attitude was evident in Padover, *Psychologist in Germany*. See also Fisher, *Disciplining Germany*.

8. Rovan, "Les relations franco-allemande." See also the 1951 report "Des perspectives d'avenir des rencontres internationales," AOFAA 42/3. For the French occupation see Hillel, *L'occupation française en Allemagne*; Zauner, *Erziehung und Kulturmission*; Defrance, *La politique culturelle de la France sur la rive gauche du Rhin*; Mombert, *Sous le signe de la rééducation*; Plum, "Französische Kulturpolitik in Deutschland."

9. Willis, *The French in Germany*, 168–70, 178, 247.

10. On BILD see Jean-Charles Moreau, "Nature et Convergence des initiatives officielles et privées du rapprochement franco-allemand dans le domaine de la vie associative," in Jurt, *Von der Besatzungszeit*, 196–208; for *Documents/Dokumente* see René Wintzen, "Le role des 'Services d'Education populaire' et des inititatives privées (rencontres franco-allemandes d'écrivains, *Documents/Dokumente*)," ibid., 209–36.

11. F. Roy Willis discusses all of this in more detail in *The French in Germany*.

12. Siegel and Harjes, "Disarming Hatred."

13. This was in keeping with the general posture, in private, of the French government, which recognized the need to reconcile and stabilize Germany though officials did not say so publicly. See Creswell and Trachtenberg, "France and the German Question."

14. Zahra, *The Lost Children*, 146–72.

15. Biess, "Moral Panic in Postwar Germany."

16. Commandement en Chef Français en Allemagne, "Rapport sur les contacts organisés par les étudiants et members des mouvements de jeunesse et d'education populaire allemand par la Direction de l'Education Publique du G.M.Z.F.O. en 1946 et 1947," 19 June 1947, 1, AOFAA AC69/2a.

17. "Bilan moral des rencontres internationales de jeunesse en Z.F.O. durant l'été 1948," 2, AOFAA AC69/2b.

18. "Les rencontres de jeunesse organisées par la Direction de l'Education Populaire," 12 December 1948, 3, AOFAA AC69/2a.

19. "Extraits de letters de jeunes Allemands ayant assisté à des rencontres de vacances," 30 January 1948, 1, AOFAA AC69/2a.

20. Allied Control Authority, "Report on the Relations between German Youth and the Youth of Allied Countries: Report from the American Zone," 30 July 1947, 1–3, UKNA, FO 1050/1086. More information on American attitudes can be found in Office of Military Government for Germany (U.S.), "Youth Activities: Report on German Youth, Second Year of Occupation."

21. Tent, *Mission on the Rhine*, 303.

22. Jarausch, *After Hitler*, 108.

23. Allied Control Authority, "Report on the Relations between German Youth and the Youth of Allied Countries: Report from the British Zone," 30 July 1947, 1–6, UKNA, FO 1050/1086.

24. "Survey of the Principal Projects Sponsored by the Education Branch of the C.C.G. in the British Zone, 1948/49," AOFAA AC261/3. The Soviet report is brief, lacks any detail, and is quite vague on the activity in their zone. For a detailed overview of the reform of education in West Germany see Puaca, *Learning Democracy*.

25. Allied Control Authority, "Report on the Relations between German Youth and the Youth of Allied Countries: Report from the French Zone," 30 July 1947, 1, UKNA, FO 1050/1086.

26. Karen Adler, "Making a French Home Abroad: The Zone Française d'Occupation in West Germany, 1945–60" (paper presented at Society for French Historical Studies Annual Conference, Charleston, SC, February 2011).

27. Zahra, *The Lost Children*, 150.

28. Allied Control Authority, "Report on the Relations between German Youth and the Youth of Allied Countries: Report from the French Zone," 2.

29. Office of Military Government for Germany (U.S.), "Youth Activities: Report on German Youth, Second Year of Occupation."

30. See, for example, Tiemann, *Deutsch-französische Jugendbeziehungen der Zwischenkriegszeit*; Hellman, *The Communitarian Third Way*; Elana Passman, "Civic Activism and the Pursuit of Cooperation in the Locarno Era," in Germond and Türk, *A History of Franco-German Relations in Europe*, 101–12; Bock, Meyer-Kalkus, and Trebtisch, *Entre Locarno et Vichy*.

31. Raymond Schmittlein, "Briser les chaines de la jeunesse allemand," *France-Illustration*, 17 September 1949, 18.

32. Commandement en Chef Français en Allemagne, "Rapport sur les contacts organisés par les étudiants et members des mouvements de jeunesse et d'education populaire allemand par la Direction de l'Education Publique du G.M.Z.F.O. en 1946 et 1947," 1.

33. "Instruction," n.d., AOFAA AC 258/1.

34. Commandement en Chef Français en Allemagne, "Rapport sur les contacts organisés par les étudiants et members des mouvements de jeunesse et d'education populaire allemand par la Direction de l'Education Publique du G.M.Z.F.O. en 1946 et 1947," 2–4. See also "Les rencontres de jeunesse organisées par la Direction de l'Education Populaire," 12 December 1948, AOFAA AC69/2a.

35. "Les rencontres de jeunesse organisées par la Direction de l'Education Populaire," 1.

36. Commandement en Chef Français en Allemagne, "Rapport sur les contacts organisés par les étudiants et members des mouvements de jeunesse et d'education populaire allemand par la Direction de l'Education Publique du G.M.Z.F.O. en 1946 et 1947," 2.

37. Robert Vannet, "Mes histoires . . . ," 50, Association pour l'autobiographie et le patromoine [hereafter APA], 2:74 APA 249.

38. "Sejours et camps de vacances de la jeunesse française en Allemagne et en Autriche occupées," 1946, 1–4, ANF F44/55/art.2.

39. M. Acolas, "Les camps internationaux de jeunesses au Tyrol," 25 November 1946, ANF F44/55/art.2.

40. See M. Acolas, "Rapport sur les rencontres de jeunesse et les contacts culturels," 19 November 1947, ANF F44/55/art.2; M. Becart, le Directeur de l'Education Populaire, "Inspection Générale," 25 February 1948, ANF F44/105/art. 1; Acolas, "Les camps internationaux de jeunesses au Tyrol." Although French authorities considered the Austrians to be victims of Nazism rather than guilty perpetrators, the occupation policies pursued in the respective French zones of occupation were markedly similar. See Dussault, "Politique culturelle et dénazification dans la zone d'occupation française en Autriche."

41. "Jugend über den Grenzen," *Rhein-Zeitung*, 1 September 1948, AOFAA AC264/4.

42. "Derniers échos des rencontres internationales universitaires," *Nouvelles de France*, 17 September 1948, AOFAA AC264/4.

43. Lafféach, "An *Avant-garde* for Europe," 42–43.

44. "Bilan moral des rencontres internationales de jeunesse en Z.F.O. durant l'été 1948," 10–11.

45. *Rheinischer Merkur*, 5 June 1948 and 23 July 1949, as quoted in Willis, *The French in Germany*, 283n99.

46. "Bilan moral des rencontres internationales de jeunesse en Z.F.O. durant l'été 1948," 10.

47. Levsen, "Kontrollierte Grenzüberschreitungen,"185–86.

48. Wolf-Dieter Wardeiner is a pseudonym. DTA 489.3, 489.4.

49. A summary of these projects and their goals and outcomes is in the 1951 report "Des perspectives d'avenir des rencontres internationales," AOFAA 42/3.

50. Geneviève Carrez, "Les Rencontres internationales," in *Les Relations internationales de l'Allemagne Occidentale*, ed. Alfred Grosser, Cahiers de Fondation nationale des Sciences politiques, no. 78 (Paris: A. Colin, 1956), 193, 195.

51. François-Poncet to Schuman, 5 May 1951, 1, AOFAA AC 57/3.

52. "Des perspectives d'avenir des rencontres internationales," 2.

53. Ibid., 4. France had aggressively targeted the Saarland with similar youth contact programs as part of efforts to Europeanize the Saarland as a state independent of West Germany. Even though the Saarland voted in 1955 to remain a part of West Germany, these sorts of programs continued undisrupted but within the larger Franco-German context. See Mission Diplomatique Française en Sarre à Bureau chargé des Relations Internationales, Centre des archives contemporaines, Fontainebleau [hereafter CAC] 860445/art.1. For more French cultural policies in the Saarland, see Long, "The Saar Dispute."

54. T. H. Marshall, "Programme for German Youth," 20 December 1950, 1, UKNA, FO 317/93658.
55. Pierre Baletaud à Monseiur Tarbe de Saint-Hardouin, "Enquête sur la jeunesse allemande," 14 March 1949, 3–5, AOFAA AC69/3.
56. See Westphal, *Jugend braucht Demokratie, Demokratie braucht Jugend.*
57. Allied Control Authority, "Report on the Relations between German Youth and the Youth of Allied Countries: Report from the French Zone," 2.
58. "Le train-exposition de la jeunesse française va parcourir l'Europe," *Le Monde*, 20 February 1948, 8.
59. Willis, *France, Germany and the New Europe*, 61.
60. This is a key argument of Willis, *France, Germany and the New Europe*. More recently see, Victor Gavin Munte, "A New Framework for Franco-German Relations through European Institutions, 1950–1954," in Germond and Türk, *A History of Franco-German Relations in Europe*, 165–75.
61. Raoul Dautry, "La jeunesse européenne," *L'Eveil de Europe*, December 1950, 2.
62. Rémy Montagne and Hans Mertens, "Gibt es seine Europäisches Jugend?," *Dokumente* 7, no. 3 (1951), Bundesarchiv, Koblenz [hereafter BAK], B/268/549.
63. Deutsch, *Political Community and the North Atlantic Area*, 53, 151–54.
64. Marcel Niedergang, "Cet été, la jeunesse du monde avait rendez-vous en Europe," *Réforme*, 15 September 1951, AOFAA AC 364/1.
65. Treue, "Europareisen und Europabewußtsein in der Neuzeit."
66. Dr. Danckwortt, "International Exchange Programs for Young People: Social Science Methods of Inquiry and Results," in UNESCO Institute for Youth, *An Analysis of the Impact of International Travel and Exchange Programmes on Young People*, November 1960, 1.
67. "Bonner Jugend geht auf große Fahrt," *Generalanzeiger für Bonn*, 10 July 1951, BAK B/268/548.
68. Carrez, "Les Rencontres internationales," 187, 189.
69. In German, French, and English, the spelling is inconsistent as "Lorelei" or "Loreley"; in German, it is more often "Lorelei," and that spelling more accurately reflects the pronunciation in English than does "Loreley." However, the HAEU uses "Loreley," so I have adopted their usage.
70. There had been similar efforts, though on a much smaller scale. For example, in 1949, the British occupation authorities had helped German youth leaders coordinate a three-week International Youth Camp on the Isle of Sylt, a traditional holiday destination in the North Sea. The camp's purpose was to enable young Germans, who constituted approximately half of the 250 campers, to interact with youth from elsewhere in northern and western Europe. See Education Branch to Herr Eriksson, "International Youth Camp, Isle of Sylt," 6 April 1949, UKNA, FO 1050/1086.
71. The Germans paid well over half, the French a quarter, with the British and Americans splitting the remainder. The campers paid 12 marks, or about 1 pound, for their stay. "Aide américaine pour le camp de la Loreley,"

15 June 1951, AOFAA AC 57/3. See the food complaints made by the French, BAK B/153/2624.

72. "Bilan moral des rencontres internationales de jeunesse en Z.F.O. durant l'été 1948," 5.

73. See "Projet de camp de la jeunesse européenne," 10 January 1951, AOFAA AC 57/3.

74. BAK B/153/2624, Heft 2, doc. 350.

75. "Rencontres de la jeunesse européenne à la Loreley," 15 March 1951, 3, AOFAA AC 57/3.

76. Ibid., 4.

77. Ibid.

78. See, for example, the speech by Maurice Cayron, AFFOAA AC 362/2. For more on the conceptual use of youth as the future in the postwar period see Jobs, *Riding the New Wave*.

79. "Youth of Europe Meets on Rhine," *New York Times*, 23 July 1951, 7.

80. *Camp* considered itself "the first European youth magazine" and was published in English, French, and German. "80 000," *Camp*, no. 1 (n.d.): 1, AOFAA 57/3.

81. "That is why we will not shoot again." Ibid., 6.

82. Gerhard Brunn details the organizational and planning aspect of the meeting in "The European Youth Meeting on the Loreley Rock in 1951 and the Failure to Establish a European Youth Movement," in *La construction européenne dans une perspective historique et culturelle* (Madrid: Euroius Editorial Juridica, 1997), 15–29.

83. See Jean Moreau, "Rapport sur les rencontres européene de jeunesse à la Loreley," AOFAA 57/3.

84. Jo-M. Grinnaert, "L'esprite français et l'organisation allemande ou la recette du succès," *La Cité Bruxelles*, 28 August 1951, AOFAA 364/1.

85. Willis, *France, Germany and the New Europe*, v.

86. However, in the spring camp organizers had predicted 80,000. Moreau, "Rapport sur les rencontres européene de jeunesse à la Loreley," 9–10.

87. Ibid., 21.

88. Ibid., 14, 16, 27. Others, such as Alexandre Marc, had a different opinion. Marc did not think they were all that interested in the politics of building Europe, but instead were absorbed with themselves as the young tend to be. Brunn, "The European Youth Meeting on the Loreley Rock," 26.

89. See the document files on the press, BAK B/268/548 and BAK B/268/550. The emphasis on a German audience is evident in a press release from early August that said a divided Germany was a fundamental problem for the future of Europe, but that the best way to lay a foundation for the reunification of Germany would be to build Europe. Press release, 7 August 1951, BAK B/268/548.

90. See the Loreley press file summaries in "La Presse des zone occidentals," 5–6, 11–12, AOFAA AC 57/3.

91. Moreau, "Rapport sur les rencontres européenne de jeunesse à la Loreley," 21.
92. Michael Buddrus, "Die Jugend der DDR und der Ausland," in Reulecke, *Rückkehr in die Ferne*, 125–50.
93. Nick Rutter, "The Western Wall: The Iron Curtain Recast in Midsummer 1951," in Babiracki and Zimmer, *Cold War Crossings*, 78–106.
94. See the July and August reports from the Office of the United States High Commissioner for Germany, file "572-World Youth Festival," National Archives and Records Administration, Washington, DC [hereafter NARA], RG 466/250/68/15/3, box 134.
95. Ibid.
96. Robert Borzat, "Neidersachsens Polizei als 'Transportunternehmen': Illegale Reisende zu den Berliner 'Wjfs' warden zurückgeschict," *Neue Zeitung*, 1 August 1951.
97. Sheffer, *Burned Bridge*, 85.
98. Rutter, "The Western Wall," 98–99. On the instability and frequent violence along the border, see Part 1 in Sheffer, *Burned Bridge*.
99. For details on the UK affair, including newspaper clippings, correspondence, and government inquiry, see UKNA, FO 371/99833 and NCUACS 54.3.95/K.308–10.
100. "Yugoslav Youth Railway," *Manchester Guardian*, 3 July 1947, 4.
101. Sheffer, *Burned Bridge*, 6, 34.
102. Rutter, "The Western Wall," 83–86, 98–99.
103. For contemporary overview accounts of both events, see "La rencontre de la jeunesse européenne au camp de la Lorelei," *Réalités Allemandes* 32 (August 1951): 25–29; and "Le festival de la jeunesse mondiale à Berlin," *Réalités Allemandes* 32 (August 1951): 31–39.
104. See "German Youth Camp Invites Foreigners," *New York Times*, 10 July 1951, 16; Frances M. Vale, "Youth Assemblies: To the Editor of The Times," *Times*, 13 August 1951, 5.
105. "Youth of Free Europe Plan for Tomorrow," *Christian Science Monitor*, 29 August 1951, 9.
106. See André Fontaine, "Sous le drapeau européenne: Des milliers de jeunes se sont rencontres sur le rocher de la Loreley," *Le Monde*, 9–10 September 1951, 3.
107. G. C. Allen to Mr. Warr, Chancery, 23 July 1951, 1, UKNA, FO 371/93660.
108. "German Youth," 9 February 1951, 1–4, UKNA, FO 371/93658.
109. Roger Alain, "Jeunesse allemande—jeunesse européenne (les suites d'une enquête)," n.d., AOFAA AC42/3.
110. André Thomas, "Pour le salut de l'Europe et pour donner un idéal commun à sa jeunesse," AOFAA AC42/3. See also Brunn, "The European Youth Meeting on the Loreley Rock," 20.
111. This was a policy particularly attractive to the French. See Schwabe, "The Cold War and European Integration"; Creswell and Trachtenberg, "France and the German Question."

112. "Auszüge aus Briefen von Teilnehmer und Teilnehmerinnen am Loreley-lager," BAK B/268/550.

113. Jo-Marie Grinnaert, "Les rencontres de la Loreley ont-elles atteint leur but?," *La Cité Bruxelles*, 15 September 1951, AOFAA AC 364/1.

114. "Europäische Gemeinschaft im kleinen Rahmen," *Die Neue Zeitung*, 7 August 1951, 6.

115. "To Unknown Places," *Camp*, no. 1 (n.d.): 7, AOFAA 57/3.

116. Jeanne Cappe, "Où La Lorelei accueille les jeunesses européennes," *La Nation Belge*, 28 July 1951, AOFAA AC 364/1.

117. Moreau, "Rapport sur les rencontres européenne de jeunesse à la Loreley," 23. Indeed, young Germans who became avid travelers sought a sense of community among the other young of Europe. See Schissler, "Postnationality"; Confino, "Traveling as a Culture of Remembrance."

118. In the wake of Loreley, Germany sponsored all kinds of similar but smaller-scale programs, such as the annual European Youth Week, to help young Europeans find their place in a new Europe, while also providing non-Germans with a concrete understanding of Germany, and young Germans with an appreciation of their neighbors. Hanns Ott looks at these programs in detail in "Die Europäischen Jugendwochen." Even before Loreley, in the fall of 1950, West German youth organizations held rallies on the theme of Europe with more than 100,000 participants. Brunn, "The European Youth Meeting on the Loreley Rock," 15–16.

119. "Bilan moral des rencontres internationales de jeunesse en Z.F.O. durant l'été 1948," 5–6, 8, 11–13.

120. "Rapport sur les activités d'échanges entre le Land Rhénanie-Palatinat et la Bourgogne: Réalisations de Juin à Novembre 1953," AOFAA AC294/2.

121. Flora Lewis, "Franco-German 'Twins'—A Startling Fact," *New York Times*, 29 May 1960, 14.

122. Le Ministre des Affaires Etrangères à M. Le Ministre de l'Education Nationale, "Réunion du sous-comité franco-allemand des échanges non-universitaires," 7 January 1958, CAC 860445/art.1. A 1978 study about Franco-German contacts between the twin cities of Ingolstadt and Grasse documents the effect of youth exchanges on national stereotypes and attitudes. See Treffer, *Jugendaustausch Innerhalb Einer Städtepartnerschaft*.

123. For a detailed look at the private initiatives of the 1950s that laid the groundwork for the FGYO, see Hans Manfred Bock, "Les raciness de l'OFAJ dans la société civile: Les initiatives privées de rapprochement en République fédérale et en France de 1949 à 1964," in Bock et al., *Les jeunes dans les relations transnationales*, 15–38.

124. For a brief overview of Charles de Gaulle's policies and attitudes toward Germany, see Pierre Maillard, "La politique du Général de Gaulle à l'égard de l'Allemagne (1945–1969): Continuité et discontinuité," in Jurt, *Von der Besatzungszeit*, 50–60.

125. For a brief overview see Willis, *France, Germany and the New Europe*, 305–11. For a more thorough account of the treaty itself, see Defrance and Pfeil, *Le traité de l'Elysée et les relations franco-allemandes*.

126. De Gaulle, *Discours et messages*, 18. Or as Michel Debré, de Gaulle's premier, said to the National Assembly, "young Frenchmen should see their future in the eyes of young Germans, and, in turn, in the eyes of the children of France, the children of Germany should perceive theirs." As quoted in Willis, *France, Germany, and the New Europe*, 293. This period is replete with a discourse of youth as the future, particularly in France, but elsewhere in Europe, too. See Jobs, *Riding the New Wave*.

127. The best overview of the Franco-German Youth Office in its first twenty-five years is Ménudier, *L'Office franco-allemand pour la jeunesse*. For a recent examination of FGYO activities with an emphasis on transnationality, see Bock et al., *Les jeunes dans les relations transnationales*. For a detailed political science assessment of the FGYO, see Delori, "De la réconciliation franco-allemande à la 'guerre des dieux.'"

128. Levsen, "Kontrollierte Grenzüberschreitungen," 195.

129. Heinrich Barth, "Jeunesse: Cooperation franco-allemande," *Documents* 18, no. 5 (September–October 1963): 45–49.

130. *L'Office franco-allemand pour la jeunesse, rapport d'activité, 1963–1968*, 41, CAC 770303/art.1.

131. Ibid., 19.

132. Ibid., 5.

133. Ibid., 52–57. The FGYO would have more success with this in the 1970s when it shifted its emphasis to educational and professional training. See, for example, Jürgen Prott and Ute Stoltenberg's study of youth trade-unionist meetings and exchanges in the 1970s, *Wege zur internationalen Solidarität*.

134. See "Fremdsprachenkenntnisse der Bundesbürger," *Divo-Pressendienst*, July 1965, 5–7; and "Junge Menschen sprechen Sprachen," *EMNID-Informationen* 32, no. 22 (1966): 10–11, A6–A9.

135. Thérèse Guitton, "Taches de l'Office franco-allemand pour la jeunesse: Aborder le problème linguistique et développer l'information politique," *Le Figaro*, 25 November 1968.

136. "Connaissance de la France/Wir entdecken Deutschland," 1966, CAC 860444/art.30.

137. "Wir entdecken Deutschland," 1966, CAC 860444/art.30. See also Helga Cording, "Wir entdecken Deutschland," *Deutsch Jugend* 14, no. 2 (1966): 77–82.

138. *L'Office franco-allemand pour la jeunesse, rapport d'activité, 1963–1968*, 35–39.

139. Tinker, *Mixed Messages*, 83–92.

140. See Chris Tinker, "Rock 'n' Roll Stardom: Johnny Hallyday," in Gaffney and Holmes, *Stardom in Postwar France*, 87–88.

141. "L'Allemagne des jeunes," *Salut les copains* 41 (December 1965): 115–23, 146, 150.

142. *L'Office franco-allemand pour la jeunesse, rapport d'activité, 1963–1968*, 130.

143. *L'Office franco-allemand pour la jeunesse, rapport d'activité, 1963–1973*, 29, CAC 770303/art. 8.

144. Anne Dulphy and Christine Manigand, "Les jeunes Français et l'Europe," in du Réau and Frank, *Dynamiques européennes*, 225–26.

145. *Bulletin de liaison de l'Office franco-allemand pour la jeunesse*, no. 1 (1973): 14, CAC 770303/art. 7.

146. Isabelle Mouré is a pseudonym. "Une Germaniste française en RDA entre 1972 et 1989," 41, 7:260 APA 1737.

147. Gaby Lafitte is a pseudonym. "Carnets de voyages au coeur de l'Europe," 12, 2:87 APA 303.

148. See Merritt and Puchala, *Western European Perspectives on International Affairs*, 281–317; Inglehart, "An End to European Integration?"; *Die Einstellung der deutschen Jugend zur Vereinigung Europas* (Allensback: Insitut für Demoskopie, 1967); and Société française d'enquêtes par sondage, *Attitudes des français à l'égard des implications socio-économiques du Marché commun* (Paris: SOFRES, 1968).

149. See Inglehart, "An End to European Integration?" For more on these studies, see chapter 1.

150. *L'Office franco-allemand pour la jeunesse, rapport d'activité, 1963–1968*, 23.

151. "Après le rapprochement une politique d'integration," *Pariser Kurier*, 1 June 1975.

152. "L'Office franco-allemand pour la jeunesse: Un exemple à l'échelle européenne," *Le Populaire du Centre*, 29 September 1971.

153. "Ein Modell für Europa," *Frankfurter Allgemeine*, 11 August 1975.

154. See "Moins de dollars, plus de deutschemarks," *Le Monde*, 29 August 1973, and "Les Américains boudent," *Le Monde*, 2 March 1974.

155. *L'Office franco-allemand pour la jeunesse, rapport d'activité, 1963–1968*, 4.

156. Office franco-allemand de la jeunesse, *15 Ans: Office franco-allemand pour la jeunesse, 1963–1978* (Versailles: Presse et d'information de l'Office franco-allemand pour la jeunesse, 1978), 19.

157. See Bulletin der Presse- und Informationsamtes der Bundesregierung, no. 117 (6 July 1963), BAK B/106/3734 doc. 021–024.

158. "Antrag der Fraktion der SPD, betr. europäisches Jugendwerk," 22 January 1964, BAK B/304/4254.

159. Internal report, CAC 770744/art.26. For more on the disagreements surrounding the treaty and the office, see Ansbert Baumann, "L'Office franco-allemand pour la jeunesse: Une fondation controversée," in Bock et al., *Les jeunes dans les relations transnationales*, 39–58.

160. "Les échanges entre jeunes Français et Allemands element majeur de l'avenir de l'Europe," *Le Figaro*, 31 July 1965.

161. See the interview with Heinz Westphal in *Jugendpolitischer Dienst-jpd*, 11 November 1967.

162. Hermann Kumpfmüller, "Die Rolle der Auslandreise als Mittel Internationaler Erziehung," in Hahn, *Internationaler Jugendtourismus*, 27; and "Vers la création d'un Office européen pour la jeunesse," *Bulletin de l'office de presse et d'information du gouvernement fédéral*, no. 31 (30 August 1967). See also Christiane Wienand, "Reverberations of a Disturbing Past: Reconciliation Activities of Young West Germans in the 1960s and 1970s," in Bird et al., *Reverberations of Nazi Violence*, 215–32.

163. Hanns Ott, "Die Bedeutung der Jugendreisen in der Internationalen Jugendpolitik," in Hahn, *Internationaler Jugendtourismus*, 109.

164. See the 29 October 1965 issue of *Jugendpolitischer Dienst-jpd*.

165. See Office franco-allemand de la jeunesse, *15 Ans*; for the shift in emphasis of the FGYO, see Katja Marmetschke, "Crise et reorganization de l'OFAJ dans les année 1970," in Bock et a.l, *Les jeunes dans les relations transnationales*, 89–116.

166. Roger Cans, "Les artisans du tour d'Europe: Trois cent mille jeunes Français à l'étranger," *Le Monde*, 21 December 1979, 34; François Fouquet, "Les différentes phases de la démarche pédagogique à l'OFAJ," in *Echanges et mobilité des jeunes en Europe*, ed. Jeanne Kraus, Document de l'INJEP, 20 (Marly-le-Roi: INJEP, 1995), 53–61.

167. Minute Sheet, UKNA, ED 121/1152.

168. Bailkin, *The Afterlife of Empire*, 83–85.

169. Hitchcock, *The Struggle for Europe*, 233, 155.

170. Volle, *Deutsch-Britische Beziehungen*, 58.

171. Report to Parliament of the Review Committee on Overseas Representation (Sir Val Duncan, Chairman), Cmnd 4107, 1969. This was part of a general shift to focus on Western Europe in British foreign policy starting in 1967. See Ellison, "Separated by the Atlantic."

172. "Interdepartmental Study of Cultural Relations with Europe," 28 October 1971, 1, UKNA, BW 31/63.

173. See, for example, Maurice Edelman, M.P., "Anglo-French Relations and the Visit of M. Pompidou," 30 June 1966, UKNA, FO 924/1624; Evans, *Youth Exchanges*; "Interdepartmental Study of Anglo-French Cultural Relations," 27 July 1971, UKNA, BW31/63; Cockerill, *Report on Youth Exchanges*, 9.

174. Donaldson, *The British Council*, 259–65.

175. This was all a component of the "European Extension Programme" launched in 1972 to coincide with British entry into the EC. See "Interdepartmental Study of Anglo-French Cultural Relations," 27 July 1971; "British Council Expansion in France," 1971, UKNA, BW 31/63; and Donaldson, *The British Council*, 262.

176. For more on the IAYC, see chapters 5 and 6 in Klimke, *The Other Alliance*.

177. IAYC, Anton W. DePorte, "French Young Elites," 88, 103, 113; Paul E.

Sigmund, "British Young Elites," 56, 66, 71; Fritz Stern, "German Young Elites," 42–44, all in "Airlie Conference on European Youth" folder, RG 353/P5/box 1, NARA.

178. "Service sociaux: Organization des camps de vacances en italie pour la jeunesse," European Commission Historical Archives, BAC 1/1970 620.

179. See Reinhold Bocket, "Report on a European Community Programme to Promote Youth Exchanges," *European Documents*, doc. 1–78/83 (1983/0078), European Commission Library [hereafter ECL].

180. See Norwig, "A First European Generation?"; and Bantigny, "Genèses de l'Europe, jeunesses d'Europe."

181. Harribey traces this in detail in *L'Europe et la jeunesse*. For a brief overview, see Belot, "Les jeunes face à l'intégration européenne"; and Creagh and Lockett, "La forum jeunesse, voix européenne des jeunes."

182. Bocket, "Report on a European Community Programme to Promote Youth Exchanges."

183. European Commission, *Bulletin of the European Communities* 19, no. 2 (1986): 45–46.

184. Bocket, "Report on a European Community Programme to Promote Youth Exchanges"; European Commission, "Proposal for a Council Decision Adopting the Action Programme for the Promotion of Youth Exchanges in the Community—YES for Europe—1987–1989," 5 March 1986, ECL COM (86) 52 final. See also Commission of the European Communities, *General Report on the Activities of the European Communities* (Brussels: Commission of the European Communities, 1986), 199; Commission of the European Communities, *General Report on the Activities of the European Communities* (Brussels: Commission of the European Communities, 1989), 216; Commission of the European Communities, *General Report on the Activities of the European Communities* (Brussels: Commission of the European Communities, 1990), 204–5. See also *Bulletin of the European Communities* 19, no. 2 (1986): 45–46.

185. *Bulletin of the European Communities* 26, no. 10 (1993): 40.

186. "M. Pompidou: La securité européenne suppose que nous sachions harmoniser nos politiques," *Le Monde*, 7 July 1971, CAC 770707/art.4.

187. See Milward, *The European Rescue of the Nation-State*. For an example of how national interests drive integration policy choices, see Griffiths, *The Netherlands and the Integration of Europe*; on how Europe could be an instrument of nation building, see Romero, "L'Europa come strumento di nation-building."

188. See, for example, the essay by Rainer Hudemann, "Frankreichs Besatzung in Deutschland: Hindernis oder Auftakt der deutsch-französischen Kooperation?," in Jurt, *Von der Besatzungszeit*, 237–54.

189. That internationalism relies on culture and interpersonal interaction is a key argument of Walton, *Internationalism, National Identities, and Study Abroad*.

190. "Resolution," Meeting of the European Youth, Loreley, 7 August 1951, BAK B/268/550.
191. See Palayret, "Eduquer les jeunes à l'Union"; and Brunn, "The European Youth Meeting on the Loreley Rock."
192. Something political scientist Ulrich Krotz has described as "parapublic underpinnings" in "Parapublic Underpinnings of International Relations."
193. Zahra, *The Lost Children.*
194. Illustration by Fritz Behrendt, "Deutsch-Französisches Verhältnis: Das Bild des anderen in Wandel der Zeit," *Frankfurter Allgemeine Zeitung,* 23 January 1988.
195. See Joseph Hurt, "Le couple franco-allemand: Naissance et histoire d'une métaphore," in Götze, *France-Allemagne,* 51–60; and Cyril Buffet and Beatrice Heuser, "Marianne-Michel: The Franco-German Couple," in *Haunted by History,* 174–205.

CHAPTER THREE

1. Holmes, *Footsteps,* 73–74.
2. Ibid., 74–75.
3. Ibid., 78.
4. Scholarship, particularly in the last decade, has emphasized the transnational and global nature of 1968. Examples include Fraser et al., *1968: A Student Generation in Revolt;* Katsiaficas, *The Imagination of the New Left;* François, *1968—ein europäisches Jahr?;* Agosti, Passerini, and Tranfaglia, *La cultura e i luoghi del '68;* Fink, Gassert, and Junker, *1968: The World Transformed;* Gilcher-Holtey, *1968: Vom Ereignis zum Gegenstand der Geschichtswissenschaft;* Marwick, *The Sixties;* Ortoleva, *I movimenti del '68 in Europa e in America;* Suri, *Power and Protest;* Daum, Gardner, and Mausbach, *America, the Vietnam War, and the World;* Horn, *The Spirit of '68;* Klimke and Scharloth, *1968 in Europe;* Davis et al., *Changing the World, Changing Oneself;* Brown, " '1968' East and West"; Jürgens et al., *Eine Welt zu gewinnen!;* Silvia Casilio, "Una 'Internazionale' di uomini di 20 anni': I Giovani e la contestazione in un mondo senza frontier: linguaggi, immagini, e azioni del movimento del '68," in Dogliani, *Giovani e generazioni,* 59–72; Klimke, *The Other Alliance;* Slobodian, *Foreign Front;* Brown, *West Germany and the Global Sixties;* Gildea, Mark, and Warring, *Europe's 1968.*
5. For a history of cultural internationalism, see Iriye, *Cultural Internationalism;* for a focus on the post-1945 era, see Iriye, *Global Community.*
6. Ginier, *Les touristes étrangers en France,* 302.
7. Michel Friedman, "La grande révolte des jeunes du monde entier," *Formidable* 15 (December 1966): 33.
8. Roger Delagnes, "Débats Parlementaires Sénat: Séance du 25 novembre 1966," *Journal Officiel de la République Française,* no. 57 (1966–67): 2024.
9. Gloaguen and Trapier, *Génération routard,* 186.

10. Holmes, *Footsteps*, 76.
11. Fraser et al., *1968*, 81.
12. Davis, "A Whole World Opening Up," 255–73.
13. James Mark and Anna von der Goltz, "Encounters," in Gildea, Mark, and Warring, *Europe's 1968*, 131–63, 133.
14. Ginier, *Les touristes étrangers en France*, 380.
15. Mack, *1968 and I'm Hitchhiking through Europe*, 71–89, 99–100, 244–60.
16. Paolo Ferro is a pseudonym. "Cara Mila," Archivio diaristico nazionale, Pieve Santo Stefano [hereafter ADN] E/94.
17. Richard Davy, "Mutual Inspiration but No International Conspiracy," *Times*, 30 May 1968, 4.
18. See Klimke, *The Other Alliance*.
19. Ehrenreich and Ehrenreich, *Long March, Short Spring*, 163.
20. See Jobs, *Riding the New Wave*.
21. Férrând, *La jeunesse, nouveau Tiers Etat*, 60, 61; for the Italian case see Casilio, "Una 'Internazionale' di uomini di 20 anni.'"
22. Mack, *1968 and I'm Hitchhiking through Europe*, 275.
23. UNESCO Institute for Youth, *An Analysis of the Impact of International Travel and Exchange Programmes on Young People*, November 1960, 33, UNESCO.
24. Ibid., 32.
25. "Provos Now in London," *Times*, 23 June 1966, 11; Cohn-Bendit, *Nous l'avons tant aimée*, 49.
26. Hilwig, *Italy and 1968*, 102–3.
27. Pas, "Images d'une révolte ludique," 368. For a more thorough account of the Provos, see Pas, *Imaazje!*
28. "Meet the Provos," Provo Archief 30/1, IISG.
29. "Dutch Sailors Throw Out 'Provos,'" *Times*, 6 April 1967, 6.
30. Niek Pas, "Subcultural Movements: The Provos," in Klimke and Scharloth, *1968 in Europe*, 14.
31. Jacques Dalny, "Les 'Provos' n'ont rien inventé," *Le Figaro littéraire*, 4 August 1966, 1.
32. Georges Belmont and Evelyne Sullerot, "Le mouvement 'Provo' gagne la France," *Arts et Loisirs*, 6–12 July 1966, 8.
33. Pas, "Images d'une révolte ludique," 343–73.
34. "Cent cinquante 'beatniks' manifestent au quartier Latin," *Le Monde*, 21 June 1966, 14; and "Manifestation de 'Provos' au Quartier Latin," *Le Monde*, 21 March 1967, 7. The reporter summarized a Provo as a "violent form of beatnik."
35. Passerini, *Autobiography of a Generation*, 52. Interestingly, the Situationists advocated the practice of *dérive*, whereby the individual seeks to encounter the unknown and unfamiliar through the disorientation produced by randomly wandering around. *Dérive* was "the practice of a passionate uprooting through the hurried change of environments," meant to result in a politicized and revolutionary consciousness using mobility to "construct

the situation." See Guy Debord, "Report on the Construction of Situations and on the Terms of Organization and Action of the International Situationist Tendency," in *Guy Debord and the Situationist International: Texts and Documents*, ed. Tom McDonough (Cambridge, MA: MIT Press, 2004), 46.

36. Thomas Ekman Jørgensen, " Scandinavia," in Klimke and Scharloth, *1968 in Europe*, 247.

37. Ali, *Street Fighting Years*, 246.

38. See Paulina Bren, "1968 East and West: Visions of Political Change and Student Protest from across the Iron Curtain," in Horn and Kenney, *Transnational Moments of Change*, 124–26.

39. Fraser et al., *1968*, 194.

40. Author interview of Alain Chermann, October 2007.

41. *Le Monde*, 12–13 May 1968, 6.

42. Gordon, "Immigrants and the New Left in France," 108.

43. Daniel Gordon has pointed out the prominence of Germans, both SDSers and others, in Paris—although rather than seeing a conspiracy, he notes that most were simply eager to get to France only after the events broke out. Ibid., 135–37.

44. William Wordsworth, *Wordsworth: Poetry and Prose* (Cambridge, MA: Harvard University Press, 1963), 367.

45. Horn, *The Spirit of '68*, 74.

46. "Rome: La visite d'étudiants de Nanterre prelude à une relance des manifestations," *Le Monde*, 31 May 1968, 12.

47. Author interview of Ron Hijman, August 2007.

48. Author interview of Ika Sorgdrager, August 2007.

49. Davy, "Mutual Inspiration but No International Conspiracy."

50. For a genealogy of how Marxist ideas circulated, see Michel Trebitsch, "Voyages autour de la revolution: Les circulations de la pensée critique de 1956 à 1968," in Dreyfus-Armand, Le Puloch, and de Baecque, *Les Années 68*, 69–87.

51. "M. Cohn-Bendit se voit interdire l'entrée du territoire Belge," *Le Monde*, 22 May 1968, 7.

52. In fact, as early as March, Peyrefitte had wanted to expel Cohn-Bendit, but Interior Minister Christian Fouchet had refused on grounds of university privilege and the possibility of exacerbating the situation at Nanterre. See Seidman, *The Imaginary Revolution*, 74.

53. "A l'interdiction de séjour de M. Cohn-Bendit," *Le Monde*, 24 May 1968, 5.

54. "Le leader du mouvement du 22 mars ne rencontre guère de succés à Amsterdam," *Le Monde*, 24 May 1968, 5.

55. "M. Cohn-Bendit est soutenu par des étudiants allemande et français," *Le Monde*, 25 May 1968, 4; "One Day in the Students' Revolt," *Times*, 24 May 1968, 10.

56. "M. Cohn-Bendit est soutenu par des étudiants allemande et français"; "One Day in the Students' Revolt."

57. Michael Hornsby, "Cohn-Bendit Refused Entry," *Times*, 25 May 1968, 1.

58. "M. Cohn-Bendit est soutenu par des étudiants allemande et français."

59. For more on fortified French frontiers see Panchasi, "'Fortress France.'"

60. In fact, Cohn-Bendit thought he would be allowed to return to France in a few weeks, perhaps by the end of the summer, but it was not until ten years later that Valery Giscard d'Estaing pardoned his prohibition in 1978.

61. Fraser et al., *1968*, 226.

62. "Le reapparition de Daniel Cohn-Bendit à Paris," *Le Monde*, 30 May 1968, 8.

63. Students in Revolt File, BBC Written Archive Center [hereafter BBC WAC], T32/1934.

64. Student Unrest and Demonstrations 1968 file, BBC WAC, R78/694/1.

65. Windsor Davies, "Red-Eyed Maniac Fear Dispelled," *Daily Telegraph*, 14 June 1968.

66. Extract from "24 Hours," 12 June 1968, BBC WAC, Talk Scripts 24 Hours.

67. Letter from Harry Robinson, Students in Revolt File, BBC WAC, T32/1934.

68. Ali, *Street Fighting Years*, 303.

69. "M. Cohn-Bendit fait l'objet d'une mesure d'interdiction en France," *Le Monde*, 23 May 1968, 22.

70. Cohn-Bendit, *Nous l'avons tant aimée*, 63.

71. Fraser et al., *1968*, 173.

72. Cohn-Bendit, *Nous l'avons tant aimée*, 9.

73. As quoted in Seidman, *The Imaginary Revolution*, 221–22.

74. This is an interesting note because, though his German nationality was emphasized extensively in the French press, he remained "M. Cohn-Bendit."

75. Charles Hargrove, "De Gaulle Bans All Demonstrations," *Times*, 12 June 1968, 1. Germany seems to have been the only government that protested this measure. See "Plusiers dizaines d'explusions," *Le Monde*, 14 June 1968, 2.

76. For a detailed account of these expulsions, see chapter 4 in Gordon, "Immigrants and the New Left in France"; for more on France's use of political expulsion as a means of bolstering the nation-state, see Gordon, "The Back Door of the Nation State."

77. Gordon, "Immigrants and the New Left in France, 30–45.

78. Ibid., 111–15.

79. Ibid., 130; for detailed numbers of arrests on a nightly basis, see 112–31.

80. Seidman, *The Imaginary Revolution*, 243.

81. See *Sun*, March 19, 1968, 16; *Guardian*, June 13, 1968, 8; *Times*, 5 September 1968, 1.

82. Bren, "1968 East and West," 130.

83. Paulina Bren, "Looking West: Popular Culture and the Generation Gap in Communist Czechoslovakia, 1969–1989," in Passerini, *Across the Atlantic*, 301–2.

84. Cuskey, Klein, and Krasner, *Drug-Trip Abroad*, 6–7.

85. Schneider, *Lenz*, 43, 44, 56. *Lenz* is based in part on the author's own travels and experiences. An activist, in late 1968 he left Berlin for Rome and

hitchhiked around Italy, namely, through Trento. See Schneider, *Rebellion und Wahn.*

86. "A l'interdiction de séjour de M. Cohn-Bendit."
87. See Slobodian, *Foreign Front*; Davis, "A Whole World Opening Up," 263–65.
88. Even Franco and Papadopoulos in Spain and Greece, respectively, thought the origins of their student movements lay with foreign agitators. See Kostis Kornetis, "Spain and Greece," in Klimke and Scharloth, *1968 in Europe,* 260.
89. See Hansen and Jonsson, *Eurafrica*; Cooper, *Citizenship between Empire and Nation.*
90. See Marker, "France between Europe and Africa."
91. Both speeches are reproduced in Collings, *Reflections of a Statesman.*
92. See Bailkin, *The Afterlife of Empire.*
93. Martha Gellhorn, "So Awful to Be Young: Or, Morning to Midnight in Espresso Bars," special issue on "The Younger Generation," *Encounter,* May 1956, 42–48.
94. Ali, *Street Fighting Years,* 284.
95. Lucien Febvre, "*Frontière*: The Word and Concept," in *A New Kind of History: From the Writings of Febvre,* ed. Peter Burke, trans. K. Folca (New York: Harper & Row, 1973), 213.
96. See the essays on "Le Territoire" in Nora, *Les lieux de mémoire II.*
97. Balibar, *We, the People of Europe?,* 109.
98. This is the argument of Maier, "Consigning the Twentieth Century to History."
99. Akira Iriye, "Foreword," in Klimke and Scharloth, *1968 in Europe,* vii.
100. See, for example, Ross, *May '68 and Its Afterlives*; Gordon, "Immigrants and the New Left In France"; or Davis, "A Whole World Opening Up."
101. See, for example, Robert Frank, "Imaginaire politique et figures symboliques internationals: Castro, Hô, Mao et le 'Che,'" in Dreyfus-Armand, Le Puloch, and de Baecque, *Les Années 68,* 31–47; and Geneviève Dreyfus-Armand and Jacques Portes, "Les interactions internationales de la guerre du Viêt-Nam et Mai 68," ibid., 49–68.
102. For more on this, see Gordon, "Immigrants and the New Left in France, 201–5.
103. See Judt, *Postwar,* 398.
104. Though I would not claim that this demonstrates the emergence of a European polity, it does suggest that 1968 can be considered a significant development in the "Europeanization" of contentious politics. Though still influenced largely by domestic concerns, the emphasis on Europe by some protesters was significant. See the work of Sidney Tarrow, especially "The Europeanisation of Conflict"; Imig and Tarrow, *Contentious Europeans*; and Tarrow, *The New Transnational Activism.* See also the work of Donnatella della Porta, especially "1968—Zwischennationale Diffusion und Transnationale Strukturen," in Gilcher-Holtey, *1968,* 131–50.

105. As quoted in Klimke and Scharloth, "1968 in Europe: Introduction," in *1968 in Europe*, 6. There was even a U.S. diplomatic conference held on the subject in Bonn in June 1969.

106. "Le 13 mai au soir," Sorbonne, in *Tracts de mai 1968*, Bibliothèque nationale de France, Paris [hereafter *Tracts de Mai 1968*], doc. 1404.

107. Parliamentary Debates, House of Commons, Official Report, vol. 766, no. 133, Thursday, 13 June 1968, 441.

108. "M. Cohn-Bendit est soutenu par des étudiants allemands et français."

109. "M. Cohn-Bendit se voit interdire l'entrée du territoire Belge."

110. See Jean-Marie Mayeur, "Une mémoire-frontière: L'Alsace," in Nora, *Les lieux de mémoire II*, 63–95.

111. For more on how borders can serve as staging grounds for political protest, see Leizaola, "Mugarik ez!"

112. "Motion du Comité de Solidarité Franco-Allemande," *Tracts de mai 1968*, docs. 4544 and 4545. Beate Klarsfeld and her husband, Serge, would go on to become quite famous for their activism in exposing former Nazis and documenting the Holocaust. In 1984, they were awarded France's Legion of Honor by President Mitterand.

113. Cornelis, *Europeans about Europe*, 53, 60, 126, 111–12.

114. Comité pour l'independence de l'Europe, untitled flyer, *Tracts de mai 1968*, doc. 4568.

115. "Ce que veulent les étudiants européens," *Tracts de mai 1968*, doc. 3752.

116. "Pour l'abolition du statut des étrangers en France," *Tracts de mai 1968*, docs. 4644 and 4647.

117. "C.A.A.F," *Tracts de mai 1968*, doc. 4950.

118. "Nous sommes tous européens," *Tracts de mai 1968*, doc. 4951.

119. Lafféach, "An *Avant-garde* for Europe," 48.

120. "Appel à la jeunesse européenne," *Tracts de mai 1968*, doc. 6805.

121. "Fédéralisme Européen Universitaire," *Tracts de mai 1968*, doc. 9681.

122. See Gildea, *The Past in French History*, 336. More specifically, this is the subject of ongoing research by Todd Shepard, as yet unpublished.

123. Mario Toscano, "La politique européenne à l'heure de la verité," *Le Monde*, 6 July 1968, 1, 7.

124. This is Suri's argument in *Power and Protest*.

125. See Shore, *Building Europe*.

126. "Address by Pierre Werner," *Bulletin of European Communities*, no. 2 (February 1970): 47, online at http://www.cvce.eu/.

127. "Address by Mariano Rumor," ibid., 45.

128. "Final Communiqué of the Meeting of the Heads of State or Government of the Member States at The Hague," 2 December 1969, online at http://www.cvce.eu/.

129. Eberhard, *The Council of Europe and Youth*, 5.

130. Valéry Giscard d'Estaing, "Towards a European Confederation," Britain in Europe Meeting, 7 May 1968, 2, UKNA, FCO 13/405.

131. As quoted in Bren, "1968 East and West," 134n23.

132. Ali, *Street Fighting Years*, 149.

133. Schwartz, *Prague's 200 Days*, 19, 26.

134. Rachel Applebaum, "A Test of Friendship: Soviet-Czechoslovak Tourism and the Prague Spring," in Gorsuch and Koenker, *The Socialist Sixties*, 219–20.

135. Golan, *The Czechoslovak Reform Movement*, 262n.

136. Golan, "Youth and Politics in Czechoslovakia," 11.

137. Some 300,000 Czechoslovaks visited the West during the spring and summer of 1968; see Levy, *So Many Heroes*, 163.

138. Bren, "1968 East and West," 124–26, quotation from 128.

139. Paul Hoffman, "For Those under 30, Prague Seems the Right Place to Be This Summer," *New York Times*, 12 August 1968, 13.

140. Mack, *1968 and I'm Hitchhiking through Europe*, 213–15.

141. Gloaguen and Trapier, *Génération routard*, 177.

142. Susanne Müller is a pseudonym. Davis, "A Whole World Opening Up," 261.

143. Fraser et al., *1968*, 266–67.

144. Mark and von der Goltz, "Encounters," 134.

145. Ibid., 136.

146. McDougall, *Youth Politics in East Germany*, 215–29.

147. Piccini, "Travel, Politics, and the Limits of Liminality," 1, 9–10.

148. Mark and von der Goltz, "Encounters."

149. Nick Rutter, "Look Left, Drive Right: Internationalisms at the 1968 World Youth Festival," in Gorsuch and Koenker, *The Socialist Sixties*, 193–212.

150. Korda, *Journey to a Revolution*, 112.

151. Holmes, *Footsteps*, 15.

152. Ibid., 74–75.

153. Colin Crouch was a participant who then wrote a sociological thesis on the topic; see Crouch, *The Student Revolt*.

154. Ginier, *Les touristes étrangers en France*, 297.

155. Walton, *Internationalism, National Identities, and Study Abroad*, 144, 160–69.

156. Hoffman, "For Those under 30, Prague Seems the Right Place to Be." For a recent historical work that applies Turner's theories to travel, see Rennella, *The Boston Cosmopolitans*.

157. See Turner and Turner, *Image and Pilgrimage in Christian Culture*. See also Turner, *The Ritual Process*; Turner, *Dramas, Fields, and Metaphors*. There has been a reluctance to use Turner's theory of *communitas* as applicable to young backpacker tourists because backpackers tend to remain quite self-absorbed and do not become "immersed" within the community. However, the travel I have traced here was specifically an expression of intentional solidarity, complete with activism and protest articulating it as such. See Erik Cohen, "Backpacking: Diversity and Change," in Richards and Wilson, *The Global Nomad*, 43–59.

158. Notably, Cohn-Bendit has remained politically active, becoming a Member of the European Parliament, and one of his issues has been to create a

cosmopolitan Europe to replace the homogeneous nation-state, especially regarding immigration policy. See Daniel Cohn-Bendit, "Europe and Its Borders: The Case for a Common Immigration Policy," in Ogata et al., *Towards a European Immigration Policy*, 22–31; and Cohn-Bendit and Schmid, *Heimat Babylon*.

159. "Restless Youth," Study no. 0613/68, CIA, September 1968, 19, 14, iii, NSF, Files of Walt Rostow, Youth and Student Movement, CIA report, box 13, Lyndon Baines Johnson Library, Austin, TX. For more detail on this report and the Johnson administration response, see Klimke, *The Other Alliance*, 194–213.

160. George McGhee to President Johnson, "World Student Unrest," in George McGhee: Writings, vol. 2: 1960–1969, 335, George McGhee Papers, Georgetown University Library, Special Collections, Washington, DC. For much more on McGhee and his role and attitudes, see chapters 5 and 6 in Klimke, *The Other Alliance*.

161. IAYC, "An Overview of Student Unrest," n.d., probably 1971, 21, NARA RG 353/P5, box 9, folder "Student Unrest, 1965–69–71.

162. Such an interconnection is explored in detail in Papadogiannis, *Militant around the Clock?*

163. This is the argument of Rosenau, *Turbulence in World Politics*.

164. The Left in general has relied on such informal political actors and networks. See Eley, *Forging Democracy*.

CHAPTER FOUR

1. Author interview of Lawrence Mark Lipin, June 12, 2012.
2. Ibid.
3. Ibid.
4. Ibid.
5. Ibid.
6. Ibid.
7. Marco Tullio Giordana, *La meglio gioventù* (2003); theatrical release *The Best of Youth/Nos meilleures années*.
8. Ibid.
9. Bouvier, *L'usage du monde: Récit*.
10. Bouvier, *The Way of the World*, 13, 311.
11. Cremer, *I, Jan Cremer*.
12. Seymour Krim, "Introduction," ibid., vii.
13. For more on the place of the Second World War in such literature see Jones, *Journeys of Remembrance*; for more on the drug trip of the text, see Grant, "Death-Trips, Power-Trips, and Head-Trips."
14. Jones, *Journeys of Remembrance*, 99.
15. Greg Richards and Julie Wilson, "Backpacker Icons: Influential Literary 'Nomads' in the Formation of Backpacker Identities," in *The Global Nomad*, 123–47.

16. For example, Granahan, *Voyager*, 10; Guarnaccia, *Beat e mondo beat*, 152–57; Philippe Gloaguen, "Tous les routards," *Le Monde*, 19 April 1980, 17; Alessandro Portelli, "The Transatlantic Jeremiad: American Mass Culture and Counterculture and Opposition Culture in Italy," in Kroes, Rydell, and Bosscher, *Cultural Transmissions and Receptions*, 128; Ireland and Gemie, "From Kerouac to the Hippy Trail."

17. See references throughout Gloaguen and Trapier, *Génération routard*; Portelli, "The Transatlantic Jeremiad," 128; Roberto De Angelis, "Il beat italiano," in Ghione and Grispigni, *Giovani prima della rivolta*, 73–84; Ireland and Gemie, "From Kerouac to the Hippy Trail."

18. See, for example, Noonan, *The Road to Jerusalem*; Moretti, *The Way of the World*; Ross, *The Emergence of Social Space*.

19. Koshar, "'What ought to be seen.'"

20. Stanley Elkin, "The World on $5 a Day: The Saga of Arthur Frommer, First of the Small-Time Spenders," *Harper's Magazine* 245 (July 1972): 41–46.

21. Buryn, *Vagabonding*, iii.

22. Rozenberg, *Tourisme et Utopie aux Baléares*.

23. See Detlef Siegfried, "The Emergence of the Post-National Subject: Identity Constructions in European Alternative Milieus, 1966–83," in Villaume, Mariager, and Porsdam, *The 'Long 1970s.'*

24. For example, see the chapters by Juliane Fürst and Valeria Manzano in Jobs and Pomfret, *Transnational Histories of Youth*; Zolov, *Refried Elvis*; Risch, "Soviet 'Flower Children.'"

25. Neville, *Play Power*, 207, 210.

26. For the Canadian case, see Mahood, "Hitchin' a Ride in the 1970s."

27. See Tim Cresswell, "The Vagrant/Vagabond: The Curious Career of a Mobile Subject," in Cresswell and Merriman, *Geographies of Mobilities*, 239–53; Hacking, *Mad Travelers*; Ross, *The Emergence of Social Space*, 55–59.

28. Ginier, *Les touristes étrangers en France*, 294.

29. "Gammler," *Der Spiegel*, no. 39 (1966): 70–80, quotations from 72.

30. Kosel, *Gammler Beatniks Provos*. For more on *die Gammler* as a fluid social identity in mid-1960s West Germany, the related political undercurrents, and the moral panic they inspired, see Brown, *West Germany and the Global Sixties*, 62–68; and Siegfried, *Time Is on My Side*, 399–428.

31. See Klaus Weinhauer, "The End of Certainties: Drug Consumption and Youth Delinquency in West Germany," in Schildt and Seigfried, *Between Marx and Coca-Cola*, 376–97; Stephens, *Germans on Drugs*, 64–68.

32. "Roma Inesauribile," undated clipping from *Capitolium*, 92–93, ASC, file: 1969_08_09_095–110.

33. Marwick, *The Sixties*, 495.

34. Mayer, *Lettere dei capelloni italiani*, 24.

35. De Martino, *Capelloni e ninfette*.

36. As quoted in Neville, *Play Power*, 204.

37. Turner and Ash, *The Golden Hordes*, 258–72.

38. As quoted in MacLean, *Magic Bus*, 216.

39. Alexandre Marchant, "The Roads to Kathmandu in the Francophone Literature of the 1960s–70s: The Drug Travel Narrative as an Apprenticeship Novel" (paper presented at the 108th Annual Conference of the Pacific Ancient and Modern Language Association, Honolulu, Hawaii, 13–14 November 2010).

40. Timothy Hall, "The Migration of the Great Unwashed," *Observer*, 24 September 1967, 2.

41. "Alarm over British Youths on Drugs in Istanbul," *Guardian*, 18 November 1967, 3.

42. Kenneth Allsop, "Across Europe and out of Sight, Man: Kenneth Allsop Inspects the Eurofreaks," *Punch*, 2 August 1972, 130–32.

43. Donna Carlson, "Thumbs Out: Ethnography of Hitchhiking," in Spradley and McCurdy, *The Cultural Experience*, 137–46; Mukerji, "Bullshitting"; Mahood, "Hitchin' a Ride in the 1970s," 214.

44. Guarnaccia, *Paradiso psichedelico*, 6–7.

45. Mahood, "Hitchin' a Ride in the 1970s," 219–20.

46. Buryn, *Hitch-hiking in Europe*, i.

47. Ibid., 18, 27, 29, 40.

48. Penelope Carstens is a pseudonym. MO R2247, Summer 2000 Directive: Travelling, 4–7, MOA.

49. Chiara Albero is a pseudonym. "Una partenza ogni giorno," ADN DV/86, 26–27.

50. Grassl and Heath, *The Magic Triangle*, 113.

51. Mahood, "Hitchin' a Ride in the 1970s," 220–22; Canadian Welfare Council, *Transient Youth: Report of an Inquiry in the Summer of 1969* (Ottawa: Canadian Council on Social Development, 1969).

52. "Report of the Special Commission on the Needs of Youth," from "Documents for the Twenty-Eighth Conference," August 1970, 2–4, 9, HIA.

53. Anton Grassl, "Address by the President at the Opening of the 29th IYHF Conference," from *Documents for the Twenty-Ninth Conference*, August 1972, 4, HIA.

54. "Youth Tourism through Hostelling," from *Documents for the Thirty-Fourth Conference*, August 1982, 1–2, HIA; "Les auberges de jeunesse à la recherche d'un second souffle," *Le Monde*, 27–28 November 1983, vi (supplementaire). For the case of the German Youth Hostel Federation, see Otto Wirthensohn, "Neuorientierungen seit den sechziger Jahren," in Reulecke and Stambolis, *100 Jahre Jugendherbergen*, 391–97.

55. Van den Berg, *Youth and Their Holidays*, 7, 15, 26–27, 45, IISG. For Dutch youth tourism numbers, see *Jeugdtoerisme* (Den Haag: Stichting Recreatie, 1975), 154–56.

56. International Youth Hostel Federation, "International Survey of Youth Travel and Youth Hostels," October 1977, 74, IISG.

57. Ibid., 4, 5.

58. Ibid., 8, 28, 29, 82, 88.
59. Ibid., 91–108.
60. F. Emma Beyn, "Tourists, Travelers, and Transients: Hostel Culture in Southwestern Ireland" (Division III examination thesis, Hampshire College, 1996).
61. "Travel Notes: The Continuing Saga of Eurailpass," *New York Times,* 25 February 1973, 4; author interview with Rachel Morton-Young of Eurail Group, Utrecht, Netherlands, 8 July 2009.
62. "Eurail Passengers since 1959," spreadsheet, Eurail Group, Utrecht.
63. Jay Brunhouse, "All Aboard!," *International Travel News,* April 2008, 72.
64. Helen Tyrrell, "Hippies Galore," *New York Times,* 19 September 1971, XX4.
65. Travel Notes: The Continuing Saga of Eurailpass," *New York Times,* 25 February 1973, 4.
66. Amsterdam, London, and Paris, for example. Guarnaccia, *Paradiso psichedelico,* 57; Bernard Weinraub, "Cheap Lodging Scarce as Big Influx Nears," *New York Times,* 1 June 1971, 12; Levenstein, *We'll Always Have Paris,* 226.
67. Liston, *Young Americans Abroad,* 149.
68. Hugh A. Mulligan, "The Young Migration to Europe: Together, Unhassled, and Cheap," *Hartford Courant,* 31 August 1971, 35.
69. Gottlieb, *Hell No, We Won't Go!,* 15–23.
70. Kornetis, " 'Everything Links'?," 41.
71. Author email interview with Arthur Goldhammer, 1 May 2010.
72. "Travel International," *Travel Market Yearbook,* 1975/1976, 57–71.
73. Liston, *Young Americans Abroad,* 56–62.
74. Bryson, *Neither Here nor There,* 14.
75. Paul Goldberger, "On the Champs-Elysees: 'Hey, Aren't You the Girl Who Sits across from Me in Abnormal Psych?," *New York Times,* 13 June 1971, XX1, 15, 18.
76. Hoffa and DePaul, *A History of U.S. Study Abroad,* 26, 128, 163.
77. I make this statement on the basis of my own personal experience.
78. Piccini, "Travel, Politics and the Limits of Liminality," 3.
79. Goldberger, "On the Champs-Elysees."
80. Author interview with Rachel Morton-Young, 8 July 2009.
81. "InterRail Passengers 1972–2008," spreadsheet, Eurail Group, Utrecht.
82. Schönhammer, "Youth Tourism as Appropriation of the World," 24–25.
83. Brunhouse, "All Aboard!," 72.
84. Alexandra Marshall and James Carroll, "The Serendipitous Appeal of Eurailpass," *New York Times,* 22 October 1989, XX29.
85. The articles were originally written for the *Christian Science Monitor* and published from late June to early August 1972.
86. Goldberger, "On the Champs-Elysees," 18.
87. John Davis, " 'Die Briten Kommen': British Beat and the Conquest of Europe in the 1960s," in Conway and Patel, *Europeanization,* 237.
88. Weinraub, "Cheap Lodging Scarce as Big Influx Nears."
89. "Roughing It," *Economist,* 25 September 1971, xxii–xxiv.

90. Lorelies Olslager, "Tourists of Many Varieties," *Financial Times*, 31 May 1974, 19.
91. Mulligan, "The Young Migration to Europe."
92. Christina Tree, "Two Cities Vie for Youth Capital Title," *Boston Globe*, 14 May 1972, B3.
93. Weinraub, "Cheap Lodging Scarce as Big Influx Nears."
94. Buryn, *Vagabonding*, 234.
95. See Mamadouh, *De stad in eigen hand*; Righart, *De eindeloze jaren zestig*; ten Have, "The Counter Culture on the Move," 309.
96. This is James C. Kennedy's argument in "Building New Babylon: Cultural Change in the Netherlands during the 1960s" (PhD diss., University of Iowa, May 1995), translated and published in Dutch as *Nieuw Babylon in aanbouw*.
97. Trevor L. Christie, "Tourism and the Common Market," *ASTA Travel News* 33 (February 1963): 56–57.
98. Guarnaccia, *Paradiso psichedelico*, 133.
99. "Zomerdagen in 'Surprising Amsterdam,'" *Nieuwe Rotterdamse Courant*, 26 August 1967, 1.
100. *Together*, 1970, 1, IISG PM 16066. *Together* was a free newspaper produced and distributed by the city of Amsterdam.
101. Gerard Haas, "Magisch Amsterdam kan invasie niet ann," *De Nieuwe Linie*, 17 May 1969, 1.
102. Kamsma, "Greetings from Amsterdam Holland," 88.
103. *Gemeenteblad Amsterdam* 1969, II, afd. 2, 1635–45. See also Kamsma, "Greetings from Amsterdam Holland," 88–92.
104. "Rapport Werkgroep Jeugdtoerisme," 11 February 1970, Stadsarchief Amsterdam [hereafter SAA] 15009:1401.
105. *Jongeren op de Dam augustus 1970* (Amsterdam: Bureau van Statistiek der Gemeente Amsterdam, 1971), 8, SAA 15030: 110883.
106. Ibid., 5–32. For a more sociological typology of the *Damslapers*, see MacGillavry, "Amsterdam beobachtet den Jugendtourismus der nahen zukunft," 72–78.
107. "Amsterdam Riots Started by Local Rowdies," *Guardian*, 26 August 1970, 3.
108. "Tegenstanders politie werpen molotow-cocktails," *Het Parool*, 27 August 1970, IISG, P. Kral Collection 02/5; "Ik ben op de Dam niet voor de sensatie, maar uit solidariteit," *De Telegraaf*, 28 August 1970, SAA 15002: 34.
109. Tasman, *Louter kabouter*, 203–5.
110. *Gemeenteblad Amsterdam*, 1970, afd.2: 1857.
111. "Politie stelt vast: 'Groot deel jonge toeristen verdwenen,'" *Het Parool*, 2 September 1970, IISG, P. Kral Collection 02/5.
112. Guarnaccia, *Paradiso psichedelico*, 28.
113. Jeugdtoerisme 1971, "Rapport van de Werkgroep Jeugdtoerisme aan Burgermeester en Wethouders," 10 November 1971, IISG Bro 1542/12 fol.
114. Ten Have, "The Counter Culture on the Move," 299–300.

115. Comité Redt 'n park to the City Council, 27 August 1971, SAA 15009:14100.
116. "Vondelpark: 1974 Use It," SAA 15009: 14099.
117. Kagie, "Het magisch centrum is verdwenen."
118. Ten Have, "The Counter Culture on the Move," 308.
119. Roland Bökkerink et al., *Jeugdtoerisme in Amsterdam 1972: Enkele bevindingen van een onderzoekje op basis van participerende observatie*, Universiteit van Amsterdam Sociologich Institut 1972, 12, Universiteit van Amsterdam.
120. Leuw, *Druggebruik in het Vondelpark 1972*, 58–60; ten Have, "The Counter Culture on the Move," 304.
121. Stephens, *Germans on Drugs*, 68–72.
122. Papadogiannis, *Militant around the Clock?*, 239.
123. Rudolph Chelminski, "Open Season on Drug Smugglers," *Life*, 26 June 1970, 28–35.
124. See General Records of the State Department, Bureau of Public Affairs, Office of Public Communications, Records Relating to Major Publications, 1949–1990, RG 59 250/67/19/2, box 16, and RG 59 250/67/19/1, box 13, entry 1589, NARA.
125. Kinnon McLamb, "Amsterdam: 'Mecca from Intolerance,'" *Washington Post*, 21 May 1972, F1.
126. Kennedy, "Building New Babylon," 337–40.
127. Jansen, *Cannabis in Amsterdam*, 39, 156; A.C.M. Jansen, "The Development of a 'Legal' Consumers' Market for Cannabis: The 'Coffee Shop' Phenomenon," in Leuw and Marshall, *Between Prohibition and Legalization*, 169–81.
128. Cuskey, Klein, and Krasner, *Drug-Trip Abroad*, 24.
129. Ibid., 33.
130. "Freeway Amsterdam," IISG Bro 238/1.
131. Lewis, *Amsterdam after Dark*, back cover; Mankoff, *Mankoff's Lusty Europe*.
132. Ten Have, "The Counter Culture on the Move," 309.
133. Kennedy, "Building New Babylon," 263.
134. Bökkerink et al., "Jeugdtoerisme in Amsterdam 1972," 20.
135. See Gert Hekma, "A Radical Break with a Puritanical Past: The Dutch Case," in Hekma and Giami, *Sexual Revolutions*, 60–80.
136. Guarnaccia, *Paradiso psichedelico*, 7.
137. As quoted in the oral history by Jonathon Green, *It*, 234.
138. Guarnaccia, *Paradiso psichedelico*, 165–66.
139. Committee for Youth Tourism, *Use It Weekly*, no. 1 (1973), IISG.
140. Cohen, *Drugs, druggebruikers en drug-scene*.
141. Gadourek and Jenson, "Proscription and Acceptance of Drugs-Taking Habits in the Netherlands."
142. Cuskey, Klein, and Krasner, *Drug-Trip Abroad*, 3.
143. Ten Have, "The Counter Culture on the Move," 302.
144. Sociologisch instituut Universiteit van Amsterdam, "Jeugdtoerisme," December 1971, 12, SAA 15009:14102.
145. Neville, *Play Power*, 29.

146. Guarnaccia, *Paradiso psichedelico*, 9–14.
147. Alberto Camerini, ibid., 129–31.
148. Jim Woodman, "Copenhagen: Eden to Love Generation," *Los Angeles Times*, 19 September 1971, R5; Tree, "Two Cities Vie for Youth Capital Title."
149. Mulligan, "The Young Migration to Europe."
150. Jensen, *Ungdomsturister i København 1971*, 6, 10, 12, 14.
151. See Siegfried, "The Emergence of the Post-National Subject."
152. Mulligan, "The Young Migration to Europe."
153. Hekma and Giami, *Sexual Revolutions*, 10.
154. See chapter 4, "Pleasure and Rebellion," in Herzog, *Sexuality in Europe*.
155. Herzog, *Sexuality in Europe*, 137; Heineman, *Before Porn Was Legal*, 125–27.
156. Lena Lennerhed, "Sexual Liberalism in Sweden," in Hekma and Giami, *Sexual Revolutions*, 37.
157. As quoted in Marwick, *The Sixties*, 74–77, 386–87.
158. Schmidt and Sigusch, "Patterns of Sexual Behavior in West German Workers and Students."
159. Davies, *Permissive Britain*, 65.
160. Herzog, *Sex after Fascism*, 147. For a synthesis of West German youth sex research of the era, see Sigusch and Schmidt, *Jugendsexualität*.
161. Littlewood, *Sultry Climates*, 11–27, 94–95.
162. Anne E. Gorsuch and Diane P. Koenker, "Introduction," in *Turizm*, 3.
163. Papadogiannis, *Militant around the Clock?*, 150.
164. This study was carried out in southwest England in 1990 among tourists aged sixteen to twenty-nine. Eisner and Ford, "Sexual Relationships on Holiday."
165. As quoted in Green, *It*, 118, 339.
166. Dagmar Herzog, "Sexuality in Twentieth-Century Austria: An Introduction," in Bischof, Pelinka, and Herzog, *Sexuality in Austria*, 16.
167. Françoise Jeannot is a pseudonym. "Le long du couloir," 211–13, APA v.4, n.185.
168. Giorgio Lamberti is a pseudonym. "Diario," ADN DV/06, 12, 25.
169. See http://www.bbc.co.uk/comedy/likelylads/.
170. The study, by Helmut Kentler, was published in two parts: *Urlaub auf Sizilien* and *Urlaub als Auszug aus dem Alltag*.
171. Astrid Podsiadlowski, "Urlaub als Auszug aus dem Alltag—die Catania-Studie von Helmut Kentler," in Hahn and Kagelmann, *Tourismuspsychologie und Tourismussoziologie*, 587–90.
172. Mayer, *Lettere dei capelloni italiani*, 65–66, 153–54.
173. Gayler, *Jugendliche Tramper*, 91.
174. Bryson, *Neither Here nor There*, 14.
175. Kaplan, *French Lessons*, 89.
176. Elkin, "The World on $5 a Day," 41.
177. *If It's Tuesday, This Must Be Belgium* (dir. Mel Stuart, 1968).
178. As quoted in Green, *It*, 11.

179. Fraser, *Tajos*, 224.
180. Buryn, *Vagabonding*, 39.
181. Walton, *Internationalism, National Identities and Study Abroad*, 172.
182. Buryn, *Vagabonding*, 179–81.
183. See Sofka Zinovieff, "Hunters and Hunted: Kamaki and the Ambiguities of Sexual Predation in a Greek Town," in Loizos and Papataxiarchis, *Contested Identities*, 203–20.
184. Buryn, *Vagabonding*, 39.
185. "Proces pour viol . . . ," *Les Petroleuses*, no.7 (December 1976): 25.
186. See Mossuz-Lavau, *Les lois de l'amour*, 231–50.
187. Halimi, *Viol*, 379–80.
188. "Marseilles," *Les Petroleuses*, no. 5 (1975): 5; Halimi, *Viol*, 145.
189. Mahood, "Thumb Wars," 661.
190. Cresswell, *The Tramp in America*, 88–109.
191. Allsop, "Across Europe and Out of Sight, Man," 132.
192. See Walton, *Internationalism, National Identities, and Study Abroad*.
193. Hoffa and DePaul, *A History of U.S. Study Abroad*, 146.
194. Löfgren, *On Holiday*, 100.
195. Buryn, *Vagabonding*, 49.
196. Mahood, "Hitchin' a Ride in the 1970s," 215–16.
197. Schönhammer, "Youth Tourism as Appropriation of the World," 26.
198. Carol M. Orsborn, "For the Single Girl, the Best Way to See Europe Is Alone," *Boston Globe*, 14 May 1972, B1, B17.
199. Furlough, "Making Mass Vacations." 285.
200. Nooteboom, *Nomad's Hotel*, 3.
201. See the chapter "Telling Stories" in Löfgren, *On Holiday*.
202. See Noy, "Narratives of Hegemonic Masculinity"; Noy, "Traversing Hegemony"; Maoz, "Backpackers' Motivation"; Noy and Cohen, *Israeli Backpackers*.
203. O'Connor, *Vagrancy*, 87.
204. Cohen, "Nomads from Affluence," 89.
205. Vogt, "Wandering," 25.
206. Graburn, "The Anthropology of Tourism."
207. Alexandra Marshall and James Carroll, "The Serendipitous Appeal of Eurailpass," *New York Times*, 22 October 1989, XX29.
208. Towner, "The Grand Tour."
209. Adler, "Youth on the Road."
210. Schönhammer, *Jugendliche Europa-Touristen*. For an English summary of the findings, see Schönhammer, "Youth Tourism as Appropriation of the World," 19, 23, 26.
211. Schönhammer, "Youth Tourism as Appropriation of the World," 21.
212. Ibid., 23.
213. Ibid., 21.
214. Ibid., 22–23.
215. See Eurobarometer 28.1, "Young Europeans in 1987," September 1988, and

Eurobarometer 34.2, "Young Europeans in 1990," May 1991, GESIS Data Archive for the Social Sciences, Leibniz-Institut für Sozialwissenschaften, Cologne.

216. Committee for Youth Tourism, *Use It Weekly*, no. 1 (1973): 1, IISG.

217. Buryn, *Vagabonding*, 191–93.

218. Schönhammer, "Youth Tourism as Appropriation of the World," 22.

219. Ruffino, *An Assessment of Organized Youth Mobility in Europe*, 19.

220. Michael Hai Young Chiang, Oral History Interview, reel 3 of 7, timecode 6:00–10:00, Accession Number 003475, National Archives of Singapore.

221. Cohen, "Nomads from Affluence," 92.

222. Vogt, "Wandering," 37.

223. Wenger, *Communities of Practice*.

224. A very good introduction to the concept is Marie-Laure Djelic and Sigrid Quack, "Transnational Communities and Governance," in *Transnational Communities*, 3–36, quotations from 7 and 21. Emanuel Adler has used the concept to think about international relations as a global system of transnational communities of practice, such as those of diplomats, activists, traders, and so on, who are defined by the habits of shared practice and interest. See in particular the first chapter of his book *Communitarian International Relations*.

225. Weinraub, "Cheap Lodging Scarce as Big Influx Nears."

226. Schönhammer, "Youth Tourism as Appropriation of the World," 26.

227. Fabrizio Abbate, "I giovani estranei al future della città," *Capitolium*, February–March 1975, 2–11, ASC file: 50_1975_02_03_03–12.

228. Leed, *The Mind of the Traveler*, 249.

229. Constant Nieuwenhuys, "New Urbanism," *Delta: A Review of Life and Thought in the Netherlands* 10, no. 3 (1967): 52–61; see also Kennedy, *Nieuw Babylon in aanbouw*.

230. Gerard Haas, "Magisch Amsterdam kan invasive niet ann," *De Nieuwe Linie*, 17 May 1969, 1.

231. "A Pilgrimage to Amsterdam? A Look Back," *Use It Weekly*, no. 12 (1973): 1, IISG.

232. Simon Vinkenoog, "Amsterdam Magic Center," *Aloha*, 15 May 1970, 3.

233. Van den Berg, *Youth and Their Holidays*, 7.

234. The official title of the EC was "European Communities," referring to three communities (ECSC, Euratom, and EEC) that had operated independently but were reorganized under the umbrella organization of the EC. Colloquially, however, the EC was more commonly referred to as the "European Community."

CHAPTER FIVE

1. Steve Hochman, "A Global Event," *Chicago Tribune*, 15 July 1990, B3; Marc Fisher, "Wall to Wall in Berlin," *Washington Post*, 23 July 1990, C1, C6.

2. Fisher, "Wall to Wall in Berlin"; Christian Caryl, "Berlin Wall Site Turned into Rock Music Spectacle," *Chicago Tribune*, 22 July 1990, C3.

3. Andrew O'Hehir, "Pedro Almodóvar: An 'Irrational Passion' for Movies," Salon.com, 13 November 2009, http://www.salon.com/2009/11/14 /almodovar_2/.

4. Author interview of Lawrence Mark Lipin, 12 June 2012.

5. Ian Coburn is a pseudonym. MO C2722, Spring Directive 2000: Travelling, MOA.

6. Enrica Capussotti, "Scenarios of Modernity: Youth Culture in 1950s Milan," trans. Graeme Thomson, in Lumley and Foot, *Italian Cityscapes*, 169–84.

7. Fabio Maggioni is a pseudonym. "Irish Round," ADN DV/88.

8. Mark and von der Goltz, "Encounters," 141–43.

9. Gurevich, *From Lenin to Lennon*, 128.

10. As quoted in Zhuk, *Rock and Roll in the Rocket City*, 1.

11. Bar-Haím, "Eastern European Youth Culture," 56–58.

12. Tinker, *Mixed Messages*, 78–97.

13. Feldman, "We Are the Mods."

14. Horgby and Nilsson, *Rockin' the Borders*.

15. Poiger, *Jazz, Rock, and Rebels*; Briggs, *Sounds French*; Risch, *Youth and Rock in the Soviet Bloc*.

16. For the Netherlands, see van Elteren, *Imagining America*; Righart, *De eindeloze jaren zestig*; Righart, *De wereldwijde jaren zestig*; and Henk Kleijer and Ger Tillekens, "The Lure of Anglo-American Popular Culture Explaining the Rise of Dutch Youth Culture," in Bosscher, Roholl, and van Elteren, *American Culture in the Netherlands*, 97–113. For Italy, see Gundle, *Between Hollywood and Moscow*. For Germany, see Siegfried, *Time Is on My Side*; and Edward Larkey, "Popular Music in Germany: The Genesis of a New Field of Discourse," in Junker, *The United States and Germany in the Era of the Cold War*, 445–50. For Greece, see Papadogiannis, *Militant around the Clock?*

17. Bar-Haím, "Eastern European Youth Culture."

18. Michael David-Fox, "The Iron Curtain as Semipermeable Membrane: Origins and Demise of the Stalinist Superiority Complex," in Babiracki and Zimmer, *Cold War Crossings*, 14–39.

19. Sheffer, *Burned Bridge*.

20. Schneider, *The Wall Jumper*.

21. Buryn, *Vagabonding*, 195, 219.

22. Suri, "The Rise and Fall of an International Counterculture."

23. Juliane Fürst, "Swinging across the Iron Curtain and Moscow's Summer of Love: How Western Youth Culture Went East," in Jobs and Pomfret, *Transnational Histories of Youth*, 236–59.

24. Taylor, *The Berlin Wall*, 313.

25. Poiger, *Jazz, Rock, and Rebels*, 208–9, 196, 200–201.

26. McDougall, *Youth Politics in East Germany*, 163–64.

27. Fenemore, *Sex, Thugs and Rock 'n' Roll*, 173–75.

28. McDougall, *Youth Politics in East Germany*, 179–89.

29. Fenemore, *Sex, Thugs and Rock 'n' Roll*, 198–200.

30. See Davis, " 'Die Briten Kommen.' "

31. Ibid. See also Peter Wicke, "Music, Dissidence, Revolution, and Commerce: Youth Culture between Mainstream and Subculture," in Schildt and Siegfried, *Between Marx and Coca-Cola*, 109–26.

32. Stark, *Meet the Beatles*, 209.

33. As quoted in Miller, *The Rolling Stone Illustrated History of Rock 'n' Roll*, 176.

34. Brown, " '1968' East and West," 85–90.

35. Detlef Siegfried, "Music and Protest in 1960s Europe," in Klimke and Scharloth, *1968 in Europe*, 57–70.

36. Niek Pas, "Mediatization of the Provos: From a Local Movement to a European Phenomenon," in Klimke, Pekelder, and Scharloth, *Between Prague Spring and French May*, 168.

37. Konrad Dussel, "The Triumph of English-Language Pop Music: West German Radio Programming," in Schildt and Siegfried, *Between Marx and Coca-Cola*, 127–47.

38. Ibid., 131.

39. Prato, "Selling Italy by the Sound," 441–62.

40. See Phillipson, *Linguistic Imperialism*.

41. See Zuberi, *Sounds English*; Briggs, *Sounds French*.

42. Giachetti, *Anni Sessanta, comincia la danza*, 88, 132–33.

43. Siegfried, "Music and Protest in 1960s Europe," 63.

44. Van Elteren, *Imagining America*, 147.

45. Righart, *De eindeloze jaren zestig*, 264.

46. Clipping from *Nieuwe Rotterdamse Courant*, 26 June 1970, 7; William Mann, "Europe's First," *Times*, 2 July 1970, 7.

47. Guarnaccia, *Paradiso psichedelico*, 65.

48. Clippings from *Nieuwe Rotterdamse Courant*, 29 June 1970, 7, and 4 July 1970, 1.

49. Guarnaccia, *Paradiso psichedelico*, 128–33.

50. Hinton, *Message to Love*, 111.

51. Bernard Weinraub, "Isle of Wight Festival Turns Slightly Discordant," *New York Times*, 31 August 1970, 3.

52. Allen, *Isle of Wight 1970*, 56–57.

53. *Message to Love: Isle of Wight Music Festival* (dir. Murray Lerner, Pulsar Productions, 1995).

54. Weinraub, "Isle of Wight Festival Turns Slightly Discordant."

55. Allen, *Isle of Wight 1970*, 57.

56. Hinton, *Message to Love*, 172.

57. John Harrison in Earle et al., *A Time to Travel?*, 13.

58. John Major, "Conservative Party Conference Speech 1992," http://www.johnmajor.co.uk/page1208.html.

59. "Criminal Justice and Public Order Act 1994," Part V, Section 63, http://www.legislation.gov.uk/ukpga/1994/33/section/63.
60. Gary in Lowe and Shaw, *Travellers*, 147.
61. Em in Dearling, *No Boundaries*, 93.
62. Shannon in Lowe and Shaw, *Travellers*, 241.
63. Bruce Kent in Dearling, *No Boundaries*, 95.
64. Miranda, ibid., 175, 176.
65. Lizzy Bean, "The Adventures of Phoebus @pollo: The Rough & Ready Guide to Europ@," ibid., 106, 109.
66. Ibid., 113. As a response to their depiction in the British media, Travellers began self-publishing edited volumes that accounted for their individual and collective history and lifestyle. I have treated these writings as primary sources rich with personal testimony.
67. Ibid., 115, 117.
68. Riley, "Road Culture of International Long-Term Budget Travelers"; Richards and Wilson, *The Global Nomad*, 20.
69. Gloaguen and Trapier, *Génération routard*, 23, 78.
70. As quoted in Tomory, *A Season in Heaven*, 11.
71. As quoted ibid., 8, 14, 19.
72. Buryn, *Vagabonding*, 213–14, 230–31, 243–44, 228.
73. As quoted in Tomory, *A Season in Heaven*, 3–4.
74. See Gloaguen and Trapier, *Génération routard*; Gloaguen, *Une vie de routard*.
75. MacLean, *Magic Bus*, 199.
76. Sobocinska, "Following the 'Hippie Sahibs,'" 3.
77. MacLean, *Magic Bus*, 87, 82.
78. Author phone interview with Deena Atlas, 12 April 2016.
79. Editor, "Tous des routards," *Le Monde*, 19 April 1980, 17.
80. As quoted in MacLean, *Magic Bus*, 90.
81. Hyland, *Space Cake in Chicken Street*, 6.
82. MacLean, *Magic Bus*, 19, 108.
83. Angelika Bergmann is a pseudonym. "Reisetagbuch Indien," DTA 325.1.
84. Sobocinska, "Following the 'Hippie Sahibs.'"
85. See, for example, Furlough, "Une leçon des choses"; and John M. MacKenzie, "Empires of Travel: British Guide Books and Cultural Imperialism in the 19th and 20th Centuries," in Walton, *Histories of Tourism*, 19–38.
86. See David M. Pomfret, "Colonial Circulations: Vietnamese Youth, Travel, and Empire, 1919–1940," in Jobs and Pomfret, *Transnational Histories of Youth*, 115–43; and Pomfret, *Youth and Empire*.
87. See Hsu-Ming Teo, "Wandering in the Wake of Empire: British Travel and Tourism in the Post-imperial World," in Ward, *British Culture and the End of Empire*, 163–79.
88. Hampton, *Backpacker Tourism and Economic Development*, 6.
89. Sobocinska, "Following the 'Hippie Sahibs.'"

90. Hyland, *Space Cake in Chicken Street*, 129.

91. For a very smart discussion of this, see Sobocinska, "Following the 'Hippie Sahibs.'"

92. For a brief historical overview, see Ruth Leiserowitz, "Unerkannt durch Freundsland: Subversiv reisen mit Transitvisa," in Rauhut, Kochan, and Dieckmann, *Bye Bye, Lübben City*, 134–42; for an anthology of writing produced by such travelers themselves, see Klauss and Böttcher, *Unerkannt durch Freundesland*.

93. Fürst, "Swinging across the Iron Curtain."

94. Anne E. Gorsuch and Diane P. Koenker, "Introduction," in *Turizm*, 13; Koenker, "The Proletarian Tourist in the 1930s: Between Mass Excursion and Mass Escape," ibid., 125.

95. Gorsuch, *All This Is Your World*, 54.

96. Ibid., 1, 13, 121, 151, 124.

97. Pack, *Tourism and Dictatorship*, 5.

98. Markov, *The Truth That Killed*, 92–98.

99. Kristin Roth-Ey, "'Loose Girls' on the Loose? Sex, Propaganda and the 1957 Youth Festival," in Ilic, Reid, and Attwood, *Women in the Khrushchev Era*, 75–95.

100. McLellan, *Love in the Time of Communism*, 38, 45–46.

101. See Risch, *Youth and Rock in the Soviet Bloc*; Babiracki and Zimmer, *Cold War Crossings*; Gorsuch and Koenker, *The Socialist Sixties*; Zhuk, *Rock and Roll in the Rocket City*; Ryback, *Rock around the Bloc*.

102. Hitchcock, *The Struggle for Europe*, 293–300.

103. Jarausch, *After Hitler*, 67, 105, 218.

104. Dale, *Popular Protest in East Germany*, 82–97.

105. Lisiecki, "Die Auslandstouristik der westdeutschen"; Westermann, "Gedanken zum deutsch-deutschen Jugendaustausch," 3.

106. Student für Europa-Student für Berlin, BAK B/153/1738.

107. Saunders, *Honecker's Children*, 14, 79.

108. Lutz, "Junge Deutsche im Ausland"; Gisela Helwig and Detlef Urban, "Jugendaustausch zwischen beiden deutschen Staaten," in *Kirchen und Gesellschaft in Beiden Deutschen Staaten Herausgegeben* (Cologne: Deutschland Archiv im Verlag Wissenschaft und Politik, 1987), 191–200.

109. Christiane Schildt is a pseudonym. DTA 936/1.4.

110. Sheffer, *Burned Bridge*, 197.

111. Brown, "'1968 East and West," 85–89.

112. Plenzdorf, *The New Sufferings of Young W.*

113. Fulbrook, *The People's State*, 70.

114. See Kate Gerrard, "Punk and the State of Youth in the GDR," in Risch, *Youth and Rock in the Soviet Bloc*, 153–82.

115. Peter Wicke, "The Times They Are a-Changin': Rock Music and Political Change in East Germany," in Garofalo, *Rockin' the Boat*, 81–92.

116. Jarausch, *After Hitler*, 218.

117. Kate Gerrard, "Punk and the State of Youth in the GDR," in Risch, *Youth and Rock in the Soviet Bloc*, 159–60.

118. Robert Hilburn, "American Music Uber Alles: The Sound of America's Greatest Ambassadors" *Los Angeles Times*, 29 July 1984, 70, 79.

119. "Meanwhile, in East Berlin," *Time*, 22 June 1987, 20; Robert J. McCartney, "East German Rock Fans, Police Clash," *Washington Post*, 9 June 1987, A1, A28; "DDR Niedrig hängen," *Der Spiegel*, 15 June 1987, Archiv der Jugendkulturen, Berlin [hereafter AJK]; Saunders, *Honecker's Children*, 69.

120. Anna Tomforde, "East Ponders Wall Clash Lessons," *Guardian*, 10 June 1987, 8.

121. Robert J. McCartney, "Katarina vs. Michael: Berlin's Dueling Concerts," *Washington Post*, 20 June 1988, B1, B7.

122. See Kirschbaum, *Rocking the Wall*.

123. German Foreign Office Twitter account, @Germanydiplo, 11 January 2016.

124. Jarausch, *After Hitler*, 199; "Brennende Uniform," *Der Spiegel*, no. 47 (1977): 65–66.

125. Michael Rauhut, "I Can't Get No SEDisfaction," *Die Zeit*, 4 June 1998, AJK; clipping from *Maerkische Allgemeine*, 7 October 1969, AJK.

126. Mark and von der Goltz, "Encounters," 137.

127. Fulbrook, *The People's State*, 139.

128. See Berg, "Jugendtourismus in der DDR"; Schmidt, *Der Deustche Jugend-Tourist*.

129. Sheffer, *Burned Bridge*, 234–35.

130. Jarausch, *After Hitler*, 248.

131. Wicke, " 'The Times They are a-Changin,' " 88.

132. Ross, "Before the Wall."

133. For more on the film, see Ken Woodgate, " 'Young and in Love': Music and Memory in Leander Haussman's *Sun Alley*," *Screening the Past* 18 (2005), http://www.screeningthepast.com/2014/12/young-and-in-love-music-and-memory-in-leander-haussmanns%C2%A0sun-alley/; and Anna Saunders, " 'Normalizing' the Past: East German Culture and *Ostalgie*," in Taberner and Cooke, *German Culture, Politics, and Literature*, 89–104.

134. Hensel, *After the Wall*, 16–17, 160, 165, 97, 164.

135. Gayler and Kroiss, *Osteuropareisen*.

136. Hensel, *After the Wall*, 35, 129–31.

137. Pack, *Tourism and Dictatorship*.

138. Ibid., 145–46.

139. Fraser, *Tajos*, 218–20, 224–26.

140. Michener, *The Drifters*, 38, 356.

141. Ibid., 322.

142. Ibid., 38, 88, 141, 310, 335, 506, 507.

143. Cremer, *I Jan Cremer*, 275.

144. Robert Gildea and James Mark, "Conclusion: Europe's 1968," in Gildea, Mark, and Warring, *Europe's 1968*, 330.

145. "The Class Structure of Hippiedom," *Economist*, 4 April 1970, 38–39.

146. "Hippie Exodus from Ibiza," *Financial Times*, 19 July 1971, 1.

147. Rozenberg, "Tourisme et identités culturelles."

148. Alethea Sellars, "The Influence of Dance Music on the UK Youth Tourism Market," *Tourism Management* 19, no. 6 (1988): 611–15.

149. D'Andrea, *Global Nomads*.

150. Grassl and Heath, *The Magic Triangle*, 130–31.

151. Ibid., 163.

152. See Dragan Popović, "Youth Labor Action (*Omladinska radna akcija, ORA*) as Ideological Holiday-Making," in Grandits and Taylor, *Yugoslavia's Sunny Side*, 279–302.

153. See Anne E. Gorsuch, "Time Travelers: Soviet Tourists to Eastern Europe," in Gorsuch and Koenker, *Turizm*, 205–26; Wendy Bracewell, "Adventures in the Marketplace: Yugoslav Travel Writing and Tourism in the 1950s–1960s," ibid., 248–65.

154. Neville, *Play Power*, 204.

155. Lanfant, "Introduction"; see also Doris Christidis-Frohne, "Der westeuropäische Tourismus als Entwicklungsfaktor Griechenlands," in Gumpel, *Griechenland und die Europäische Gemeinschaft*, 151–58.

156. Papadogiannis, *Militant around the Clock?*, 29.

157. Kornetis, " 'Everything Links'?," 41; Federico Romero, "Cross-Border Population Movements," in Wallace, *The Dynamics of European Integration*, 176.

158. Ruffino, *An Assessment of Organized Youth Mobility in Europe*, 10.

159. Thomas Mergel, "Europe as Leisure Time Communication: Tourism and Transnational Interaction since 1945," in Jarausch and Lindenberger, *Conflicted Memories*, 139–42; Papadogiannis, *Militant around the Clock?*, 28–30.

160. Papadogiannis, "Travel and the Greek Migrant Youth."

161. Berlinghoff, " 'Faux Touristes'?"

162. Cohen, "Les circulations entre France et Algérie."

163. Ibid.; Berlinghoff, " 'Faux Touristes'?"; Möhring, "Tourism and Migration."

164. François Durgel, "La police arrête les agresseurs à Toulouse," *France-Soir*, 16 November 1983, 1, 4; Françoise Gaspard, "Danger de mort," *Le Monde*, 23 November 1983, 12; Sylvain Stein, "Le train 343," *L'Express*, 2 December 1983, 12. The Grimzi Affair inspired a 1985 film by Roger Hanin, *Le train d'enfer*, and a 1986 novel by Ahmed Kalouaz, *Point Kilométrique 190*. See Deborah S. Reisinger, "Writing Memory: *Point Kilométrique 190* and the Grimzi Affair," in Hardwick, *New Approaches to Crime*, 191–203.

165. Phillips, *The European Tribe*, 102.

166. For a brief overview, see McCormick, *Understanding the European Union*, 159–62.

167. Roberto Aliboni, "The Mediterranean Dimension," in Wallace, *The Dynamics of European Integration*, 155–67.

168. Table, "Ventes Inter Rail," 1992, spreadsheet, Eurail Group, Utrecht.

169. Kozakowski, "Making 'Mediterranean Migrants.' "

170. Romero, "Cross-Border Population Movements," 171.

171. Hollier and Subremon, *Le tourisme dans la Communauté européenne*, 5, 10, 23, 53–72, 120.

172. Pack, "Revival of the Pilgrimage to Santiago de Compostela."

173. Abdel-Ghaffar, "Youth Tourism," 793.

174. Mintel Publications, "Independent Travel."

175. Martinegro and Savoja, *Giovani e turismo*, 49, 63, 70.

176. Acquaviva and Scarsini, *Giovani sulle strade del terzo* millennio, 83–88.

177. Eurobarometer 34.2, "Young Europeans in 1990," May 1991, 57–73, GESIS Data Archive for the Social Sciences.

178. Lotte Thorsen and Jacob Markers, "Secret Haven for Rail Travellers," *Guardian*, 16 August 1991, 22.

179. Hartmann, "Youth Tourism in Post-Industrial Society."

180. Gayler, *Wettbewerb Jugend reist und lernt Europa kennen*; Gayler, *Jugendliche Tramper*.

181. Gayler, *Jugendliche Tramper*, 115.

182. Roberto Suros, "Venice Yearns for Tourists Who Sleep in Hotels," *New York Times*, 9 August 1986, 2.

183. Giorgio Cecchetti, "Tornano I saccopelisti a 'invadere' Venezia," *La Repubblica*, 2 August 1988, 20.

184. Hans Baumann, "L'Europe des jeunes est déjà là . . . ," *Le Monde*, 6 December 1977, 6.

185. Xavier Allouis, "Une génération communitaire," *Le Monde*, 7 September 1978, 2.

186. Madame M. Lucy Dumas-Soula, "L'Europe, c'est foutu?," *Le Monde*, 14 December 1983, 2.

187. Bocquet and Delleur, *Génération Europe*, 231, 250.

188. Chisholm, du Bois-Reymond, and Coffield, "What Does Europe Mean to Me?," 5; Eurobarometer 34.2, "Young Europeans in 1990," May 1991, 107, GESIS Data Archive for the Social Sciences.

189. Belot, "Les jeunes face à l'intégration européenne."

190. See Risch, *Youth and Rock in the Soviet Bloc*.

191. Jonathyne Briggs, "East of (Teenaged) Eden, or, Is Eastern Youth Culture So Different from the West?," ibid., 267–83.

192. See Loersch and Arbuckle, "Unraveling the Mystery of Music"; and Ian Cross, "Music as a Social and Cognitive Process," in Rebuschat et al., *Language and Music as Cognitive Systems*, 315–28.

193. Stuart Hall and Paddy Whannel, "The Young Audience," in Frith and Goodwin, *On Record*, 27–37.

194. For an excellent study of this in the case of France, see Briggs, *Sounds French*.

195. See Siegfried, "The Emergence of the Post-National Subject."

196. Balibar, *We, the People of Europe?*, 162.

197. Ibid., 173, 176, 177.

198. Patel, "Where and When Was Europe?"; Frevert, *Eurovisionen*, 78–100.

199. Marker, "Obscuring Race," 10.

200. Lévi-Strauss, *Tristes tropiques*, 40–41.

201. Musée d'ethnographie de la Ville Neuchâtel, *Être nomade aujourd'hui*.

202. For the French case, see Sherman, *French Primitivism and the Ends of Empire*.

RIGHTS OF PASSAGE

1. Wijnand Boon's website is http://www.twalkwithme.eu/home.html. There are links to a variety of news coverage, mostly in Dutch. See also Louisa Schaefer, "Dutch Pilgrim Sets Out to Prove Social Media Unites," 26 November 2010, http://www.dw.com/en/dutch-pilgrim-sets-out-to-prove -social-media-unites/a-6266578.

2. Wakeman, "Veblen Redivivus," 439.

3. "Eurail Passengers since 1959" and "InterRail Passengers 1972–2008," charts and data from Eurail Group, Utrecht, 2009.

4. See Michael O'Regan, "Hypermobility in Backpacker Lifestyles: The Emergence of the Internet Café," in Burns and Novelli, *Tourism and Mobilities*, 109–32; Peter M. Burns and Michael O'Regan, "Everyday Techno-social Devices in Everyday Travel Life," ibid., 146–86.

5. See Urry, *Mobilities*; Cresswell, *On the Move*.

6. Wakeman, "Veblen Redivivus," 439.

7. Cresswell, "Towards a Politics of Mobility."

8. Cees Nooteboom, "Birth of a New Nation?," *Guardian*, 8 May 1992, 23.

9. Nooteboom, *Nomad's Hotel*, 2.

10. Hensel, *After the Wall*, 35, 129–31; Hartmann, "The Significance of Youth Mobility."

11. Nadine Cattan, "Gendering Mobility: Insights into the Construction of Spatial Concepts," in Uteng and Cresswell, *Gendered Mobilities*, 90.

12. Antonio Coimbra Martins, "Report on Student Mobility and the Proposal from the Commission of the European Communities to the Council for a Decision on Adopting ERASMUS: The European Community Action Scheme for the Mobility of University Students," European Parliament Documents 1986/0022 A2, 7 April 1986, ECL.

13. Teichler and Maiworm, *The ERASMUS Experience*, iii, 130–32, 202–6.

14. Bertoncini, *Encourage Young People's Mobility in Europe*.

15. Bantigny, "Genèses de l'Europe, jeunesses d'Europe."

16. Horak and Weber, "Youth Tourism in Europe," 39, 41.

17. Mintel Publications, "Independent Travel," 4, 13, 18.

18. For an analysis of contemporary backpacking, see Richards and Wilson, *The Global Nomad*.

19. Horak and Weber, "Youth Tourism in Europe," 40.

20. O'Reilly, "From Drifter to Gap Year Tourist," 1013.

21. Jonathan Zimmerman, "Requiem for the Backpacker: Today's Youth Risk Missing Out on the Joys of Spontaneous Travel," Salon.com, 17 July 2016,

http://www.salon.com/2016/07/17/requiem_for_the_backpacker_todays
_youths_risk_missing_out_on_the_joys_of_spontaneous_travel/.

22. Peter Mason, "The 'Big OE': New Zealanders' Overseas Experience in Britain," in Hall and Williams, *Tourism and Migration*, 87–101.

23. Grassl and Heath, *The Magic Triangle*, 115–16, 127–28.

24. See Sobocinska, "Following the 'Hippie Sahibs' "; Teo and Leong, "A Postcolonial Analysis of Backpacking."

25. Grassl and Heath, *The Magic Triangle*, 117–23.

26. Annual Report of the International Youth Hostel Federation for 1970–71, Section 3, 8, HIA.

27. See Mittag and Wendland, "How Adventurers Become Tourists"; Hartmann, "The Significance of Youth Mobility."

28. Riley, "Road Culture of International Long-Term Budget Travelers."

29. Sobocinska, *Visiting the Neighbours*, 10, 11, 126.

30. See Noy and Cohen, *Israeli Backpackers*.

31. See Hampton, *Backpacker Tourism and Economic Development*.

32. Feng Yi Huang, "Western and Asian Backpackers in Taiwan: Behavior, Motivation and Cultural Diversity," in Cochrane, *Asian Tourism*, 171–81.

33. Merry I. White, "All Roads Lead to Home: Japanese Culinary Tourism in Italy," in Guichard-Anguis and Moon, *Japanese Tourism and Travel Culture*, 207; Conte-Helm, *The Japanese and Europe*, 49.

34. Teo and Leong, "A Postcolonial Analysis of Backpacking."

35. Rong Huang, "Are Chinese International Students in the UK Tourists?," in Cochrane, *Asian Tourism*, 157–69.

36. Nyíri, *Mobility and Cultural Authority in Contemporary China*, 69–76, quotation from 76.

37. Appadurai, *Modernity at Large*.

38. See Maira and Soep, *Youthscapes*.

39. See Mahood, "Thumb Wars"; Zolov, *Refried Elvis*; Valeria Manzano, "On the Revolutionary Road: Youth, Displacements, and Politics in the 'Long' Latin American Sixties," in Jobs and Pomfret, *Transnational Histories of Youth*, 167–87.

40. For more on this and other road movies, see chapter 5 in Higbee, *Post-Beur Cinema*.

41. Silverstein, *Algeria in France*, 217.

42. Stephen Castles, "Immigration and Asylum: Challenges to European Identities and Citizenship," in Stone, *The Oxford Handbook of Postwar European History*, 201–19.

43. See Boswell and Geddes, *Migration and Mobility in the European Union*.

44. Sheffer, *Burned Bridge*, 352.

45. Michael Wintle, "The Question of European Identity and the Impact of the Changes of 1989/90," in Shahin and Wintle, *The Idea of a United Europe*, 11–30.

46. Mergel, "Europe as Leisure Time Communication," 147–48.

47. Tim Coles, "Telling Tales of Tourism: Mobility, Media and Citizenship in the 2004 EU Enlargement," in Burns and Novelli, *Tourism and Mobilities*, 65–80.

48. Suzanne Daley, "Denmark Leads Nationalist Challenge to Europe's Open Borders," *New York Times*, 25 June 2011, A1, A5.

49. Wallace, "Rescue or Retreat?," 70; Office for National Statistics, "Travel Trends: 2014," 20 May 2015, http://www.ons.gov.uk/peoplepopulationand community/leisureandtourism/articles/traveltrends/2015–05–20.

50. Steven Erlanger, "Worries over Turkey Inflame 'Brexit' Debate," *New York Times*, 14 June 2016, A9.

51. See John Burn-Murdoch, "Brexit: Voter Turnout by Age," *Financial Times*, 24 June 2016, http://blogs.ft.com/ftdata/2016/06/24/brexit-demographic -divide-eu-referendum-results/; Damian Lyons Lowe, "How Will Europe's Migration Crisis Affect UK Attitudes to the EU?," *Survation*, n.d., http:// survation.com/how-will-europes-migration-crisis-affect-britains-attitudes -to-the-european-union/; Ashley Kirk and Daniel Dunford, "EU Referen- dum: How the Results Compare to UK's Educated, Old and Immigrant Populations," *Telegraph*, 27 June 2016, http://www.telegraph.co.uk/news /2016/06/24/eu-referendum-how-the-results-compare-to-the-uks-educated -old-an/.

52. Aftab Ali, "Brexit Result: What Does It Mean for UK's Higher Education Sector and Students?," *Independent*, 24 June 2016, http://www.independent .co.uk/student/news/eu-referendum-result-brexit-leave-remain-higher -education-sector-students-a7100106.html.

53. Rhiannon Lucy Cosslett, "Britain's Young People Will Suffer Most from an EU Divorce," *Guardian*, 20 June 2016, https://www.theguardian.com /commentisfree/2016/jun/20/britain-young-people-eu-older-generation -brexit-vote.

54. Claire Barthelemy and Kimiko de Freytas-Tamura, "Among Young Britons, Fear and Despair over Vote to Leave E.U.," *New York Times*, 25 June 2016, http://www.nytimes.com/2016/06/25/world/europe/among-young-britons -fear-and-despair-over-vote-to-leave-eu.html.

55. Alex Matthews, " 'This Vote Doesn't Represent the Younger Generation Who Will Have to Live with the Consequences': Millennials Vent Fury at Baby Boomers for Voting Britain OUT of the EU," *Daily Mail*, 24 June 2016, http://www.dailymail.co.uk/news/article-3658671/This-vote-doesn-t -represent-younger-generation-live-consequences-Millennials-fury-baby -boomers-voting-Britain-EU.html.

56. See Blitz, *Migration and Freedom*.

57. See Ohligher, Schönwälder, and Triafilopoulos, *European Encounters*.

58. See Eurostat, *Standard Eurobarometer* 79 (2013), 17–23, http://ec.europa.eu /public_opinion/archives/eb/eb79/eb79_en.htm.

Bibliography

Abdel-Ghaffar, Amr, et al. "Youth Tourism." *Annals of Tourism Research* 19, no. 4 (1992): 792–96.

Acquaviva, Sabino, and Fiorenzo Scarsini. *Giovani sulle strade del terzo millennio: I giovani degli ostelli; Tra peregrinaggio interior e turismo culturale.* Milan: San Paolo, 1999.

Adler, Emanuel. *Communitarian International Relations: The Epistemic Foundations of International Relations.* New York: Routledge, 2005.

Adler, Judith. "Youth on the Road: Reflections on the History of Tramping." *Annals of Tourism Research* 12, no. 3 (1985): 335–54.

Agosti, Aldo, Luisa Passerini, and Nicola Tranfaglia, eds. *La cultura e i luoghi del '68.* Milan: Angeli, 1998.

Aldrich, Richard J. *The Hidden Hand: Britain, America and Cold War Secret Intelligence.* London: John Murray, 2001.

Ali, Tariq. *Street Fighting Years: An Autobiography of the Sixties.* London: Verso, 2005.

Allen, Rod. *Isle of Wight 1970: The Last Great Festival.* London: Clipper Press, 1970.

Appadurai, Arjun. *Modernity at Large: Cultural Dimensions of Globalization.* Minneapolis: University of Minnesota Press, 1996.

Babiracki, Patryk, and Kenyon Zimmer, eds. *Cold War Crossings: International Travel and Exchange across the Soviet Bloc, 1940s–1960s.* College Station: Texas A&M Press, 2014.

Badenoch, Alexander, and Andreas Fickers, eds. *Materializing Europe: Transnational Infrastructures and the Project of Europe.* New York: Palgrave Macmillan, 2010.

Bailkin, Jordanna. *The Afterlife of Empire.* Berkeley: University of California Press, 2012.

Balibar, Etienne. *We, the People of Europe? Reflections on Transnational Citizenship.* Translated by James Swenson. Princeton: Princeton University Press, 2004.

Bantigny, Ludivine. "Genèses de l'Europe, jeunesses d'Europe: Entre enchantement et détachement." *Histoire@Politique* 20 (January–April 2010): 1–15.

Baranowski, Shelley, and Ellen Furlough, eds. *Being Elsewhere: Tourism, Consumer Culture, and Identity in Modern Europe and North America.* Ann Arbor: University of Michigan Press, 2001.

Bar-Haím, Gabriel. "Eastern European Youth Culture: The Westernization of a Social Movement." *International Journal of Politics, Culture, and Society* 2, no. 1 (1988): 45–65.

Barth, Heinrich. "Jeunesse: Cooperation franco-allemande." *Documents* 18, no. 5 (September–October 1963): 45–49.

Bauman, Zygmunt. *Liquid Modernity.* Cambridge: Polity Press, 2000.

Baumann, Hans. "Die Stellung Deutschlands im internationalen Reiseverkehr." *Der Fremdenverkehr* 19/20 (1953): 4.

Belot, Céline. "Les jeunes face à l'intégration européenne." *Agora: Débats jeunesses* 20, no. 1 (2000): 35–48.

Berg, Detlef. "Jugendtourismus in der DDR." *Deutsche Studien* 27 (March 1989): 49–59.

Berlinghoff, Marcel. " 'Faux Touristes'? Tourism in European Migration Regimes in the Long Sixties." *Comparativ* 24, no. 2 (2014): 88–99.

Berrino, Annunziata. *Storia del turismo in Italia.* Bologna: Il Mulino, 2011.

Bertoncini, Yves. *Encourage Young People's Mobility in Europe: Strategic Orientations for France and the European Union.* Centre d'analyse strategique, July 2008. http://freref.eu/docs/en/Encourage-young-people%92s-mobility_EN_-_V3_2008-11-25_VF.pdf.

Biesanz, John. "Nazi Influence on German Youth Hostels." *Social Forces* 19, no. 4 (May 1941): 554–59.

Biesanz, John, and Mavis Biesanz. "Social Distance in the Youth Hostel Movement." *Sociology and Social Research* 25 (January–February 1941): 237–45.

Biess, Frank. "Moral Panic in Postwar Germany: The Abduction of Young Germans into the Foreign Legion and French Colonialism in the 1950s." *Journal of Modern History* 84, no. 4 (2012): 789–832.

Bird, Stephanie, Mary Fulbrook, Julia Wagner, and Christiane Wienand, eds. *Reverberations of Nazi Violence in Germany and Beyond: Disturbing Pasts.* London: Bloomsbury Academic, 2016.

Bischof, Gunter, Anton Pelinka, and Dagmar Herzog, eds. *Sexuality in Austria.* New Brunswick, NJ: Transaction, 2007.

Blitz, Brad K. *Migration and Freedom: Mobility, Citizenship and Exclusion.* Cheltenham: Edward Elgar, 2014.

Bock, Hans Manfred, Corinne Defrance, Gilbert Krebs, and Ulrich Pfeil. *Les jeunes dans les relations transnationales: L'Office franco-allemand pour la jeunesse 1963–2008.* Paris: Presses Sorbonnes nouvelle, 2008.

Bock, Hans Manfred, Reinhart Meyer-Kalkus, and Michel Trebtisch, eds. *Entre Locarno et Vichy: Les relations culturelles franco-allemandes dans les années 1930.* Paris: CNRS Editions, 1993.

Bocquet, Dominique, and Philippe Delleur. *Génération Europe*. Paris: François Bourin, 1989.

Borchert, Wolfgang. *The Man Outside*. Translated by David Porter. London: Hutchinson International Authors, 1952.

Böröcz, József. "Travel-Capitalism: The Structure of Europe and the Advent of the Tourist." *Comparative Studies in Society and History* 34, no. 4 (1992): 723–24.

Bösch, Frank, Ariane Brill, and Florian Greiner, eds. *Europabilder im 20. Jahrhundert: Entstehung an der Peripherie*. Göttingen: Wallstein Verlag, 2012.

Bosscher, Doeko, Marja Roholl, and Mel van Elteren, eds. *American Culture in the Netherlands*. Amsterdam: Vrei University Press, 1996.

Boswell, Christina, and Andrew Geddes. *Migration and Mobility in the European Union*. New York: Palgrave Macmillan, 2011.

Bouvier, Nicolas. *L'usage du monde: Récit*. Geneva: Droz, 1963.

———. *The Way of the World*. Translated by Robyn Marsack. New York: New York Review of Books, 1992.

Briggs, Jonathyne. *Sounds French: Globalization, Cultural Communities and Pop Music, 1958–1980*. Oxford: Oxford University Press, 2015.

Brown, Timothy Scott. "'1968' East and West: Divided Germany as a Case Study in Transnational History." *American Historical Review* 114, no. 1 (February 2009): 69–96.

———. *West Germany and the Global Sixties: The Anti-Authoritarian Revolt, 1962–1978*. Cambridge: Cambridge University Press, 2013.

Bryson, Bill. *Neither Here nor There: Travels in Europe*. New York: Perennial, 1992.

Bucholtz, Mary. "Youth and Cultural Practice." *Annual Review of Anthropology* 31 (2002): 525–52.

Buffet, Cyril, and Beatrice Heuser, eds. *Haunted by History: Myths in International Relations*. Providence, RI: Berghahn Books, 1998.

Burns, Peter M., and Marina Novelli, eds. *Tourism and Mobilities: Local-Global Connections*. Wallingford: CABI, 2008.

Buryn, Ed. *Hitch-hiking in Europe: An Informal Guidebook*. San Francisco: Hannah Associates, 1969.

———. *Vagabonding in Europe and North Africa*. Berkeley: Bookworks, 1973.

Calleo, David P., and Eric R. Staal, eds. *Europe's Franco-German Engine*. Washington, DC: Brookings Institution Press, 1998.

Casson, Lionel. *Travel in the Ancient World*. Baltimore: Johns Hopkins University Press, 1994.

Chisholm, Lynne, Manuela du Bois-Reymond, and Frank Coffield. "What Does Europe Mean to Me? Dimensions of Distance and Disillusion amongst European Students." In *The Puzzle of Integration*, vol. 1 of *European Yearbook on Youth Policy and Research*, edited by CYRCE, 3–31. Berlin: de Gruyter, 1995.

Cini, Michelle, and Angela K. Bourne, eds. *Palgrave Advances in European Union Studies*. New York: Palgrave Macmillan, 2006.

Clark, Robert. *Dark Water: Art, Disaster, and Redemption in Florence*. New York: Random House, 2008.

Cline, Justin J. "Youth Hosteling: Social Travel toward Democracy." *Educational Method* 20, no. 5 (1941): 251–56.

Coburn, Oliver. *Youth Hostel Story.* London: National Council of Social Service, 1950.

Cochrane, Janet, ed. *Asian Tourism: Growth and Change.* Amsterdam: Elsevier, 2008.

Cockerill, G. F. *Report on Youth Exchanges.* London: Foreign and Commonwealth Office, 1983.

Cohen, Erik. "Nomads from Affluence: Notes on the Phenomenon of Drifter-Tourism." *International Journal of Comparative Sociology* 14, no. 1–2 (1973): 89–103.

Cohen, H. *Drugs, druggebruikers en drug-scene.* Alphen aan den Rijn: Samson Uitgeverij, 1975.

Cohen, Muriel. "Les circulations entre France et Algérie: un nouveau regard sur les migrants (post)coloniaux (1945–1985)." *French Politics, Culture & Society* 34, no. 2 (2016): 78–100.

Cohn-Bendit, Daniel, and Thomas Schmid. *Heimat Babylon: Das Wagnis der multikulturellen Gesellschaft.* Hamburg: Hoffmann and Campe, 1992.

Cohn-Bendit, Dany. *Nous l'avons tant aimée, la révolution.* Paris: Bernard Barrault, 1986.

Cole, Alistair. *Franco-German Relations.* Harlow: Pearson, 2001.

Collings, Rex, ed. *Reflections of a Statesman: The Writings and Speeches of Enoch Powell.* London: Bellew, 1991.

Confino, Alon. *Germany as a Culture of Remembrance: Promises and Limits of Writing History.* Chapel Hill: University of North Carolina Press, 2006.

Conte-Helm, Marie. *The Japanese and Europe: Economic and Cultural Encounters.* London: Athlone, 1996.

Conway, Martin, and Kiran Klaus Patel, eds. *Europeanization in the Twentieth Century: Historical Approaches.* New York: Palgrave Macmillan, 2010.

Cooper, Frederick. *Citizenship between Empire and Nation: Remaking France and French Africa, 1945–1960.* Princeton: Princeton University Press, 2014.

Cornelis, Petrus-Arsène. *Europeans about Europe: What European Students Know and Expect of the Unification of Europe.* Amsterdam: Swets & Zeitlinger, 1970.

Creagh, Mary, and Tony Lockett. "La Forum jeunesse, voix européenne des jeunes." *Objectif Europe,* no. 34 (1994): 14–23.

Cremer, Jan. *I, Jan Cremer.* New York: Shorecrest, 1965.

Creswell, Michael, and Marc Trachtenberg. "France and the German Question, 1945–1955." *Journal of Cold War Studies* 5, no. 3 (Summer 2003): 5–28.

Cresswell, Tim. *On the Move: Mobility in the Modern Western World.* New York: Routledge, 2006.

———. "Towards a Politics of Mobility." *Environment and Planning D: Society and Space* 28, no. 1 (2010): 17–31.

———. *The Tramp in America.* London: Reaktion Books, 2001.

Cresswell, Tim, and Peter Merriman, eds. *Geographies of Mobilities: Practices, Spaces, Subjects.* Farnham: Ashgate, 2011.

Crouch, Colin. *The Student Revolt.* London, 1970.

Cuskey, Walter R., Arnold William Klein, and William Krasner. *Drug-Trip Abroad: American Drug-Refugees in Amsterdam and London*. Philadelphia: University of Pennsylvania Press, 1972.

Dale, Gareth. *Popular Protest in East Germany, 1945–1989*. London: Routledge, 2005.

D'Andrea, Anthony. *Global Nomads: Techno and New Age as Transnational Counter-cultures in Ibiza and Goa*. London: Routledge, 2007.

D'Angelis, Erasmo. *Angeli del fango: La "meglio gioventù" nella Firenze dell'alluvione*. Firenze: Giunti, 2006.

Daum, Andreas W., Lloyd C. Gardner, and Wilfried Mausbach, eds. *America, the Vietnam War, and the World: Comparative and International Perspectives*. New York: Cambridge University Press, 2003.

Davies, Christie. *Permissive Britain: Social Change in the Sixties and Seventies*. London: Pitman, 1975.

Davis, Belinda, Wilfried Mausbach, Martin Klimke, and Carla MacDougall, eds. *Changing the World, Changing Oneself: Political Protest and Collective Identities in West Germany and the U.S. in the 1960s and 1970s*. New York: Berghahn Books, 2010.

Dearling, Alan, ed. *No Boundaries: New Travellers on the Road (Outside of England)*. Dorset: Enabler, 1998.

Defrance, Corine. *La politique culturelle de la France sur la rive gauche du Rhin (1945–1955)*. Strasbourg: Presses universitaires de Strasbourg, 1994.

Defrance, Corine, and Ulrich Pfeil, eds. *Le traité de l'Elysée et les relations franco-allemandes 1945-1963-2003*. Paris: CNRS, 2005.

De Gaulle, Charles. *Discours et messages: Pour l'effort, 1962–1965*. Paris: Plon, 1970.

Delori, Matthias. "De la réconciliation franco-allemande à la 'guerre des dieux': Analyse cognitive et discursive d'une politique publique voluntariste d'éducation à la cause de la paix; L'office franco-allemand pour la jeunesse." Doctoral thesis, Université Pierre Mendès-France, 2008.

De Martino, Gianni, ed. *Capelloni e ninfette: Mondo Beat 1966–1967; Storia, immagini, documenti*. Milan: Costa e Nolan, 2008.

Demossier, Marion, ed. *The European Puzzle: The Political Structuring of Cultural Identities at a Time of Transition*. New York: Berghahn Books, 2007.

Deutsch, Karl W. *Political Community and the North Atlantic Area: International Organization in the Light of Historical Experience*. Princeton: Princeton University Press, 1957.

Djelic, Marie-Laure, and Sigrid Quack, eds. *Transnational Communities: Shaping Global Economic Governance*. Cambridge: Cambridge University Press, 2010.

Dogliani, Patrizia, ed. *Giovani e generazioni nel Mondo contemporaneo: La ricerca storica in Italia*. Bologna: CLUEB, 2009.

Donaldson, Frances. *The British Council: The First Fifty Years*. London: Jonathan Cape, 1984.

Dreyfus-Armand, Geneviève, Robert Frank, Marie-Françoise Lévy, and Michelle Zancarini-Fournel, eds. *Les Années 68: Le temps de la contestation*. Paris: Complexe, 2000.

Duggan, Christopher, and Christopher Wagstaff, eds. *Italy in the Cold War: Politics, Culture, and Society, 1948–1958*. Oxford: Berg, 1995.

Du Réau, Elisabeth, and Robert Frank. *Dynamiques européennes: Nouvel espace, nouveaux acteurs 1969–1981*. Paris: Publications de la Sorbonne, 2002.

Dussault, Eric. "Politique culturelle et dénazification dans la zone d'occupation française en Autriche (Tyrol et Vorarlberg) et à Vienne de 1945 à 1955." *Guerres mondiales et conflits contemporains*, no. 221 (January 2006): 83–92.

Earle, Fiona, Alan Dearling, Helen Whittle, Roddy Glasse, and Gubby. *A Time to Travel? An Introduction to Britain's Newer Travellers*. Dorset: Enabler, 1994.

Eberhard, Laurence. *The Council of Europe and Youth: Thirty Years of Experience*. Strasbourg: Council of Europe, 2002.

Ehrenreich, Barbara, and John Ehrenreich. *Long March, Short Spring: The Student Uprising at Home and Abroad*. New York: Monthly Review Press, 1969.

Eisner, J. Richard, and Nicholas Ford. "Sexual Relationships on Holiday: A Case of Situational Disinhibition?" *Journal of Social and Personal Relationships* 12, no. 3 (1995): 323–39.

Eley, Geoff. *Forging Democracy: The History of the Left in Europe, 1850–2000*. Oxford: Oxford University Press, 2002.

Ellison, James. "Separated by the Atlantic: The British and de Gaulle, 1958–1967." *Diplomacy & Statecraft* 17, no. 4 (2006): 853–70.

Endy, Christopher. *Cold War Holidays: American Tourism in France*. Chapel Hill: University of North Carolina Press, 2004.

Epstein, Jonathon S., ed. *Adolescents and Their Music: If It's Too Loud, You're Too Old*. New York: Garland, 1994.

Evans, Alan. *Youth Exchanges: The Way Ahead*. London: European Educational Research Trust, 1970.

Faist, Thomas, and Eyüp Özveren, eds. *Transnational Social Spaces: Agents, Networks and Institutions*. Aldershot: Ashgate, 2004.

Farquharson, John E., and Stephen C. Holt. *Europe from Below: An Assessment of Franco-German Popular Contacts*. New York: St. Martin's Press, 1975.

Feldman, Christine Jacqueline. *"We Are the Mods": A Transnational History of a Youth Subculture*. New York: Peter Lang, 2009.

Fenemore, Mark. *Sex, Thugs and Rock 'n' Roll: Teenage Rebels in Cold-War East Germany*. New York: Berghahn Books, 2007.

Férrând, Jerome. *La jeunesse, nouveau Tiers Etat*. Paris: Robert Laffont, 1968.

Fieldston, Sara. "Little Cold Warriors: Child Sponsorship and International Affairs." *Diplomatic History* 38, no. 2 (2014): 240–50.

Fink, Carole, Philipp Gassert, and Detlef Junker, eds. *1968: The World Transformed*. Cambridge: Cambridge University Press, 1998.

Fisher, Jaimey. *Disciplining Germany: Youth, Reeducation, and Reconstruction after the Second World War*. Detroit: Wayne State University Press, 2007.

François, Etienne, ed. *1968—ein europäisches Jahr?* Leipzig: Leipziger Universitätsverlag, 1997.

Fraser, Ronald. *Tajos: The Story of a Village on the Costa del Sol.* New York: Pantheon, 1973.

Fraser, Ronald, et al. *1968: A Student Generation in Revolt.* New York: Pantheon, 1988.

Frevert, Ute. "Europeanizing Germany's Twentieth Century." *History and Memory* 17, no. 1–2 (2005): 87–116.

———. *Eurovisionen: Ansichten guter Europäer im 19. und 20. Jahrhundert.* Frankfurt/Main: Fischer Taschenbuch Verlag, 2003.

Friend, Julius W. *The Linchpin: French-German Relations, 1950–1990.* New York: Center for Strategic and International Studies, 1991.

Frith, Simon, and Andrew Goodwin, eds. *On Record: Rock, Pop, and the Written Word.* New York: Pantheon Books, 1990.

Fulbrook, Mary. *The People's State: East German Society from Hitler to Honecker.* New Haven: Yale University Press, 2005.

Furlough, Ellen. "Making Mass Vacations: Tourism and Consumer Culture in France, 1930s to 1970s." *Comparative Studies in Society and History* 40, no. 2 (1998): 247–86.

———. "Une leçon des choses: Tourism, Empire, and the Nation in Interwar France." *French Historical Studies* 25, no. 3 (2002): 441–73.

Gadourek, I., and J. L. Jenson. "Proscription and Acceptance of Drugs-Taking Habits in the Netherlands." *Mens en Maatschappij* 46 (1971): 376–410.

Gaffney, John, and Diana Holmes, eds. *Stardom in Postwar France.* New York: Berghahn Books, 2007.

Garofalo, Reebee. *Rockin' the Boat: Mass Music and Mass Movements.* Boston: South End Press, 1992.

Gayler, Birgitte. *Jugendliche Tramper: Beiträge zum Wettbewerb 'Jugend reist und lernt Europa kennen.'* Starnberg: Studienkreis für Tourismus, 1986.

———. *Wettbewerb Jugend reist und lernt Europa kennen.* Starnberg: Studienkreis für Tourismus, 1986.

Gayler, Birgitte, and Elke Kroiss. *Osteuropareisen junger Deutscher vor und nach der politischen Wende.* Starnberg: Studienkreis für Tourismus, 1991.

Germond, Carine, and Henning Türk, eds. *A History of Franco-German Relations in Europe: From "Hereditary Enemies" to Partners.* New York: Palgrave Macmillan, 2008.

Ghione, Paola, and Marco Grispigni, eds. *Giovani prima della rivolta.* Rome: Manifestolibri, 1998.

Giachetti, Diego. *Anni Sessanta, comincia la danza: Giovani, Capelloni, studenti ed estremisti negli anni della contestazione.* Pisa: Seratini, 2002.

Gilcher-Holtey, Ingrid, ed. *1968: Vom Ereignis zum Gegenstand der Geschichtswissenschaft.* Göttingen: Vandenhoeck & Ruprecht, 1998.

Gildea, Robert. *The Past in French History.* New Haven: Yale University Press, 1994.

Gildea, Robert, James Mark, and Anette Warring, eds. *Europe's 1968: Voices of Revolt.* Oxford: Oxford University Press, 2013.

Ginier, Jean. *Les touristes étrangers en France pendant l'été.* Paris: Génin, 1969.

Ginsborg, Paul. *A History of Contemporary Italy: Society and Politics, 1943–1988.* New York: Palgrave Macmillan, 2003.

Glaser, Hermann. *The Rubble Years: The Cultural Roots of Postwar Germany.* New York: Paragon House, 1986.

Gloaguen, Philippe. *Une vie de routard.* Paris: Calmann-Lévy, 2006.

Gloaguen, Philippe, and Patrice Trapier. *Génération routard.* Paris: JC Lattès, 1994.

Golan, Galia. *The Czechoslovak Reform Movement: Communism in Crisis, 1962–1968.* Cambridge: Cambridge University Press, 1971.

———. "Youth and Politics in Czechoslovakia." *Journal of Contemporary History* 5, no. 1 (1970): 3–22.

Gordon, Daniel A. "The Back Door of the Nation State: Expulsions of Foreigners and Continuity in Twentieth-Century France." *Past & Present,* no. 186 (February 2005): 201–32.

———. "Immigrants and the New Left in France, 1968–1971." PhD diss., University of Sussex, 2001.

Gorsuch, Anne E. *All This Is Your World: Soviet Tourism at Home and Abroad after Stalin.* Oxford: Oxford University Press, 2011.

Gorsuch, Anne E., and Diane P. Koenker, eds. *The Socialist Sixties: Crossing Borders in the Second World.* Bloomington: Indiana University Press, 2013.

———, eds. *Turizm: The Russian and East European Tourist under Capitalism and Socialism.* Ithaca, NY: Cornell University Press, 2006.

Gostmann, Peter, and Lars Schatilow. *Europa unterwegs: Die europäische Integration und der Kulturtourismus.* Berlin: Lit, 2008.

Gottlieb, Sherry Gershon. *Hell No, We Won't Go! Resisting the Draft during the Vietnam War.* New York: Viking, 1991.

Götze, Karl-Heinz, ed. *France-Allemagne: Passions croisées.* Aix-en-Provence: Université de Provence, 2001.

Goudsblom, J. *De nieuwe volwassenen: Een enquete onder jongeren van 18 tot 30 jaar.* Amsterdam: De Salamander, 1959.

Graburn, Nelson H. H. "The Anthropology of Tourism." *Annals of Tourism Research* 10, no. 1 (1983): 9–33.

Granahan, Brendan. *Voyager: An American Prayer.* N.p.: Xlibris, 2001.

Grandits, Hannes, and Karin Taylor, eds. *Yugoslavia's Sunny Side: A History of Tourism in Socialism (1950s–1980s).* Budapest: Central European University Press, 2010.

Grant, Matthew T. "Death-Trips, Power-Trips, and Head-Trips: Bernward Vesper's *Die Reise.*" *Border/Lines,* 1 July 1996, 4–10.

Grassl, Anton, and Graham Heath. *The Magic Triangle: A Short History of the World Youth Hostel Movement.* N.p.: International Youth Hostel Federation, 1982.

Green, Jonathon. *It: Sex since the Sixties.* London: Secker & Warburg, 1993.

Greenblatt, Stephen. *Cultural Mobility: A Manifesto.* Cambridge: Cambridge University Press, 2010.

Griffiths, Richard T., ed. *The Netherlands and the Integration of Europe, 1945–1957.* Amsterdam: Neeha, 1990.

Guarnaccia, Matteo. *Beat e mondo beat: Chi sono i beats, i provos, i capelloni*. Rome: Stampa alternative, 2005.

———. *Paradiso psichedelico: Amsterdam 1976–74; La mecca degli hippies*. Bertiolo: AAA Edizioni, 1998.

Guérin, Daniel. *The Brown Plague: Travels in Late Weimar and Early Nazi Germany*. Translated by Robert Schwartzwald. Durham, NC: Duke University Press, 1994.

Guichard-Anguis, Sylvie, and Okpyo Moon, eds. *Japanese Tourism and Travel Culture*. New York: Routledge, 2009.

Gumpel, Werner, ed. *Griechenland und die Europäische Gemeinschaft*. Munich: R. Oldenbourg, 1980.

Gundle, Stephen. *Between Hollywood and Moscow: The Italian Communists and the Challenge of Mass Culture, 1943–1991*. Durham, NC: Duke University Press, 2000.

Günther, Armin, Hans Hopfinger, Jürgen Kagelmann, and Walter Kiefl, eds. *Tourismusforschung in Bayern: Aktuelle sozialwissenschaftliche Beiträge*. Munich: Profil Verlag, 2006.

Gurevich, David. *From Lenin to Lennon: A Memoir of Russia in the Sixties*. San Diego: Harcourt Brace Jovanovich, 1991.

Hacking, Ian. *Mad Travelers: Reflections on the Reality of Transient Mental Illnesses*. Charlottesville: University of Virginia Press, 1998.

Hahn, Heinz, ed. *Internationaler Jugendtourismus*. Starnberg: Studienkreis für Tourismus, 1966.

Hahn, Heinz, and H. Jürgen Kagelmann, eds. *Tourismuspsychologie und Tourismussoziologie: Ein Handbuch zur Tourismuswissenschaft*. Munich: Quintessenz, 1993.

Halimi, Gisèle, ed. *Viol: Le procès d'Aix-en-Provence*. Paris: Gallimard, 1978.

Hall, C. Michael, and Allan M. Williams, eds. *Tourism and Migration: New Relationships between Production and Consumption*. Dordrecht: Kluwer, 2002.

Hampton, Mark P. *Backpacker Tourism and Economic Development: Perspectives from the Less Developed World*. London: Routledge, 2013.

Hannam, Kevin, and Irena Ateljevic, eds. *Backpacker Tourism: Concepts and Profiles*. Clevedon: Channel View, 2008.

Hansen, Peo, and Stefan Jonsson. *Eurafrica: The Untold History of European Integration and Colonialism*. London: Bloomsbury, 2014.

Hardwick, Louise, ed. *New Approaches to Crime in French Literature, Culture and Film*. Bern: Peter Lang, 2009.

Harp, Stephen L. *Au Naturel: Naturism, Nudism, and Tourism in Twentieth-Century France*. Baton Rouge: Louisiana University Press, 2014.

Harribey, Laurence Eberhard. *L'Europe et la jeunesse: Comprendre une politique européenne au regard de la dualité institutionnelle Conseil de l'Europe-Union européenne*. Paris: L'Harmattan, 2002.

Hartmann, Jürgen. "The Significance of Youth Mobility and Travel in Western Europe: The Case of Sweden." *European Yearbook on Youth Policy and Research* 1 (1995): 63–74.

———. "Youth Tourism in Post-Industrial Society." *Sociologia urbana e rurale* 13, no. 38 (1992): 377–90.

Heath, Graham, ed. *The International Youth Hostel Manual.* Copenhagen: International Youth Hostel Federation, 1954.

Heineman, Elizabeth. *Before Porn Was Legal: The Erotica Empire of Beate Uhse.* Chicago: University of Chicago Press, 2011.

Hekma, Gert, and Alain Giami, eds. *Sexual Revolutions.* New York: Palgrave Macmillan, 2014.

Hellman, John. *The Communitarian Third Way: Alexandre Marc's Ordre Nouveau, 1930–2000.* Montreal: McGill-Queen's University Press, 2002.

Hendriks, Gisela, and Annette Morgan. *The Franco-German Axis in European Integration.* Cheltenham: Edward Elgar, 2001.

Hensel, Jana. *After the Wall: Confessions from an East German Childhood and the Life That Came Next.* Translated by Jefferson Chase. New York: Public Affairs, 2004.

Herzog, Dagmar. "'Pleasure, Sex, and Politics Belong Together': Post-Holocaust Memory and the Sexual Revolution in West Germany." *Critical Inquiry* 24, no. 2 (1998): 393–444.

———. *Sex after Fascism: Memory and Morality in Twentieth-Century Germany.* Princeton: Princeton University Press, 2005.

———. *Sexuality in Europe: A Twentieth-Century History.* Cambridge: Cambridge University Press, 2011.

Higbee, Will. *Post-Beur Cinema: North African Emigré and Maghrebi-French Filmmaking in France since 2000.* Edinburgh: Edinburgh University Press, 2013.

Hillel, Marc. *L'occupation française en Allemagne, 1945–1949.* Paris: Balland, 1983.

Hilwig, Stuart J. *Italy and 1968: Youthful Unrest and Democratic Culture.* New York: Palgrave Macmillan, 2009.

Hinton, Brian. *Message to Love: The Isle of Wight Festivals, 1968–1970.* Chessington: Castle Communications, 1995.

Hitchcock, William I. *The Struggle for Europe: The Turbulent History of a Divided Continent, 1945 to the Present.* New York: Anchor Books, 2003.

Hoffa, William W. *A History of US Study Abroad: Beginnings to 1965.* Carlisle, PA: Forum on Education Abroad, 2007.

Hoffa, William W., and Stephen C. DePaul, eds. *A History of U.S. Study Abroad, 1965–Present.* Carlisle, PA: Forum on Education Abroad, 2010.

Högselius, Per. *Red Gas: Russia and the Origins of European Energy Dependence.* New York: Palgrave Macmillan, 2013.

Hollier, Robert, and Alexandra Subremon. *Le tourisme dans la Communauté européenne.* Paris: Presses Universitaires de France, 1990.

Holmes, Richard. *Footsteps: Adventures of a Romantic Biographer.* New York: Penguin, 1985.

Honeck, Mischa, and Gabriel Rosenberg, eds. "Transnational Generations: Organizing Youth in the Cold War West, 1945–1960." Special forum, *Diplomatic History* 38, no. 2 (2014): 233–98.

Horak, Sinisa, and Sanda Weber. "Youth Tourism in Europe: Problems and Prospects." *Tourism Recreation Research* 25, no. 3 (2000): 37–44.

Horgby, Björn, and Fredrik Nilsson, eds. *Rockin' the Borders: Rock Music and Social, Cultural, and Political Change.* Newcastle upon Tyne: Cambridge Scholars, 2010.

Horn, Gerd-Rainer. *The Spirit of '68: Rebellion in Western Europe and North America, 1956–1976.* Oxford: Oxford University Press, 2007.

Horn, Gerd-Rainer, and Padraic Kenney, eds. *Transnational Moments of Change: Europe 1945, 1968, 1989.* Lanham, MD: Rowman & Littlefield, 2004.

Hyland, Pauline. *Space Cake in Chicken Street: Travelling the Hippie Trail London-to-Kathmandu, 1977.* Geelong: Pauline Hyland, 2009.

Ilic, Melanie, Susan E. Reid, and Lynne Attwood, eds. *Women in the Khrushchev Era.* New York: Palgrave Macmillan, 2004.

Imig, Doug, and Sidney Tarrow, eds. *Contentious Europeans: Protest and Politics in an Emerging Polity.* Lanham, MD: Rowman & Littlefield, 2001.

Inglehart, Ronald. "Changing Value Priorities and European Integration." *Journal of Common Market Studies* 10, no. 1 (1971): 1–36.

———. "An End to European Integration?" *American Political Science Review* 61, no. 1 (March 1967): 91–105.

———. "The New Europeans: Inward or Outward-Looking?" *International Organization* 24, no. 1 (Winter 1970): 129–39.

Ireland, Brian, and Sharif Gemie. "From Kerouac to the Hippy Trail: Some Notes on the Attraction of *On the Road* to British Hippies." *Studies in Travel Writing* 19, no. 1 (2015): 66–82.

Iriye, Akira. *Cultural Internationalism and World Order.* Baltimore: Johns Hopkins University Press, 1997.

———. *Global Community: The Role of International Organizations in the Making of the Contemporary World.* Berkeley: University of California Press, 2002.

Jansen, A. C. M. *Cannabis in Amsterdam: A Geography of Hashish and Marijuana.* Muiderberg: Dick Coutinho, 1991.

Jarausch, Konrad H. *After Hitler: Recivilizing Germans, 1945–1995.* Oxford: Oxford University Press, 2008.

———. "Die postnationale Nation: Zum Identitätswandel der Deutschen 1945–1995." *Historicum: Zeitschrift für Geschichte* 30 (Spring 1995): 30–35.

Jarausch, Konrad H., and Thomas Lindenberger, eds. *Conflicted Memories: Europeanizing Contemporary Histories.* New York: Berghahn Books, 2007.

Jensen, Jette. *Ungdomsturister i København 1971: Young Tourists in Copenhagen, 1971.* Copenhagen: Københavns Statistiske Kontor, 1972.

Jobs, Richard Ivan. *Riding the New Wave: Youth and the Rejuvenation of France after the Second World War.* Stanford: Stanford University Press, 2007.

Jobs, Richard Ivan, and David M. Pomfret, eds. *Transnational Histories of Youth in the Twentieth Century.* New York: Palgrave Macmillan, 2015.

Jones, Kathryn N. *Journeys of Remembrance: Memories of the Second World War in French and German Literature, 1960–1980.* London: Legenda, 2007.

Judt, Tony. *Postwar: A History of Europe since 1945.* New York: Penguin, 2005.

Junker, Detlef, ed. *The United States and Germany in the Era of the Cold War.* Cambridge: Cambridge University Press, 2004.

Jürgens, Hanco, Jacco Pekelder, Falk Bretschneider, and Klaus Bachmann, eds. *Eine Welt zu gewinnen! Formen und Folgen der 68er Bewegung in Ost- und Westeuropa.* Leipzig: Leipziger Universitätsverlag, 2009.

Jurt, Joseph, ed. *Von der Besatzungszeit zur deutsch-französischen Kooperation.* Freiburg: Rombach Verlag, 1993.

Kagie, Rudie. "Het magisch centrum is verdwenen." *Jeugd en Samenleving* 12, no. 7 (July 1982): 29–35.

Kaiser, Wolfram, and Peter Starie, eds. *Transnational European Union: Towards a Common Political Space.* London: Routledge, 2005.

Kamsma, Theo. "Greetings from Amsterdam, Holland: Een studie naar de jeugdtoeristische beleidspraktijk in Amsterdam 1969–1990." PhD diss., Vrije Universiteit, July 1991.

Kaplan, Alice. *French Lessons: A Memoir.* Chicago: University of Chicago Press, 1993.

Katsiaficas, George. *The Imagination of the New Left: A Global Analysis of 1968.* Boston: South End Press, 1987.

Kennedy, James C. "Building New Babylon: Cultural Change in the Netherlands during the 1960s." PhD diss., University of Iowa, May 1995.

———. *Nieuw Babylon in aanbouw: Nederland in de jaren zestig.* Amsterdam: Boom, 1995.

Kentler, Helmut. *Urlaub als Auszug aus dem Alltag.* Munich: Studienkreis für Tourismus, 1963.

———. *Urlaub auf Sizilien: Beobachtungen in einem Jugendferienlager am Mittelmeer.* Munich: Studienkreis für Tourismus, 1963.

Kirschbaum, Erik. *Rocking the Wall: Bruce Springsteen; The Untold Story of a Concert in East Berlin That Changed the World.* New York: Berlinica, 2013.

Klauss, Cornelia, and Frank Böttcher, eds. *Unerkannt durch Freundesland: Illegale reisen durch das Sowjetreich.* Berlin: Lukas Verlag, 2011.

Kleindienst, Jürgen, ed. *Mauer-Passagen: Grenzgänge, Fluchten und Reisen 1961–1989.* Berlin: Zeitgut Verlag, 2009.

Kleinschmidt, Christian. "Infrastructure, Networks, (Large) Technical Systems: The 'Hidden Integration' of Europe." *Contemporary European History* 19, no. 3 (2010): 275–84.

Klimke, Martin. *The Other Alliance: Student Protest in West Germany and the United States in the Global Sixties.* Princeton: Princeton University Press, 2010.

Klimke, Martin, Jacco Pekelder, and Joachim Scharloth, eds. *Between Prague Spring and French May: Opposition and Revolt in Europe, 1960–1980.* New York: Berghahn Books, 2013.

Klimke, Martin, and Joachim Scharloth. *1968 in Europe: A History of Protest and Activism, 1956–1977.* New York: Palgrave Macmillan, 2008.

Korda, Michael. *Journey to a Revolution: A Personal Memoir and History of the Hungarian Revolution of 1956.* New York: HarperCollins, 2006.

Kornetis, Kostis. "'Everything Links'? Temporality, Territoriality and Cultural Transfer in the '68 Protest Movements." *Historein* 9 (2009): 34–45.

Kosel, Margret. *Gammler Beatniks Provos: Die schleichende Revolution*. Frankfurt: Verlag Bärmeier & Nikel, 1967.

Koshar, Rudy. *German Travel Cultures*. London: Bloomsbury, 2000.

———, ed. *Histories of Leisure*. Oxford: Berg, 2002.

———. "'What ought to be seen': Tourists' Guidebooks and National Identities in Modern Germany and Europe." *Journal of Contemporary History* 33, no. 3 (July 1998): 323–40.

Kössler, Till, and Alexander J. Schwitanski, eds. *Frieden lernen: Friedenspädagogik und Erziehung im 20. Jahrhundert*. Essen: Klartext-Verlag, 2014.

Kozakowski, Michael A. "Making 'Mediterranean Migrants': Geopolitical Transitions, Migratory Policy, and French Conceptions of the Mediterranean in the 20th Century." *Cahiers de la Méditerranée* 89 (2014): 181–93.

Kroes, Rob, Robert W. Rydell, and Doeko F. J. Bosscher, eds. *Cultural Transmissions and Receptions: American Mass Culture in Europe*. Amsterdam: Vrije University Press, 1993.

Krotz, Ulrich. "Parapublic Underpinnings of International Relations: The Franco-German Construction of Europeanization of a Particular Kind." *European Journal of International Relations* 13, no. 3 (2007): 385–417.

Lanfant, Marie-Françoise. "Introduction: Tourism in the Process of Internationalization." *International Social Science Journal* 32, no. 1 (1980): 14–43.

Laqua, Daniel, ed. *Internationalism Reconfigured: Transnational Ideas and Movements between the World Wars*. London: I. B. Tauris, 2011.

Laqueur, Walter. *Young Germany: A History of the German Youth Movement*. London: Routledge & Kegan Paul, 1962.

Leblond, Laurent. *Le couple franco-allemand depuis 1945: Chronique d'une relation exemplaire*. Paris: Le Monde-Editions, 1997.

Leed, Eric J. *The Mind of the Traveler: From Gilgamesh to Global Tourism*. New York: Basic Books, 1991.

Lefebvre, Henri. *The Production of Space*. Translated by Donald Nicholson-Smith. Oxford: Blackwell, 1991.

Leizaola, Aitzpea. "Mugarik ez! Subverting the Border in the Basque Country." *Ethnologia Europaea* 30, no. 2 (2000): 35–46.

Leuw, E. *Druggebruik in het Vondelpark 1972*. Amsterdam: Stichting voor alcohol- en drugsonderzoek, 1972.

Leuw, Ed., and I. Haen Marshall, eds. *Between Prohibition and Legalization: The Dutch Experiment in Drug Policy*. Amsterdam: Kugler, 1994.

Levenstein, Harvey. *We'll Always Have Paris: American Tourists in France since 1930*. Chicago: University of Chicago Press, 2004.

Lévi-Strauss, Claude. *Tristes tropiques*. Translated by John Weightman and Doreen Weightman. New York: Penguin, 2012.

Levy, Alan. *So Many Heroes*. Sagaponack, NY: Second Chance Press, 1972.

Lewis, Phil. *Amsterdam after Dark*. New York: MacFadden-Bartell, 1969.

Lisiecki, Stanisław. "Die Auslandstouristik der westdeutschen: Jugend als Element der politischen Bildung und der Aussenpolitik der Bundesrepublik Deutschland." *Aktuelle Ostinformationen* 12, no. 2–3 (1980): 97–124.

Liston, Robert A. *Young Americans Abroad.* New York: Julian Messner, 1971.

Littlewood, Ian. *Sultry Climates: Travel and Sex.* Cambridge, MA: Da Capo Press, 2001.

Lodge, David. *Out of the Shelter.* London: Penguin Books, 1970.

Loersch, Chris, and Nathan L. Arbuckle. "Unraveling the Mystery of Music: Music as an Evolved Group Process." *Journal of Personality and Social Psychology* 105, no. 5 (2013): 777–98.

Löfgren, Orvar. *On Holiday: A History of Vacationing.* Berkeley: University of California Press, 1999.

Loizos, Peter, and Evthymios Papataxiarchis, eds. *Contested Identities: Gender and Kinship in Modern Greece.* Princeton: Princeton University Press, 1991.

Long, Bronson Wilder. "The Saar Dispute in Franco-German Relations and European Integration: French Diplomacy, Cultural Policies, and the Construction of European Identity in the Saar, 1944–1957." PhD diss., Indiana University, 2007.

Loth, Wilfried. "Explaining European Integration: The Contribution from Historians." *Journal of European Integration History* 14, no. 1 (2008): 9–26.

Lowe, Richard, and William Shaw, eds. *Travellers: Voices of the New Age Nomads.* London: Fourth Estate, 1993.

Luitweiler, Bob. *The Seeds of Servas: Opening Doors for Peace.* San Francisco: Richard Piro, 1999.

Lumley, Robert, and John Foot, eds. *Italian Cityscapes: Culture and Urban Change in Contemporary Italy.* Exeter: University of Exeter Press, 2004.

Lundin, Per, and Thomas Kaiserfeld, eds. *The Making of European Consumption: Facing the American Challenge.* New York: Palgrave Macmillan, 2015.

Lutz, Felix Philipp. "Junge Deutsche im Ausland: Vergangenheitsbewältigung und Vorurteilsabbau." *Beiträge zur Konfliktforschung* 19, no. 2 (1989): 91–112.

Lyons, Amelia. *The Civilizing Mission in the Metropole: Algerian Families and the French Welfare State during Decolonization.* Stanford: Stanford University Press, 2013.

MacGillavry, D. H. D. "Amsterdam beobachtet den Jugendtourismus der nahen zukunft." *Jahrbuch für Jugendreisen und Internationalen Jugendaustausch* (1971): 72–78.

MacInnes, Colin. *Absolute Beginners.* London: Farrar, Strauss & Giroux, 1959.

———. *England, Half English.* London: Hogarth Press, 1961.

Mack, Joanna, and Steve Humphries. *London at War: The Making of Modern London, 1939–1945.* London: Sidgwick & Johnson, 1985.

Mack, Joe. *1968 and I'm Hitchhiking through Europe.* Philadelphia: Solid Press, 2005.

MacLean, Rory. *Magic Bus: On the Hippie Trail from Istanbul to India.* Brooklyn: Ig, 2006.

Mahood, Linda. "Hitchin' a Ride in the 1970s: Canadian Youth Culture and the Romance with Mobility." *Histoire sociale/Social History* 47, no. 93 (2014): 205–27.

———. "Thumb Wars: Hitchhiking, Canadian Youth Rituals and Risk in the Twentieth Century." *Journal of Social History* 49, no. 3 (2016): 647–70.

Maier, Charles S. "Consigning the Twentieth Century to History: Alternative Narratives for the Modern Era." *American Historical Review* 105, no. 3 (June 2000): 807–31.

Maira, Sunaina, and Elisabeth Soep, eds. *Youthscapes: The Popular, the National, the Global.* Philadelphia: University of Pennsylvania Press, 2005.

Major, Patrick, and Jonathan Osmond, eds. *The Workers' and Peasants' State: Communism and Society in East Germany under Ulbricht, 1945–71.* Manchester: Manchester University Press, 2002.

Mamadouh, Virginie. *De stad in eigen hand: Provo's, kabouters en krakers als stedelijke sociale beweging.* The Hague: Uitgeverij Sua, 1992.

Mankoff, Alan H. *Mankoff's Lusty Europe: The First All-Purpose European Guide to Sex, Love, and Romance.* New York: Viking Press, 1972.

Maoz, Darya. "Backpackers' Motivation: The Role of Culture and Nationality." *Annals of Tourism Research* 34, no. 1 (2007): 122–40.

Marker, Emily. "France between Europe and Africa: Youth, Education and Envisioning the Postwar World, 1940–1960." PhD diss., University of Chicago, 2016.

———. "Obscuring Race: Franco-African Conversations about Colonial Reform and Racism after World War II and the Making of Colorblind France, 1945–1950." *French Politics, Culture & Society* 33, no. 3 (2015): 1–23.

Markov, Georgi. *The Truth That Killed.* Translated by Liliana Brisby. New York: Ticknor & Fields, 1984.

Martinegro, Maria, and Luca Savoja. *Giovani e turismo: Un'indagine sulle vacanze giovanili.* Milan: FrancoAngeli, 1993.

Marwick, Arthur. *The Sixties: Cultural Revolution in Britain, France, Italy, and the United States, c. 1958–c. 1974.* New York: Oxford University Press, 1998.

Mayer, Sandro, ed. *Lettere dei capelloni italiani.* Milan: Longanesi, 1968.

McCormick, John. *Understanding the European Union: A Concise Introduction.* New York: Palgrave Macmillan, 2005.

McDonough, Tom, ed. *Guy Debord and the Situationist International: Texts and Documents.* Cambridge, MA: MIT Press, 2004.

McDougall, Alan. *Youth Politics in East Germany: The Free German Youth Movement, 1946–1968.* Oxford: Oxford University Press, 2005.

McLellan, Josie. *Love in the Time of Communism: Intimacy and Sexuality in the GDR.* Cambridge: Cambridge University Press, 2011.

Ménudier, Henri, ed. *Le couple franco-allemand en Europe.* Asnières: Pia, 1993.

———. *L'Office franco-allemand pour la jeunesse: Une contribution exemplaire à l'unité de l'Europe.* Paris: Armand Colin, 1988.

Merritt, Richard L., and Donald J. Puchala. *Western European Perspectives on International Affairs: Public Opinion Studies and Evaluations.* New York: Frederick A. Praeger, 1968.

Michener, James A. *The Drifters: A Novel.* New York: Random House, 1971.

Miller, Jim. *The Rolling Stone Illustrated History of Rock 'n' Roll.* New York: Rolling Stone Press, 1976.

Milward, Alan S. *The European Rescue of the Nation-State.* Berkeley: University of California Press, 1992.

Mintel Publications. "Independent Travel—A Bias towards Youth." *Leisure Intelligence* 1 (1991): 1–32.

Misa, Thomas J., and Johan Schot. "Inventing Europe: Technology and the Hidden Integration of Europe." *History and Technology* 21, no. 1 (2005): 1–20.

Mittag, Jürgen, and Diana Wendland. "How Adventurers Become Tourists: The Emergence of Alternative Travel Guides in the Course of Standardisation of Long-Distance Travelling." *Comparativ* 24, no. 2 (2014): 36–51.

Möhring, Maren. "Tourism and Migration: Interrelated Forms of Mobility." *Comparativ* 24, no. 2 (2014): 116–23.

Mombert, Monique. *Sous le signe de la rééducation: Jeunesse et livre en zone française d'occupation, 1945–1949.* Strasbourg: Presses universitaires de Strasbourg, 1995.

Moretti, Franco. *The Way of the World: The Bildungsroman in European Culture.* London: Verso, 1987.

Mossuz-Lavau, Janine. *Les lois de l'amour: Les politiques de la sexualité en France.* Paris: Petit bibliothèque Payot, 2002.

Mukerji, Chandra. "Bullshitting: Road Lore among Hitchhikers." *Social Problems* 25, no. 3 (1978): 241–52.

Musée d'ethnographie de la Ville Neuchâtel. *Être nomade aujourd'hui.* Neuchâtel: Institut d'ethnologie de l'Université, 1979.

Neville, Richard. *Play Power: Exploring the International Underground.* New York: Vintage Books, 1971.

Ngai, Mae M. "Promises and Perils of Transnational History." *Perspectives on History*, December 2012. https://www.historians.org/publications-and-directories /perspectives-on-history/december-2012/the-future-of-the-discipline/promises -and-perils-of-transnational-history.

Noonan, F. Thomas. *The Road to Jerusalem: Pilgrimage and Travel in the Age of Discovery.* Philadelphia: University of Pennsylvania Press, 2007.

Nooteboom, Cees. *Nomad's Hotel: Travels in Time and Space.* Translated by Ann Kelland. London: Harvill Secker, 2006.

———. *Philip and the Others.* Translated by Adrienne Dixon. Baton Rouge: Louisiana State University Press, 1988.

Nora, Pierre, ed. *Les lieux de mémoire II: La Nation.* Paris: Gallimard, 1986.

Norwig, Christina. *Die erste europäische Generation: Europakonstruktionen in der Europäischen Jugendkampagne 1951–1958.* Göttingen: Wallstein Verlag, 2016.

———. "A First European Generation? The Myth of Youth and European Integration in the Fifties." *Diplomatic History* 38, no. 2 (2014): 251–60.

Noy, Chaim. "Narratives of Hegemonic Masculinity: Presentations of Body and Space in Israeli Backpackers' Narratives." *Israeli Sociology* 5, no. 1 (2003): 75–120.

———. "Traversing Hegemony: Gender, Body, and Identity in the Narratives of Israeli Female Backpackers." *Tourism Review International* 12 (2008): 93–114.

Noy, Chaim, and Erik Cohen, eds. *Israeli Backpackers: From Tourism to Rite of Passage*. Albany: State University of New York Press, 2005.

Nugent, Thomas. *The Grand Tour; or, A Journey through the Netherlands, Germany, Italy and France*. London: Printed for D. Browne, A. Millar, G. Hawkins, W. Johnston, and P. Davey and B. Law, 1756.

Nyíri, Pál. *Mobility and Cultural Authority in Contemporary China*. Seattle: University of Washington Press, 2010.

O'Connor, Philip. *Vagrancy: Ethos and Actuality*. London: Penguin, 1963.

Ogata, Sadako, Daniel Cohn-Bendit, Adrian Fortescue, Raffiq Haddaoui, and Igor V. Khalevinski. *Towards a European Immigration Policy*. Brussels: Philip Morris Institute for Public Policy Research, 1993.

Ohliger, Rainer, Karen Schönwälder, and Triadafilos Triafilopoulos, eds. *European Encounters: Migrants, Migration and European Societies since 1945*. Aldershot: Ashgate, 2003.

O'Reilly, Camille Caprioglio. "From Drifter to Gap Year Tourist: Mainstreaming Backpacker Travel." *Annals of Tourism Research* 33, no. 4 (2006): 998–1017.

Ortoleva, Peppino. *I movimenti del '68 in Europa e in America*. Rome: Riuniti, 1998.

Ott, Hanns. "Die Europäischen Jugendwochen: Konzeption und Realisierung." *Jahrbuch für Jugendreisen und Internationalen Jugendaustausch* (1975), 9–34.

Pack, Sasha D. "Revival of the Pilgrimage to Santiago de Compostela: The Politics of Religious, National, and European Patrimony, 1879–1988." *Journal of Modern History* 82, no. 2 (June 2010): 335–67.

———. *Tourism and Dictatorship: Europe's Peaceful Invasion of Franco's Spain*. New York: Palgrave Macmillan, 2006.

Padover, Saul K. *Psychologist in Germany: The Story of an American Intelligence Officer*. London: Phoenix House, 1946.

Palayret, Jean-Marie. "Eduquer les jeunes a l'Union: La Campagne européenne de la jeunesse (1951–1958)." *Journal of European Integration History* 1, no. 2 (1995): 47–60.

Panchasi, Roxanne. " 'Fortress France': Protecting the Nation and Its Bodies, 1918–1940." *Historical Reflections/Réflexions Historiques* 33, no. 3 (2007): 475–504.

Papadogiannis, Nikolaos. *Militant around the Clock? Left-Wing Youth Politics, Leisure, and Sexuality in Post-Dictatorship Greece, 1974–1981*. New York: Berghahn Books, 2015.

———. "Travel and the Greek Migrant Youth Residing in West Germany in the 1960s–1970s." *Comparativ* 24, no. 2 (2014): 67–87.

Papadogiannis, Nikolaos, and Detlef Siegfried, eds. "Between Leisure, Work and Study: Tourism and Mobility in Europe from 1945 to 1989." Special issue, *Comparativ* 24, no. 2 (2014).

Pas, Nicolas. "Images d'une révolte ludique: Le mouvement néerlandais Provo en France dans les années soixante." *Revue historique* 2, no. 129 (2005): 343–73.

Pas, Niek. *Imaazje! De verbeelding van Provo 1965–1967*. Amsterdam: Wereldbibliotheek, 2003.

Passerini, Luisa, ed. *Across the Atlantic: Cultural Exchanges between Europe and the United States*. Brussels: P.I.E.-Peter Lang, 2000.

———. *Autobiography of a Generation: Italy, 1968*. Translated by Lisa Erdberg. Hanover, CT: Wesleyan University Press, 1996.

Patel, Kiran Klaus. "Provincialising European Union: Co-operation and Integration in a Historical Perspective." *Contemporary European History* 22, no. 4 (2013): 649–73.

———. "Where and When Was Europe? Europeanness and Its Relationship to Migration." *National Identities* 15, no. 1 (2013): 21–32.

Perraton, Hilary. *A History of Foreign Students in Britain*. New York: Palgrave Macmillan, 2014.

Phillips, Caryl. *The European Tribe*. New York: Vintage, 2000.

Phillipson, Robert. *Linguistic Imperialism*. Oxford: Oxford University Press, 1992.

Piccini, Joe. "Travel, Politics, and the Limits of Liminality during Australia's Sixties." *PORTAL: Journal of Multidisciplinary International Studies* 10, no. 1 (2013). doi: http://dx.doi.org/10.5130/portal.v10i1.2372.

Picht, Robert, and Wolfgang Wessels, eds. *Motor für Europa? Deutsch-französischer Bilateralismus und europäische Integration*. Bonn: Europa Union Verlag, 1990.

Pistone, Sergio, ed. *I movimenti per l'unità europea 1954–1969*. Pavia: Università di Pavia, 1996.

Plenzdorf, Ulrich. *The New Sufferings of Young W*. Translated by Kenneth P. Wilcox. New York: Frederick Ungar, 1979.

Plum, Jacqueline. "Französische Kulturpolitik in Deutschland 1945–1955: Das Beispiel der Jugendpolitik und privaten Organisationen." PhD diss., Rhenischen Friedrich-Wilhelms-Universität zu Bonn, 2005.

Poiger, Uta G. *Jazz, Rock, and Rebels: Cold War Politics and American Culture in a Divided Germany*. Berkeley: University of California Press, 2000.

"Politik des Reisens? Eine Untersuchung über die Bedeutung von Auslandsreisen für die Schaffung eines Europabewußtseins." *Europa-Archiv* 9, no. 7 (April 1954): 6461–68.

Pomfret, David M. *Youth and Empire: Trans-Colonial Childhoods in British and French Asia*. Stanford: Stanford University Press, 2016.

Prato, Paolo. "Selling Italy by the Sound: Cross-Cultural Interchanges through Cover Records." *Popular Music* 26, no. 3 (2007): 441–62.

Pries, Ludger, ed. *New Transnational Social Spaces: International Migration and Transnational Companies in the Early Twenty-First Century*. London: Routledge, 2011.

Prott, Jürgen, and Ute Stoltenberg. *Wege zur internationalen Solidarität: Erfahrungen und Perspektiven deutsch-französischer Begegnungen junger Gerwerkschafter.* Munich: Verlag Deutsches Jugendinstitut, 1980.

Puaca, Brian M. *Learning Democracy: Education Reform in West Germany, 1945–1965.* New York: Berghahn Books, 2009.

Rasmussen, Morten, and Ann-Christina L. Knudsen, eds. *The Road to a United Europe: Interpretations of the Process of European Integration.* Brussels: Peter Lang, 2009.

Rauhut, Michael, Thomas Kochan, and Christoph Dieckmann, eds. *Bye Bye, Lübben City: Bluesfreaks, Tramps, und Hippies in der DDR.* Berlin: Schwarzkopf & Schwarzkopf, 2004.

Rebuschat, Patrick, Martin Rohrmeier, John A. Hawkins, and Ian Cross, eds. *Language and Music as Cognitive Systems.* Oxford: Oxford University Press, 2012.

Reis, Jehnie I. "Cultural Internationalism at the Cité Universitaire: International Education between the First and Second World Wars." *History of Education* 39, no. 2 (March 2010): 155–73.

Rennella, Mark. *The Boston Cosmopolitans: International Travel and American Arts and Letters.* New York: Palgrave Macmillan, 2008.

Reulecke, Jürgen, ed. *Rückkehr in die Ferne: Die deutsche Jugend in der Nachkriegszeit und das Ausland.* Munich: Juventa Verlag, 1997.

Reulecke, Jürgen, and Barbara Stambolis, eds. *100 Jahre Jugendherbergen 1909–2009.* Essen: Klartext Verlag, 2009.

Richards, Greg. *Youth Travel Matters: Understanding the Global Phenomenon of Youth Travel.* Madrid: World Tourism Organization, 2008.

Richards, Greg, and Julie Wilson, eds. *The Global Nomad: Backpacker Travel in Theory and Practice.* Clevedon: Channel View, 2004.

Righart, Hans. *De eindeloze jaren zestig: Geschiedenis van een generatieconflict.* Amsterdam: Uitgeverij De Arbeiderspers, 1995.

———. *De wereldwijde jaren zestig: Groot-Brittannië, Nederland, de Verenigde Staten.* Utrecht: Universiteit Utrecht, 2004.

Riley, Pamela J. "Road Culture of International Long-Term Budget Travelers." *Annals of Tourism Research* 15, no. 3 (1988): 313–28.

Risch, William Jay. "Soviet 'Flower Children': Hippies and the Youth Counter-Culture in 1970s L'viv." *Journal of Contemporary History* 40, no. 3 (2005): 565–84.

———, ed. *Youth and Rock in the Soviet Bloc: Youth Cultures, Music, and the State in Russia and Eastern Europe.* Lanham, MD: Lexington Books, 2014.

Robinson, Shirleene, and Simon Sleight, eds. *Children, Childhood and Youth in the British World.* New York: Palgrave Macmillan, 2015.

Röling, H. Q. *Idealisme en toerisme: 50 jaar jeugdherbergen 1929–1979.* Amsterdam: Uitgave NJHC, 1979.

Romero, Federico. "L'Europa come strumento di *nation-building*: Storia e storici dell'Italia repubblicana." *Passato e presente* 13, no. 366 (1995): 19–32.

Rosenau, James N. *Turbulence in World Politics: A Theory of Change and Continuity.* Princeton: Princeton University Press, 1990.

Ross, Corey. "Before the Wall: East Germans, Communist Authority, and the Mass Exodus to the West." *Historical Journal* 45, no. 2 (2002): 459–80.

Ross, Kristin. *The Emergence of Social Space: Rimbaud and the Paris Commune.* Minneapolis: University of Minnesota Press, 1988.

———. *May '68 and Its Afterlives.* Chicago: University of Chicago Press, 2002.

Rovan, Joseph. "Les relations franco-allemandes dans le domaine de la jeunesse et de la culture populaire (1945–1971)." *Revue d'Allemagne* 64, no. 3 (1972): 675–704.

Rozenberg, Danielle. "Tourisme et identités culturelles: Ibiza, une île en Méditerranée." *Les Cahiers du Tourisme* 162 (January 1991): 2–27.

———. *Tourisme et utopie aux Baléares: Ibiza, une île pour une autre vie.* Paris: L'Harmattan, 1990.

Ruff, Mark Edward. *The Wayward Flock: Catholic Youth in Postwar West Germany, 1945–1965.* Chapel Hill: University of North Carolina Press, 2005.

Ruffino, Roberto. *An Assessment of Organized Youth Mobility in Europe.* AFS Occasional Papers in Intercultural Learning, no. 3. New York: AFS, 1983.

Ryback, Timothy W. *Rock around the Bloc: A History of Rock Music in Eastern Europe and the Soviet Union, 1954–1988.* Oxford: Oxford University Press, 1990.

Sassatelli, Monica. "Imagined Europe: The Shaping of a European Cultural Identity through EU Cultural Policy." *European Journal of Social Theory* 5, no. 4 (2002): 435–51.

Sassoon, Donald. *Contemporary Italy: Politics, Economy, and Society since 1945.* London: Longman, 1997.

Sauder, Axel, and Joachim Schild, eds. *Handeln für Europa: Deutsch-französische Zusammenarbeit in einer veränderten Welt.* Opladen: Leske + Budrich, 1995.

Saunders, Anna. *Honecker's Children: Youth and Patriotism in East(ern) Germany, 1979–2002.* Manchester: Manchester University Press, 2007.

Saunier, Pierre-Yves. *Transnational History.* New York: Palgrave Macmillan, 2013.

Schäfer, Hermann, ed. *Endlich Urlaub! Die Deutschen reisen.* Cologne: DuMont Buchverlag, 1996.

Schildt, Axel, and Detlef Siegfried, eds. *Between Marx and Coca-Cola: Youth Cultures in Changing European Societies, 1960–1980.* New York: Berghahn Books, 2005.

Schipper, Frank. *Driving Europe: Building Europe on Roads in the Twentieth Century.* Amsterdam: Aksant, 2008.

Schissler, Hanna. "Postnationality—Luxury of the Privileged? A West German Generational Perspective." *German Politics and Society* 15, no. 2 (1997): 8–27.

Schlink, Bernhard. *The Reader.* Translated by Carol Brown Janeway. New York: Vintage Books, 1997.

Schmidt, Gunter, and Volkmar Sigusch. "Patterns of Sexual Behavior in West German Workers and Students." Translated by Fred Klein. *Journal of Sex Research* 7, no. 2 (May 1971): 89–106.

Schmidt, Harald. *Der Deustche Jugend-Tourist: Jugendsoziologische Studien über Reise-interessen und -tätigkeiten junger Leute aus Ost- und Westdeustchland 1989/90*. Berlin: Verlag für universitäre Kommunikation, 1990.

Schneider, Peter. *Lenz*. Translated by A. Leslie Willson. In *Three Contemporary German Novellas*, edited by A. Leslie Willson, 1–78. New York: Continuum, 2001.

———. *Rebellion und Wahn: Mein 68; Eine autobiographische Erzählung*. Cologne: Kiepenheuer & Witsch, 2008.

———. *The Wall Jumper*. Translated by Leigh Hafrey. New York: Pantheon Books, 1983.

Schönhammer, Rainer. *Jugendliche Europa-Touristen: Eine psychologische Studie über das Reisen im europäischen Netz von Bahn und Jugendherbergen*. Starnberg: Studienkreis für Tourismus, 1987.

———. "Youth Tourism as Appropriation of the World: A Psychological Perspective." *Phenomenology + Pedagogy* 10 (1992): 19–27.

Schwabe, Klaus. "The Cold War and European Integration, 1947–63." *Diplomacy & Statecraft* 12, no. 4 (2001): 18–34.

Schwartz, Harry. *Prague's 200 Days: The Struggle for Democracy in Czechoslovakia*. New York: Frederick A. Praeger, 1969.

Seidman, Michael. *The Imaginary Revolution: Parisian Students and Workers in 1968*. New York: Berghahn Books, 2004.

Shahin, Jamal, and Michael Wintle, eds. *The Idea of a United Europe: Political, Economic and Cultural Integration since the Fall of the Berlin Wall*. New York: Macmillan, 2000.

Sheffer, Edith. *Burned Bridge: How East and West Germans Made the Iron Curtain*. New York: Oxford University Press, 2011.

Sherman, Daniel J. *French Primitivism and the Ends of Empire, 1945–1975*. Chicago: University of Chicago Press, 2011.

Shinkfield, Michael. *A Student's Travel Guide to the Netherlands*. Leiden: Netherlands Office for Foreign Student Relations, 1958.

Shore, Cris. *Building Europe: The Cultural Politics of European Integration*. London: Routledge, 2000.

Siegel, Mona, and Kirsten Harjes. "Disarming Hatred: History Education, National Memories, and Franco-German Reconciliation from World War I to the Cold War." *History of Education Quarterly* 52, no. 3 (2012): 370–402.

Siegfried, Detlef. *Time Is on My Side: Konsum und Politik in der westdeutschen Jugendkultur der 60er Jahre*. Göttingen: Wallstein, 2006.

Sigusch, Volkmar, and Gunter Schmidt. *Jugendsexualität: Dokumentation einer Untersuchung*. Stuttgart: Ferdinand Enke Verlag, 1973.

Silverstein, Paul A. *Algeria in France: Transpolitics, Race, and Nation*. Bloomington: Indiana University Press, 2004.

Slobodian, Quinn. *Foreign Front: Third World Politics in Sixties West Germany*. Durham, NC: Duke University Press, 2012.

Sluga, Glenda. *Internationalism in the Age of Nationalism*. Philadelphia: University of Pennsylvania Press, 2013.

Sobocinska, Agnieszka. "Following the 'Hippie Sahibs': Colonial Cultures of Travel and the Hippie Trail." *Journal of Colonialism and Colonial History* 15, no. 2 (2014). doi: 10.1353/cch.2014.0024.

——. *Visiting the Neighbours: Australians in Asia*. Sydney: NewSouth, 2014.

Solnit, Rebecca. *Wanderlust: A History of Walking*. New York: Penguin Books, 2000.

Spode, Hasso, ed. *Goldstrand und Teutonengrill: Kultur- und Sozialgeschichte des Tourismus in Deutschland 1945 bis 1989*. Berlin: Institut für Tourismus, 1996.

——. *Wie die Deutschen "Reiseweltmeister" wurden: Eine Einführung in die Tourismusgeschichte*. Erfurt: Landeszentrale für politische Bildung Thüringen, 2003.

Spradley, James P., and David W. McCurdy, eds. *The Cultural Experience: Ethnography in Complex Society*. Prospect Heights, IL: Waveland Press, 1972.

Stark, Steven D. *Meet the Beatles: A Cultural History of the Band That Shook Youth, Gender, and the World*. New York: William Morrow, 2005.

Stephens, Robert P. *Germans on Drugs: The Complications of Modernization in Hamburg*. Ann Arbor: University of Michigan Press, 2007.

Stone, Dan, ed. *The Oxford Handbook of Postwar European History*. Oxford: Oxford University Press, 2012.

Stråth, Bo. "A European Identity: To the Historical Limits of a Concept." *European Journal of Social Theory* 5, no. 4 (2002): 387–401.

Suri, Jeremi. *Power and Protest: Global Revolution and the Power of Détente*. Cambridge, MA: Harvard University Press, 2002.

——. "The Rise and Fall of an International Counterculture, 1960–1975." *American Historical Review* 114, no. 1 (February 2009): 45–68.

Sutton, Michael. *France and the Construction of Europe, 1944–2007: The Geopolitical Imperative*. New York: Berghahn Books, 2007.

Taberner, Stuart, and Paul Cooke, eds. *German Culture, Politics, and Literature into the Twenty-First Century: Beyond Normalization*. Rochester, NY: Camden House, 2006.

Tarrow, Sidney. "The Europeanisation of Conflict: Reflections from a Social Movement Perspective." *West European Politics* 18, no. 2 (April 1995): 223–51.

——. *The New Transnational Activism*. Cambridge: Cambridge University Press, 2005.

Tasman, Coen. *Louter kabouter: Kroniek van een beweging 1969–1974*. Amsterdam: Babylon-De Geus, 1996.

Taylor, Frederick. *The Berlin Wall: A World Divided, 1961–1989*. New York: Harper Perennial, 2006.

Taylor, Kathrine Kressman. *Diary of a Florence Flood*. New York: Simon and Schuster, 1967.

Teichler, Ulrich, and Friedhelm Maiworm. *The ERASMUS Experience: Major Findings of the ERASMUS Evaluation Research Project*. Kassel: European Communities, 1997.

ten Have, Paul. "The Counter Culture on the Move: A Field Study of Youth Tourists in Amsterdam." *Mens en maatschappij* 49, no. 3 (1974): 297–315.

Tent, James F. *Mission on the Rhine: Reeducation and Denazification in American-Occupied Germany.* Chicago: University of Chicago Press, 1982.

Teo, Peggy, and Sandra Leong. "A Postcolonial Analysis of Backpacking." *Annals of Tourism Research* 33, no. 1 (2006): 109–31.

Thompson, Edward, ed. *The Railway: An Adventure in Construction.* London: British-Yugoslav Association, 1948.

Tiemann, Dieter. *Deutsch-französische Jugendbeziehungen der Zwischenkriegszeit.* Bonn: Bouvier Verlag, 1989.

Tinker, Chris. *Mixed Messages: Youth Magazine Discourse and Sociocultural Shifts in Salut les copains (1962–1976).* Oxford: Peter Lang, 2010.

Tomory, David. *A Season in Heaven: True Tales from the Road to Kathmandu.* London: Thorsons, 1996.

Towner, John. "The Grand Tour: A Key Phase in the History of Tourism." *Annals of Tourism Research* 12, no. 3 (1985): 297–333.

Treffer, Gerd. *Jugendaustausch Innerhalb Einer Städtepartnerschaft: Langzeitstudie über Wirkungen im Rahmen des Austausches zwischen Ingolstadt und Grasse.* Starnberg: Studienkreis für Tourismus, 1978.

Treue, Wilhelm. "Europareisen und Europabewußtsein in der Neuzeit." *Europa-Archiv* 9, no. 2 (January 1954): 6295–302.

Turner, Louis, and John Ash. *The Golden Hordes: International Tourism and the Pleasure Periphery.* New York: St. Martin's Press, 1976.

Turner, Victor. *Dramas, Fields, and Metaphors: Symbolic Action in Human Society.* Ithaca, NY: Cornell University Press, 1974.

———. *The Ritual Process: Structure and Anti-Structure.* London: Routledge, 1969.

Turner, Victor, and Edith Turner. *Image and Pilgrimage in Christian Culture: Anthropological Perspectives.* Oxford: Blackwell, 1978.

Urry, John. *Mobilities.* Cambridge: Polity, 2007.

Uteng, Tanu Priya, and Tim Cresswell, eds. *Gendered Mobilities.* Aldershot: Ashgate, 2008.

Van den Berg, S. A. *Youth and Their Holidays: A Survey of the Youth Hostel Association of the Netherlands.* Amsterdam: NJHC, 1970.

Van Elteren, Mel. *Imagining America: Dutch Youth and Its Sense of Place.* Tilburg: Tilburg University Press, 1994.

Verstraete, Ginette. *Tracking Europe: Mobility, Diaspora, and the Politics of Location.* Durham, NC: Duke University Press, 2010.

Villaume, Poul, Rasmus Mariager, and Helle Porsdam, eds. *The 'Long 1970s': Human Rights, East-West Détente and Transnational Relations.* London: Routledge, 2016.

Vogt, Jay W. "Wandering: Youth and Travel Behavior." *Annals of Tourism Research* 4, no. 1 (1976): 25–41.

Volle, Angelike. *Deutsch-Britische Beziehungen: Geschichte und Gegenwart.* Berlin: Landeszentrale für politische Bildungsarbeit, 1985.

Wallace, William, ed. *The Dynamics of European Integration.* London: Royal Institute of International Affairs, 1990.

———. "Rescue or Retreat? The Nation State in Western Europe, 1945–93." *Political Studies* 42, issue supplement s1 (1994): 52–76.

Walton, John K., ed. *Histories of Tourism: Representation, Identity and Conflict.* Clevedon: Channel View, 2005.

———. "Travel as a Force of Historical Change." *Journal of Tourism History* 3, no. 2 (2011): 85–89.

Walton, Whitney. *Internationalism, National Identities, and Study Abroad: France and the United States, 1890–1970.* Stanford: Stanford University Press, 2010.

Ward, Stuart, ed. *British Culture and the End of Empire.* Manchester: Manchester University Press, 2001.

Wenger, Etienne. *Communities of Practice: Learning, Meaning, and Identity.* Cambridge: Cambridge University Press, 1998.

Westermann, Klaus. "Gedanken zum deutsch-deutschen Jugendaustausch: Was heist 'Normalität'?" *Jugendpolitik: Zeitschrift des Deutschen Bundesjugendringes,* July 1986, 3.

Western European Union. *Youth in the Western European Union.* [London?]: Western European Union, 1957.

Westphal, Heinz. *Jugend braucht Demokratie, Demokratie braucht Jugend: Mein jugendpolitisches Engagement 1945–1974; Erinnerungen.* Rostock: Jugend und Geschichte, 1994.

Williams, John Alexander. *Turning to Nature in Germany: Hiking, Nudism, and Conservation, 1900–1940.* Stanford: Stanford University Press, 2007.

Willis, F. Roy. *France, Germany and the New Europe, 1945–1967.* Oxford: Oxford University Press, 1968.

———. *The French in Germany, 1945–1949.* Stanford: Stanford University Press, 1962.

Wolff, Larry. *Inventing Eastern Europe: The Map of Civilization on the Mind of the Enlightenment.* Palo Alto: Stanford University Press, 1994.

Zahra, Tara. *The Great Departure: Mass Migration from Eastern Europe and the Making of the Free World.* New York: W. W. Norton & Company, 2016.

———. *The Lost Children: Reconstructing Europe's Families after World War II.* Cambridge, MA: Harvard University Press, 2015.

Zauner, Stefan. *Erziehung und Kulturmission: Frankreichs Bildungspolitik in Deutschland 1945–1949.* Munich: R. Oldenbourg, 1994.

Zhuk, Sergei I. *Rock and Roll in the Rocket City: The West, Identity, and Ideology in Soviet Dniepropetrovsk, 1960–1985.* Baltimore: Johns Hopkins University Press, 2010.

Zolov, Eric. *Refried Elvis: The Rise of the Mexican Counterculture.* Berkeley: University of California Press, 1999.

Zuberi, Nabeel. *Sounds English: Transnational Popular Music.* Urbana: University of Illinois Press, 2001.

Zuelow, Eric G. E., ed. *Touring beyond the Nation: A Transnational Approach to European Tourism.* Burlington, VT: Ashgate, 2011.

Index

Made in United States
Orlando, FL
22 January 2022

13877574R00221